International Praise for Wibke Bruhns's

MY FATHER'S COUNTRY

"As unsentimental as it gets: Bruhns is under no illusion that a bunch of 'good Germans' can redeem the crimes of a nation. It is for that very reason that when she finally does discover something like sympathy for her father, her book is utterly moving and sincere." —*The Times* (London)

"*My Father's Country* interrogates the moral and material ruins of post-Nazi Europe, and bleakly conveys the risks of blind adherence to an extremist ideology." —*The Daily Telegraph* (London)

"An extraordinary story. . . . I was almost too moved and appalled to go on reading—but almost too moved and appalled to stop." —Michael Frayn

"Penetrating." —*The Toronto Star*

"An intensely personal book, lively and engrossing yet appalling. . . . Bruhns does justice to her father's tragedy, and at the same time to the vast historic tragedy of the nation he loved so well and so unwisely." —*National Post* (Toronto)

"A fascinating mix of private chronicle, contemporary reporting, and personal search for identity." —*Der Spiegel* (Hamburg)

"A sensational book, one that almost incidentally answers the question of questions: How could it have come to that?" *ntagszeitung*

"A moving, being shoc  this without : (Hamburg)

Wibke Bruhns

MY FATHER'S COUNTRY

Wibke Bruhns was born in 1938 in Halberstadt, Germany. She has worked as a journalist in both TV and print and as a TV host and news broadcaster. She was a correspondent for *Stern* magazine in the United States and Israel and headed the culture section at one of Germany's public TV stations, ORB. She has two grown daughters and now lives and works as a freelance writer in Berlin.

MY FATHER'S COUNTRY

MY FATHER'S COUNTRY

The Story of a German Family

WIBKE BRUHNS

Translated from the German
by Shaun Whiteside

VINTAGE BOOKS

A Division of Random House, Inc.

New York

FIRST VINTAGE BOOKS EDITION, AUGUST 2009

The Library of Congress has cataloged the Knopf edition as follows:
Bruhns, Wibke, 1938–
[Meines Vaters Land. English]
My father's country : the story of a German family / Wibke Bruhns ; translated from the
German by Shaun Whiteside.
p. cm.
1. Klamroth, Hans Georg, 1898–1944. 2. Intelligence officers—Germany—Biography.
3. Anti-Nazi movement—Germany—History. 4. Anti-Nazi movement—Germany—
Biography. 5. Hitler, Adolf, 1889–1945—Assassination attempt, 1944 (July 20).
6. Bruhns, Wibke, 1938– I. Whiteside, Shaun. II. Title.
DD247.K537B7813 2004
943.086'4092—dc22
[B]
2007019945

Vintage ISBN: 978-1-4000-9670-1

Author photograph © Amos Schliack
Book design by Anthea Lingeman

www.vintagebooks.com

Printed in the United States of America
10 9 8 7 6 5 4 3 2 1

For Annika and Meike

MY FATHER'S COUNTRY

PROLOGUE

Hans Georg Klamroth, aged about thirty . . . and baby Else

I've found a photograph of my father. There are hundreds of them—in albums, in envelopes, scattered among diaries, reports, letters. Hans Georg as a child, as a serious-looking adolescent, in uniforms from the First and Second World Wars, as a father with us, his children. This one was hidden away inside one of the miniatures that used to stand on my mother's bedside table.

After she died I took the three little pictures away with me: my Danish grandmother, Dagmar, with her inevitable flowery hat, Hans Georg in hunting garb sitting on the terrace steps in Halberstadt with a dead deer in front of him, and my mother, Else, as a little girl in a white lace dress, with patent leather shoes and uneven stockings. All three—the enchanting old lady, the contented huntsman, the skeptical child—have smiled at me from my desk for fifteen years, a restrained smile, detached, really, from the precious little frames which along with the fact that they had once belonged in Else's bedroom were my reason for putting them there.

But when baby Else slipped in her frame, I opened it up to put her back in place, and Hans Georg appeared before me. Else had hidden him behind her childhood portrait, a grief-stricken man of about thirty—he doesn't look so forlorn in any of the other photographs apart from the last one, before the People's Court. I've hidden the child Else behind him for now, but I'll not be able to endure that hopeless face for long. Perhaps that was why Else covered him with her memories of early childhood. Her photograph must have been taken sometime around 1900, she's barely two—nurtured, cared for, loved. Anything seemed possible back then, none of the things that were to happen could have been foreseen.

So why did she cut the face of her husband, so young and so forlorn, to fit the oval of the formal little frame? At the time when this photograph of Hans Georg was taken they were still given to laughing a lot. They were famous among their circle of friends for their quick and ready wit. And when did she switch the photographs—after his death in Plötzensee? Or before that, when the years of separation during the war estranged them, when each of them functioned alone, eroding their sense of togetherness? When Hans Georg betrayed Else?

For months I have been searching through the lives of strangers, reading letters, diaries, pages written over a period of a hundred years, which I have assembled from the catacombs of the various branches of our tribe. The Klamroths have existed for so long, and they have always seen themselves as a clan, they still do today, even though the focus of their pride—the estate in Halberstadt—was lost to them in the war. What I read there isn't really alien to me. I know who these people are. And yet I don't know them. By the 1930s, Hans Georg had a 16mm movie camera and recorded the family's parties: hunting on horseback in the Harz mountains, bowls in the garden, and the older children, still young at the time, playing on the swing. I recently received the digitalized version of the films and recognized everyone in the pictures, although I'd never met many of them, or had only as a toddler.

I see dinner jackets—goodness, they liked their dinner jackets!—and the expensively styled ladies, and I wonder why Else dressed so badly, when she had Suli Woolnough as a dressmaker whose elegant designs were considered quite exotic in Halberstadt at the time. They held extravagant fancy-dress parties on the eve of weddings, and for Grandmother Gertrud's sixtieth birthday, there were performances by Benno Nachtigall, the family's own band of balladeers. In my cupboard I store the songs they wrote, the *Bänkellieder* and *Schüttelverse*. Strange lives.

I find pictures of Hans Georg at the piano—he used to sing, everybody in this family sang, in harmony, all the time, and the whole clan played musical instruments. Cantatas, street ballads, the whole standard songbook from start to finish and back again, not to mention all the family songs. But I don't know his voice. I feel sure that I've never heard it, although that can't be so—he must have said something to me when I was a little girl. He would certainly have sung to me, too, on the rare occasions he came home from the war.

Neither do I know how he spoke, the man who was my father. It would be a great help to me in understanding who he was, how he was. Did he wave his hands about like I do, was he noisy, impulsive? When he writes, and he writes a lot, he sounds measured and correct. He never makes mistakes, not even when typing, he doesn't need to correct his syntax or his spelling, and least of all his thoughts. His handwriting is tiny, neat, and legible whether in Sütterlin, the German style of the old days, or in Roman script. His writing is just like his father's—my grandfather. Was there anyone else he respected so highly? Think of the way the two of them set out their photograph albums—white ink, borders drawn accurately around each picture, tiny inscriptions.

And then there's Else: chaos in her head and her handwriting, spilling over the edges, extravagant, scatterbrained. Enormous letters, lines rising and falling, crossed out, written over. When she fills in forms by hand, her handwriting rages like a dog imprisoned in a cage. There's a big housekeeping book—household planning and accounts for the years between 1938 and 1943. The two of them kept the book alternately—Hans Georg in marshaled columns of numbers, no mistakes, never a moment's doubt. Else trots through the columns, wanders across the page, jots down rapid question marks and footnotes—she went on battling with calculations like these long after the war. They never added up and left Else in despair—she would so have loved to be orderly.

In her letters—she wrote many—she flits from one subject to the next, batters the grammar and punctuation, leaves the pages scattered with doubtful corrections. She laughs and cries without transition, moral advice for her daughters living away from home is mixed up with descriptions of her varied experiences managing the big house with lots of guests. The battle with twenty hundred-weight of peas and unruly mason jars leads her directly to the observation that God's counsel is seldom convincing. Some idiot—damn him!—has mislaid the key to the silver cupboard, and incidentally she, Else, "would like to have had it out" with Hegel.

They laughed about their apparent mismatch, together and with others. But in later life, when I came to perceive her as a human being and not just as a mother, Else seemed rather histrionic, highly sentimental, and, above all, sad. She would have liked to die much earlier. She was almost ninety in 1987 and had lost her enthusiasm for life twenty-five years previously, when she stopped having to care for her five children. In the past, long before my time or perhaps in my early childhood, both of them, Else and Hans Georg, must have been a delight. Friends from those days have raved to me about their wit, their devotion to each other, their ability to gather people around them and keep them there. Children, I maintain, are interested in their parents only as a resource. Their relationship with them is essentially a selfish one: to what extent am I protected, nurtured, encouraged? The question of who their parents are, what they feel, whether they are happy, is one that passes children by. The child doesn't know the human being that friends have known and loved and spent time with—until the death of those parents, perhaps, when inquiry ceases to be an indiscretion. However affectionate one may be, children, my children as well, are kept at a distance and establish their own distance. One's parents' helplessness is always a threat. Parents don't impose it on their children, and while as grown-ups they might be willing to share the burden of a friend's personal failure, when it comes to parents they dread it.

During the course of my psychoanalysis in the early 1990s, I couldn't really reach my parents. I wasn't prepared—I'm still not— to blame my mother for the problems in my childhood or even later—she was annoying sometimes, of course, she was overburdened and I was often rather lonely. But was there anything she could have done about it? I had assigned a relatively innocuous role to the father: I never knew him, and as a result he didn't affect me. I never missed him—millions of daughters of my generation grew up fatherless. I kept him at arm's length—not wanting to know anything about him. He was an open wound in my mother's life, and I experienced him as her loss. She said nothing about him. Today I know that many of the widows of the July 20 conspiracy held things back from their children. It was a silence in which questions were forbidden.

In 1979 I prepared for my family's move to Jerusalem. I drove down to Italy, then sailed from Ancona to Haifa, and the entrance formalities in the harbor left no doubt: I'm in an oriental country now. I found a house on Mount Scopus, near the Hebrew University, with a wide view of the karstic desert, and an Arab village far below. A hundred years previously, the English school for the children had been an Anglican hospital. The first time I walked through the large garden, past oleander bushes and fig trees, it was clear to me that it didn't matter in the slightest whether my daughters learned math and grammar. The worn steps and crooked sandstone walls, the blooming geraniums, the milling crowd of children from forty different countries, the colors of their hair ranging from deep black to straw-blond, would later give them powerful memories of their school days—and that was exactly how it was.

At the same time I was researching the story of a Palestinian family in Hebron, West Jordan, and it was here that I learned what our everyday life would be like: profound hatred between the Arab population and the Jewish settlers from nearby Kiryat Arba. I experienced a curfew imposed on my hosts, during which I was the only one allowed into the street to buy food for the numerous members of the family. The shops were barricaded, I got in through the back door, while outside the snotty youths of the settlement went strolling with their Kalashnikovs and their Uzis. In Jerusalem, where every stone is a piece of history, I immersed myself in the almost peaceful jumble of nationalities and religions, the deafening noise in the markets, and the possessive attention of complete strangers. I battled with the authorities over our move, I fought for my accreditation, and spent hours upon hours in the bank doing something as simple as setting up two convertible accounts. They were six packed weeks, during which I was constantly worried about how my sheltered children were going to cope with the switch from their orderly life in Hamburg to this exotic confusion. They were twelve and eleven at the time, and in the event they acclimatized astonishingly quickly.

In the course of one of my many phone calls home to Germany, their nanny told me there was a documentary series about the July 20 conspiracy on television, and more or less in passing I asked her to put in a videotape next time. I flew back late, there had been a bomb alert at the airport—something else I would have to get used to. On the plane a group of Orthodox Jews held noisy prayers, standing in the aisle, with black hats and ringlets. In wonder, I studied the equipment required for the process, the tallith, or prayer shawl, and the tefillin, the prayer straps wrapped around forehead and arm. I was amazed by the rocking movements of their bodies. I still had a lot to learn.

I arrived back in Hamburg late in the night, kissed my dozing children, found out what life had been like while I had been away in this bewildering foreign country. At about three in the morning, dog-tired, I poured myself a whiskey and tried to come to terms with the contrast between my own pristine surroundings in the Hamburg district of Rothenbaum and the wild, confused city, sacred for thousands of years, that was to be our home.

A videocassette lay on top of the television. I innocently put it into the VCR. There was my father, standing in front of the People's Court. Bolt upright, looking miserable in an oversized suit, silent, he stands there in a short sequence while the voice of the chairman Roland Freisler jabs and rages. I can see myself sitting there, in a state of utter bafflement. This was thirty-five years in the past, the blink of an eye in historical terms. Thirty-five years ago—he was forty-five years old then, just five years older than me now, sitting here on my sofa in Hamburg. His life, his hopes, everything was past. Large parts of Germany lay in ruins. The war was lost, even though it was going to drag on for another tormented year. The world of that generation was over. Never would the German people, it seemed, be able to overcome the curse, the shame of those years. They paid for their hubris with the loss of their future.

Thirty-five short years. And here am I, the youngest child of that man marked for death there on television—he's actually on television! On video!—and here am I, just back from a colorful trip to the Middle East, from a Jewish country, of all places! I'm drinking whiskey—whiskey!—from Bohemian crystal, I'm surrounded by books, paintings, beautiful furniture. Thirty-five years. I stare at this man with the lifeless expression—eleven days after this footage is taken he will be dead, hung on a meat hook in Plötzensee. I don't know him, there isn't a shadow of a memory within me. I was just a year old when war broke out. From that point onward my father barely came home. But I recognize myself in him—his eyes are my eyes, I know that I look like him. I pinch my forearm. This skin wouldn't exist without him. I wouldn't be me without him. And what do I know about him? Nothing.

Why do I know nothing? What is the significance of the vague family pact of silence that prevailed throughout all those years, why did nobody ever try to track down the father? Children milk their parents, demanding food, warmth, fun, comfort, protection, and above all love, and the father didn't supply any of these—was that it? That might apply to me. But what about my older brother and my sisters, who were practically adults when he died—didn't he feature in their lives? He did, but as a legend. They armed themselves with unchanging anecdotes about the father's wit, about his pedantry. There was always this affectionate laughter reserved for the father.

But this man here before me, on television late at night, isn't a legend. He's a man of flesh and blood. There he stands in the big hall of the Berlin Supreme Court, surrounded by onlookers, and he knows he will soon die a terrible, pitifully lonely death. Composure was called for, and courage. They died "like men," people said afterward. Good God! That can't be. You need someone to take you by the hand, you need someone to go with you, not just to the gallows in Plötzensee. Because until then you had lived—and who remembers that? What was your life like beyond the memorial tablets that hang now in the Berlin Supreme Court or the German Defense Ministry, in Plötzensee or in Halberstadt, what were you like outside of the books in which your name appears under *K* for Klamroth? Your death distorted my perception of your life. You weren't yourself—you were always your death. But at the same time you are more than the carefully avoided zone of pain within my mother's psyche. I don't want to travel the highways and byways to find you. I want you. I'm your child. That night, on my return from Jerusalem, I made a promise to myself: I'll care for you.

Of course I asked them—I asked Else, I asked other people who had known him. But it was far too late, the accepted terminology had been fixed long before. Those set phrases had something to do with the heroes of the resistance movement apostrophized in state memorial speeches; to belong to that movement, even as a child, was an honor. Privately, Else divided her life into before and after: before was glitter, after was servitude. The loss of the one and the tribulation of the other were borne with composure, and mourning over both was taboo as far as the child was concerned. Only decades later, when the mother required daughterly care, did I understand that she had discharged all her misery onto my eldest sister, beginning with the fact that in 1944 Else had asked her twenty-one-year-old daughter, a chemistry student at the time, to get hold of poison for the whole family.

When Else was exasperated by my adolescent waywardness, she sometimes invoked Hans Georg as a kind of bogeyman. "You'd never have dared do that if your father was still alive," she would say, and I snorted with contempt as my weary mother resorted to arguments that couldn't touch me. Sweet, captivating, ill-treated, exhausted mother—if only you'd told me what I know today: that your marriage was worn out, that the father betrayed you, that you both worshipped Hitler in the early years, you presumably for longer than he did. If only you'd told me that you were, if not exactly "manly," as people used to say in those days, for your part unendingly brave, and that with the composure required of every-one back then, you could never scream out your horror over his death or over the failure of your life together.

I'm grateful to Else for not telling me. I couldn't have coped with it. I couldn't have negotiated my way around the ruins of her soul, if I'd had to decide between the man whose death made him impregnable and the woman I wanted to love, or at least rub myself against. The one thing I didn't want to do was pity her. Not then. When I was young, my mother was the standard against which I grew, against which I tested my own strength. I couldn't have wrestled with the shadow of the past, and I think I was content with the taboos that spared me that.

Hans Georg is executed on August 26, 1944, and presumably he walks, like everyone else, from the "house of death" in Plötzensee in prisoner's uniform, hands tied behind his back, his bare feet in wooden clogs. It is a bright summer day, ninety degrees, almost cloudless. The moment of death is established as 12:44, as recorded in the registry office in Berlin Charlottenburg "from the verbal statement of assistant guard Paul Dürrhauer, resident in Berlin, Number 10 Manteuffelstrasse." This man, it is recorded, is "well known, and declared that he was informed about the death on the basis of his own knowledge." I haven't been able to question Paul Dürrhauer; he died in 1976. I don't need to question him. Herr Gluck, the registrar, signed "as a representative" on August 28, 1944: "Cause of death: hanging."

Could it have been a mistake? And if so, whose mistake? Hans Georg and Else were both Party members. He had joined in 1933 and she in 1937; he had been a member of the SS, she was the district leader of the NS-Frauenschaft, the Nazi women's organization. In her application she confirmed that she was of "German-Aryan descent, and free of Jewish or colored blood," and her signature on the form is as expressive and confident as ever.

'He that loveth danger shall perish therein.' So it says in the Old Testament. Aside from the parents, millions of Germans had bitter experience of this truth. Did they grasp that the chief danger wasn't their military opponents, but themselves? Certainly Else didn't. As late as 1947, she writes in the diary that she kept for each of her children from birth to confirmation: "I was filled with horror at the sight of the senseless destruction and sacrifice of the people, only because one man was too cowardly to admit that he had failed." One man? Failed? Hadn't it been a dance of death from the very first?

Not for Else. In 1942 she writes jubilantly to a friend on the Eastern Front: "Things are proceeding wonderfully well—80 km from Stalingrad! Once we're there, the pincer is closed!" In the same year, in one of her Sunday letters: "If we do make it to Alexandria, what will England do with its fleet? If they have to leave, the Mediterranean is ours!!" Ours? That's how it was. A question of *Lebensraum*. Hans Georg writes from the front in Russia in 1942 that the subjugated nations must be won over: "Anyone who wants to lead a people must have a command of its language, since he will otherwise be unable to reach its soul, which must be conquered—it cannot be done with the enslavement of the body alone!" No doubt, however, about the legitimacy of the "enslavement" and the claims to leadership.

When did he understand the extent of the mess he was in? When, if ever, did Hans Georg become aware of the terrible injustice of this "Third Reich"? When did he recognize that he was being betrayed? In the verdict of the People's Court it states that Hans Georg learned of the conspiracy to assassinate Hitler on July 10, 1944, and that he did not report those involved. For that he had to hang. But the verdict also states that he and his son-in-law Bernhard Klamroth were, of the six accused, those who were "directly the closest to the murderous attack." How can those two things fit together?

I don't know the truth. Many things suggest that Hans Georg, as an experienced member of the Abwehr, the German intelligence services, deceived his questioners in Ernst Kaltenbrunner's Reich Security Headquarters, that until just before his execution, like several other men involved in the conspiracy of July 20, he played for high stakes and lost. He was acquainted with too many people from the circle of conspirators to have known nothing about the attack until ten days before it happened. Some of these men, such as Wolf-Heinrich Count Helldorf and Michael Count Matuschka, were contacts from his training as a cadet in the First World War. Hans Georg called Ewald von Kleist his "uncle," he was a fatherly friend to Axel von dem Bussche—and Hans Georg nurtured friendships, connections, and networks throughout his life.

More than twenty of the conspirators, when questioned by the Gestapo and the court, gave as reasons for their involvement in the conspiracy the persecution of the Jews, the "murders in Poland," or the treatment of prisoners of war and the civilian population in the conquered territories. But there was also an element of military outrage. These officers wanted to avoid a second Versailles, they attacked Hitler's incompetence as supreme warlord, they were concerned with bringing the war to a bearable conclusion, not with achieving atonement for irredeemable guilt. The greatness of the nation and German honor were at stake, they fought for this god-damned flag which they thought had been besmirched.

As far as the military was concerned, it was always the others who committed the atrocities. The German Wehrmacht was clean, wasn't it? Even Helmut Kohl blustered about the injustice "perpe-trated in the name of Germany," as though the gremlins had come, waving black-white-and-red banners, and had murdered, looted, gassed, expropriated, laid waste, as if it had been extraterrestrials that had come up with the idea of German blood and German soil, unceremoniously sought to eradicate "inferior" races, and bawled "One people, one Reich, one Führer," and "Today Germany, tomor-row the world."

Not Hans Georg. He didn't bawl. He sang. But he did every-thing he did for "a better future for our children." Where should that take place? In that "lousy country," as he called Russia? And why? The children were doing splendidly, and so was he. What more did he want? He had a decent family, a decent firm, decent friends, he himself had traveled halfway around the world as a decent German. Was he watching from his cloud when, at the age of eleven, I was cut off from the other children in my school in

Stockholm, because they weren't allowed to play with a German child? Did he understand my grief when we couldn't hang paper chains of the national flag on our Christmas tree as they did in Denmark or Sweden, where flag and state are no reason to be ashamed? Was he with me when I became a foreign correspondent in Israel and struggled to take a stand against my country?

"Come on, Wibke, we're going to see Father now, to ask his mercy," my eldest sister demanded of me with ultimate decisiveness. That was just before her death in 1990. For four decades she had substituted for the late Hans Georg in Else's life; she had tidied up, straightened out, mended the storm damage in our mother's life, and kept her brother and younger sisters from going astray again and again. She herself and what she could have become were buried beneath the requirements of this family. Now she wanted the almighty Hans Georg, the murdered father, to grant her absolution.

Excuse me? Just to be on the safe side, I checked: did she mean the Lord God or did she really mean our father? Yes. He was the one she wanted. His mercy. God in heaven, or whoever, thank you for the fact that I don't have to do this. I can contemplate the father, I can try to understand him, perhaps I can love him, and I would like to comfort him. I've been lucky.

It was, after all, plain luck that I didn't have to decide. I wasn't made to wear a Hitler Youth Jungmädel uniform. The only thing I had to put up with were those terrible Little Red Riding Hood outfits sewn from swastika flags after the end of the war. I've never had to brave anything I've been opposed to. Would I have then? A whole generation set an example that must never be allowed to occur in my life. The legacy of all those fathers was to be rejected. I escaped the fate of collective bondage.

The eldest sister didn't. I'm filled with rage and compassion as I read her diaries. In November 1944, aged twenty-one, she writes, "I cannot abandon him and my faith in him, whom I have served, whom I wanted to serve my whole life long. So fully do I belong to the man who murdered my father that no clear thought has so far dared rise against him." And a little later: "Mein Führer, I was one of the most faithful. I am still not free of you, mein Führer—still I want to stand before you, captured by your gaze, then order me to do what you will, I will die for you." And then: "I believed and am betrayed. I have worked for the devil—I loved, mein Führer! For the first time I feel that I could hate . . . a wild hatred that was even wilder love. Hatred and destruction for the man who has destroyed us, and if I should die, I want to die fighting you! My father's murderer!"

If I strip those words of their pathos and their crack-brained devotion, in which the sister wasn't alone, I can't see anything that could possibly have kept this young woman from succumbing to the madness that had taken hold of Germany. Here she is, at the age of eleven, standing around the grand piano with friends and family in October 1933. The father is hammering away at the keys, the children are stretching their arms radiantly into the air in the Hitler salute. Their mother, too. "We are singing Hitler songs with Father," Else writes in the children's diary—she of all people! She couldn't sing at all, for heaven's sake. She was the crow in a family of larks, the only one who couldn't hold a tune.

These diaries constantly evoke "highly political and uplifting times," Hitler's "brilliant sense" of timing for whatever. In his Sunday letters from the Eastern Front, Hans Georg describes how the Führer's radio broadcasts bring together "officers, NCOs, and men," even when "the heavy chunks of an enemy air raid are raining down on us." Outside, the world is being blown apart, but "everything is drowned out by the Führer's voice, which all the men listen to devotedly and with intense concentration."

Letters such as these also reach the children—his typewriter makes nine carbon copies, and each child receives their weekly reinforcement that everything's just fine. Even my next-eldest sister—just eleven when Hans Georg dies—is involved. Compassion is still being expressed in 1947, when Else describes in her diary the period after the assassination attempt on Hitler: "It was worst for you, having grown up to love and admire Hitler, and you loved your father so very much. How can those two things go together?" How indeed? Else explains it by using the image of a packed train rushing toward an abyss. The men of July 20 had seen the attack as a way of halting the train. To outsiders, it looked as though they wanted to hasten the accident, which was why they had to die a dishonorable death. But the true honor lay in the attempt to prevent the catastrophe, and no one could take that away from her father. The child was comforted—writes Else.

Honor. A dishonorable death. The catastrophe. Only we, the next generation, were to deal with the catastrophe that our country had wrought on others. For our parents the catastrophe was the loss of the war, the crushing of Germany and everything it stood for. My sister told me how Else learned of the extermination camps after the war. White in the face, she stood in the doorway and said, "We Germans will never be forgiven that." We Germans. Auschwitz—a mortgage. Not a word, not a single word in all those years about the victims.

This is getting me nowhere. Who am I to judge today, when I want to understand the past? Hans Georg and Else have paid, each in their turn. I have no scores to settle, and I must rein in my arrogance. "You, who will rise from the flood that has submerged us, remember too, when you speak of our weaknesses, the dark time that you have escaped," Bertolt Brecht urges those born later. Sixty years on I can't sit here ruthlessly "being right." My luck was the caesura—I began when everything had stopped. What of those who lived through both? Should they declare the first forty years of their lives invalid, as citizens of East Germany are often required to do? Eternal penance?

That can't be it. I want to understand what it was that did such damage to my generation, to those born later. For this I must return to the history of those who have written my history, to my family's forefathers. I must go to Halberstadt.

ONE

Father Kurt and son Hans Georg on their morning ride

I can immerse myself in the early photographs—the half-timbering, the baroque, ramshackle stables, the courtyards. Halberstadt had 43,000 inhabitants in 1900, the pictures suggest affluence and above all industry. Shops everywhere, markets, awnings outside the shops. The Kaiserhof patisserie by the fish market served its customers under parasols on a second-floor terrace. From 1887 there was a horse tram, replaced in 1903 by the electric one. From 1888 the people of Halberstadt were able to use the telephone. Charlemagne himself had established the diocese in 804, and even today when I drive across the incredibly flat North German landscape I see churches in the distance, many, many churches.

For me Halberstadt is a metaphor. Halberstadt is "before." My memory of the town where I was born, the town of my early childhood, begins on April 8, 1945, the Sunday after Easter, at 11:25 in the morning. Allied bombers, supposedly 215 of them, reduced 82 percent of the old town to rubble. I was six at the time. All my memories prior to that are buried under ruins, consumed in the conflagration that raged for days. After that I remember a difficult postwar time everywhere and nowhere—that was the beginning of what became my life. Halberstadt isn't part of it. Whenever I have driven there later on, what I found was gray, decaying everyday life in East Germany, brightened by family friends, but still strange to me. Today Halberstadt is a pleasure. The town always picks itself up, as it did after the destruction wrought by Henry the Lion, the Peasant War and the Reformation, the Thirty Years' War, French rule, and its storming by the Cossacks.

At some point in the meantime the Klamroths arrived. "For when our forefather came out of the woods near Börnecke in the Harz . . . dapp-i-dee," they sang later at their family parties. The forefather appeared sometime around 1500. Thereafter Klamroths were living in the villages of the Harz mountains as foresters and saddlers to the court of Saxony, master brewers, and even one town councillor in Ermsleben. Things really got intriguing with Johann Gottlieb. He was a trained businessman, he traveled with the certificate of the "Honorable Guild of Grocers and Canvas Tailors" from Quedlinburg to Halberstadt, "at which place" he founded the company I.G. Klamroth in 1790. He was twenty-two; in 1788 he first sealed his letters with the family crest that we still use today.

There was one infallible way for me to put Else in a fury. Like everyone who marries into a family of stature she was a convinced convert: the honor of the Klamroth family was sacred to her. If I compared this family—not inaccurately—with the Buddenbrooks, Else foamed at the mouth. Whenever I described the company—

that company!—as a shop selling hop poles and jute bags, there was serious trouble. Yet it's not a completely inaccurate description either.

Johann Gottlieb ran a business selling "fabric and victuals." That was how it started. He wore his hair in the style of Napoleon—how did they do that in those days, before hairspray was invented? When he got up in the morning, did he look as handsome as he does in his oil painting? How often were the lace ruffs under his velvet collar washed? And did he wear them at the counter? We don't really know anything for sure.

In 1802 he married sensibly into a flourishing leather company. His wife's father had passed away, and Johann Gottlieb moved his business into his late father-in-law's residence at No. 3 An der Woort—"house fit for a brewery, with 5 large rooms, 8 smaller rooms, 2 alcoves, 1 plaster and 2 tiled floors and 2 vaulted cellars, valued at a total of 2,011 thaler 14 groschen." It was in the ruins of this glorious building, frequently rebuilt and finally flattened, that the company withered away after the Second World War.

For Johann Gottlieb and his vivacious wife, Johanne, things went from strength to strength. No paralyzing guild regulations anymore; instead there was freedom of trade. The peasants were liberated in 1807 by Friedrich Wilhelm III and his Baron von Stein. Somehow, herring barrels and dibbles were no longer of the moment. The trade now moved to peas and wheat, poppy seeds and hemp, far beyond the boundaries of Halberstadt. Industry! It's a joy to follow the traces of these early family entrepreneurs, who efficiently absorbed each economic change, spotted each innovation on the horizon just in time, and converted it into profit.

In 1828, at the age of twenty-five, Johann Gottlieb's son Louis joined the company. He was as ugly as sin and a gifted businessman. With various different partners and a complex network of companies, he sold seeds imported from all over Europe, agricultural implements, grains, and fertilizer. In his own factories he produced beet sugar, spirits, and vinegar; he traded in cement, wine, and even money. His flourishing pawnbroker's firm bought its customers' family jewels for good cash and gave them credit on favorable terms.

Louis bought farmland that he leased out to his own factories for the planting of sugar beet. He owned houses, properties, farms, and a manor. His transport company carried goods from the new railway to the buyer; agricultural products were stacked up in warehouses for sale even beyond the boundaries of Prussia. He was one of the first to equip his factories and farms with new steam-operated machinery, sowing machines, and harvesters—Louis was heavily into the new technology. By 1840 he had in his private office a desk with a built-in copying press of which he was particularly proud, because it meant that he didn't need his letters copied out by apprentices.

Louis Klamroth advised the region's farmers of the advantages of Victoria or giant-yield peas ("a yield of 16–18 *Berliner Scheffel*"—about fifty-five liters—"per Magdeburg acre, the softer, longer straw is very healthy feed for cattle"), and Hungarian seed corn ("has proven in our last harvest to be ideal for our climatic conditions"). He included "red clover, green fescue, and timothy grass" in his assortment, and sold "English riddles," coarse-meshed sieves for separating wheat and chaff.

In his youth, Louis traveled on horseback to visit business colleagues in Leipzig and Frankfurt am Main, finding the express post chaise too slow. On these journeys he carried large sums of money in a belt wrapped around his body. It hasn't been recorded whether he carried a weapon as well, but horse riding has stayed in the family. In 1861 Louis Klamroth—his actual name was Wilhelm Ludwig—was appointed to the Royal Prussian Chamber of Commerce, and when he died twenty years later he left a princely fortune. Holding in my hands the will that he drew up together with his wife, Bertha, I was impressed. Even their young granddaughter Martha Löbbecke, whose mother had died in childbirth, was promised 330,000 marks, a vast sum of money at that time—and their son Gustav, Louis's successor in the company, paid the sum in a single installment. Gustav was also able to perform a similar service for his three living brothers and sisters, and nowhere is there any suggestion that these disbursements brought the company to its knees.

Gustav is educated like a crown prince—a year at the renowned Beyersches Trade Institute in Braunschweig, a four-year apprenticeship with the import-export business of the von Fischers in Bremen, extended internships with companies in London and Paris. Finally in 1861, at the age of twenty-four, he becomes a partner in the firm. New brooms sweep clean, and like his father before him, Gustav now seeks to ensure that an already impressive business grows even bigger.

Gustav admires the chemist Justus von Liebig, who revolutionized agriculture with his artificial fertilizer. After less than three years with the company, and much earlier than his hesitant competitors, Klamroth junior begins manufacturing superphosphates, which would very swiftly lead to the establishment of an extremely profitable fertilizer factory in Nienburg an der Weser. The Liebig label was still a presence in my childhood: in my parents' library there were imposing albums of pictures collected from Liebig's meat extract packages, and everything I know about the legend of King Arthur or the battle of Königgrätz I have gleaned from these trading cards.

The 1866 war—Prussia versus the rest of the German-speaking world—was resolved in Königgrätz after just four weeks. In those days wars tended not to last very long. Two or three big battles—I imagine them as being something like a soccer final, with brightly colored uniforms, foaming horses, banners, flags. On the commanders' mound Wilhelm I and his leather-faced General Helmuth von Moltke. "March apart, strike together," was his credo: three Prussian armies came from different directions, to the bafflement of the Austrians and the Saxons.

Things got going on July 3, 1866. The different sides lined up in the open field—the town of Königgrätz was a long way from the tumult—a trumpet sounded, and a murderous clanging of weaponry began and lasted till evening, when messengers on horseback appeared with white flags and the horrors were over. A single day. That was it. At least that was how "the greatest battle of the century," as it has since come to be known, was told in Liebig's meat extract pictures.

There was great agitation at I.G. Klamroth. The kingdom of Hanover had sided with Austria against Prussia, and relations between Prussian Halberstadt and Nienburg in Hanover were difficult. Banks had stopped credit, imports from England were being held on the River Weser, trains weren't allowed to cross the border, which was guarded with great suspicion by the Cuirassiers of Halberstadt. Louis and young Gustav walked about with concerned expressions, while packages for Bohemia were assembled at the company's headquarters, and the family picked rags for lint. But then Hanover was swallowed up by Prussia, and soon everyone was friends again.

Bismarck's North German Alliance was formed, and trade barriers fell—a blessing for business. Gustav made use of whatever could be used: steam-driven plows were brought in, there was a steam thresher, Gustav's wife, Anna, was given—long before it turned into an industry—a mechanical sewing machine. But Gustav was useful to others, too: in 1867 he became a town councillor, and remained so until 1904. He oversaw the foundation of the Halberstadt Chamber of Commerce, and became its second chairman. He represented the interests of Halberstadt in the provincial parliament and the provincial council, and he was an active member of the National Liberal Party, for many years one of Bismarck's chief parliamentary supports.

Gustav donated stained-glass windows to the reformed Liebfrauenkirche in Halberstadt, and a magnificent banner to the local grammar school, the Königliches Domgymnasium. He bought a large plot of land for a new imperial post office, donated a convalescent home to what would later become St. Cecilia's convent, and financed the building of the infant school. He was on the committee of the Fatherland Women's Association—what was he doing there?—the Shelter to Home Association—whatever that was?—and the Halberstadt Art Society. For the company's one hundredth anniversary in 1890, the town was given 30,000 marks to establish a Klamroth Memorial Foundation for distressed businessfolk, and Gustav, like his father, was awarded the title of *Königlicher Kommerzienrath,* or councillor of commerce.

He was a very kind man. Even the late photographs showing him as a patriarch, taken around the turn of the century, give a sense of the warmth that he radiated around his wife and the five surviving children. In Gustav's accounts you constantly come across special gifts, presents, and rewards for the company employees and the family's domestic staff. There was always some member of the extended family who was ill, and Frau Anna describes her husband wandering comfortingly around the house at night with babies in his arms. Two of the couple's sons died very young, and in Gustav's household accounts book I found an entry for 1868, under the heading "miscellaneous," mentioning 2 thaler 15 silver groschen for a child's coffin. The cross for Johannes Gottfried's grave cost 25 thaler. Gustav's wife, Anna, had the following words for her son inscribed on it:

> *Short was your life, beloved,*
> *But filled with pain and woe,*
> *Rest in the peace of God,*
> *You dearest little soul.*

Anna was profoundly religious, yet despite her grief over her dead sons and her own serious illnesses, she was a very cheerful woman. She wrote enchanting children's stories in her picturesque handwriting, preserved in four well-tended leather volumes, and

also love poems to Gustav. When she fell dangerously ill once
again, she allowed him to weep tears of despair in the event of her
death, but asked:

When you have granted pain its rights,
Come back, rejoin your life,
And give the children soon a mother;
Choose yourself a wife.

Man should not walk lonely on the earth,
A true heart should be by your side.
In time one spring succeeds another
And in time you shall have a new bride.

She was just fifty years old when she died in 1890, and Gustav
did not replace her. He lived alone for another fifteen years, looked
after and admired by his children, his friends, and the dignitaries
of the town, an intelligent man and a sagacious voice of caution,
who was worried to see Bismarck, the "Chancellor of Peace,"
deposed by Wilhelm II. Husband and wife had celebrated the
foundation of the Reich in 1871; when the victorious troops
returned, the euphoria in Halberstadt was uncontainable, too.
Anna's lines on the welcoming of the Halberstadt Cuirassiers were
sung in every street: "High flies the banner, in wild, warlike dance;
onward, bold horsemen, to victory advance."

Business was thriving. At I.G. Klamroth, things were consoli-
dated and expanded. The *Company Chronicle*, published in 1908,
records soaring profits from 1871 until 1880, the company having
been spared the serious downturns that affected many firms in the
early years of the Reich. Its author, Gustav's son and successor,
Kurt, enthusiastically describes "the foundation of the German
Reich, which with its patriotic verve roused all the slumbering
powers of the national economy." Because, he continued, "the five

billion of 1871"—referring to the war reparations demanded from France, a fresh spur for Franco-German hostility—"was, so to speak, the oil with which the rigid masses of the national workforce were transformed into living power, they set the big machine in motion and now it's working at full steam." May Kurt be forgiven. He had spent the first half of his life in a state of national drama. He was sixteen in 1888, when Wilhelm II ascended the throne—how could he have been any different?

I become aware that I'm gradually approaching the pain threshold. On the way to Hans Georg I would have liked still to linger with Louis and Gustav, to wander around that wonderful era in this cool Prussia, when the world was laid out in front of the forebears like a ripe field of sugar beet. If you had done your homework, all you needed to do was reap the harvest. All right then. Kurt. I'm old enought to have known him. The grandfather died in 1947—a broken man, whose son and heir had been hanged for high treason, whose proud company was destroyed, whose country and hometown lay in ruins. His family had crammed themselves into the servants' quarters as Soviet soldiers occupied his bedrooms and bathrooms and danced in their muddy boots on the Chippendale sofas in the drawing rooms.

That wasn't how things were meant to be, that wasn't the song they sang to him in his cradle. In 1872, it stood in the apartments above the premises at the Woort, where the family had lived for three generations now. At lunchtime apprentices who also lived in the house were fed and taught manners at the family table along with everyone else, amid the pungent smell of guano that forced its way from the warehouses through the cracks in the floorboards. Kurt is the first to break with family tradition. In 1897, when he marries and becomes a fourth generation partner of I.G. Klamroth, he looks for a base away from company headquarters and finds a house in Magdeburger Strasse. There, apprentices are neither fed nor taught manners. Kurt had never been meant as an heir. That role should have been filled by Gustav's eldest son, Johannes Gottlieb, which is why he was given a Christian name with the initials J.G. This initialing was what the old company now required, and what the sons of future generations would have to endure. But Johannes is having none of it, he chooses to be a farmer, and his father, Gustav, liberal as he is, lets him.

Kurt is the emergency solution and a stroke of luck. With great prudence he treads in his father Gustav's footprints, becomes a town councillor, a member of the church committee, a patron, and he leads the company competently through all kinds of peril to calmer waters. But we're not quite there yet. First Kurt attends the Dom-gymnasium, leaving at the age of sixteen to enter an apprenticeship with the Vogler Bank in Halberstadt. Its owner, Ernst Vogler, is a close friend of Gustav's, and a fellow political campaigner in the city council. Later he'll also become Kurt's father-in-law—the Klamroth sons had a knack of marrying the daughters of their employers.

But the gods were to put some very Wilhelmine hurdles in the way of this success. Queen Victoria's England, with its reputation for prudery, must have been one great big party in comparison with puritanical Halberstadt, where young lovers had to obey strict social rules. Writing about his London apprenticeship in 1896, Kurt enviously describes the natural way in which young, unengaged couples go to darkened corners or rooms at balls to "talk to one another unobserved, and no one thinks anything of it."

Nothing of the kind exists in Halberstadt. Kurt and Gertrud Vogler have known each other from childhood, because their families are friends. They probably played together in the sandpit, scampered about together at children's birthday parties and addressed each other with the familiar *du*. Now they have to address each other formally, exchange invitations to tennis in the garden of the Sternenhaus, the family's summer residence outside the town gates. Kurt writes to her as his "sehr verehrtes, gnädiges Fräulein" (most honored and gentle young lady), and at dances Gertrud has a "lady of honor" to act as chaperone.

The problem is: Kurt and Gertrud have fallen for each other and become secretly "betrothed" in November 1893. Kurt is twenty-one, Gertrud eighteen. And Kurt isn't anything yet. Certainly banker Vogler has trained him personally for his job as a future partner with I.G. Klamroth, and given him a glowing reference, saying that he has great hopes for him. But that isn't to say that the young man is allowed to get too close to his daughter. At least not yet—and this means the start of almost four years of suffering for the two lovers.

Kurt is sent out into the world for further training, and when in Halberstadt he's invited to the Voglers' for conversation around the tea table, and allowed to kiss the hand of his beloved fiancée—although nobody will acknowledge that that's what she is. Of course the parents know about the "secret," but they don't mention it. Mama Vogler has given her daughter to understand that she doesn't want to see a letter from Kurt in the house more than every second week. To circumvent this, discreet friends and distant relatives are asked to address envelopes to Gertrud in their own handwriting, so that Kurt can stockpile them and use them for his forbidden epistles. It's hard to imagine that Frau Vogler failed to see through the trick. But at least appearances are preserved.

There's no point resisting. In other parts of the world it's quite possible, as Kurt has learned in London. Friends the same age, he writes to Gertrud, the sons of "fine houses," were on "respectful but equal terms" with their parents. "It isn't a matter of subjection and pious compliance with one's parents' wishes as it is with us." If "the father's wishes don't suit the son, he calmly declares as much." Everyone is "his own master and does what he wants."

Not Kurt. The obedient son does bridle on occasion—although only in his letters. But when he's back in Halberstadt—the engagement still isn't official, because Kurt is first supposed to establish himself as a junior in the company—Gertrud leaves town for weeks, to ensure that they don't commit a faux pas when invited out together, or while spending the evening at the theater, as this would be enough to set tongues wagging. Kurt grumbles: "What terrible restrictions and constraints modern [!] society imposes on us!" and he admires his "understanding Trudelchen, bravely clenching her teeth and doing what is the correct thing, under the distorted circumstances about which, unfortunately, there is nothing to be done."

This kind of strain has been described hundreds of times in literature—we don't know it only from Fontane's tragic love story *Effi Briest*. But these aren't characters in a novel. They're real people, whose lifetimes just overlap with my early childhood. I see Gertrud's smart wedding photographs, when the time finally comes in 1897, and I hear the shrill old-lady soprano voice when, after the war, the grandmother ushered us into Holy Week at the harmonium: "When Jesus left his mother, and Holy Week began." Wafting from the white silk band with which Gertrud bundled together her fiancé's letters, I can just detect a faint, sweetish smell that I like to imagine is the perfume she wore as a bride.

I would like to have known Kurt—back then. The grandfather knew how to do magic tricks, although he had stopped doing them by the time I came along. Family legends relate how he jumped from the five-meter board into Halberstadt's open-air swimming pool with a lit cigar in his mouth, and went on cheerfully smoking in the water after bobbing to the surface. At parties in Hamburg and London he conjured rabbits from a hat and made watches on gold chains disappear. Of course he was a member of the Magic Circle, the national association of German amateur magicians, whose members used to greet one another with the words "Holla-hoppla."

He was a member of Halberstadt's Pilots' Association and Magdeburg's Airship Society, in whose balloons he flew over the Harz mountains accompanied by many dignitaries, and in June 1911 he actually undertook a successful night flight from Halberstadt to Torgau. He was a chairman of the Airedale Association, and his dogs were prize-winning pedigrees. He organized the long horse rides through the Harz mountains, and led countless hunts in the autumn. Kurt was a chairman or deputy of various genealogical associations, and when I read the plaudits he later receives for twenty-five years of busy activity in some Chamber of Commerce or other, or one of his many societies, I start getting dizzy at the thought of how a man could possibly have any time or—more important—enthusiasm left over for all this as well as for his company, his wife, and his four children.

With Kurt it makes sense. I don't see him as a potential rebel. Instead I sense the urgency of his need for active membership, a desire to belong to imperial Wilhelmine society. Such a thing existed even away from Berlin, in Halberstadt. The most important key to it was the army. Kurt is the first Klamroth to have served, and when I used to look at the silly photographs of the grandfather in his white gala uniform, at the handwritten certificates of ownership for his many medals, with all their flourishes and their royal Prussian seals, I always thought he was nuts.

Because you didn't have to serve in the force, in fact, universal conscription in Prussia wasn't as universal as all that. The aristocracy, higher-ranking officials, the teaching staff in the universities, and also the inhabitants of larger cities were exempt. Businessmen and factory owners possessing more than 10,000 reichstaler—in the Kaiser-reich that equalled 30,000 marks, more or less petty cash to Kurt—were also allowed to stay at home. You didn't have to, but you could. Whereas an army profession was practically a social duty for the younger sons of the aristocracy—what else were you supposed to do when the eldest son had inherited the land?—the sons of the upper middle class, however, had to invest a considerable amount in order to be allowed in. Once they had successfully finished eleventh class in grammar school, at the age of sixteen, they could be trained as a "one-year volunteer" reserve officer. In order to do this, you undertook to pay for your own lodging, food, clothing, and equipment. I'd love to know how much Papa Gustav paid for that.

Because Kurt didn't serve just anywhere, but with the Halberstadt Cuirassiers—or more precisely, in the Third Squadron of the Royal Prussian Cuirassier Regiment von Seydlitz (Magdeburg Region) No. 7, which was set up in 1815 and which was headed by old Prince Bismarck during the last years of his life. On the occasion of Bismarck's eightieth birthday, Kurt is reverently among the company in Friedrichsruh when the emperor and the regiment pay the old gentleman their respects.

But devotion alone doesn't make up for such expense: horses, gala uniforms, visits to their officers' mess, weapons—everything had to be paid for. The young man even learned to fight with a lance—and he must have bought that with his own money. Why, then? Because once promoted to lieutenant—in Kurt's engagement announcement (finally!) he went by the title Second Lieutenant of the Reserve—these young men were entitled to be called *Hochwohlgeboren* (well born), which was otherwise reserved for the aristocracy.

That was nothing to be sneezed at. On his early visits as his father's junior partner to the farms in the duchy of Anhalt, for example—we're in the year 1896—Kurt was dismissed by "their lordships the fine Barons of Berssel and Stötterlingenburg in a very loutish manner" when he handed over the card "of the old and respectable company I.G. Klamroth." Quivering with rage, he wrote to Gertrud: "Had I shown them the wretched Reserve Lieutenant card instead, the doors would have been thrown open."

That was how it was. Businessmen fell between the stools of aristocracy, professoriate, and the officer corps, and even a "wretched Reserve Lieutenant" had a standing. The famous writer Theodor Fontane says: "The chief idol, the Vitzli-putzli of the Prussian cult is the lieutenant, the officer of the reserve." And Carl Zuckmayer, in his play *Captain von Köpenick,* has the uniform tailor Wormser grumble: "The doctor is the visiting card, the reserve officer is the open door, that's how it is."

Sons of bourgeois families who went to university and brought enough money with them achieved an entrée to the upper circles of society via an appropriate student fraternity. As an alternative to officer training, it was in the fencing halls that these young men were inducted into the code of honor that was indispensable if one wished to belong to the upper class of Wilhelmine society. It paved the way for members of the student fraternities into the hierarchy of the imperial administration or the university. Since he was needed by the family business, Kurt was unable to study, and as successful as he was, he wouldn't even have made it as a second-league player in the strictly demarcated society of the Reich if he hadn't been a reserve officer in a renowned regiment.

In Louis's and Gustav's day that wasn't yet required. The Prussian urban bourgeoisie was strong and confident, its political influence was comfortably ensured by the Prussian three-class franchise system, which favored wealthy voters, and the demarcation between the bourgeoisie and the aristocracy was accepted by both sides. But with the growing power of the industrial workforce of the Reich, a new front was arising. This was the "red menace" constantly evoked by Bismarck, which led large parts of the upper bourgeoisie to seek frightened refuge under the coattails of the nobility. The haute bourgeoisie "Junkered up," as the opposition maliciously observed.

The code of entrance to the upper circles of society was called *Satisfaktionsfähigkeit*—literally, "capability of delivering satisfaction," or willingness to duel. Dueling was forbidden in imperial Germany, but the establishment turned a resolutely blind eye to it. After all, its own members belonged to the same dueling society, and didn't wish to call their own superior status into question. It was just a matter of preserving secrecy. If one of the adversaries was killed, there was always a doctor who was himself capable of delivering satisfaction, who would be willing to certify a natural death, while the survivor disappeared abroad for a little while, to lie low until the dust had settled.

I find it hard to imagine Kurt's taking a coach into the Harz mountains through the early morning fog to engage in a shooting match with some landed lout. Presumably the danger of being hurt wasn't great in Halberstadt, and in any case that wasn't really the issue. The issue was having a place on the right side of the dividing line between wheat and chaff in Wilhelmine society, where the upper class had closed itself off from the rest of the world. This included the nobility, bourgeois officers in "respectable" regiments, senior officials, and academics, as long as they were former fraternity members with the right connections. All of these people were considered "capable of delivering satisfaction."

Businessmen and Jews, however rich they might have been, were not. In any case, only wealth that was inherited or acquired through marriage was considered befitting of the requisite social standing. Money acquired through work didn't count. Kurt had both, and in good supply, but he circumvented this essentially agreeable handicap in skintight white trousers and high-sided boots, with sword, sashes, and tassels, with a silver spiked helmet on his head and an accumulation of medals across his chest. Later his promotion to *Rittmeister* (cavalry captain) was signed by the Kaiser himself.

Kurt and Gertrud marry on October 9, 1897. He is twenty-five, she twenty-two; they look terribly young in the photographs, so much energy in their faces, and so hampered by the convention of the time. Kurt's forbidden letters to his bride are a treasure trove to me—but if I'd been Gertrud, I'd have felt chilled to the bone. Every single object from his immediate surroundings is described in detail—everything except his passion for her. There is no tenderness except in the opening and the sign-off: "Your loving Kurt Klamroth."

At the wedding feast there is an expensive sequence of dishes from partridges with truffles, asparagus (in October!), Strasbourg goose-liver terrine, Rhine salmon with sauce béarnaise, and shoulder of veal with mushroom sauce and roast potatoes. This is all washed down with 1874 Château Parveil or 1889 Hochheimer Domdechant, while Pommery and Greno accompanied the fattened French hens. To me it looks like a buffet, because nobody could eat and drink as much as that, one course after another. Kurt marries in civilian clothes, the band of the Halberstadt Cuirassiers plays, among other things, the "Triumphal March" from the opera *Aida* (solo using the Theban trumpets, whatever those may have been). In the boisterous songs delivered to the newlyweds they were loudly praised for their patience during the four-year wait: "But today marks the end of that long separation, of such painful years, and happy joy may now blossom to the young and happy pair."

And what does this young and happy pair do? They go on honeymoon to England, where Kurt had encountered such a liberal way of life, and he fills a gold-framed photograph album, *Our Honeymoon 1897,* with (yes, that's right) landscape photographs. Imagine that? They keep a honeymoon diary in which they alternately record every royal rhododendron bush, every museum, every sea view ("we spent most of our time on the beach and the pier, where we sang German songs out across the English Channel"). Dinner on the steamer *Kaiser Wilhelm der Grosse* is described (turbot, parsley sauce, melted butter, calf's head à la Cavour). Not a word about their togetherness, finally achieved, nothing about happiness, plans, or the future.

But somehow or other their son Hans Georg came into being— in my head, incidentally, he is HG. Nine days after his birth in 1898 the overjoyed father writes in the baby's childhood diary about how he "thanked God with paternal pride and joy for his merciful protection and infinite benevolence." Apart from that, these childhood diaries, which were kept for all the Klamroth scions, weren't really revealing: first teeth and dislike of spinach, birthdays with games of "hit-a-pot" and blindman's buff, nothing about the times the children grew up in, nothing "adult," although they will be more or less adults by the time they come to read them.

So there is nothing in HG's childhood diary to say that the German Fleet Association was founded in the year of his birth—an astonishing PR machine that would only a few years later have millions of members, Kurt among them, of course. Its aim was to turn the global status of the German naval forces, the "giant toy" of Wilhelm II and Grand Admiral Alfred von Tirpitz, into a cause for intense national pride.

HG, his brother, and all the little boys in imperial Germany innocently contributed to this by wearing white sailors' uniforms on Sunday. We know the photographs from those days: children all over the place in their little sailor suits. For weekdays there was a dark blue version, and a similar horror was inflicted on little girls— the Bleyle company grew fat on the profits.

Otherwise HG's childhood diary teaches me that nowadays we no longer know how difficult life was back then, without antibiotics and multivaccines. Everyone—not just children—was sick all the time, for weeks on end. Every cold, every inflamed scratch on the leg was a genuine source of danger, death lurked around every corner, and mothers, exhausted from their long nocturnal vigils— exhausted despite their domestic staff—often have to accompany their convalescent charges to cures in Pyrmont or Badgastein. I read an entry from the autumn of 1900, written in Gertrud's rapid hand, that "days without spanking" are rare, and HG is just two at the time. Around his sixth birthday, she returns to the theme: "Unfortunately the temper tantrums are very frequent, and very often the rod must come and provide a good reason for the racket." Smacking "so that you've got something to cry about!" stopped only in my children's generation, if it ever did.

HG is a greedy child—his mother Gertrud writes of the four-year-old's waking up one morning and beaming as he tells her, "I dreamt I was allowed to eat incessantly, and got full up." He is never full up, and eats accordingly, leading inevitably to "stomach fever," which becomes a constant theme in the childhood diary. Did his parents ever have him checked for a tapeworm? In any case, it didn't do HG any harm in later life—all the photographs show him as a slender boy, and in pictures of the swimming team his washboard stomach is most impressive.

Even aged three, HG is a pedant. Anyone coming in from the garden has to wipe his shoes, and if anyone leaves the room the boy turns the light out behind him. Every morning he checks the calendars in the house because, his father, Kurt, writes, he can't bear it if a calendar "is a day behind." He counts the candles on the Christmas trees—there are five of them in the big hall at his grandparents' house—and if he discovers that one tree has fewer candles than another, he whines until they are balanced out. Numbers are his passion long before he goes to school, and both parents look with delight at the promising heir of I.G. Klamroth.

The name is a story in itself. My father is christened Johannes Georg, and the family calls him Hans Georg with the stress on the second syllable—Ge*org*—and that remains the case throughout the whole of his life. His name will never be abbreviated or turned into anything else. HG will never have a nickname, not at school, not in the army, and not during his professional training. His sister Anna Marie will always be known as "Annie," his other sister, Erika, is 'Ka'chen.' She's the only one who sometimes calls HG "Nonno," but it doesn't last. The crown prince already grapples with his name when he's speaking baby talk: "Hann-Org," he calls himself, according to the childhood diary. I imagine how unwieldy it must have been calling after him, "Hans Ge-*ohorg!*"—that doesn't sound right. I try to soften the jagged name with a coating of tenderness. That doesn't work either. Nevertheless, his future wife, Else, will always call him Hans Georg.

In 1911, the family—parents, four children, large staff, and five horses—moves to an expensively built "country house" with a huge garden at Bismarckplatz, designed by the then fashionable architect Hermann Muthesius. In the garden there was a goldfish pond, edged with sandstone, which all the children and grandchildren—myself included—fell into at some time or other. There was a bowling green, the size of a football pitch, or so it seemed to me then. I was born in this house, and my rabbit died on the balcony outside my room. Behind tall white poplars there was a tennis pavilion and tennis court—during the occupation the Soviet commanders stored their briquettes there, and we stole them at night. There was a playground with a swing, a sandpit, and gymnastics equipment—rings for grand circles and a barre. That's the kind of thing they had in those days. There was the tree house under the crown of a massive fir tree, and an area for exercising the horses. There were gooseberry bushes and a rose garden with beds laid out in the shape of the Union Jack. At its corner stood—and still stands—the "little temple," with its domed roof and arched windows. Having survived the air raids, the house was turned into a hotel in the Democratic Republic, and that's what it is again today—quite different, though.

Running the length of the magnificent herbaceous borders in Kurt and Gertrud's garden was a white pergola, draped over with vines. Three generations later, when marguerites and delphiniums had long since been replaced by runner beans and red cabbage, I fell through it once when climbing on the struts—the rotten wood couldn't even withstand the weight of a child. There was—and still is—a white, plastered terrace of Paderborn brick around the house, with sizable sandstone walls that you leaned over to look at the garden and the goldfish pond a few meters below.

On this terrace the children, including myself, held races with wooden go-carts—they were called Dutchmen, and were steered with hand gears. Photographs show the young HG setting a complicated sailing vessel in motion on this same terrace. Also photographed here were the serving ladies, ten or twelve of them, lined up in black dresses with lace caps, who ensured the well-being of the guests at the many house parties. Enormous hydrangeas in wooden tubs stood here in the summer, and were taken to overwinter in an orangerie at company headquarters. Into the rhododendron hedge on the other side of the wall I disposed of the cod liver oil capsules which I so detested, and which were so indispensable in the time of food shortages after the war. I got a terrible beating for it.

The house itself: room after room, coachman's apartment, comfortable servants' quarters, wonderful kitchen with sideboard, larders, laundries, storerooms, shed, stables, hayloft. At the end of the war in 1945, fifty-eight people were cramped in here, mostly refugees and bombed-out relatives, including almost twenty children. The outside of the building is sandstone with balconies; a loggia, called an air bath; lovingly designed, precisely detailed sills; eyebrow windows; and beavertail shingles on the roof. Inside, Jugendstil in mahogany, built-in cupboards, attics, a storeroom behind every piece of wooden paneling. Hermann Muthesius had congenially combined prestige and practicality.

The dining room could seat forty people, and the stucco ceilings in the ladies' rooms were dainty and elegant. In the gentlemen's rooms, oak dominated in the paneling, and the curved "Sunday staircase" led to the big front hall. In a niche with columns and benches on either side was (still is, always frightens the life out of me) the heavy fireplace, which sets in chiseled stone Kurt's weakness for rhyming couplets: "Warmer Herd Harm erwehrt" (A warm hearth keeps harm at bay).

All this was fitting, at least for a businessman in Halberstadt. Even by the start of the century, and ten years before the building of his house, Kurt had already arrived in the social conditions of which the journalist Bernhard Guttmann wrote: "The haute bourgeoisie was not, for the sake of liberal ideas, inclined to follow trends that would have kept their sons out of the officer corps and prevented their daughters from dancing with lieutenants." Walther Rathenau, himself an industrialist and later the foreign secretary of the Weimar Republic, had a sharper and a more embittered comment to make: the upper middle class had "in favor of the reserve lieutenant, the corps student, the government assessor, and the commercial councillor not only blocked the wellsprings of democracy, it had poisoned them."

Like his father and his grandfather, Kurt was made a Prussian councillor of commerce, and in 1912 he was also awarded the Medal of the Red Eagle, a Prussian medal more or less equivalent to the German Cross of Merit. In every official photograph taken until the 1940s, the old gentleman wears this decoration on his civilian lapel. But as to poisoning the wellsprings of democracy— he hadn't the faintest idea what democracy was. Why should he? His many workers and employees were fine, most of them stayed with the company for decades. When they retired they were given a pension, and their widows and offspring could depend on the patriarch's active benevolence. Responsibility for subordinates was not only a duty in Kurt's small-scale cosmos, it was an inclination, and to Kurt, as to many of his kind, it was far from obvious that any difference existed between favors granted and certified claims.

In any case, where was he supposed to learn democracy? In the Halberstadt council chamber the well-heeled dignitaries, nonpartisan and independent, sat together pondering the well-being of the community, and if any disagreements arose, they were resolved over a good cigar. The Reich was an almost absolutist system, in which the Kaiser decided who was to be Chancellor and policy was determined between them. They couldn't be appointed or deposed by the Reichstag, and the government wasn't answerable to any serious parliamentary checks. The Reichstag was able to pass laws on the nod, and "help to determine" the economy. It was a toothless lion, and Wilhelm II dismissed parliament, not without reason, as a "babbling shop."

Kurt was also content to leave politics to the people who had always conducted it, and not to his disadvantage. After all, he had "Junkered up" out of conviction, and out of conviction he had become an officer. Reasonably enough, he held Wilhelm II and his government responsible for the unparalleled economic boom from which he, like many other entrepreneurs, had benefited. Only the "comrades without a fatherland" of social democracy represented a danger against which the military maintained and defended traditional values.

It was an honor and a duty to serve the fatherland, and the rules of Kurt's class were fear of God, manly courage, and self-control. Gertrud had resolutely set about bringing up HG and his brother in this very spirit. HG was fearful, she scolded in 1904, he was a "craven little coward," afraid of dogs, fire, and spiders. A year later she writes that he was a boaster when it suited him, but that he always burst into tears when things got serious. "Cry-baby, coward, and braggart," his mother calls him with some anxiety—and his father, Kurt, adds in his neat hand: "Let us hope that you will be a brave and virtuous man. May God grant it!" I can't hear the word "brave" without bristling. But how could Kurt have guessed how much "bravery," how much "manliness" would be demanded of his son in Plötzensee?

There's a great deal of talk about "achievement" in the childhood diary, of games involving "practice for later on"—we know that don't we? The toys and the board games, from Pelmanism to Pullock, a kind of prototype of Scrabble, were all as pedagogical as anything used in schools today. But words like "good," "well-behaved," and "obedient" crop up more frequently than they might today, and praise is dished out when the boy does well by his parents. Anyway, both parents repeatedly express the wish that their son may bring his parents and grandparents "much joy"—little thought is given to the question of whether he himself should derive some pleasure from his life.

I don't think this is heartless—at least it isn't meant that way. The time they were living in made the parents speak in these terms. A fear of coddling their "little men," and an absence of emotional warmth, runs throughout the Wilhelmine years. Boys should be "bold," in line with Nietzsche's Zarathustra: "Praised be that which hardens"—or later, in Hitler's version, "hard as Krupps steel." Honor was more important than love, unless it was love of Kaiser and fatherland, and soon afterward they looked death "joyfully in the eye." I fear those weren't just empty phrases.

HG is trained early for this world. When he has just turned two, the diary records that "marching is being practiced with guns and flags" under Kurt's direction. He's also allowed to play "Kaiser parade"—the child rides on his father's shoulders, Gertrud pretends to be the Kaiser, and the boy salutes her. At Christmas 1907, both sons are dressed up in Cuirassier and Uhlan uniforms, and the royal Domgymnasium organizes large-scale "war games" in the countryside, in which Kurt, as an "impartial observer," rides back and forth between the fronts.

War games are also the chief pastime during the annual summer holidays on the North Sea island of Juist, where a crowd of cousins and friends always assembles. Kurt draws up complicated deployment plans for the blue company in their fight against the red company, and the many children, in their inevitable sailor suits, "patrol, storm, defend" the "Lembke Grove" before breakfast, heavily armed with Heureka rifles and pistols brought by Kurt "from Hanover." These are weapons that fire rubber-tipped darts—they could put your eye out. Once their campaign is over, "the young warriors march, to the sound of the fife and the drum, to the beach," where breakfast finally awaits.

The adolescent girls are organized as well. In one photograph in HG's diary for the summer of 1913, the "Green Amazon Corps" parades on the beach in impressive formation. Uniforms, flags, inspections, at least four hours of "duty" a day keep the child-soldiers on the go, and the pictures show great crowds of adults who clearly have nothing better to do with their holiday than organize war games and march-pasts. Kurt is "Commander of Honor" and has to be greeted by everyone, as his son proudly records.

They are actually playing war. The last one was more than forty years before. It was short, relatively low in casualties, and victorious, and it established the Kaiserreich and Germany's greatness.

None of the players of these games has experienced war as anything other than the flag-waving parades on Sedan Day, Germany's unofficial national day—what's wrong with war? Who could guess that a war was in the offing which would last four years, cost 1.8 million Germans their lives—including three of HG's cousins and playmates from Juist, still little more than children—and leave four and a quarter million men wounded? Who would have dreamt that at the end of this war in four empires the monarchy would collapse, and the German kings, dukes, and princes would vanish into oblivion? That their black-white-and-red flag, behind which Kurt and his loved ones marched so happily, might be replaced by the black-red-and-gold flag of 1848, of which they were so suspicious?

They lived in an age outside of time. Kurt and his family were solidly immured in the new sandstone house on Bismarckplatz, which was so big that at first the family must have rolled about in it like marbles, and which called for new means of communication. I myself have only ever known the house filled with refugees and bombed-out relatives, and even then there were forgotten corners and hiding places. I love the idea that Kurt's four children disappeared into the vastness of the house and no one could find them, because they too must have explored possible escape routes via secret doors and hidden staircases. But did they make use of them?

Today things are different—children withdraw to their rooms after the family dinner (if such a thing still exists), to switch on televisions, computers, or video games. In those days, "Go to your room!" was a punishment; it meant being excluded. The custom then, the source of family harmony, was sitting together around the sitting-room table—reading aloud, games, discussions. And that had nothing to do with the fact that in many households only one room was heated, and if you were up in your bedroom your nose turned blue from coldness. In HG's and later my parental home, there was central heating from the outset. Coal supplies permitting, it went on working until 1995 and would probably have done so for years if natural gas hadn't been installed instead of coal. So you didn't freeze in your room—although in a sense you did. You weren't simply left on your own, you were ostracized, excluded. And that hurt.

But HG did shut himself away for some time. He enters puberty at a very young age—although Gertrud would never put it that way. She does complain of his "closed, unlovable nature," worries about "dark wrinkles on your brow," and a photograph of HG, just turned fifteen, really does show a very confused young boy with the first shadow of a beard and distinct traces of acne. Sport helps with this, riding above all. He owns a pony—HG is quite small, and will never grow taller than five feet nine—and he often rides around the grounds alone. Best of all are the dawn rides with his father. The two talk about God and the world, which Kurt would patiently explain to his son. The "world" predominantly refers to the company, but also to the flora and fauna of the Harz mountains, the rules of hunting, and Kurt's experiences in the United States, in England, which he so admires, and in the Caribbean, where I.G. Klamroth has shares in a phosphate mine.

The son learns that Gerhart Hauptmann's plays about the class struggle are poison to the people. Kurt draws his attention to the painter Adolph Menzel, in contrast to Max Liebermann," and tells him "he really needn't read" the satirical poet Heinrich Heine. I can't say whether Kurt was deliberately singling out two Jews for opprobrium—Jews are in his terms "the descendants of Abraham." At any rate, the adult HG loved both Liebermann and Heine.

Father and son also discuss the difficulties involved in encounters with girls, who exercise a frightening appeal for HG, and on one of these early-morning rides HG is given a manly and informative chat on the subject by his father. That's in 1909, HG is eleven, and after the war he describes in a commemorative essay for his three fallen cousins how he was able to impress the older boys with his knowledge in their shared bedroom on the island of Juist. For a while the equestrian father and son speak a kind of kitchen Latin—"in silva copia fossarum est. Aqua est in fossis. Aqua puerum delectate. Puer bestiis in silva isidias parat." Hello? HG had been ill for several months and missed a lot of school. The "beasts" that he was ambushing in Latin were salamanders that he fished from the *fossis* (ditches) for his aquarium.

Kurt is a demanding father, but also a devoted one, and from their morning rides together the son's deep love for him grows, along with great respect. All his life HG solicited Kurt's acceptance, copying his father's handwriting and even his body language—Kurt's younger sister describes the "big man and the little one," strolling side by side "through the garden like two peas in a pod, with a manly swagger."

As late as Christmas 1921—HG is twenty-three, and has by now three years' military service, apprenticeship, and a lengthy stay in the Curaçao phosphate works behind him—he sends his father a poem:

> *Ah, if you know how hard I try*
> *To be your son, not only as I am*
> *By flesh and blood; no, that your essence*
> *Draws me powerfully ever upward.*

TWO

Cavalry Captain Kurt Klamroth

There's a war on. Today it's hard to understand why an old association with Austria should have driven Germany into such a terrible conflagration. The fact is: each country wanted the war for different reasons, and war—in the experience of the previous century, short, not painless, then somehow "purifying"—was, in the perception of everyone involved, nothing but the way to a quick and profitable victory. Still you wonder about the indescribable jubilation prompted throughout so much of Europe by the start of this devastating conflict. Jubilation was certainly felt by Kurt, and by sixteen-year-old HG.

Mobilization begins on August 1, 1914, a Sunday. Kurt, a reserve cavalry captain, still goes to church in the morning with all his loved ones, but by lunchtime he is already wearing his field-gray coat, driving out of the gate "with three cheers to Kaiser and fatherland." That's what it says in his war diary, and in it I also read that "our Kaiser, inspired by a sacred love of peace, has striven to protect Europe from the horror of this war." That's more or less the case, but Wilhelm II was no longer really master in his own house. Neither was Reich Chancellor Theobald von Bethmann Hollweg. The final say rested with the generals, and they had been preparing for this war for years: "Germany's sword, sharpened by years of work in peace"—in Kurt's words—"flies from its sheath to protect the fatherland."

On the way to his place of mobilization in Berlin, Kurt and his driver are repeatedly stopped by jubilant people handing flowers to them, by flag parades and spontaneous processions in the streets. His first disappointment awaits him in Berlin. He is put in charge of a supply unit—Etappen Train Escadron Nr. 1, Garde—which has been hastily assembled and is to go immediately to Belgium. Kurt "had always yearned to be able to fight a campaign with my old regiment, the Halberstadt Cuirassiers, but my own desires must remain silent"—and besides, he's forty-two.

The invasion of Belgium takes place without a declaration of war, and the incensed populace behind the front immediately reach for kitchen knives and poison. The slow supply units behind the lines are particularly badly affected by this, and from this point onward everything Kurt knows from his maneuvers and war games with the children on Juist retreats into the past. Disillusioned, he notes in his diary that "Belgian farmers' wives" are contaminating wells, slaughtering field cooks with butcher's knives hidden under their aprons, and, at dawn, cutting the throats of the German soldiers billeted in their bedrooms."

They show little respect for the Hague Convention concerning War on Land. Neither do the "francs-tireurs," the snipers, who lay ambushes in woods and hidden ravines, nor those "educated people!! Lawyers, pharmacists," who turn their small-town attic rooms into nests for snipers. Kurt detects a rebellious character even in the horses he has requisitioned in Belgium: one gelding bites an ear off one of his soldiers, two others are so furiously unwilling that no one dares go near them and they have to be shot. Did Kurt really expect that the Belgians, their sovereignty violated, will obligingly clear the streets when enormous armies pass along them, commandeering their railway lines and canals for troop transports, emptying their cellars and barns for board and lodging for umpteen thousand hungry soldiers? He certainly did. So now Kurt thinks the Belgians are "nasty."

Equally "nasty" are his formerly beloved Englishmen, who have no option other than to enter the war against Germany because of the violation of Belgian neutrality. Kurt has to acknowledge that they "fight like the very devil," but "they also tend to hoist the white flag, and then use their machine guns to mow down the German soldiers who innocently approach them." Besides, "perfidious Albion" uses dumdum bullets, horrible shrapnel ammunition manufactured in the vicinity of Calcutta, which cause serious flesh wounds that are very difficult to heal, and are strictly forbidden by the Hague Convention. Kurt sends several of these repellent objects home as souvenirs to Halberstadt.

His faith in the purity of war has been shaken. War is no longer waged according to rules of any kind—war as a men's game based on reliable agreements is a thing of the past. "This is a hard school," Kurt observes. "War reveals the vilest and most underhand characters"—this applies above all, and here speaks the voice of disappointed love, to the English. But "it also liberates man's highest instincts," and here Kurt is referring to his own soldiers. "Every day I am delighted by my boys," he writes to Gertrud. "No doubt some among them were reds at home. But war has had its effect, a cleansing fire: the clinker has fallen away, and the noble ore remains. All hail to Germany! Victory must be yours, when you send such men to war." Kurt is happy that "he can be there and do his little bit to help!" And now it's Gertrud's turn: "Don't you think so too, my love? Share my happiness! You are a German woman! You are a mother of German children, who look forward to a great future."

The father of those children holds "German culture" in high esteem, painstakingly ensuring that in French towns where he is installed as garrison commander, "the streets will finally be cleaned," proper toilets are built instead of the traditional holes in the ground with steps for the feet on either side. As a tourist off the beaten track, Kurt would probably be lost in France even today. He sets up garbage collections and organizes the liquidation of messenger pigeons as possible enemy informants. The occupied French probably think he has a screw loose.

Death is everywhere, even behind the front. In a field, Kurt's horse rears up at the sight of two dead Frenchmen, "one very young and one about thirty. Even in death they held one another close." It makes Kurt think "about the mother, who still doesn't know that she has lost her son, the young wife, perhaps playing even now with her innocent children, unaware that she has been widowed." The "misery of war" clutches him "directly by the heart," and he sometimes "becomes weak, but time and again I overcome it." Nothing in his soul revolts. Without a hint of horror he writes in his war diary, upon learning of the "heroic death" of a nephew, that the man's father sent a telegram from the front to his wife: "Take courage! Victory is needed, not life!" Are they mad? What kind of boundless hubris is that, placing Germany and the Germans above the death of sons?

Kurt in 1914, writing from France to his son HG, who has just turned sixteen: "Isn't it remarkable how many efficient, wonderful men God has awoken among our people in these difficult times? Does any other nation have a Hindenburg? Can French, Kitchener, Joffre"—referring to the highly successful warlords on the opposing side—"compare with our own military leaders, not one of whom has failed? The British and the French fight like lions, but guilt eats away at the marrow of those nations; their struggle will be in vain."

And later: "The news of our first sea battle has just come in. Hurrah! That is wonderful! Our fine navy! England—the big-mouths! Rulers of the waves, retired! Just a few more Zeppelin bombs on London—right on the Bank of England! How lovely that would be!" What on earth's got into him? England, of all places, a country he has always been so fond of! Does war mean losing your mind? I can't be sure, thanks to the aberrations of my forefathers. Such a war has not occurred in my lifetime, and I have never had to get worked up about anything patriotic, not even a soccer team.

Kurt's sons—HG and his little brother, Kurt junior—want to have their own war at home. They make themselves useful in the auxiliary scouts. Kurt junior writes in stiff Gothic script to his father: "There's a great deal to do here. In the morning I went to the dike and brought the soldiers shirts, trousers, and boots. Yesterday morning Hans Georg and I [Hans Georg is a scout as well] went to the police station in Kühlingerstrasse. We had to deliver letters, and I brought Hans Georg's bicycle. Hans Georg rode on your bicycle, and I rode on his. We did the same thing again in the afternoon. This morning I was at the town hall and brought the policemen beer and did errands for them, or showed some soldiers the way. Here at home I don't notice much about the war, except that sometimes someone is arrested and shot. Recently there was a lot of shouting and shooting, and there was a report that it was a Russian who wanted to cut the telegraph wires. But he didn't succeed. I can't write anything more. Warm greetings from your son Kurt Klamroth."

The boy is ten, and won't have made any of that up. How should I imagine it? We are in a small town in the middle of Germany, in the autumn of 1914. The war has lasted only three months so far, its theaters are a long way away, and there's no suggestion that little boys shouldn't show their patriotic eagerness by fetching beer for policemen. But who was arrested and shot, and why, in Halberstadt of all places, and how did a Russian saboteur manage to get all the way to such an out-of-the-way town?

Gertrud runs the Red Cross auxiliaries in the military hospital. Already all hands are required, because new transports of casualties are coming in every day. To Halberstadt! The fronts are six hundred miles away in both directions, so what would things be like in Eastern Prussia or the Rhineland? Kurt and his men often have to take hundreds of wounded men to railway stations, and writes of huge numbers of prisoners—90,000 Russians after the battle of Tannenberg, many tens of thousands of French and British soldiers on the Western Front. "The fact that they all have to be fed," Kurt writes, "makes the slowness of supplies even worse." Hunger—by the winter of 1914–15 this new enemy can be seen on the horizon and will put the Germans under ever greater pressure year by year.

There are men billeted in Bismarckplatz, too. Gertrud writes of two young lieutenants who irritatingly never turn the light off, and who "chase" the serving girls. She has to be "very strict" with them. One would like to know whether the young ladies found ways and means of getting around that strictness. Food is hoarded, and charitable gifts are packed for the front—at Christmas 120 parcels are dispatched, one each for everyone in Kurt's column. But they never arrive. Even the packages for Kurt seldom reach their destination, and his "mouth waters when I see the list of contents." He receives these by normal forces' postal service, and now knows "what it was like for Tantalus. He has my sympathy."

Kurt and his men are transferred to the Eastern Front: "Hindenburg needs more columns." The news doesn't gladden the heart, "but the soldier performs his duty with equal joyfulness wherever he is." Says Kurt. The soldiers are given furs, warm underwear, and lined boots, "so that each individual feels that the army leaders are keeping us well supplied, and that gives everyone a sense of security and confidence." Claims Kurt. After a march of 1,300 kilometers west, with sixty vehicles, 162 horses, minus four men—one is missing, three are in the field hospital—they turn around and head east. It is November 30, 1914.

And Russia is the same as ever. Kurt and his men, like Napoleon before them and Hitler's men after them, sink into the deep mud of the endless plains. Bearing this in mind, the German-Austrian successes are astonishing. At the end of September 1915 the front line runs from Bukovina to the Gulf of Riga, which means that an area several times larger than the former Federal Republic has been occupied.

Kurt can't take the strain—an old amoebic parasite that he caught years before in Curaçao breaks out again, and in the spring of 1915 he has to have an operation. It is performed in Halberstadt, and while travelling there he is astounded by the changes at home. "Everything had become more German," he writes in his war diary. "The gold sign saying 'Café Piccadilly' no longer stood over the magnificent building on Potsdamer Platz, but instead one that read simply 'Fatherland.'" On the tram, where once there had been conductors there were now conductresses, and "from the post office there streamed a crowd of cheerfully chatting postwomen."

At Bismarckplatz, he experiences a great triumph in the middle of the night: "Never will I forget, my dear wife, how I took off my coat and you saw the Iron Cross on my chest—the way you looked at me!" The news that he had been awarded the Iron Cross, Second Class, had not reached as far as Halberstadt. Now Gertrud's pride helps him through his operation and convalescence. Besides, he is concerned to note how the economy of scarcity is growing. The British naval blockade, intended to starve Germany's civilian population, is working almost exactly according to plan, just as it did in the Boer War. Bread and many other foodstuffs are rationed, there is no chocolate and no soap, and Kurt, who is himself, after all, unstinting in his insults against "our former cousins on the other side of the Channel," is stunned by the level of bitterness that he sees all around him.

His eldest son, HG, now sixteen, startles him when he gives a furious and dramatic rendition of Ernst Lissauer's "Song of Hatred against England." Lissauer was a Berlin author who had hardly been noticed until then, and who has since fallen back into oblivion where he belongs. His "Song of Hatred" was on every tongue in those days. Its last verse:

> *We will hate you with long hatred*
> *We will not stint in our hatred*
> *Hatred on water and hatred on land*
> *Hatred of hammer and hatred of crown,*
> *Throttling hatred of seventy million,*
> *They live united, united they hate,*
> *United by a single foe:*
> *ENGLAND*

Lissauer, incidentally, distanced himself from this shoddy effort later on—once the war was over.

HG is champing at the bit. Almost all the final-year pupils in Halberstadt's Domgymnasium have signed up in the army as volunteers. Young men, school friends, are strutting through the town in uniform. There is the additional problem that the school has a new headmaster. While the old one looked benevolently upon the young HG, the new headmaster is unfamiliar with the town's hierarchy, and is persnickety in his insistence on the learning of Latin and math. Should HG take an interest in these dreary subjects, when the world is on fire and he could be throwing himself into battle for the fatherland? Yes, says Father Kurt: "You will do your duty where it is required. The country needs well-educated men!"

History does not reveal whether HG grumbles in reply. But he will certainly be hurt by the fact that his father thinks he is too young at seventeen to be a soldier, and, above all, unfit for service.

He suspects, no doubt correctly, that his parents are in this respect hand in glove with their longtime family doctor, so HG secretly gets as much training in as he can: swimming, route marching, cycling. Kurt, however, goes back to Russia "with the consolation," as he writes to Gertrud, "that the boy is being looked after at home, safely by your side."

In April 1916 Kurt is transferred to Grodno on the Memel. Halberstadt's mayor, Hans Weissenborn, has been ordered there as town captain, and Kurt, his council chairman, is to help him set up a German administration in the strife-torn town. Grodno's present-day name is Hrodna, and it lies in Belarus, just over the border from Poland and Lithuania. In Kurt's time it was part of tsarist Russia, and had just been taken by the Germans. The fact that a German administration was to be established there suggests that this war was clearly not about national defense alone. The most daring plans for extensive territorial gains were under discussion—the whole of Belgium to the west, large parts of western Russia, all of Poland. So Hitler's plans twenty years later weren't all that new.

Kurt doesn't say whether or not he is devoted to such dreams of Germany as a major power. At first he and his mayor find themselves sinking into a bottomless pit. The retreating Russians have taken all their files and the city treasury with them—here is a town, clearly a delightful little town, on both banks of the Memel, with its 24,460 inhabitants, spinning around in an administrative vacuum, forced to find groceries on the black market, keep their children out of school, unable to take patients to the hospital. Access to electricity and water is possible only after shady negotiations with the suppliers.

Thirty-one Germans, 21 Latvians, 113 Lithuanians, 67 Estonians, 465 White Russians, 570 "other" Russians, 7,609 Poles, 15,583 Jews, and 1 Greek (I'd like to have met him!): that's a total of 24,460 people—oh, Kurt! The Halberstadt businessman doesn't leave out a single Polish child, or a single elderly Hasid. Since being conquered by the Germans, all these people have skillfully resisted the orders of the new military authorities. It's chaos. But it's well-documented chaos—Kurt records everything, and it makes my head spin, because he really has no idea about Jews—and Eastern Jews at that.

There was a significant Jewish community in Halberstadt. Its dignitaries were at least as affluent as the Klamroths, and their international business connections far superior to those of the Klamroths. Jews were members of the town council; like Kurt's father, Gustav, and like Kurt himself, they were influential patrons and benefactors of the town. But in the private life of Kurt's family they made no appearances. In the guest books of the Klamroth household, I have not found a single one, nor in the "games book" of the tennis pavilion or on the lists of riders into the Harz mountains.

True—the Halberstadt Jews, Orthodox as they were, probably didn't go riding or play tennis. They couldn't eat from the Klamroths' nonkosher crockery or drink their nonkosher wine. But neither is there anywhere the slightest indication that the Klamroths and the Jews ever had any contact with one another—not at concerts, receptions, in the Chamber of Commerce, or at community events, and this in a town where the upper crust numbered only a hundred people, Jews and non-Jews. But the boundary was, I think, accepted on both sides.

Kurt and his mayor are drowning in work, so they call in chums from Halberstadt, wherever they happen to be stationed. Kurt has his young accountant, Willy Lodahl, from I.G. Klamroth, tracked down to his trenches in the Balkans, and by early June he's in Grodno, to get the city treasury in order. The editor in chief of the Grodno newspaper comes from Halberstadt. A stout matron is brought in from St. Cecilia's Convent in Halberstadt; she doesn't understand a word of the local language, but she does get the hospital shipshape in record time. Herr Sinning, a member of the Landsturm, Prussia's National Guard, and in peacetime Halberstadt's town surveyor, is brought to Grodno to sort out the water supply, and a skilled lawyer is called in from Quedlinburg to take charge of civilian law.

They wage a war on two fronts: against the anarchy prevailing in the town and against the German military authorities. General Field Marshal Paul von Hindenburg, Supreme Commander of the East, and his general chief of staff Erich Ludendorff have given unequivocal orders. Hindenburg: "The supreme task of the administration is the ruthless exploitation of the country to supply the army, the population, and Germany. If anyone is to live in want, then the population of the occupied area should be the first to do so. I expect energetic seizure of supplies by the relevant members of the administration, ensuring that local interests take second place to the requirements of the German people."

While Kurt sends 70,000 eggs and barrels of butter—all properly paid for—to Germany once a week, he also attempts to bridge the gap between orders from the military authorities and the needs of the local population by setting up public soup kitchens. To do this, he recruits the assistance of Jewish businessmen, who promise themselves long-term advantages from their collaboration with the German civilian administration. There is, of course, a strictly forbidden black market, and there are unofficial sources for everything. So Kurt pays the businessmen, and their wives who do the cooking—Kurt to Gertrud: "We're learning Levantine customs here"—with only a small sum from the town budget, but on the other hand he has supposedly no idea where the ingredients for the soup kitchen and the other black market goods are coming from. The businessmen complain that too much meat has to go into the pot. Kurt's rejoinder: "Nu, woas kenn mer machen, woas kenn mer tun?"—Well, what can we do, what's to be done?

But it's still not enough. Kurt receives anonymous, despairing letters: "I worry about my child. He's crying and calling: Mama, Mama, give me bread! And where am I to get bread? If there is any, it costs 60 pfennigs a pound. And the money? Where are we to get it? And on top of everything they're asking us for a 'poll tax,' as though we were cattle, not human beings. Yes, Germans are the only human beings, the rest of the European population are cattle! It goes with their helmets, their cruel, medieval helmets."

That really gets to Kurt, but in the end he still considers it only fair that the occupied regions should bleed for Germany, "when Germany itself is suffering from England's attempts to starve it." He hears this from his wife, Gertrud, who writes every day, and the mail between Halberstadt and remote Grodno only takes two days, even in these chaotic times.

Back at home, there are by now four goats on the big lawn, and Gertrud distributes milk to the mothers of newborn babies in the neighborhood. Chickens have been brought to the house, and a few rabbits that HG looks after and intends to slaughter "without the slightest compunction." Gertrud does battle with caterpillars in the vegetable garden—"they're just as hungry as we are"—and can't make preserves, because sugar is impossible to come by. According to the food cards, the meat ration has been reduced to one pound a week, sometimes only half a pound, without bones, and by no means always available. Gertrud and her servants, who are still in the house, do the big weekly wash without soap—"the sun will bleach it." This is early summer 1916.

Kurt quickly understands that he won't be able to manage without "the long-established Jewish trade." Some of his fellow officers in neighboring districts have tried to do just that and failed miserably. They "deeply mistrust the Jews, and try to use police powers to enforce the purchase of goods at prices fixed by the state." So all of a sudden there are no eggs or butter in the market. Kurt, on the other hand, strikes a deal with the Jewish businessmen—tradespeople among themselves. He imports goods from Germany that the German producers desperately want to get rid of, and which vanish in a flash into the market in Grodno and its hinterland: "cheap penknives, combs, glass necklaces, icons, cards, pocket mirrors, cheap jewelry and the like." It sounds awfully like the economy of the new African colonies. But clearly it works.

Kurt increases the prices by 10 percent for the benefit of the town treasury, and through this trade he acquires the military raw materials and foodstuffs demanded by Oberost—the German military regime in the Baltic countries—and both sides are content. Although he couldn't have made his profit without them, Kurt finds the Jews of Grodno weird, and he doesn't like them. Not even the representatives of their upper class, of whom he writes: "These Eastern Jews haven't the slightest sense of decency when it comes to business. What we would deem common fraud they consider shrewd negotiation and cunning. For that reason it's impossible to deal with them."

Elsewhere Kurt observes: "Weissenborn was very surprised to learn that when a Jewish businessman tried to swindle me too outrageously, I took my horsewhip and inscribed a receipt for the man's behavior on his back. This response struck the town captain as rather dubious." But the mayor is a quick learner. "A few days later I saw him applying the same treatment to a fishmonger who was shamelessly exploiting the poor population in contravention of a bylaw proclaimed a short time before."

These scenes, performed "in the style of Russian landlords," have been recommended to Kurt by Polish business partners. Back home in Halberstadt it would never have occurred to him that "the Jew feels such treatment to be entirely just, and that it is more effective than the fines imposed upon him for the infringement of bylaws. In this case the trader I had punished returned to my office the following day with new offers. It is this alien behavior on the part of the Jew that makes him so disagreeable to us."

"The Jew"—the singular for the genus. Like "the earthworm." Distinguishing oneself from the unknown leads to arrogance— "what can become of this country, when German culture develops its soil?" What pains Kurt most is the refusal to yearn for the "superiority" of German culture. He doesn't understand the self-sufficiency of this Jewish world, which seems willing enough to reach accommodations with external necessities, but won't actually let them in, let alone accept them as the standard for its own Jewish identity. Kurt admires "the intimacy of Jewish family life" and the "strictly moral lifestyle of Jewish women and girls." He is also impressed by "Jewish charity"—what he is experiencing is the solidarity of an Eastern Jewish community that exploits the outside world for its own survival. He and the whole of the German administration, like the Russian administration before it and the Polish before that, are being used, but without fraternization. It is a matter of seeking advantages, averting danger, and securing a livelihood in a generally hostile environment. All Jewish groups have collapsed at some time or another when they have relied on the benevolence of the outside world. Courting favor won't protect you—not from Russian pogroms or from Hitler's extermination camps.

Kurt doesn't understand anything. How could he? In his generation assimilation is the watchword in Germany. Wilhelm II had his *Kaiser-Juden*—imperial Jews—like the industrialist Walther Rathenau, the shipowner Albert Ballin, and the banker Max Warburg. He valued their economic competence. Conservative and Christian as he was, however, he remained an anti-Semite throughout his life. Despite their formal equality, unbaptized Jews were second-class citizens in the Wilhelmine decades. In the upper class they were tolerated at best, access was granted them as an act of generosity—although not to the reserve officer corps, the "right" student associations, or the upper levels of the administration, the most important doorways to social acceptance. There was a distinct gap between those who strove for recognition—the Jews—and those with the power to grant or withhold it.

In Grodno in 1916 that gap doesn't exist. Here, two different formations face each other head-on, forget the riding crops. Each side needs the other. They both strike reciprocal deals. The Jewish traders trick the German occupying powers whenever they can, and Kurt isn't going to have the wool pulled over his eyes by anyone. He has duties to perform: butter and eggs for Germany, military raw materials, the poll tax. The population of Grodno is starving, and the town treasury is unstable. What Kurt needs now is gold.

The gold reserves of the Reichsbank are in urgent need of replenishment, and all over the country people are being called upon to part with their stocks, voluntarily and in return for payment. Quotations with facsimile signatures appear as small advertisements in the newspapers: " 'He who hoards gold mistakes the hour'—Ludendorff," and " 'In war our gold belongs to the fatherland'—Hindenburg." The proposed fashion for wearing iron jewelry didn't really catch on. But ladies appear in public wearing no jewelry except for wedding rings—anything else is considered politically incorrect.

In Grodno, Kurt meets with wide-eyed astonishment when he approaches his trading partners for gold. "The Russians have already collected it all," he is supposed to believe, and tries to come up with a remedy. He applies to Oberost to have the town and district monopoly on alcoholic spirits transferred to him, and when long lines form outside the outlet on the first day, "I shut the shop and stuck a piece of paper on the door saying that the small remaining stock would be sold the following day, but only by the bottle and in exchange for a gold coin. The following morning the gold rained in, and soon after that I was able to send the Reichsbank the first 20,000 rubles in pure gold." Despite this subterfuge, Kurt remains correct. The customers, most of them the same traders who so recently had nothing at all, are able to sell their gold at the regular exchange rate, and buy their spirits at a slightly lower rate than that set down by Oberost. "After all, they're supposed to be coming back with even more gold!"

For Gertrud in Halberstadt, things aren't quite so simple. In June 1916 she is appointed to the honorary gold-collection committee, and considers it ludicrous that wedding rings are exempt "lest our poverty become known abroad." Instead, it should become a "duty of honor" to wear thin silver rings, which would allow the nation to have the pure gold of millions of wedding rings, even without having to deal with the question of the artistic merit of other items of jewelry, which are, in addition, so often bound up with so many personal memories.

No one asks her, so Gertrud herself struggles to decide what exactly she should hand over: Kurt's watch chain will clearly have to go, but what about HG's watch chain, the one he inherited from his grandfather? Kurt's cuff links—"yes, that's fine"—her own long chain with its christening coin—"that's not so easy." Should she hand over her "jingle bells," a bracelet of brilliants that Kurt gave her for their tenth wedding anniversary? "Of course we have to set a good example, and it's not such a great sacrifice to give away your gold when others are asked to lay down their lives for the fatherland," but it is still hard for her, and she has pangs of guilt about it.

In the end, Gertrud parts with the jingle-bells, and receives in return a certificate adorned with a laurel wreath interwoven with black, white, and red laces, the colors of the German flag. Its text says that she has given up her jewels "in order to strengthen the gold treasury of the Reichsbank and thus the financial defensive force of our German fatherland." In September 1916, the "Government Diamond Company" sells it in Copenhagen for the sum of 850 reichsmarks, which she is invited to kindly collect from the Städtische Sparkasse. Kurt will later note on the certificate that the bracelet cost 1,500 reichsmarks—both figures were then enormous amounts. At any rate, the gold stock of the Reichsbank almost doubled, to the tune of about a billion marks.

Everything is collected, not just gold. Children collect things, parents collect things, teachers, companies, offices, and hospitals collect things—there are special collecting weeks for Hindenburg's birthday, wild vegetable weeks. Gertrud finds herself on the board of the Halberstadt Refuse Exploitation Committee, whose report mentions, among many other things, 520 kilos of eggshells, 319 kilos of women's hair, 22,148 kilos of pottery fragments, 10 mouth-wash bottles, 1 cigar holder, and 8,950 Danish milk bottles—why Danish? At peak times more than three hundred children stream into the collection point every day, to exchange their treasures—bottle tops, beechnuts, fish bones—for vouchers or lottery tickets, with which they could win live rabbits.

Gertrud calms agitated mothers looking for their cooking pots and baby linen among the objects that have been collected—the children will bring in anything that isn't actually nailed down. Gertrud writes to Kurt: "I have strictly instructed the little ones not to take away anything that Schneemann or I haven't seen"—Schneemann is the housekeeper—"and I think it's working." In addition she's extremely busy looking after her own children, who are taking turns being ill. Only HG is in good health, but his nose is out of joint because his friends and cousins are doing their Notabitur, the specially instituted emergency school-leaving exam, and going away for officer training. This is June 1916.

HG is seventeen now, and he's thoroughly fed up with school. Also, he doesn't feel like doing defense exercises with the scouts anymore, and he's worried "that life and the war are passing me by." That he writes in a letter to a cousin, whose Notabitur party and farewell to civilian life he endures through gritted teeth, although Gertrud remains oblivious: "Hans Georg has been behaving very sensibly in response to the Notabitur, Fritz's farewell party and so on—I've been proud of him." HG speaks more directly to his father, Kurt: "I could have had all that myself today, and I could have joined in the party wholeheartedly. Admittedly I did join in, and it's the first time in my life that I've been a bit unsteady on my feet. Well, it's the kind of thing you have to learn."

At the same time he is such a baby face. Smooth, unformed—three-year-olds show more character. So did HG as a little boy, when rage and fun still radiated unfiltered. Now he is—like every-one at seventeen—a product of expectations, his own and other people's. He's "educated," he sits there gravely in a confirmation suit as if he's just understood Hegel's philosophy, or else he loiters about the place in his hunting outfit like a miniature John Wayne (if John Wayne had been around at the time). Pleasant, this kid, but still wet behind the ears. You want to blow his nose and give him a woolly cap to keep the cold away, and I can understand that Gertrud doesn't want to let her little boy go to war.

But that's not at all what's happening. She's visibly unsettled, and it takes me a while to work out why she's suddenly in such a hurry. She wants to forestall a possible draft, which is in the cards for 1898, HG's year of birth, because frontline casualties are so high. The draft could mean that HG—heaven forfend—would have to join the infantry or the support, "decent" people, certainly. Serving the fatherland, of course, but not just anywhere. To avoid the draft and join the army as a Fahnenjunker, an officer cadet, HG has to volunteer. Not only does a Klamroth from Halberstadt have to be a Junker, an officer, he has to be working with horses, cavalry if you please—Cuirassiers, dragoons, hussars, Uhlans. It has to be the "right" regiment. War or no war, this is a matter of social status. This is where the course is set for the future. A cavalry captain like Kurt is somehow more elegant than an infantry captain—horses mean aristocracy. This is Prussia.

It goes like this: first of all a young man must be fit for field duty, then he needs a regiment that will take him on as a volunteer. Then, and only then, can he do his Notabitur, because school won't stand in the way of duty to the fatherland. Certainly not. The regiment will take the would-be Junker only if he really has passed his Abitur—so the heat is on, both for the examinee and the school. And in certain schools—the Domgymnasium, for example—the headmaster, the new headmaster, doesn't want the Abitur to be compromised by the requirements of the fatherland. The people of Halberstadt call him a red behind his back. He isn't a socialist at all, he's more of a democrat, but he's still an obstacle as far as HG is concerned.

First of all, however, there are his parents to deal with. Kurt's experience of war is one of darkness and cruelty, and for all his patriotism he wants to keep his son out of it. No telegram, please, saying "victory is needed, not life," as his cousin wrote in his telegram to his wife after their son's "heroic death." Gertrud in Halberstadt has a different approach, seeing the world through HG's yearning eyes. In homeopathic doses she convinces Kurt in Grodno of the urgent need to make a decision: "In Baden they have drafted the boys born in 1898," or "At school they're constantly asking Hans Georg about the early exam," or "Everyone expects a boy his age to put himself at the disposal of the fatherland. And it can hardly be held against us, his parents, if we want to keep him out of the infantry if at all possible." And, repeatedly: "Is your wife doing the right thing?" or "If only you were here to decide about things." And best of all: "Mothers aren't good for big boys. I can't hold him back, it takes his father to do that." She's quite something, my grandmother.

And then comes July 11, 1916: "My beloved husband! Yesterday Hans Georg came home in a state of bliss: 'Paul Springorum [the family doctor] declared me fit to fight.' He had secretly made an appointment, and secretly gone to it. Now Paul wants to talk to me again, and I'm going to see him this afternoon. Dear old man, it was my only option. Hans Georg said to me, 'Mother, Father sees things differently from a distance—it's my honor that's at stake.' The crucial factor was probably the fact that frail, weak Kühne from his class had found a regiment. I told you that I had told Paul about your feelings on the matter, and that if possible he should hold the boy back if he still detected any weakness in him. If Paul now says, you're healthy and fit for military service, we can be convinced that this is the case."

Gertrud goes on: "Now the consequence of this, of course, is that he wants to sign up for the exam immediately after vacation. Sadly there is no longer any doubt that he must become a soldier, which is to say that the war is lasting so long that we can't really keep HG waiting. The hardest thing for you will be that he cannot become a Cuirassier"—the Halberstadt Cuirassiers, Kurt's regiment, have stopped recruiting—"because of course he needs his certificate of acceptance as a Junker before he can do the Notabitur. But in practice many more regiments are still willing to take on Junkers than theory might suggest."

Gertrud assumes command. But to her husband in Grodno she is still every bit the little woman: "My dear husband, I am so sorry that this is all happening now, and you alone [!], far away as you are, must make the decision. But you know your boy, and I am sure you have already given the subject considered reflection. You know that I would give thanks for every extra day that I could keep him at home, but we are all home to be grateful that he is completely healthy." That should preferably remain the case, and if Kurt thinks that war is injurious to the health, he's not far off the mark, after all. Of course he doesn't say so. The soldier should carry out his duty "joyfully," shouldn't he, and in doing so risk life and limb. But does it have to be your own son? Kurt can't assume that not much will happen to HG in this war, at least not physically. A lot of things will happen in his soul, and its defensive and repressive reflexes will stay with him for the rest of his life—they form and deform him. The "big boy" really was very small when he blundered into this war.

Kurt first receives only a brief note from HG: "Hurrah! Hurrah! Fit for field duty!!! Your delighted son H.-G." And the following day a letter, under the etched initials H.G.K.: "Dear father! So now I've finally achieved the goal of fitness for military service. I imagine you'll be as happy as Mother and I are. But I have also worked toward this reward, I have made great demands on my body for months, and seen that I can endure anything, anything. And not being alone in my knowledge, to have medical certification of the fact that my body is fit in every respect, has been such a great source of joy to me! Now even you will no longer object, can no longer object, dear father, to my becoming a soldier. I hope I have removed your qualms over the possibility that a lengthy period as an officer might spoil me for becoming a businessman later on. I'm aware that by joining up now I am making a warlike sacrifice concerning precious time, and I am not alone in making that sacrifice, since it affects you to at least the same extent. Because it may put off the date when I can work beside you in the family company. But I think that we must sacrifice this extra time just as joyfully as others assume the burden of sacrifices much heavier to bear."

Just look at that: baby face turning his father's own guns against him. Didn't Kurt fill his wartime diary with bombastic screeds about how important it was to carry patriotism and "Germanness" to every land? Didn't he praise Gertrud as a German mother of German children? Didn't he portray everyone's willingness to make sacrifices as the supreme virtue? HG must have read the first parts of that wartime diary, because he was the one who put in the photographs. Now Kurt has clearly tried to curb his son's ambitions, using his own needs and those of the family firm, to reduce his horizons to the concerns of Halberstadt. You can't do that, not with impunity, to a boy who's had to absorb "three cheers for Kaiser and fatherland" with his mother's milk.

THREE

Lieutenant Hans Georg Klamroth

An extensive, detailed search is launched throughout the whole of Germany for cavalry regiments. Letters are dispatched to the Sixteenth Allenstein Dragoons and the Hussars in Leobschütz, the Twelfth Hunters in St. Avold and the Uhlans in Insterburg. The Uhlans in Züllichau immediately reject the application, and the cavalry brigade in Saarbrücken hasn't any room either. The same applies to the Riesenberg Cuirassiers. Gertrud has prepared her applications with meticulous attention to detail. Every former tennis partner, every brother-in-law of an uncle of a former friend from ladies' training college, everyone who knows someone who commands horses is dragged in. Gertrud and HG are on tenterhooks, Gertrud because she wants to find a prestigious position for her son, to which HG has no objections either. But the more urgent matter for him is to be able to sit his Notabitur immediately after the holidays, because then—HG writes to his father, Kurt— "three draftees from my class have to do the exam, so I could join them and wouldn't be the only one sitting the exam with this new headmaster."

And so it comes to pass. Two days after the end of the summer holidays in 1916 the relieving news arrives that HG has been accepted as a cadet by the Prince Albrecht of Prussia (Lithuanian) First Dragoon Regiment in Königsberg—"a good regiment," according to Kurt. He dispatches his agreement posthaste, and the next morning HG writes his Notabitur essay on the subject "Stand by your nation. It's your proper place." The boy has learned this lesson from earliest childhood, and accordingly finds it all "rather easy." But the next day "they examined me in Latin, Math, and History, pretty nasty on the boss's part, it lasted more than an hour. I wouldn't wish an oral like that on anybody."

What could have been driving the headmaster? Love of mankind, because he wanted to keep young men from dying in the thick of battle? Or was it a kind of defiance: do educational standards have to be thrown to the four winds just because there's a war on? HG just scrapes through the Abitur, but once it's over nobody cares. He comes home adorned with laurels, and he's spared himself six months of school. He's a Fahnenjunker, and his mother, at the harmonium, sings Schubert's "Frühlingsglaube": "Nun muss sich alles, alles wenden" (Now everything, everything must change).

A week later HG is to join his regiment in Königsberg, and only now does Gertrud start worrying about her motherly courage. Königsberg is hardly around the corner, even Grodno isn't as far away. "Have you thought," she moans in a letter to Kurt, "that the boy will have to find his way all alone in that very strange town, where we don't even know of a hotel? I'm sure he'll have to rent an apartment, because he can only take the bare minimum to the barracks." Shouldn't at least one of them go with him? "We'd have to leave here at four o'clock in the morning to be in Königsberg at eight in the evening, or else we'd set off at 3:55 in the afternoon and take the train in Berlin at three minutes past eleven, which gets you in at 8:35 in the morning. Then you might be able to welcome him there and be sure that he gets a good rest and doesn't turn up at the regiment looking white as a sheet."

That's what Kurt does. He combines the journey with a buying expedition for his Grodno haberdashery, and on September 7, 1916, after a last comfortable night in a hotel, he delivers his son to the Königsberg-Rotenstein barracks. He first exchanges a word with HG's new boss, Major von Mandelsloh, as one officer to another. This pays off—in future the major will send his comrade the cavalry captain regular reports on HG's progress.

The first weeks aren't easy. HG is the only Junker in the place, neither fish nor fowl. He's supposed to associate with the men only in an official capacity—how does that work, when he shares a dormitory with them, for example? He isn't allowed to dine in the officers' mess, because he isn't yet an officer. But eating with the others isn't allowed either. Kurt warns him: "Of course you can't keep turning up with your mess tin. If it only happens occasionally nobody's going to worry too much, but it can't happen more often than that." So he has to go in search of food elsewhere. He does that alone, because neither the officers nor the men can go with him.

He's not to mention that he goes riding every day at home. Kurt says: "If you do, somebody's going to find an opportunity to portray you as a bungler"—and he must take care to have his uniforms pressed every now and then, "because a Junker always has to look very smart at all times." HG's uniforms are, incidentally, made in Halberstadt, as are the boots, which is difficult because fabric and leather are almost impossible to come by. But even during the war officers—and candidates—still have to supply their own kit beyond the basic equipment, which means that Dad has to pay for it. And that remains the case in the present day—even though uniforms are compulsory, officers in the German army still have to supply their own, apart from a wardrobe subsidy that comes to just 15 euros a month.

In their letters, both parents flutter around HG. Gertrud: "Here's some fresh linen. You pack your dirty things in the cardboard box, I enclose a franked label, and you can reuse the packing tape." Kurt: "If you think you're 'above' this NCO by the name of L., and that you're being presented to him as an example, it isn't going to encourage comradeship. Examples are generally seen as disagreeable. So be careful!" Gertrud: "Do you sleep on the top bunk or the bottom, and can you perhaps get your case under the bed?" Kurt: "Certainly you can ask the major to let you off stable duty." (HG has to brush out ten horses a day.) Gertrud: "I hope your comrades have good manners." That's what it's like when you "grant your son his independence." Gertrud again: "Do you need Hirschtalg [a cream to prevent soreness]? Are you saddle-sore? Go to bed early and don't smoke so much!" In every photograph with his regiment, HG has a cigarette in his mouth.

After just four weeks barracks life is at an end, and HG moves into two furnished rooms nearby. The landlady cooks his meals and his father pays. Now HG sets off to report for duty every morning the way other people go to the office. He's had a chance to unpack his suitcase, in which he has found underpants and biscuits hidden by Gertrud. He gets little pots of plum puree sent from home, and in return he supplies Gertrud with soap, which is still available in Königsberg.

At the beginning of October 1916, just four weeks after HG arrived in Königsberg, the draft board in Halberstadt calls HG in for a medical examination—so that was close, and Gertrud is "pleased, after all, that you are already a soldier. Who knows where you might have been sent." Königsberg is a reasonable place, above all because family connections provide sufficient estates and manor houses in the surrounding area, where the young man spends his weekends, kisses the hand of his kind hostess, and goes off to shoot ducks with his host. The fact that HG is charged with riding the young horses at the barracks says something about his horsemanship, and by the end of November, having turned eighteen, he is promoted to lance corporal. Gertrud: "We're delighted that you've got past the highest level of the common herd [!] so quickly. But commanding twelve to fifteen recruits immediately—best of luck. I'd like to see you doing it."

At the end of 1916, Kurt is ordered from Grodno to Magdeburg, where he is made leader of the newly established "war office." This was an instrument of "total war," even if that name didn't yet exist. Germany's military situation in 1916 was far from rosy: the hell of Verdun, five months of carnage at the Somme, losses in Italy, the Russian invasion of Bukovina, Romania's entry into the war, the pointless marine battle in the Skagerrak, pointless because while the Germans might have been tactically successful against the British—good for the German ego!—in strategic terms the slaughter came to nothing. The Germans and their allies held their ground in every direction, but at what cost.

On August 29, 1916, Hindenburg and his quartermaster general Ludendorff assume supreme command of the army—basically the beginning of a military dictatorship. From then on Germany was in a "state of siege," with press censorship, no gatherings without official consent, random arrests, and drumhead courts-martial. These were the responsibility of the Deputy General Command, which effectively supplanted the civilian administration. The goal was the total mobilization of the home front. The Hindenburg Plan was intended to deploy the last reserves of men and matériel at the front, and so the production vital to the war effort was cranked even higher, and all healthy men were to be seconded from the factories into the army.

Replacements were to be recruited from the general population, and the "Law Concerning the Summons to the Defense of the Fatherland in Time of War" obliged all men between the ages of seventeen and sixty to work in administrative offices, the war industry, agriculture, nursing, transport, or wherever gaps had been left by workers sent to the front. It was the task of the war offices to enforce this, to guarantee the energy supply as far as possible, and at the same time to make sure that everyone involved in the war effort had enough to eat.

Particular attention is devoted to the women who are now to perform men's work. At the Leuna works in Merseburg, for example, three thousand women are taken on "to shift earth," five thousand work in the Reinsdorf explosives factory, and the same number in the ammunition plant in Gerwisch. Kurt sets up a special women's department in his war office, dealing with cribs, breastfeeding times, breaks, and "workloads suitable for women," and above all the avoidance of any threats to their virtue.

Pretty soon, Kurt insists on sending a woman supervisor to every base where women are to be employed as secretaries, cooks, and telephone operators, thus freeing up men to be deployed at the front. These supervisors see to it that the ladies are accompanied to and from work, and that they stay in their lodgings when work is over. Kurt: "Many unsuitable girls had applied for these jobs, whether out of a spirit of adventure or for worse reasons. Thereupon disciplinary sanctions were applied, and morally unsuitable girls were sent home." Certainly, they were supposed to work, but there was to be no fun, and in Magdeburg they kept a close eye to ensure that barracks rats didn't bring their girlfriends with them— Kurt doesn't allow anybody anything.

Meanwhile Gertrud is kept very busy with her kitchen garden, her goats and rabbits, any number of chickens, and now she's fattening a pig as well. The coachman is at the front, so is the caretaker, and the number of company employees who might have been able to help her has been cut by half. Apart from the housemaids, she has only an old rheumatic gardener left, and her everyday life is determined by shortages—well, all right, shortages relatively speaking. Gertrud doesn't complain, but she does talk about it.

She can't get hold of starch—"what am I going to do with your shirts?" She unravels old socks for darning thread—"there must be a nail in one of your boots, the hole's always in the same place," she complains to HG. She wants his briefcase for Kurt junior, so that she can give his satchel to a younger boy—"schoolbags are impossible to find." Her ten-year-old daughter, Erika, had spent the summer running around barefoot like a "brave little German girl," because shoes were in such short supply. Gertrud has stoves set up in the house, only three for almost thirty rooms, not much when you think that Halberstadt winters in those days were absolutely freezing, fourteen degrees Fahrenheit and below for weeks at a time. But the coal allowance is no longer enough for central heating. The copper gutters are replaced by zinc—copper's needed for the war effort.

HG trots through Königsberg, the capital of East Prussia, in search of artificial honey for Halberstadt's Christmas baking; sometimes he sends an army loaf, which is received with jubilation, and occasionally manages to get hold of Königsberg marzipan, which his sisters reverently devour with a knife and fork. He actually succeeds in tracking down a box of cigars for his father—in Magdeburg or Halberstadt they are now being sold singly. On weekends he also tries his luck as a huntsman on the local estates, and cheers up his loved ones back home with hares or snipe—a good thing the postal service is still so fast!

In Magdeburg, Kurt organizes a factory kitchen committee, on call every day at noon for complaints about the quality of the food in the works canteen, and if necessary to instigate spot checks. Since this committee has been in existence, complaints have abated—either the canteen cooks are cooking better or, as Kurt suspects, the complaints were the result of "provocateurs who wanted to stir up unrest among the workers." Problems gnaw away at everyone's nerves. The populace is edgy, because the power cuts are increasing and the only jam to be found is made of turnips. The army is quarreling with civilian officials. Everyone has someone at the front to be worried about. In Kurt's war office, too, the army is repeatedly testing people for their fitness for military service, and the older officials are particularly worried that they might still be caught. So Kaiser Wilhelm's 1916 Christmas message to his adversaries is balm for sore hearts. He offers peace and, when his offer is rejected, still gives the population a sense "that it isn't our fault."

This imperial offer of peace was by no means unchallenged. A bitter argument had broken out in Germany about the goals of the war: "peace through agreement" on the one hand, "peace through victory" on the other. Above all, the Social Democrats and the Center Party wanted "a peace based on agreement and lasting reconciliation between nations. Forced cession of territories and political, economic, or financial violations are irreconcilable with such a peace." In his speech from the throne at the beginning of the war on August 4, 1914, the Kaiser had said: "We are not driven by a need to conquer"—and that was to remain the case. On the other hand, conservatives and National Liberals, the nationalist "All-Germans," and many hundreds of reactionary university teachers, supported by Grand Admiral von Tirpitz and the rabble-rouser Erich Ludendorff, are calling for *Lebensraum* for the German people and a "Pan-German Central Europe"—Hitler could follow on seamlessly.

At the start of the war, Kurt was very much the conqueror, though now in his letters to HG he tends cautiously toward the idea of a peace that is "honorable, of course, and appropriate to German victories." The high losses at the front and above all his experience of the misery of the civilian population lead him to wish "that there will be a just end." The tone between father and son has changed. Kurt writes to his son as one man, one soldier to another. HG is now on a Fahnenjunker training course in Döberitz near Potsdam. At last the difficult protocol issues of the military hierarchy are a thing of the past; officers of the same rank from the whole of Germany all find themselves in the same boat. On March 20, 1917, HG is promoted to NCO; things are accelerating now. While in Döberitz he forms friendships with a whole series of young men that will last well into the Second World War and the circles of the resistance movement. Then in July 1917, he transfers to barracks in Tilsit for final training, spends some time in the military hospital with a severe intestinal infection, and all of a sudden the war begins for HG.

After the German occupation of 1915, peace had reigned in Kurland for two years. The province had been governed by Russia until the Teutonic Knights conquered it in the thirteenth century and established the area as a German province. Located in the south of Latvia, in 1917 it was the northernmost point of the occupation line running from Bukovina to the Gulf of Riga. The city of Riga hadn't yet been taken by Germany, and suddenly that was precisely the issue. Supreme Army Command needed a free hand at the Eastern Front, since the United States had entered the war in spring 1917. They wanted to conclude a separate peace with Russia, which was weak in any case. A revolution had swept away Tsar Nicholas in March, and three days after the American declaration of war Ludendorff had allowed the man who called himself Lenin to travel across Germany from Switzerland to Petrograd. He and his Bolshevik revolution—this was Ludendorff's plan—would completely destabilize Russia, and peace would fall into the laps of the Germans like a ripe peach.

Before the signature of any peace treaty, Ludendorff wants to get his hands on Riga and the islands in the gulf quickly—it's a step in the right direction, and Petrograd is just around the corner. The successful battle of Riga lasts from September 1 until September 5, 1917, and it's HG's first action on the battlefield. His faraway father writes with a certain longing: "I'm so happy that you're able to be there. I'm delighted with all my heart that you're about to have such a lovely time"—he really does mean the battle. "It's the finest thing that can happen to a young cavalryman. But take care that for all your guts and daredevilry you do not risk your life needlessly. The main thing, when the cavalry vanguard is reconnoitering, is to ensure that reports come back correctly, and this goal is achieved only when the leader isn't shot down unnecessarily." When he's right, he's right.

HG doesn't get shot down, but he is wounded on the second day. He takes a bullet to the shoulder, mitigated by the fact that the bullet first shattered his telescope. This injury doesn't suit HG at all. At last there's a war, and he's fallen at the very first hurdle. He wants to get back to his troop as quickly as possible, because otherwise he has a sense, once again, that life is passing him by. His mother and his sister Annie immediately set off on the long journey to Tilsit, where the young warrior is lying in the military hospital. Kurt expresses his sympathy in a letter: "A shame they caught you so quickly. Because staying so hard on the heels of the defeated Twelfth Army"—the Russian one—"as a cavalryman, is a splendid, even if an insanely arduous task." He goes on to say at last: "I thank God that he protected you so mercifully."

Less than three weeks later, HG is awarded the Iron Cross, Second Class—either it's being handed out at an inflationary rate as the war progresses, or the boy really did excel in battle before taking his injury. At any rate, his parents are proud, and his father says with a slight edge, "I myself had to wait a lot longer." But after all, Kurt was based only behind the lines. "You're quite right," he writes with a hint of regret, "I've never been really involved in gunfire."

What on earth is going on with these men? In almost every letter they mention the fact that someone from their family or circle of friends has fallen. Three of the cousins with whom HG grew up are dead. One of them anticipated in Flanders that he wouldn't survive the battle of Ypres, and left moving letters of farewell to his parents: "I hope I will be mercifully spared too severe a battle with death. It's only a shame that death must come so soon after life began to be really beautiful since my promotion to the rank of officer. Don't grieve for me, for you can't know the deeper purpose of my early death. Farewell, may God protect Germany and ease your pain." Cousin Albrecht was twenty-one.

Kurt manages a two-line description of the funeral—"I was deeply moved"—before passing rapidly on to "two quick pieces of news: the food in the Excelsior Hotel is really good now"—Kurt is in Berlin—"Soup, main course, and a pudding for 4 marks. I was surprised how good the food was. Then I came across a little wine bar, 'Pfuhl,' in Königgrätzer Strasse, there's a big sign by the door saying Naturally Pure Wines. To be highly recommended." What am I supposed to do with a letter like that? And worse, what is HG to do with it? He loved his cousin! Or this: "How are things going with the Russian artillery, are they firing gas-grenades as well? We've got them, splendid new things now that were very useful to us in Flanders." This is the same man who was so furious that the "perfidious British" were using dumdum bullets.

HG spent eight weeks—September–October 1917—in a static war on the Dvina. Much later he would say it was "disgustingly dangerous," and "I'm still amazed that I got out of it alive." Now he writes: "Every night some Polski troops turn up and want to attack us. By and large I'm enormously pleased to be able to take part in so much war, but I'd really rather have a big war than all this creeping around in forests and bogs." For recovery HG is then sent off with eight others to the woods in the hinterland of Wilna, and here he practices being a superior. "Fighting gangs in Lithuania" it says in his military papers for this period, but he sees and hears nothing of it. By now he is nineteen and bored to death because he does nothing apart from mucking out horses.

Gertrud tries to console him: "Remember that you've just experienced such a cheerful bit of war, and you were left so mercifully safe!" Of course she's relieved that the threat of another bullet has passed for the time being, and she happily babbles her maternal concern on the page: "You'll be getting some candles, but remember your eyes and don't try to read by such a faint light. Please try to give up drinking. And think about your bowels—you shouldn't mess with things like that. And stay away from bad water!" She was slightly alarmed to learn that HG was hunting wolves, "but then again you're a good shot."

HG whiles away the boredom with almost daily letters home, and if it was up to him, I read, the political situation would be quite different. The Brest-Litovsk peace negotiations begin shortly before Christmas 1917, and HG fumes: "Kühlmann is a first-class weakling." This was Richard von Kühlmann, the head of the Foreign Office, who represented the German side in the negotiations. In the face of resistance from Ludendorff, he was trying—in vain—to keep his eye on the postwar period, when Germany would still need Russia as a partner. "A traitor to the German cause," HG rages, "Kühlmann is the only person I would happily stand up against the nearest tree, except that it would be a waste of an honest German soldier's bullet."

Kurt, a truly patient father, replies on three closely written pages, although with gentle mockery: "People who stand on the mountain generally see farther than those squatting in the Lithuanian valley. So you may happily assume that Kühlmann and the people instructing him have a better overall view." He explains Germany's precarious situation despite earlier military successes and admits: "I still have hopes of a reasonably favorable peace through agreement." Finally he warns his little know-all: "Holding out in your godforsaken little Lithuanian hole out there is easier than living here in Germany."

That was probably true. At another base—Gut Dobuski, which I've never found on a map—HG, along with a lieutenant and three other NCOs, was responsible for thirty soldiers, and here too there were no "gangs" for miles around. On the other hand, "I usually wake up at eight, when Armutat fetches my boots"—that's his "cleaner," probably something like a groom, but his function seems to be that of an orderly. The boy "clicks his spurs together, whispers 'Herr Junker requires?,' pokes the fire in the stove, and brings hot water. Then I splash away vigorously at my washstand—built by

Armutat—so much so that the two farm girls next door asked my 'cleaner' in astonishment whether I washed myself every day."

After that the young gentleman breakfasts: "Milk, eggs, sausage, and bread—while the lieutenant is still asleep. Then there are exercises from ten till eleven. I've been assigned half a column, which I maneuver around all by myself, practicing at being a commander. At half past eleven we have lunch, from the field kitchen, which is great. After lunch the lieutenant and I sink into the deep upholstered armchairs in the sitting room [where they come from, God alone knows!], smoke, and wait for the mailman. Then I ride for a while—it's minus twenty outside—or take a walk on skis until tea at four. After that we read or write till supper at seven. Tonight we're having pork chops and fried potatoes, yesterday we had scrambled eggs. With them we drink milk as always. At half past eight I take my leave and go to bed, while the lieutenant goes on reading until long into the night."

It's a drone's life compared with the truly murderous service of the troops in the west or the struggle for survival of the strained population back at home. That's how HG sees things, too. All right, he's on night duty twice a week, and has to sleep with his clothes on. Now and then he rides at night with a patrol to other villages, where the soldiers search houses and stables for "gangs," and frighten the inhabitants with their carbines. Sometimes, too, there are unexpected exercises, for which the soldiers have to be ready to march at a moment's notice, but it's all a bit pointless. HG has his schoolbooks sent to him, and starts reading English and history again. He studies specialist military literature and reads several newspapers, since Kurt wrote to tell him that his immature political views are the product of a lack of information. But that's not enough for him—he feels superfluous.

On February 8, 1918, HG writes to Kurt: "I feel I have the strength to achieve something. In the west, all my comrades from Döberitz are being awarded the Iron Cross, First Class, one after the other, and I've been condemned to inactivity. I don't think,

Father, that I will be able to stand it for very much longer. My initial enthusiasm and my thirst for blood [!] have subsided, things like that vanish remarkably quickly, through the first test of fire, in fact. They have made way for the calm and reasonable reflection that where strength is present it must be exploited. But the First Cavalry Division [HG's regiment] will stay here as a police force until peace is concluded, since it has the greatest number of Lithuanian and Polish-speaking NCOs and units.

"Over the next few weeks the decision will have to be made as to whether we go to war with Russia. If that proves not to be the case, would you have any fundamental objections to my volunteering for a different regiment in the west? In the next few days I'm going to be made an ensign. Promotion to officer could follow immediately, if I got an instant transfer. It would be hard for me to leave the regiment, to which I've belonged for over a year and a half, but you can't allow yourself to be swayed by sentimental feelings with your eye on the greater cause. On the quiet, I already have a particular regiment in mind, in a place where it would be easy to distinguish oneself, and easier still to do one's duty. But first, of course, I'd like your opinion."

HG *does* know what he would be in for. Risking his life for a pathetic piece of tin that he's not going to get out here in the Lithuanian pampas? His cousins have fallen, along with his best friend from Junker training school in Döberitz, Horst von Rosenberg, whose death continues to trouble him. Nonetheless, HG keeps quoting that stupid sentence, *Dulce et decorum est pro patria mori*. It was nonsense even when Horace said it. *Decorum*—honorable—well, could be. Perhaps. But *dulce*—sweet? Since when has it been sweet to die of a bullet in the belly, in a rain-soaked, plowed-up battlefield? HG adds his own touch. "Lucky man!" he writes in such cases in his letters. He's nuts. But Kurt was exactly the same.

Not anymore. Now, as HG drones on about duty and strength, he hears what the boy really wants: braids, bars, stripes. And he won't let him have them. He can sympathize with him for wanting to be awarded the Iron Cross, First Class, and soon to become an officer. But: "1. No one doubts your courage and your keen sense of duty. You demonstrated that at Riga and afterward. 2. The Iron Cross, First Class, is a goal worth striving for, but not to the point where all calm consideration can be allowed to disappear behind it.

"3. With your regiment you have proven with your blood that you are prepared to give your life for the fatherland. If your regiment is deployed again, you will do it again, and if God has so willed, we, your parents, will bend to His will and bear even the worst. But if I imagine myself having given you my permission to expose yourself unnecessarily, and indeed without any moral need, to the coming struggle in the west, which is going to be terrible, and if something happened to you, if you were crippled, for instance, or blinded, then the thought that I could have prevented it all would never leave me in peace. 4. Always bear in mind, my dear boy, that you will not remain a professional soldier forever, but that you have a great and also a fine task ahead of you with your fathers' old firm, which you must not leave in the lurch."

Should I object that the father puts the parents' wishes before those of the son? When HG was a child, it was much the same: "You are to bring your parents joy." Should I bristle at the fact that he has messed up his son's military career, but possibly spared him an early death? I'll say that I believe Kurt was thinking along these lines when he told HG that volunteering for the battlefields in the west wouldn't be good for "us, your parents." Had he said that HG's crackbrained idea was not good for him, his son, the boy would have gone on endlessly about how he was a grown-up by now. So he obeyed his father, as always. In the event, this was farsighted. Because shortly afterward, things really did "get going" in the east. The Baltic Germans, tormented by Russia since the outbreak of war, were freed; first the Russian Army, then Lenin's Red Guard were defeated. And HG was there, and he finally became a lieutenant. But before we get to that, there are some other things that need to be told.

For example, that HG keeps the family at home supplied with groceries. With his "cleaner" Armutat, he patrols the Lithuanian villages and buys up whatever he can get hold of. For Gertrud's birthday at the end of January a box arrives containing veal, a goose, butter, military bread, flour, tea, and dried vegetables. HG learns—and I greatly admire him for it—to pack eggs in such a way that almost all of them arrive unbroken. He wraps thirty-pound hams and whole sides of bacon in brand-new scouring cloths and old pillowcases, and uses a captured shotgun to shoot hares—animals highly valued in Halberstadt, not least for their fur.

On his horseback patrols, HG gets to know the country and its people: "Yesterday I found myself at a funeral. The corpse, an old lady, lay in her coffin in the cleanly swept room. All around were four clean tables covered with tablecloths and laden with the most delicious food—ham, bacon, potatoes, *kapuste* (sauerkraut), bread, butter, and so on. There was also *alaus,* a fabulous home-brewed beer. I had to drink more of it than I would have wished, because it contains a great deal of alcohol and has the corresponding effects. All the *panjes* bowed low to me, saying 'Nastroviak, Pani!' Quite against my will, they made me a kind of chairman of their festivities, almost completely ignoring my three dragoons. Funny people.

"At the end came the corpse kiss, which I resolutely resisted. Luckily they understood, and the general kiss of consolation, with which I joined in, because there was a crowd of very pretty little *paninkas* there. Then the corpse was laid on sleds, among terrifying lamentations, and the sexton charged off alone with it. Everyone else immediately started dancing. A proper *Krakowiak* is really quite different from our German dances; it clicks and clacks, claps and clatters, quite delightful. The girls looked very charming in their brightly colored costumes. We 'Germanski soldieri' were, of course, much sought after as dancing partners, and even I, 'Pan

NCO!,' was forced to join in although I don't really care to dance with the simple *panjes* because it harms discipline."

Discipline—what he probably means is the ban on fraternization by German troops. What's the problem, if the whole place is supposed to be German territory? But HG's discipline with regard to girls remains a delicate subject anyhow: "Once when patrolling in deep snow I discovered, in a woodman's hut, a beautiful, clean Polish girl out of a fairy tale, who was very nice to me. Sometimes these days it's quite off-putting the way the women here force themselves on our soldiers with their simple, animal need for a man!"

He wished! And he would surely be pleased to play the benefactor. Father Kurt suspects ground a: "I've looked on the map and found the area you've been patrolling for pretty Polish girls. I'm surprised that you've found a 'clean' one. Or do you mean that not in the literal, but in the extended sense of the word? As far as I can remember I've never met a Polish girl who was scrubbed clean. And by the way, be careful! I've seen some sad things while I was out there. But you know all that."

"Masculine pressure" keeps the boy busy. He plays sports, takes cold baths, rides till he's exhausted, and writes to his father: "You'll know from your own experience that at my age the body urgently needs such distraction, and often enough it still cries out for release." That's worth a snatched hour of the father's time, busy though he is, and Kurt replies: "I completely understand your physical needs, and can quite imagine them. They are intensified by rich food and by the fact that you are underemployed.

"At your age I discovered that if one consorts with girls from the better social circles, one is most easily encouraged in one's abstinence *in venere* [abstinence of the flesh]. The joys of the grape also have a crucial part to play here. Must you drink so much? I would worry, because drinking also stimulates the body to an enormous degree. Good reading greatly encourages intellectual discipline. Gymnastics and sport alone won't do it. Distraction of the thoughts from all things erotic is also required. It takes you beyond the challenges that plagued even hot-blooded Luther, and made him throw his inkpot at the source of his temptation. For the body, abstinence *in venere* is by no means damaging; nocturnal emissions take care of that. So in this respect as in others, be brave and strong. Later on, you will be all the more grateful when you become the father of a healthy pack of children, and I pray that God may let me experience that. Most cordially—your old man, who always wants to be a friend to you."

Kurt is replying to his son just as he spoke to him on their chatty morning rides. HG asks at the beginning of January, "What are we actually living on now, Father? You must be spending hundreds every month, Mother's spending is in the thousands, and you also give me three hundred every month. It can't be coming out of your captain's salary, and what's happening to the business? Is it earning anything at all in these hard times? Can the factory still operate?" Six days later the answer is there, this time in four closely written double-sized sheets—Kurt has taken his time.

No, in truth Kurt's officer's income won't cover the family outgoings, the wages of the company employees, the running costs of the transport fleet, which is still in existence, storage capacities, silos, and numerous properties. He lost all his foreign benefits on his return to Germany, he can no longer claim any expenses, he has to pay for the flat in Magdeburg by himself, and feed himself. But the firm is going from strength to strength. It's been in operation for 127 years, and is making considerable profits thanks to the energetic direction of Kurt's brother-in-law Heinrich Schulz, who married Gertrud's sister. Kurt made him a partner shortly before the war. "An authorized signatory could never have done what he has managed as a partner."

Kurt lists his significant assets, his shares in the company and Gertrud's money, which was earning considerable interest in her father's bank. He explains to his son how he should one day finance the inheritance for his siblings, lists tax burdens and amortizations, secret reserves and capital investments. The father is treating his very young son as the partner he will eventually become.

That's how Kurt is with his son. He never says, "It has nothing to do with you," or "Don't talk about things you don't understand." He wants HG to understand. He isn't impatient or arrogant toward his precocious lad in far-off Lithuania. While the father has sympathy with the exhaustion of the war-weary population, HG crows with approval when strikers are shot down in Berlin: "I hope the government will stay hard. Those people shall see who's master in his own house." Kurt replies: "And who will build the house? And besides, my dear young man, you've never gone hungry." HG is immediately ashamed: "Perhaps I don't always get the right perspective on things from here."

FOUR

HG with Lenin and Trotsky

All of a sudden HG finds himself in the thick of it. On February 10, 1918, Trotsky breaks off the peace negotiations in Brest-Litovsk. Ludendorff uses this as an excuse to carry out his long-nurtured plans to conquer Estonia and Livonia, officially to free the Baltic Germans from the clutches of the Red Army, but in reality because he had always had his eyes on the region—Petrograd is only 150 kilometers from the mouth of the Narova River. And what's Livonia, exactly? I've found out in the meantime: it no longer officially exists, it's on the Baltic coast, it was German a long time ago, then Polish, and Swedish for a time, and from 1721 it spent two hundred peaceful years as one of the Russian Baltic provinces, with its capital in Riga. After the First World War it was divided between Latvia and Estonia.

Livonia is the place that the Eighth Army is to march into, on the double. Just in case peace negotiations resume, Ludendorff wants to make sure he gets what he wants and can hold on to it. "It's going to be splendid," HG writes delightedly, putting all desires for a westward transfer on hold. By now he's an ensign with the cavalry, and quickly sets to work as a commander. In eleven days, marching fifty kilometers a day in deep snow, they cover the distance from Riga to the Gulf of Finland—"it's almost impossible to believe that the horses survived the journey." The whole advance, "as far as we were concerned," HG writes, "passed without any clashes with the Russians, who were always running closely ahead of us. Until the day before yesterday." With a strong ten-man patrol, they take a whole Russian squadron in a village by surprise; forty officers and seventy-two men with all their equipment are disarmed and taken prisoner. "When we had almost completed our arrest, a patrol of Russian officers came riding over the bridge, not suspecting a thing."

HG does what he has learned to do: "At thirty paces I called to the officer: 'Stoi!' You should have seen the man's stupid face, it was a picture! But he wasn't as cowardly as the others, and after a moment's reflection he pulled his horse around and drew his pistol. I'd been waiting for him to do just that, and my good old parabellum rang out twice, whereupon he slid sideways from his saddle, but was dragged over the bridge by his horse. That was where we found him, it was the captain, both bullets had lodged in his left lung. The first person I've ever deliberately killed. War!"

This event will never be referred to again. Not by HG, and Kurt and Gertrud don't so much as mention it, unless we take Gertrud's words—"We share your delight in all your many marvelous experiences"—as a commentary. No one rebukes him for his unspeakable tone, no one is uneasy about his overbearing attitude—as though HG hadn't just killed a human being, but done something else. What, in fact? He's brought down a trophy, a twelve-point stag, but hunters grant their booty more respect than HG does his Russian.

HG's letter continues without a break: he has managed to get hold of a raincoat and several pairs of socks from the booty, because when they were on their way to Riga the officers' luggage car was looted, and now he hadn't a thing to wear. The boy's tone becomes civilized again, and that's the only clue I have that the Russian officer's death has shaken him, and that being so coarse is his only way of escaping it. And no one talks to him. No one helps him out of this damned "manliness."

The soldiers are welcomed into northern Estonia with a forest of German flags and great jubilation—"Welcome, German liberators!" The scene must have been like Hitler's army marching into Vienna twenty years later. The Baltic knights in whose castles and farms the Germans are quartered talk of terrible acts of cruelty on the part of the Red Guard, and once again Gertrud in Halberstadt hammers out her piece of Schubert at the harmonium: "Now everything, everything must change!" She is at least as enthusiastic as her son: "It's a good thing that the Russians are being shown once again who they're dealing with."

HG thinks much the same, but he is even more stirred by the enthusiasm of the Baltic population—he, the little soldier, suddenly in the savior's role: "It's as though we're living in Germany among Germans, and that's equally true of the Estonians, who are just like Germans except they speak an incomprehensible dialect. It would be the gravest error and at the same time the meanest sort of whim if the German government, out of some sort of sentimentality toward Russia, spurned these loyal, German-minded people, who have for decades hungered for German rule and German care, when the fulfillment of their wishes seems so close." HG evokes his loved ones at home: "You can ask anybody you want, you'll hear it in Estonian, Latvian, German, and Russian: anything but independence! We want to belong completely to Germany!" He can hardly contain himself. He is experiencing the "ideal Germans" here, because "such a combination of kindness, hospitality and helpfulness, efficiency and love of the distant fatherland is something that one would search long and hard to find at home!"

Gertrud is equally keen: "We pounce eagerly on the army report every day. What great and magnificent days these are, with you bringing freedom to the Germans over there." Only Kurt is more reticent: "You write that everyone there, even the Estonians and the Latvians, desires *Anschluss* with Germany, and I do believe of course that they will say nothing else to your face. But in neutral countries abroad one hears from Estonian and Latvian deputies that most people in the country want an autonomous state. So we should let things settle, because we aren't yet in a position to judge."

HG isn't concerned with letting things settle. The Germans establish a civil administration, and suddenly the young man finds himself in a similar role to that of his father in Grodno. When they withdrew, the Russians had taken with them all the files and funds of the little town of Arroküll. Now HG sits in an office in the castle, behind a door bearing the legend "Local Kommandantur Dept. II," with a list of all the things he is dealing with, or perhaps we should say, supposed to be dealing with: arms licenses, captured materiel, machinery, forestry, feeding of the local population, distribution of supplies, police, sanitation, and veterinary matters, information. Kurt's son asks him if any of this sounds at all familiar, saying, "At least I'm pretty indispensable." Kurt replies laconically: "Well, I suppose you must be learning something."

The Germans settle down for a lengthy stay in the town. The peace of Brest-Litovsk has finally been signed in March 1918, after an exhausting period of to-ing and fro-ing. As expected, Russia loses Livonia and Estonia, along with Lithuania. The Russians sign the treaty because Lenin wants to have free rein in his own country for the Revolution, and he also expects that given the weakness of the Germans and Austrians this contractual stuff won't apply for long anyway. He wasn't wrong there. But no one foresaw just how chaotic the Russian situation would be, and so—unlike in Lithuania—there really are gangs of young people calling themselves the "new revolutionary army," keeping the German soldiers busy. HG can abandon his basic course in administration for the time being and, like everyone else, lies in wait fully equipped somewhere in the snow:

"We're waiting to give the appropriate reception to the 'new revolutionary army,' should they do anything stupid. We have enough ropes ready, because if any of those peace breakers, the Jewish louts of the Red Guard, have the good fortune to fall into our hands, we're stringing them up. A few days ago, in our own village, three Red Guards were hanged, serious criminals who had cruelly tortured a farmer before murdering him. It's a shame the sun wasn't good enough to take a picture, the lads looked good, hanging side by side from the branch of a big fir tree. But now word reaches us that the Bolsheviks have changed their minds and decided to withdraw their 'troops' from the neutral zone agreed along the Narova, and have declared themselves willing to ratify the peace. Which means that they'll be sparing our horses the violent march on St. Petersburg."

Should I allow the "Jewish louts"—*Judenlümmel*—to pass without comment? At this point the word isn't yet a synonym for murder and extermination; it's only the beginning of the journey in that direction. In HG's presumptuous arrogance, the term is a cliché for the fear of the "other," the kind of thing people use to protect the alleged superior status of their own group. "Nigger" could be said to have once fulfilled a similar function in America. But there it is again, that tone. Not quite as bad as when he was talking about the death of the Russian cavalry captain, because presumably HG didn't "string up" the men himself. That's the kind of thing you get private soldiers to do. But I sense that this unusually vulgar talk on HG's part is his attempt to keep the whole thing at a distance. I sense both his machismo and his fear.

The fear is lost in HG's normal day-to-day business, when he's sitting in a raised hunting hide at four o'clock in the morning with Baltic knights waiting to shoot capercaillie and, after a princely breakfast, going to his command office with its census of people and animals, and plans to feed the population and the troops and satisfied captain. The two of them have set about cataloging all the administrative processes—"He's such a maniac for order, he has to label every single cupboard and every single shelf." HG is wallowing in "Diary Number *x*" and "File mark *y*," and endless incomprehensible abbreviations like *Abw., Fa., Ben, Sa, Fo, Rei,* and *Esr.* "I've always liked doing this kind of thing, but I've never had the chance to do it on such a big scale." He really is his father's son, the same orderly handwriting, the same ordered mind with all those firstlies, secondlies, thirdlies. Poor Else! My mother, in all her chaos, was surrounded by right angles.

But it's not Else's turn yet. The young man to whom she would become engaged only three years later will no longer be the one I have accompanied thus far. His own chaos breaks out on April 22, 1918, when he is nineteen. Three days later he writes to Kurt: "Dear Father! My captain will by now have told you of the event that will probably turn me into a different person forever. In short, what happened is this. On the afternoon of your birthday, April 22, I volunteered for a patrol, since I had spent the whole day working in the office, and wanted to go for a nice ride to recover. News had come in that a pig had been stolen in a village by two Germans and an Estonian soldier. I rode there, but on the way I had to leave behind the two dragoons I had brought with me, as the horse of one of them had seriously injured itself. So I rode on alone, accompanied only by our interpreter Hoffmann, although he was not considered a member of the military.

"Arriving at the scene of the crime, I quickly hunted down the thieves, two German infantrymen, one of whom, the leader, was inebriated and thus twice as dangerous as he might otherwise have been. After my initial order to lay down his weapons (pistol, bayonet, knife), he threatened that he would stab and shoot me and everyone around if I tried to arrest him. From that point onward I was fully convinced that one of us would not survive this. Nonetheless, I went on trying for about three-quarters of an hour until I noticed that I was getting into ever greater danger.

"In the course of the conversation I had maneuvered him into the open, as I was entirely powerless in the forest, where he could suddenly have jumped behind cover and shot at me. All attempts to learn his name and his company during our conversation had been in vain. Instead he threatened me several times that he would defend himself to the death if I tried to do anything. So without his noticing I got my pistol ready to force him to hand over his weapons immediately. As I was walking with him across an open path of ground, I leaped aside, drew my pistol, and shouted, 'Drop your weapons,' to which he replied, 'You've cheated me, you dog!'

"With these words he lunged so aggressively for his pistol that it was clear to me that he would shoot as soon as he could take aim. So I fired. As the first shot missed, and the man shouted, 'You dog, I'll kill you!' I immediately fired again. Then he slumped to the ground and lay completely still. I ran quickly to the other infantryman, who was in the process of being arrested by the interpreter. He didn't put up the slightest resistance.

"You can't begin to imagine what I felt like, because you've never shot a man. Dear Father, I was that close to putting a bullet in my own head. The idea that a member of the Klamroth family should stand before a court-martial on a murder charge was terrible to me, and remains so. Today, now that the first judicial hearings are over, I'm somewhat calmer. I now say to myself first of all that I acted as a patrol leader who had been sent out as a matter of duty. Secondly, in the hearing of witnesses it turns out that I really did fire at the very last moment. For several witnesses agreed that the infantryman, shortly before I acted, and without my being aware of it, had released his safety catch. So it would only have taken a few moments and the situation would have been reversed.

"When the court-martial is over I hope for a holiday, so that I can tell you everything in person. I hope the court will find me not guilty. And if not, can I still be your son? Yours, Hans Georg."

He can. Kurt writes: "My dear, good boy! Yes, you have been through a serious experience, and I can feel the mental struggles you are going through. In my view, you have proved yourself a match for the situation, and have no reason to hang your head. And it's better for the man than if he had shot you first. Then he would have been driven to the sand pile for resisting a superior officer at gunpoint and summarily shot. Come to us, my dear son, we will welcome you with open arms, and want to help you get over your grave concerns. Your father, who loves you all the more, Kurt Klamroth."

His mother writes: "Remember—'everything that happens to me is God's will, and His will is good'—so I hope you won't shed any tears over such a seditious wretch. Thank God the situation wasn't reversed. Today we received such a lovely parcel of butter from you, we all thank you, and for the time being no one will know about the other matter."

The captain writes to Kurt: "I can only assure you that throughout this matter Hans Georg has acted as an extremely sensible, calm, and efficient man and soldier. I am glad that I have also been able to report in these terms to the regiment. I very much hope that he will soon overcome his melancholy."

The commander of the First Cavalry Division issued the following order of the day. "I should like to express my appreciation to Ensign Klamroth (First Dragoons) for his prudent and energetic actions in the arrest of two military staff who had committed a theft in Sallotak. The above should be conveyed to Ensign Klamroth."

Yes, all that helps HG. But it doesn't cure him. Over the decades he will be haunted by Gunner Franz Vitt, the man he shot on April 22, 1918. He appears in his diaries, in letters to his fiancée, his future wife, Else. In the spring of 1942, just after HG was transferred to Pleskau as an intelligence officer in the Russian campaign, he traveled hundreds of kilometers farther to Sallotak, looked for and found the farm where the pig had been stolen, and walked across the field where he had killed Franz Vitt.

That Gunner Vitt was a human being—HG to Kurt: "You've never shot a man"—and the Russian officer a trophy, I must somehow accept. The Russian's death disturbs me less—things like that happen in war. I hate the tone he used subsequently, the contempt laid on with a trowel. Franz Vitt, however, was "one of us" for HG, a German, not an enemy. True, he behaved like an enemy, just like the Russian captain. They both wanted to shoot HG. In both cases HG was a second faster.

There is no mockery of the late Franz Vitt, on the contrary. HG asks Kurt to find out whether Gunner Vitt's family needs support, and to send them money from HG's own savings: "Usually money does no good, but in this case it just might. You will understand that I don't yet want to write to them; a correspondence would certainly not be good for either side." Kurt attaches the note "put on file" to HG's letter: "I shall do nothing for the time being. The family might misunderstand the support and attempt blackmail. The state must look after the family if they are in poverty, and if the man who was shot was their only mainstay." Welfare proceedings for the Vitt family don't get under way until August 1920, almost two years after the war—who knows what they lived on for all that time?

And why does this story prey upon HG to such an extent? "You dog, you've cheated me," shouts Vitt when HG, pistol drawn in the field, orders him to hand over his weapons. And this is true. The court records state that HG struck a fake deal with Vitt, accepting money from him—100 marks—to buy the stolen pig from the farmer. Then HG suggested a glass of schnaps to seal the contract, and called upon Franz Vitt to accompany him to the brandy shop.

That was how he enticed him out of the forest. HG's superiors considered his action prudent and energetic, because his task was quite clearly to capture the criminal. But Gunner Vitt must have believed he had escaped an apparently hopeless situation at the small price of 100 marks. He presumably didn't suspect anything when he left the sheltering forest, and became furious when he worked out that the bill didn't add up. Was it the deception that so tormented HG?

First of all, despite his sense of guilt he is simply happy to be alive: "When I look at the beautiful world around me, I am heartily glad that I didn't hesitate before firing. I feel as though I have been granted a new gift of life, and I hope that's what it will be, after the trial." But there was to be no trial. HG's interrogations were examined, as were the accounts of many other witnesses—the farmers, the villagers, the interpreter. They all spoke up for HG, and why not? Franz Vitt was dead, after all.

Even with his new lease on life, HG finds it difficult to get back to normal. He gets thrown off his horse, which shatters his jaw and knocks out several teeth. I don't think this is accidental—the boy has been repeatedly punished most cruelly by his horses, whenever he causes difficulties or finds himself in trouble. HG has to have his face reassembled, tediously and painfully, in Königsberg, and while he is there he clearly loses it. He drinks and fools around with "little actresses," although he "didn't go the whole way." Kurt gratefully takes note of that but still finds it necessary to warn: "Alcohol and springtime in the company of loose women can easily wreck the best intentions."

He is more unsettled by what HG writes to his sister, namely that he is thinking about "putting an end to it all, and atoning for the deed with my life." Another variation is "volunteering for the most dangerous place at the Western Front." Kurt writes: "Heavens above, how many times have I read my children the words of their forefathers from the Klamroth archive: 'If, when your little boat is sailing on the ocean of the world, harsh storms and adverse winds instill fear in your soul, just remember the lord God!' Old man, have you completely forgotten the good Lord and His commandments, that instead of thinking of Him, you erect the false altar of an exaggerated and misleading code of honor? That in your darkest hour you did not think of Christian conviction, nor did your faith extend the hand of salvation to you, and instead you stumbled without finding it—that makes me very sad."

HG truly is stumbling, and he turns to the other extreme: "I am hurling myself strenuously into the maelstrom of pleasure and self-expression, so that I may quickly see how enjoyable life can be, and how even this lighter side of life makes it worth living," he writes to his sister.

The fact that HG doesn't take a break from those exhausting exercises even when his mother and little brother spend the evening waiting for him in a hotel leads Kurt to fire off a furious harangue: "This really won't do. You seem to me like a good wine with sediment, that someone has taken in his fist and given a good hard shake. The events of April 22 and the war in general have left you in a state of utter confusion. Things will have to 'settle' within you again, and then the clarity that I now miss in you will return."

That clarity comes with a marching order from HG's captain. On June 5, 1918, the young man follows his regiment to Odessa. Why Ukraine? It declared independence after the Russian Revolution and at the Brest-Litovsk negotiations early in February 1918 a special peace was concluded with the Central Powers. That doesn't interest the Bolsheviks in the slightest, who want to bring the valuable country back under Soviet control. They quickly occupy Kiev and expel the young government, which then calls on its new friends for help. They come promptly, 400,000 of them. One of them is HG.

His journey to Kiev takes him four days and four nights, equipped with salami, sand cake, and a bottle of red wine from his manor house friends in East Prussia. After this came twenty hours in an open cattle wagon to Mirgorod—all in all, a very long way! I was amazed when I looked it up in the atlas, amazed because after four uninterrupted years of warfare the German Reich still had a few hundred thousand spare troops with all the appropriate logistics, with horses, carts, riflemen, field hospitals, field kitchens, bivouacs, and everything else they needed, to be sent all the way to the Ukrainian steppe. Moreover, Supreme Army Command is dreaming once again of another colony, a "German settlement on the Black Sea," in the words of the second man on Hindenburg's leadership squad, Erich Ludendorff.

" 'Steppe' sounds so hungry," Gertrud worries in a letter to HG shortly after his arrival. On closer inspection, she is driven not so much by concern about his nutrition as by the hope that her son might again be able to find flour, semolina, and rice for the kitchen in Halberstadt, as he did before. "You could line a box with paper, pour in the flour and bury eggs in the flour if you get any," she suggests. Because back home eight chickens have died of cholera—who'd have thought it! The remaining eight are swiftly slaughtered, but Gertrud doesn't dare offer them to the family to eat: "Does cooking help against cholera bacilli?"

HG forbears to answer such a difficult question, but promises to send eggs if he can get hold of a box. First he has to find his feet, which isn't easy in a godforsaken hole where he is surrounded by villagers with that "sly Slavic expression on their faces." His superiors had given him a friendly welcome, "even with a degree of appreciation and respect," because of the business with Gunner Vitt. The matter has by now been completely erased from his papers.

HG is pleased about this, but he still doesn't feel good: "This really is an awful kind of war." Germans are being ambushed and shot down in the street, and the troops can travel only in a convoy, because the majority of the population sees the strangers not as allies but as an occupying power. HG sits with his squadron far from civilization, with the sun beating down on him, and goes swimming with his horses in a nearby river—"at first the animals didn't know why they should get into the water. And now they don't want to come out again"—gets bored and suffers from homesickness: "I'm now constantly filled with an unspeakable longing for home. It's unmanly [!], so one shouldn't write it down, but resolutely fight it."

He is also still tormented by Gunner Vitt. "Outwardly the whole story is over and done with," HG writes to Gertrud, "now I have to deal with it internally as well." But Gertrud replies: "We are very, very pleased that the unpleasant matter of April 22 has been removed from the world and even wins you praise, my dear boy. Now it won't be at all hard for you to deal with it internally as well, if you adopt the correct military attitude and impose a sense of duty on your emotions."

What nonsense! Does the "correct military attitude" mean kindly not making a fuss about shooting someone who'd stolen a pig when out on a binge? Does "duty" forbid reflection on one's own role in this fate? Kurt and Gertrud were worried about the possible external consequences of HG's "misfortune": court-martial, end of career—whatever. They couldn't or wouldn't see the turmoil raging within him. The first time his life takes a really serious turn, both parents refuse to help their son when he turns to them. HG is left alone with Gunner Vitt.

It must have tormented him during the hot Ukrainian nights. HG can't sleep in the oppressive air, the constant alerts because of marauding gangs are eating away at his nerves, and his dragoons are on edge. He's "managed to find an old harmonium that only has one major disadvantage: all the C's and G's are missing, the keys have fallen out, which means you have to sing the notes in between." I like to imagine HG's singsong echoing out over the sultry Ukrainian night—a harmonium in itself is already a kind of challenge. But necessity is the mother of invention: HG plays only in A major, which means that he doesn't need any C's or G's, and soon he can play that Schubert song as well: "Now everything, everything must change!"

Everyone hopes it will. HG finds it hard to come to terms with the uncertain atmosphere in his host country. Gertrud fires up everybody's courage: "Germany won't fail now," but she admits, "We all get tired sometimes!" Kurt grieves over the "hungry, exhausted, underfed populace," and notes: "Business isn't looking good. We have no raw materials left, and so the war will eventually have a serious economic effect on us as well. I only hope that we aren't going to have any unpleasant surprises with Curaçao. That would hit me very hard." He had transferred his I.G. Klamroth shares early enough to neutral Holland, but the consortium also includes Englishmen and Americans, "and who knows what they will do." Kurt recalls wistfully: "Do you remember playing war in Juist? Such lovely times!"

Because of business worries in Halberstadt, HG offers to request a transfer from the expensive cavalry to an infantry regiment, where life in the officers' mess is less expensive, and his meager funds won't have to run to saddles, bridles, and the like. Kurt, however, reassures him, saying that the money he spends on his son is practically nothing in comparison with his other expenses. The Hugo Stinnes company has made him an offer "to sell them the factory in Nienburg and the whole business, for a very high price. But I would have had to pay horrendous taxes on the profits, and I want to—I have to—keep my forefathers' business going for my sons. So we refused. But this may give you an idea what the postwar prospects of our industry look like. At any rate, you will stay with your regiment for as long as possible." People only ever leave the prestigious cavalry in an emergency; they have to think about what will happen later, after all. And besides, the infantry is fighting in the west, and Kurt definitely wants to keep his son out of that.

He asks his junior partner to fulfill his company duties. On July 1, 1918, the authorized signatory Alexander Busse will have spent forty years with I.G. Klamroth: "Please write to congratulate him. We're giving him 5,000 marks in war loan, and I have applied for the Order of the Crown, Fourth Class for him, and the Cross of Merit." Four decades—that's twenty years longer than Kurt himself has been in the business, and such anniversaries aren't exceptional in the company. At a special ceremony Gertrud hands the meritorious employee the order and the cross. The war loan probably won't have been much use to him anymore.

Gertrud sometimes prescribes self-control exercises for her son: his cousin Fritz, whose Notabitur HG had celebrated glumly and less than soberly two years ago, "was awarded the Iron Cross, First Class, in France. Please share his happiness without envy, rather than the opposite!" She also worries about HG's intellectual development: "Use your time to learn Russian. Have you any good books to read?" The boy picks up the language as easily as he picked up Estonian. After a few months he no longer needs an interpreter, and he can also read Cyrillic script. Twenty-four years later, on the Eastern Front in the Second World War, he will retrieve the knowledge from his memory to engage for hours in ideological discussions with Soviet prisoners of war after the end of official interrogations.

As far as his intellect is concerned—hmm. HG asks his mother to send him Alice Berend's "latest work": *The Bridegrooms of Babette Bomberling*. I bravely read it myself; it's only 155 pages long, published by Fischer's Library of contemporary novels in 1915. Frau Berend also wrote *The Burned Bed* and *The Flea and the Fiddler*—very popular in her time. HG is asking for junk novels. He also wanted to read Agnes Günther's sentimental story *The Saint and Her Fool* to while away his solitary hours. I very dimly remember picking up both volumes as a twelve-year-old, and however close I might want to get to HG, I'm not sure I could bring myself to repeat the experience.

In Ukraine, tensions between the various parties are mounting. The military, the right-wing conservative partisans, the Bolsheviks, and the German troops are clashing in ever new series of assaults and punitive expeditions. The Germans are allowed to intervene only if they're being attacked directly, so HG's little outpost is spared for the time being. As a newly promoted lieutenant he's now leading both squadrons—"I'll have to learn to issue orders even to grumpy faces"—but that's merely occupational therapy, because there's nothing to do. The soldiers can't go riding, because it's too dangerous, so the horses are lunged for hours at a time and everyone's down in the dumps.

By now, contradictory and alarming reports are coming in, the newspapers are weeks old, and the mail arrives only occasionally. HG to Kurt: "We don't know anything here, and I feel inactive and impotent. Rumors are whizzing around the place that the war will soon be over." It doesn't occur to HG that it might already have been lost. No one expects that, neither the soldiers nor the populace. For the Germans, the end of the war means victory, or at least a negotiated peace. For four long years they had actually remained "undefeated in the field." They have fought simultaneously and successfully against the mighty armies of the British, the French, the Russians, and the Italians, an enormous military achievement. And no one has even begun to prepare them for a defeat, not the Kaiser, not the government, and certainly not Supreme Army Command.

Until mid-July 1918, the all-powerful General Ludendorff was still conveying radiant certainty of victory to the senior members of the government and to his generals. At the end of the next war the same loss of reality will recur with Hitler. The news from the Western Front, however, was worse than ever. The great offensives of spring 1918 failed, but Ludendorff had promised the "final victory" for July. That cost the Germans 800,000 casualties, whether dead, wounded, or missing, and now masses of American soldiers were flooding into France. With them they brought their deadly tanks, the first ever seen, and when the French, followed by the British and finally the fresh American troops, went on the counteroffensive, another 700,000 German soldiers perished between August and November. Altogether—in a parallel with Hitler's inferno—

about one and a half million Germans died in the last nine months of the war.

And nobody knew about it? Of course they did. But no one imagined that this would mean defeat, that the war would end "dishonorably" for Germany. In fact the war was omnipresent throughout the country, but the battles were far away. Unlike in the Second World War, there were no foreign troops on German soil, no aerial warfare over German cities, no nights of hiding from bombs in air-raid shelters. A few months previously, early in 1918, the U.S. president Woodrow Wilson had outlined his fourteen-point program for peace in Europe after the war. Germany was to lose all its conquered territories—Belgium, the French provinces, Alsace-Lorraine, all the territory it had stolen in Russia, from the Baltic to Ukraine. It wasn't only Supreme Army Command and its compliant government that had contemptuously waved the program aside. To the German people, Wilson's conditions were a joke, and the Reichstag's response was one of complete rejection. An armistice based on those fourteen points? The very idea!

In faraway Ukraine, HG has no notion of any of this, and Kurt, better supplied with information in his Deputy General Command in Magdeburg, doesn't share his forebodings. HG sends home preserving sugar, cauliflower, eggs, and above all flour, which is desperately needed. The town council has just granted Gertrud an allowance of fifty grams (less than two ounces) per person in her household "for the meatless week." But she wouldn't let it get her down: "Cleaning the house without cleaning agents isn't easy. We're trying sand at the moment." Or: "We've made some clothes for Annie and Erika out of the thin English plaids. They look very pretty." In mid-September she writes: "It gets chilly by evening. We can only heat two rooms, but the family sits close together." A little later this becomes: "God is setting our German people a very severe test, but we will withstand it with His help."

Gertrud is seriously concerned about the mounting cases of influenza. Her younger daughter, Erika, has been in bed for weeks:

"Thank God she isn't in mortal danger. We're having funerals every half hour at the cemetery at the moment." The schools are closed, public events are canceled, and Kurt writes from Magdeburg: "The factories are silent, a third of the clerks are ill even here in my war office, and many of the cases are fatal." What they are experiencing is the Spanish flu, an epidemic of influenza coming from Gibraltar, which killed 20 million people worldwide in 1918 and 1919. In Germany almost 300,000 people died. Whole families were wiped out, as though the war hadn't been enough. You have to imagine that: someone manages to survive the lethal retreats in Flanders or the Saarland while parents and siblings at home are perishing from influenza. Once the Lord strikes, He scores.

Back in Ukraine, HG is still completely unsuspecting. He understands nothing of the tumult that has exploded around him, he hasn't a clue who's fighting whom and why in the battles between the gangs. How could he, in his backwater of houses made of cow dung, facing the endless horizon, which they search with field glasses for partisans. HG has been given two greyhounds, which he calls Lenin and Trotsky, and in all likelihood that's as far as his involvement in Russian politics goes. Like all soldiers everywhere in the world he waits for someone to tell him what to do, and until that happens he sinks into boredom.

He goes bustard shooting with Ukrainian landowners. He wonders whether he should have his father's horses Nelly and Lord brought from Bialystok in Poland to his new posting near Odessa—they had accompanied Kurt through Belgium, France, Russia, and in Grodno, and now that Kurt is in Magdeburg there's a danger that they might be lost in the bedlam of the war. HG: "In the end we're the police force for the Ukrainskis. We'll certainly be here for another two years, and I could even use the horses here." He practices Bach's organ works on the battered harmonium, and thinks once again about volunteering, along with a friend, for the Western Front—"Here I'm completely useless." He writes this on October 5, 1918, and doesn't know just how right he is.

On that same day the German public, completely unprepared for the news, learns that their state is now a parliamentary democracy, and that they have a new Reich Chancellor, Prince Max von Baden, the third within fifteen months. Effective immediately, the Social Democrats, the Center Party, and the Progressive Party, meaning the hitherto powerless Reichstag majority, are now sitting in government. And what does that brand-new government do? On the day they enter office, these "pitiful wretches, footlers, bunglers, birds of ill omen, and croaking toads from the depths," as one conservative flyer greeted them, address a request for peace and armistice to the American president on the basis of the aforementioned fourteen points.

Can a whole nation's heart stop beating at the same moment? Everyone yearned for an end to the war, but on these conditions? HG's horror—inevitably postponed, because it takes the newspapers a while to get to Ukraine—is played out up and down the country in countless variations: "All the pride, all the honor, all joy in life and work is irrevocably lost for our generation, and no twisting and quibbling will do anything about it. Haven't we always known that these men wouldn't be strong enough to see the iron necessity of a victorious war for Germany?" HG's fury shrills through one letter after the other. "One could never have imagined such a humiliating peace offer from the German Reich—the relinquishment of Alsace-Lorraine, reparations to Belgium, the revision of the peace in the east! But the worst thing is this: the happy pride that comes from being a German is lost for ever."

No one is spared: "Our nation was thoroughly unworthy of the great time that it was briefly allowed to experience, and its natural instinct for servitude is breaking through once more. This is obvious just by looking at the representatives of the German people. We owe it to the massive hecatombs"—the things he writes in his Ukrainian hayloft! In Homer, hecatombs are sacrifices of one hundred bulls—"We owe it to the massive hecatombs of our dead to go on fighting, even if our whole country is occupied. Anyone with a spark of honor in his body, men, women, children [!], would rather kill himself than submit to the yoke!"

It isn't fair, and may HG forgive me: but I do have to laugh at his letters. But I can see the puffed-up little lieutenant—he turns twenty in a week—sitting there in Ukraine, perhaps not in the greatest comfort, but a long way from the gunfire, cursing the loss of the German Reich's dream. It really isn't nice of me to laugh— what sort of nonsense was I coming out with at twenty? For me it was Marxism, and I was deadly serious about it. Nowadays I find both ridiculous. In 1918 everyone talked like HG, everyone dreamed like that, and millions had died for it.

They could have lived, if fate had spared them men like Ludendorff. Hindenburg's mighty chief of staff in Supreme Army Command not only determined the course of the war during the two years of his dictatorial rule, but time and again stood in the way of a "negotiated peace." He had reduced the Kaiser and the government, along with Hindenburg himself, to the status of mere puppets. Contrary to all the articles of the constitution he had high-handedly changed Chancellors and foreign ministers, transported Lenin to Russia, and turned Parliament into a shadow institution.

This Parliament was now to pull the chestnuts out of the fire for him and shoulder responsibility for the defeat. For this to happen, the Reichstag majority, so despised by Ludendorff and his consorts, had to enter the government, for it was they—not Supreme Army Command, under any circumstances—who were to deliver the request for armistice to Wilson. On the weekend of September 28–29, 1918, Ludendorff informed the Kaiser and the government of this. It wasn't until Sunday evening that his nominal boss, Hindenburg, learned of Ludendorff's plan. Over the next two days the officers of Supreme Army Command and the Reichstag were informed, and in both cases—although it's hard to believe—the men were completely stunned.

"Groaning and sobbing," the high-ranking officers absorbed the fact that the war was lost, and a breakthrough by the enemy was to be expected at any minute on the Western Front. What had these gentlemen been up to prior to this, to be so surprised? Similar scenes were played out in the Reichstag. The journalist Erich Dombrowski wrote: "The delegates were completely shattered. Friedrich Ebert turned deathly pale, Stresemann looked as though he'd been stabbed. There were half-stifled cries, and eyes welled up with tears. An awakening from narcosis, rage, fury, shame, reproach: we have been lied to by the military for years, and we believed in it as gospel."

If that's the case, then the devout HG has every right to be out-raged as well. Except he's raging against the wrong people. His fury is directed at the representatives of the center-left parties and their sudden request for an armistice. He, along with millions of others, believes they betrayed the fatherland from the moment they entered government. No one knew that it was Ludendorff who had drawn up the request and commissioned the useful idiots in the Reichstag. These are the roots of the legend of the *Dolchstoss,* the "stab in the back," according to which the home front and the "left-wing representatives of the people" attacked the "undefeated" army from the rear with their request for an armistice.

From his war office in Magdeburg, Kurt has been able to work out what has been going on. In a page-long epistle written in mid-October, he puts HG in the picture on condition that his son immediately destroys the letter. Luckily he didn't. Kurt was partic-ularly concerned to mitigate HG's harsh judgment of the Reichstag members and the new Reich Chancellor Prince Max von Baden: "The prince is fulfilling his difficult task with great loyalty to the fatherland, and we must be grateful to the Social Democrats for assuming responsibility for the masses, although from a party polit-ical point of view it would have made more sense for them not to do so." That's arguably true—a year later they were the "November criminals" who had delivered the "victorious army" into the jaws of defeat.

Kurt also knows that it wasn't the "footlers and bunglers" of the new government but the Supreme Army Command itself—meaning Ludendorff—that had categorically demanded the armistice: "They had to ensure, at all costs, that war did not reach Germany." It doesn't occur to Kurt to revolt against the leaders of his state, even in his quiet little room. He does suffer: "I feel like an instrument with a broken string. It hurts me almost physically when I think of the collapse." But his anger is directed at President Wilson and his harsh conditions for the armistice: withdrawal from the occupied territories, ending of submarine warfare, reparations for the Allied civilian population, and—sacrilege!—the abdication of the Kaiser.

No sacrilege. No one gives a fig about the fact that Wilhelm II has disappeared to Holland, that all the governing princely houses in the German Reich have dissolved into air, that the exasperated Prince Max von Baden is tending his family vineyards, and Friedrich Ebert has assumed the post of Reich Chancellor. Two hundred and seventeen years after the first Prussian king was crowned and forty-seven years after the king of Prussia had become the German Kaiser, the monarchy in Germany is a thing of the past.

Not a single sentence in Kurt's or HG's notes records this event. Only Gertrud writes on November 10: "Today we really woke up in the Republic of Germany," and that in church, for the first time, there had been no prayer for "our Kaiser." How can that be? They have spent their whole lives in reverence for the monarchy. Even as a little boy, HG learned to salute the Kaiser, and Kurt, in his smart operetta uniform, had felt that he was a smooth-ironed part of the imperial whole. Three cheers for Kaiser and fatherland, with all the flags and pennants, was the core of their world; they would have laid down their lives for it. And now? Nothing. Not even an obituary.

At least not for the Kaiser. The fatherland keeps them busy enough during these weeks; never before have they seen such upheaval. In the war office, they're already secretly preparing for soldiers returning from the front—"this is confidential information. Don't mention it to anyone!" Demob committees try to ensure food and lodgings for the soldiers flooding back into the country; military equipment that is brought home has to be stored and protected against looting. The armament factories have to switch to making civilian products—the question is: which ones? The many women working in the plants have to be found other jobs—the question is: where? In Halberstadt, Gertrud anticipates billeting twelve returning Cuirassier officers—"although I hope I won't have to feed them." She doesn't know how she will heat the rooms, "but then again, they've also been freezing at the front."

And besides, there's a revolution going on, or what passes for a revolution in Germany. It breaks out in a place where no one had expected it—not among the starving workers in Berlin, but far away in Schillig-Reede, on the coast near Wilhelmshaven, where the imperial fleet is at anchor. Since the battle of the Skagerrak in 1916 the fleet—unlike the submarines—had been lying idly and uselessly at harbor, partly because of the British blockade, but also because the Kaiser wanted to spare his "giant toy." Now the navy officers, who felt they'd been given something of a raw deal, wanted some of the fame and to make sure that the army didn't get all the credit for fighting the war.

In strict secrecy, the senior naval officers ordered a suicide mission, pointless, meaningless, a colossal act of carnage—the whole imperial fleet against Great Britain, and an indirect attack on the "slack" German government and its request for an armistice. It was an act of mutiny by the officers around Admiral Reinhard Scheer, a revolt against all the decisions that had been made in Berlin and in Spa to end the war. They even thought of inviting the Kaiser to take part in the furious finale aboard the flagship of the fleet, excellent subject matter for the seascape painters of future generations. Officers don't want to capitulate despicably, they want to die fighting.

That's not what the crews want, certainly not in a war that's already lost. On October 28 they mutiny themselves, only a few at first, against the mutineers on the command decks, preventing the fleet from leaving harbor. This resistance spreads like wildfire across the whole of Germany, and at first it is—has such a thing ever happened before?—an uprising not against, but *in favor of* the government. The civilian Social Democratic bourgeois government is supported against the supremacy of the military powers which repeatedly kept the war going and have held the civilian population in a "state of siege" for years.

On November 9, 1918, the revolution reaches Berlin. At noon, speaking from a Reichstag window, Philipp Scheidemann, the Social Democrat politician soon to be Germany's first prime minister, proclaims the German Republic. A short time later Socialist Karl Liebknecht stands, as the Kaiser did at the start of the war, on a balcony of Berlin Castle, and proclaims the Free German Socialist Republic. The impending row on the German left is inevitable. Whether and how the tens of thousands of people outside the Reichstag and the castle can hear both speakers remains unclear. There were no electric megaphones in those days. That doesn't diminish the jubilation, and—until its violent suppression by the right-wing Freikorps—it is a peaceful, rather benign revolution without lynch mobs and kangaroo courts. There are hardly any casualties, there's no looting, and if the rebellious soldiers and workers tear off the officers' stripes and hoist the red flag on public buildings, that's about as extravagant as things get.

In Magdeburg, Kurt sighs in his war diary: "So horror has become reality: the collapse, the revolution are here, and can't be halted!" That's about it when it comes to lamenting; by November 9 he has regained control of things. When "marauding artillerymen, swinging sabers—mostly purloined officers' sabers" force their way into the war office, he has them led into the conference room and sits them down at the negotiating table. He advises them to speak in turn, "because in all the hubbub I couldn't understand a word," and draws up a list of those present. His adjutant takes the minutes, "as is customary at all important war office conferences."

The baffled revolutionaries explain that the soldiers' council has demanded the suspension of all military institutions. Kurt: "I replied that the war office, although instituted on a military basis, dealt primarily in economic matters that could not be interrupted, and handed them a mountain of files to persuade them that work here must continue. They were lost for words, and passed the files from one to the next." So that's that, and the minutes record a little later that "the delegates of the Magdeburg soldiers' council have been persuaded that the work of the war office could not be disturbed." With this paper additional troops are turned away at the front door, and here at least the revolution is over.

The more senior officials in Magdeburg's General Command have a harder time of it. Two generals demand to be excused from sessions with the city's soldiers' council, because they fear losing their composure in negotiations with inferior officers. Kurt has no such problems, and neither does he mind going to the office in civvies from one day to the next: "I'm not going to hand that gang out there a pretext." A representative of the workers' and soldiers' council is assigned to work beside him, a trade union leader called Bauer from the woodworkers' union, to whom Kurt presents, every morning and with exquisite politeness, the problems that need to be addressed. Each time he does so the distraught man says, "Just do everything you think is right, Captain. It's a good thing all you gentlemen are going on working. It would be over our heads, and chaos would have broken out," quotes Kurt.

There aren't any real revolutionary excesses in Halberstadt either. A little red flag flutters on the roof of the staff building of the Twenty-seventh Infantry Division, a bakery hands over its bread to the hungry demonstrators, and some meat paste for spreading on it is purloined from Heine's sausage factory. The following day, the workers' and soldiers' council describes this petty theft in the *Halberstadt Gazette and Intelligence Sheet* as a "regrettable event" that "would not be repeated." And, in bold script, they announce: "The private property of every citizen must remain untouched!" Revolutions can be very civil.

In the first town council meeting after that, it's business as usual. Council chairman Kurt, always reelected to the post despite his constant absence, has traveled specially from Magdeburg—it's the first time he is heading this committee again since the beginning of the war. In a programmatic speech, he swears in the town fathers with a phrase by Friedrich Ebert about what's to come: "There are many people in this room who will find it hard to work with the new men who have undertaken to lead the Reich." And later: "Many of us have been inclined, by our whole upbringing, to turn our eyes toward the past—we must resolutely turn them toward the future!"

This means that they must now move on to the business of the day, and that's exactly what the councillors do. The charges for the removal of sewage are increased, strict regulations on bricks are maintained, so that they won't—in Kurt's words—be used for luxury buildings. The registry office is given additional rooms to accommodate the extra staff taken on to cope with the increased mortality due to influenza and deaths at the front, and the cemetery has to be extended. In the labor exchange, separate waiting rooms are set up for male and female job seekers—even in confused times, Kurt keeps his eye on the things that matter.

Gertrud is clearly more shaken than her husband. Even in Halberstadt, officers in the street are being stripped of épées, rosettes, and epaulets. "Oh, my boy," she writes to HG, "your blood will boil when you read this, and you won't understand why they don't fight to the last man. But even the Cuirassiers are running around all over the place with red flags and ties—tears came to my eyes when I saw the first of them." Her world, which was never knocked out of kilter by hunger, avian cholera, and worries about heating, is reeling now. The man in the street, hitherto someone she would have felt responsible for, has suddenly become a threat to her. Gertrud writes gratefully that "the worst thing that could have happened to Kurt was that they took his saber away and tore off his epaulets," and that he was spared that because "like all the men in the war office he was already wearing civilian clothes." "The worst": for Gertrud that means the loss of insignias that declare her class status.

Gertrud flees to Schiller. "The old world falls, time changes, and new life blossoms from the ruins," she quotes from *William Tell,* and she has a good idea of what that new life should be like, namely that "the nature of Germanness will assert itself once more." To recover from the horrors in the outside world, in the evening they read Wilhelm Raabe's novel *The Starving Pastor,* which fits very nicely with the times, in at least two respects. The book's anti-Semitic tone recurs in anonymous flyers which, already in December, are being distributed in Magdeburg factories. Kurt: "These flyers say that the relative number of Jews within the overall population of Germany totals one and a half percent, but that eighty percent of the present government are Jews." There they are again, the "All-Germans," the "Fatherland Party" and all the others who lay the blame for the German defeat at the door of a "global Jewish-Freemason conspiracy."

After a considerable delay German history even reaches Ukraine. While massive demonstrations of soldiers and workers paralyze the towns back home, HG is dancing with the local beauties at a maneuver ball. On the day of the signature of the armistice, November 11, 1918, he is on a pub crawl in Kiev with a few officers and Ukrainian businessmen—Kurt censors the description of this juicy night, which HG had sent to his father, copying it out and softening it before passing it on to Gertrud: "The boy wrote to me man to man. Not suitable for mothers." Not for daughters either, sadly. The original letter has disappeared.

It isn't until November 21 that the news of revolution and overthrow reaches the unsuspecting HG, when he comes back to base from a machine-gun training course ("I've never drunk so much in my whole life!"). Head over heels, his excited soldiers in the squadron unanimously elect him, their officer, to the soldiers' council—the last newspapers they have seen are from November 4, and how a revolution is supposed to go no one really knows. They just know they want to get home as quickly as possible. HG: "They say we'll not be going by train, but that we'll have to ride the whole distance"—from Odessa to Tilsit!—"which is going to be great, frankly. Keep my civilian stuff ready, I won't stay a soldier a moment longer than I absolutely have to. If you don't hear anything from me for a while, don't worry about me. I'm as safe in Abraham's bosom with my comrades!"

He's not. An orderly retreat of the German army from Ukraine is no longer possible, and HG can't tell whether their assailants are robber gangs or military formations—everyone wants to steal their weapons, their ammunition, their horses, their equipment. They get caught in heavy fighting. HG writes in one of the few letters that get through: "We were galloping on horseback in dense columns through rapid machine-gun fire, a hairy business!" Horror stories pour in about units being loaded onto trains unarmed, still trusting in their former Ukrainian partners, only to be robbed and blown up after a few kilometers. HG: "Normally that would have meant war," but nothing in the German army works anymore.

Rumors spread among the officers about an imminent pogrom of the Germans, and HG gloomily describes a lifelong lesson: "Two months ago we were the only, undisputed masters—what a change!! But we rightly saw that only power leads to success, so-called 'law' is only an utopia. In accordance with 'law,' we want to stay neutral here, and retreat in an orderly fashion, but we incautiously handed over our power, and look where we are now!"

The regiments, reinforced by an artillery division from Königsberg, literally have to battle their way through. HG finds himself in close-quarters combat on two occasions, surviving unharmed, but both times his horse kicks him, breaking first his leg and then his shoulder blade. As in the spring, when he survived his encounter with Gunner Vitt, HG again learns of his mortality, again from a kick from his horse. But he rides on, his leg and shoulder in makeshift splints, it's bitterly cold, the soldiers are suffering from frostbite and hunger. In the villages they catch lice and worms.

HG is required as an interpreter when they need free passage, and above all when the point is not to be disarmed. Clearly his skill as a negotiator is called for here, too. HG is his father's son, who, however furious he might be feeling inside, knows how to strike the right tone. No letters survive from this period, but he later writes. "That was war, a dirty, disgusting war, one in which we were retreating, soldiers of a lost war, without honor, without pride, but also no longer willing to die."

After four hard weeks, on January 23, 1919, they reach Bialystok, a railway junction, where a German rearguard is coordinating the transport of the entire retreat from Eastern Europe. It isn't until now that HG is able to have his broken bones treated, and the base commandant, an old friend of Kurt's from their time on the Eastern Front, wants to send him home immediately to avoid possible deformation. HG refuses. He doesn't want to leave his troop, and curiously enough he is left with no lasting damage.

A month later the regiment is moved to Tilsit—HG hasn't been in Germany since the previous spring, and he hasn't been to Halberstadt for more than two years. Kurt greets him with great concern: "Welcome, my dear boy, a hearty welcome home. But oh, I hoped you would have a very different homecoming. You will have to get used to a lot of things, which will be difficult for you. It isn't the old Germany anymore! We have experienced the transformation more slowly, and even for us many things have happened too quickly. It'll be harder for you, because the transition will be more sudden."

My Father's Country

The transition begins as soon as he arrives in Tilsit. Previously, the regiment would have marched into the town in triumph to the sound of a military band, all the houses would have been draped with flags, and the jubilation of the people would have warmed the warriors' hearts. Now they arrive by night, the train having waited for nightfall on open tracks far from the station, and only a few sleepless inhabitants of Tilsit can have been aware of the silent columns making their way to the barracks.

FIVE

Kurt and Gertrud with their children

The return to civilian life takes time. HG is a professional officer, and his discharge into reserve status doesn't happen overnight, particularly since the regiment really wants to keep him. But Kurt applies pressure. Apprenticeships are hard to come by: "The young officers and ensigns are jostling each other into bourgeois jobs in alarming numbers, and soon all the good posts will be occupied." HG's wish to bring his orderly back to Halberstadt and keep him on as a servant meets with mild horror on the part of his parents. Gertrud: "What are you going to feed him on? However nice it might be for you—we've got enough people here already." Kurt: "An apprentice with a personal servant! Forget it!"

Kurt's contacts lead to a job for HG in the Carl Prior transport company in Hamburg, from which an apprehensive Herr Michaelsen writes a letter to "Herr Councillor of Commerce" to say that he assumes "that your son is aware of the difference between an apprentice relationship and the responsibilities of an officer." Kurt replies: "I take it fully for granted that he will submit to all orders given by his master, and keep to customary business hours." What was that song he used to sing at the harmonium? "Now everything, everything must change"—poor boy! He is scheduled to start work on May 13, 1919.

I'm trying to put myself in HG's position: first military service behind the lines with feasts in the officers' mess, revelries, the maneuver ball, bustard shooting. Dragoons clicking their heels, an orderly to fill his bath. Then "rapid machine-gun fire," former allies threatening a pogrom of the Germans. Terrifying retreat, close-quarters combat at four degrees below zero Fahrenheit. Broken leg, broken shoulder, negotiating, negotiating, negotiating—two thousand men depending on your being skilled at it. In Russian. After all that you creep back to the barracks at night like a dog, and outside there's a world—a German world—that you don't know. Instead, you've got the perspective of "orders given by a master," "customary business hours," letters of indemnity, customs applications in the free port—without a break. No time to think. No one to hug you, no one to say: "Take your time, just ease yourself into it."

On April 20, HG travels in civvies on packed trains from Tilsit to Halberstadt—the age of comfortable special compartments for officers is long gone, and there isn't an orderly to look after his luggage. HG had so much wanted to walk through the town just once as a lieutenant, capped and gowned in his uniform. Kurt, who has by now been discharged from his duties in Magdeburg, consoles him in a letter: "An impeccable single-breasted suit awaits you, and we think you'll like it." I know the photographs: HG looks as

though he's on his way to confirmation once more. In Halberstadt
he is glad to see again his father's battle horses Nelly and Lord,
which Kückelmann the coachman—he's been with the family for
years—had tracked down somewhere near Breslau. In the photographs, they look as though they must have had a cart horse
grandfather at the very least. Small wonder that they survived the
war so well, even without HG's rescue mission to Ukraine. But
morning rides in the Spiegelsberge are out of the question. Any
"Junker" trappings would only attract mockery from the town's
hooligans.

Because the revolution has stopped being civil. The disagreements between the various socialist groups have intensified. The
counterrevolution, in the form of regiments that have not yet been
demobilized and the hastily constituted Freikorps, is literally waiting with guns at the ready. In early January 1919, on the orders of
Ebert's Social Democratic government, the Social Democrat Gustav Noske smashes the Spartacus uprising in Berlin with those
far-right Freikorps. On January 15, Rosa Luxemburg and Karl
Liebknecht are ambushed and murdered by government troops.
Germany is in a state of civil war.

In the midst of all this chaos, how is somebody to cope when
he's lived strictly according to the rules up until now? Quite simply: he goes on living exactly as before. Both HG and his parents
come to terms with the adversities of the postwar period—starvation rations, unheated rooms, trains that are delayed if they run at
all. And besides, the civil war is happening elsewhere, in the workers' districts of Cologne, for example, above all in Berlin, devastat-
ingly in Bavaria. In Halberstadt it all prompts tedious discussions,
but does not lead to the overthrow of traditional values. You can go
on living, though not exactly as before.

National Assembly elections are held and, for the first time without the three-class franchise, elections to the Prussian regional
parliament. Kurt stands as a candidate in Halberstadt for Gustav
Stresemann's German People's Party (Deutsche Volkspartei, or

DVP), which represents the great German industrialists. He doesn't do so with any great enthusiasm, but sets "all his might against the Social Democrats." The point was to strengthen the conservative element in the National Assembly against everything "left-wing," and with a sigh Kurt, a senior representative of the old order, followed the urging of his distraught fellow members of the social elite—sugar manufacturers, bankers, businessmen: "In these difficult times, we mustn't leave the field open for the others." But that's exactly what they did, because the German People's Party was, like the other conservative parties, an also-ran, and Kurt was able to stay at home. When the right achieved clear gains in the next Reichstag election, Kurt was no longer with them.

Almost as soon as he starts learning the transport business with Carl Prior and Co., HG finds himself in the middle of the "Hamburg brawn riots," one of the many food protests of the civil war. Well, not exactly in the middle. He's living in Harvestehude, and the disturbances are in Wilhelmsburg. Despite the fact that he is now working quite often in the port, he experiences nothing of the violent excesses going on just around the corner. Nonetheless, he's unsettled by these riots, one of the many protests over food during the civil war: "Must I not come to the help of the fatherland, and sign up with my regiment again?" Shrewd Kurt puts the needs of the fatherland in perspective: "No one is right in this struggle, and no one's motives are honorable. I'll be happy if you stay out of it. The fatherland needs men to boost the economy, and you will be one of them."

His son does as he is told, goes to the office at eight o'clock in the morning; during lunch break from one until three he eats his homemade sandwiches by the Alster—"there's a curious kind of synthetic lard here now, but with the help of a little imagination you can just about force it down"—and rarely leaves work before seven. After hours he studies English, takes business classes, and discovers two new passions: city life and the thrill of doing business on a freelance basis. He hustles herring barrels to East Prussia, devotes himself to the export of turnip seeds, and plans to import farm machines from the United States. He organizes wood transports to Hessen, and dispatches a cargo of live goslings to Nuremberg—or at least they were alive when they set off. Otherwise, almost everything else somehow goes wrong, and HG's meager funds, which he advances on loan, melt away like butter in the sun.

Kurt watches all this for a while before intervening: "Turnip seeds are subject to quotas and can only be sold under the counter. That's illegal, I wouldn't have anything to do with it and you should steer clear of it, too. Importing farm machinery from the United States is economic nonsense. Our native engineering industry has its own finished products. Your company account is now in the red to the tune of 702.75 marks including postal costs. Businessmen know how difficult money is to make, and treat it differently from green lieutenants!! Cordial greetings—your old man."

So far the "old man" could still forbid his son to do stupid things—HG, the officer and, until recently, the commander of several dozen dragoons, comes of age only in October 1919. Without Kurt's signature no apprenticeship contract with the Prior company, and without his father's consent no rental agreement with the Biebers in the Klosterallee, where HG lives in an unheated little room as part of the family. But this father isn't given to issuing prohibitions. He continues to trust in the power of argument, even if he sometimes blows his top. When HG plots a supposedly fantastic deal to export bread-slicing machines—HG: "This time it's definitely going to work, it's all absolutely certain and we'll earn loads of money!"—Kurt has to pay several thousand marks for the interim financing and find a buyer in the United States who will at least pay the purchase price.

Kurt writes sarcastically: "I'm delighted with your interest in business. If only it were coupled with the requisite caution and farsightedness and an ability to assess profit and loss, I would be more than enthusiastic. And what are you going to do when one of your customers finds out that you're just an apprentice in a transport company and nothing else? What will you do when your master learns about your 'deals'? You've got a name that you must nurture so that you can one day join the company as a respectable businessman, not someone with questionable stories about his past."

That strikes home. HG vows abstinence: "I wanted to show you that I can be successful in our profession with ideas of my own, but I see that I'm going to be relying on your advice for a long time to come." Kurt's advice alone is not enough. He and Gertrud take concerted action when they work out that HG is succumbing to the temptations of the big city, far beyond what his purse will allow. Gertrud: "Father is very displeased about this third restaurant bill from the Vier Jahreszeiten—and champagne, too! Must you swank so?"

Once again, Gertrud's irritation over HG's extravagant lifestyle goes hand in hand with concern for his intellectual nourishment: "Can't you go and hear a good concert or go to the theater? In these hard times you can do that even without evening wear. And what are you reading? Shall I send you something? Are you getting enough sleep?" When HG orders expensive fuel to heat his little room, Kurt can no longer understand his son: "Was that absolutely necessary? Can't you do your writing and reading and so on in Bieber's heated rooms? I freely admit that it's very unpleasant not to have a warm room of your own. But many people are living like that these days. As I write this, I'm freezing dreadfully in my office. It isn't nice, but what can you do?"

But Kurt pays up: 214.50 marks for wood and peat, and an electrician gets 120 marks—HG has had electricity installed in his room. Kurt, sharply: "Oil lamps aren't enough anymore??" Kurt buys him patent leather shoes for the tails and lugs his dinner jacket to a tailor in Hanover in a packed train. Apart from HG's failed investments in his "deals," Kurt transfers 500 marks for food and lodging every month, as well as 300 marks for pocket money, and a food parcel arrives from Halberstadt every second week.

I get quite agitated when I add up all these expenses—couldn't he just have thumped the table? He has four children, after all. Is he like this with all of them? Careful! What would I do with my children if they'd just emerged safe and sound from the horror of war, while my friends were all in mourning over the loss of their young hopes? Kurt's brother Johannes had lost two sons, his sister Gertrud, one—the list goes on. Nonetheless, it puts my back up to read: "By the way, have you written to anyone to tell them I'm keeping you short, or something like that? Something along these lines has reached my ears indirectly. If you have wishes of that nature, my dear boy, then speak to me directly about it."

Why does HG go so completely off the rails during his first months in Hamburg? Didn't he worry every so often, as a soldier, about whether life as a cavalryman wouldn't stretch his father's finances to the limits? Perhaps he didn't. Perhaps all his concerns about the high costs of equipment, the officers' mess, bingeing in the regiment, HG's repeated offers to transfer to the cheaper artillery, were merely one of those parlor games so often played out between sons and fathers. When the son acts conscience-stricken, and the father pays up all the more easily because he feels that his son appreciates the burden? HG knew full well that former Cuirassier Kurt would pinch and scrape so as not to spoil his son's career opportunities in a cavalry regiment. Moreover he knew that his father didn't really need to pinch and scrape, even during the war.

But now? Things are tough, the hunger blockade laid down by Germany's opponents is still hitting home, and no raw material is entering the country. Kurt expects the reds to impose "nationalizations that'll make our eyes water." That doesn't actually happen, but such fears paralyze the entrepreneurial spirit. The demobilization law demands that all those who were working in 1914 have to be reemployed at full wages by their company, even if the company in question, like I.G. Klamroth and many others, has hardly any work to offer. Accordingly, Kurt's enterprise is clearly employing too much staff—things aren't really going badly, but they aren't going as well as before. Kurt has to do some hard sums, and he feels that his son and future partner should do the same. So why now, of all times, does HG start spending with such gay abandon?

Perhaps because he can't cope. Apart from the experience with Gunner Vitt, life in the army was quite straightforward. HG knew his place, and the officer's lifestyle, with all its corresponding privileges, struck him as appropriate. As a schoolboy in Halberstadt he never had to fight for his status. Now he's one of several badly paid apprentices under the prickly head clerk, Michaelsen, who refuses to see HG as the jewel he considers himself to be. Among his father's business colleagues and the East Prussian Junkers to whom he pays visits in Hamburg, and who subsequently invite him to their estates, it's just like being home, except that the house in Halberstadt as an equivalent is not available for HG. He can't invite anyone to morning rides or tennis matches, so instead of eating synthetic lard sandwiches in the Bieber family's cold little room, he sometimes feels compelled to put on his best bib and tucker and go to the Vier Jahreszeiten.

HG clearly feels that there's an imbalance in his life. After celebrating his twenty-first birthday with friends in the "Atlantic" in Hamburg singing at the grand piano "Now everything, everything must change" for the bewildered musicians in the bar, he wonders the following day where his life is going to take him. On his birthday he receives forty-two letters, parcels, flowers, plus food ranging from an East Prussian goose to a layer cake to keep him going for the next few weeks. "I'm really rather flabbergasted at how many people take an interest in me," he writes to his parents. For this new year in his life he had "wished for one particular thing, namely becoming 'a bit more myself.' Up till now I've always been too reliant on other people, and then I do lots of things to please them, and that's not always the right thing. I must practice being independent."

Who isn't familiar with the need to be everybody's darling? Kurt will have seen this soapbox speech for what it was. But he takes his son seriously again. So he watches with concern as HG flees the difficult task of self-discovery for the security of the only group he knows outside of the family: his regiment. A few officers from Tilsit have formed a club in their Hamburg exile, and during the fierce debates about the Versailles Treaty they discuss "whether everyone with a spark of honor in his body is not duty-bound to fight it, gun in hand." Luckily the young people don't concern themselves with the Freikorps and their hunt for "Bolsheviks." The class struggle isn't their main issue; it's the external enemy, specifically anyone who might be about to invade Germany. Kurt calms HG down: "We can put up no resistance, not least because we're not in a position to supply our troops with ammunition and equipment. The franc-tireur war"—today we'd call it a guerrilla war—"preached by conservative fanatics, would be the greatest nonsense and the greatest misfortune for Germany."

All in all, HG's idea that he must now defend the fatherland as a soldier isn't appropriate to the circumstances, says Kurt. "Instead, we will all have to respond to the situation created by the loss of the war in as dignified a manner as possible—although I fear many people will be undignified—and attempt to regain our lost respect through our behavior." I can hear Kurt in 1914. What an arduous journey since the time when he still felt he had to bring "German culture and the essence of Germanness" to the whole world.

Now Kurt advises his son: "Above all you are in an employment situation, which you cannot single-handedly break over an adventure with a dubious outcome. An apprentice contract isn't a piece of scrap paper. In business, everything is based on good faith. In the event of an occupation of Hamburg by the British, your company will probably be kept very busy, and your boss would be astonished if you wanted to leave him. Have you discussed it with him?"

As before, when Kurt ensured that HG didn't get his brains blown out on the Western Front for the sake of the Iron Cross, he now prevents him from joining a kamikaze unit inspired by outrage over the Versailles Treaty. That is to say: he can't prevent him from doing anything anymore. By now HG is twenty-one. Instead, Kurt uses arguments, and it is pleasing to hear his paternal diplomacy: "I consider your decision to go straight to your regiment to be wrong, and it was rather precipitate of you to have written to the commander and the adjutant already, even if you did so out of a very respectable sense of loyalty to the fatherland. It is true that we don't want to see you crouching behind the stove when the fatherland is in trouble. We want to see you in the place where you belong. But I don't agree with you about *where* you belong if you're to serve the fatherland most effectively."

The father has a knack of getting to the nub: "Examine carefully whether your decisions aren't really based on your heart's desire to be back in your former circles, leading your former life with your comrades, that—I freely admit—is much more agreeable than the life of a business apprentice. I can imagine that your former life compares most unfavorably with the one you are leading now; but one should beware of crucial decisions concerning one's future life made on the basis of a passing mood."

Presumably Kurt is right about HG's yearnings. But the explosion of national ire in Germany over the Versailles Treaty was unanimous, and it wasn't only young hotheads like HG who were unwilling to submit to its outrageous conditions. In the 440-article treaty, I see nothing but a desire to destroy and humiliate. The Germans were particularly upset by war-guilt article 231: Germany and her allies are responsible "for causing all the loss and damage" to which the allies have been subjected as a consequence of "the war imposed upon them."

Not to mention the loss of territories—Danzig Corridor!—or the reduction of the Reich Army to 100,000 men with meticulously counted-out rounds of ammunition. An army that size wouldn't have been enough to defend a miniature state. The navy is boiled down to 15,000 sailors, Germany is forbidden to have so much as a single submarine or an air force, for that matter, and all but a rump of the High Seas Fleet, Kaiser Wilhelm's giant toy, is to be handed over to the Allies. This is forestalled, a week before the signature of the treaty, by the dramatic self-scuttling of the fleet in the Scottish bay of Scapa Flow on the orders of Admiral von Reuter—I wonder what seascape painters made of that!

OK: Germany has lost the war, and what the Kaiserreich imposed on the Russians in the treaty of Brest-Litovsk gives us a clue about what might have happened if Germany had been victorious this time too. But look how many nations climbed aboard at Versailles! Twenty-seven states suddenly assembled, not counting the Commonwealth countries like India, Canada, Australia, South Africa, and New Zealand. What on earth did they, what did Cuba, Siam, and Haiti have to do with the war?

I guess it's understandable enough that the king of the Hedjas—modern-day Saudi Arabia—should get back the original Koran, assembled in about A.D. 650 by Mohammed's son-in-law, the third caliph Othman. The Turks had stolen the ancient treasure from Medina to give it to Wilhelm II—you really don't do that kind of thing! But did that make the desert king a participant in the war? If the Liberians no longer want to have one (!) German customs official on their soil, as they had contractually agreed with the Kaiserreich in 1911, does that really constitute grounds for war? The British now laid a claim to the skull of Sultan Mkwawa, which was "removed from the Protectorate of German East Africa and taken to Germany." Why the British? But there it is in the treaty.

HG and his friends in the dragoons probably didn't examine the document very closely, and in all likelihood they don't pay much attention to how much livestock is to be delivered to France and Belgium—the French get five hundred stallions between the ages of three and seven, the Belgians two hundred. The French lay claim to fillies and mares of Ardennais, Boulonnais, or Belgian bloodlines, 30,000 in all. The Belgians are awarded only 10,000, but those are draft horses of the "large Belgian type." France orders

10,000 goats, while 15,000 sows go to Belgium. As ordered by the treaty.

But some things really do matter: 85 million tons of coal are to be delivered to France, Belgium, and Italy each year, even though Germany had lost a third of its coal supplies. The occupation of the German territories west of the Rhine for a period of fifteen years is a humiliation, but more than anything else it is expensive, because Germany has to pay for "the keep of men and beasts, lodging and billeting, pay and allowances, salaries and wages, bedding, heating, lighting, clothing, equipment, harness and saddlery, armament and rolling-stock, etc., etc." Those are the terms of the treaty, and the fear that France might move many more troops than necessary to the region, just as a way of having its army financed by Germany, was quickly confirmed.

And then the reparations—everyone knows that these are illusory sums, an easy way of punishing Germany over and over again by occupying its territories, imposing food blockades, closing avenues of communication if the country, already bled to death, didn't pay, couldn't pay—a continuation of war by other means. At first these were set at an astronomical 269 billion gold marks plus substantial deliveries in kind, such as 80,000 locomotives and 150,000 railway wagons, ships, heavy machinery, chemical products, and so on, and so on. But Germany's adversaries realized that you shouldn't kill the goose that laid the golden egg: the new sum halves the figure, although it's still ludicrously high, 132 billion gold marks plus interest. The first billion, please, within twenty-five days of the signature of the contract. Germany doesn't have the money. But Germany does have presses for printing money, and soon she has massive inflation.

It is now the start of the far from Golden Twenties. One government crisis follows another, the economy goes into free fall, there are strikes and uprisings all across the political spectrum, murderers and gangs of thugs terrorize the streets. The Klamroths stride through the chaos surprisingly unscathed. My agitation about this absurd time has little to do with their lives. Two months after the enforcement of the Treaty of Versailles, for example, we have the Kapp Putsch. Five thousand heavily armed members of the Ehrhardt Freikorps Brigade, wearing swastikas on their steel helmets for the first time, march on Berlin. The government flees to Dresden, the Reich Army doesn't lift a finger to help its masters, Friedrich Ebert and his comrades. To rescue themselves they call a general strike, which sets the country ablaze from north to south. The putsch collapses, the protagonists—"Reich Chancellor" Wolfgang Kapp, founder of the German Fatherland Party; General Walther von Lüttwitz, "Father of the Freikorps"; Captain Pabst, the murderer of Karl Liebknecht and Rosa Luxemburg; and, yes, him again, Erich Ludendorff—escape to safety with false passports.

That's on Saturday, March 13, 1920. On Wednesday, March 17—all hell's let loose—the factory owner and Councillor of Commerce Curt Klamroth, his brother, landowner Johannes Klamroth, and their wives turn up at the notary's office in Halberstadt. And what do they do there? With the authority of other relations they found the Klamroth Family Association. They take with them a "constitution," printed expensively in Gothic script on fifteen pages of the finest handmade paper, to be deposited with the local court. The purpose of this association is the "union of all descendants, if possible, of Johann Caspar Klamroth, born on January 29, 1689, in Alterode (Eastern Harz), died May 2, 1764, in Ermsleben, insofar as they bear the name of Klamroth, and their wives, for the fostering of shared family matters."

And these are—I'll keep them brief: 1. To ensure greater cohesion among the family members. 2. To maintain and extend the Klamroth archive. 3. To hold family reunions. 4. To supervise and administer the family foundations. 5. To support family members with words and deeds. 6. To settle feuds between family members. 7. To deal with all matters described by the family council or the family reunion as family matters. So, basically: "Be nice to each other." Do you really need an association for that?

Well, they did. I know of other such middle-class family associations. It had to do with the "Junkerization" of their social class—meaning: we do exactly the same things as the aristocracy. And if the Klamroths inaugurated their association at a time when "the old order" around them was in pieces, I see this as the need to preserve order at least in the family. I don't wish to make too much of the fact that this long-prepared ceremony by a landowning haut bourgeois family coincided with the Kapp Putsch. The founding grandparents probably had no idea what was going on in the outside world—there was a general strike: no newspapers, no mail, no telephone. A few days later, however, Kurt fumes about "this crime and the incredible stupidity of these right wing fanatics and members of the general staff."

So: family. Genealogical research was all the rage, and Kurt had involved himself in it even long before the war. His first extensive family chronicle was published in 1908—a wonderful source for me! The family archive is his work, and his correspondence with genealogical societies fills several files. Where did he get the time? He scoured church records, rifled through land registers, buried himself in parish records, copied out feudal duties and tenancy records. There's an exchange of letters in Latin between Kurt and a church provost in Poland about some forebear of his father Gustav's wife—Kurt knew enough Latin for this. I find it hard to see this dotty research as entirely innocent, because we know where it was all going to end up, and because I know that the "immaculately Aryan" family trees of all the Klamroths came to represent the family's "breed value" less than twenty years later.

Not yet, though. In 1920, the Klamroths considered even Southern Germans extravagant, and connections with Jews, blacks, Arabs—whoever—didn't even cross the minds of these Harz-mountain people. The Jews in Halberstadt were Orthodox and lived their separate lives. The non-Jews in Halberstadt would never attempt any chumminess—the world was fine as it was. The members of the family were probably more concerned with the evidence for their social rank, their family crest testifying to their membership in an exclusive circle. Kurt was a tireless archivist. His meticulously kept folio volumes, twelve in all and grandiosely labeled, reappeared after the fall of the Berlin Wall, in the attic of the Liebfrauenkirche in Halberstadt, from where I gratefully lugged them away.

Kurt collected ancestors the way people today collect the little figures out of Kinder eggs, and I'm always tickled by his efforts to trace bloodlines back to Goethe or Lucas Cranach. Particularly because just about any of us can trace our ancestry back to kings and generals if we really take the trouble. Kurt did take the trouble, documented in the various editions of the "Gazette of the Klamroth Family Association," where, among others, he introduced Charlemagne as a member of the Klamroth family.

Then, at family reunions, the members would sing. At first there are about sixty of them, and the access criteria are strict. You can't have just any old cousin four times removed jostling her way in. Certainly not! But those who belong sing: "Auntie Nettchen, right as rain—Jupp-i-dee, jupp-i-da—Claims descent from Charlemagne—Jupp-i-dee-i-da and her sons, they do report, stem from old Pippin the Short, Jupp-i-dee, jupp-i-da, jupp-i-dee-fiderallala" and so on. These are tunes that everyone knows, and there are little black moleskin notebooks with the lyrics stuck in—*The Songbook of the Klamroth Family Association*—and then off they go: "Sing the song, oh Klamroths all, let it ring through house and hall!"

And so they do, in harmony. The house has a grand piano, a harmonium, and an upright. There's Kurt junior, who composed the choral introit for the family reunion: "Blessed be he who commemorates his forefathers." He also plays the violin, and how! There are lutes and accordions and flutes, and everybody sings. Constantly. Every innocent phrase is canonized. Even the new arrivals move up and down with the melodies. The only one who doesn't is Kurt the Elder. He doesn't sing, he doesn't play an instrument, he doesn't make up rhymes. But everyone else does: "Accord and family are what the German nation needs—Without family tradition discord grows like weeds!"

I wasn't there. The last family reunion of the "old days" took place in 1938, when Else was pregnant with me. But these songs, the whole repertoire of the family ballad-mongers Benno Nachtigall and Son, have crept under my skin. However ghastly the rhymes, however clumsy the tunes, however terrible I may find the idea of them all sitting there associating with one another, in harmony—why should it be ghastly? It somehow touches me. I know all those songs by heart, heaven knows how:

> *All you beloved members of the family association,*
> *Aunts and uncles, cousins all, shake hands 'midst jubilation,*
> *For once again today we see what cannot be denied,*
> *Nice people to a man we are, and to our family tied!!*

But there's also this one, which they sing in 1935:

> *Unified and young and strong is the noble land that breeds us,*
> *And it does glorious homage pay to the great man who leads us.*
> *So come then, fellow Klamroths all, and join in merrily:*
> *Hail to the Führer, hail to our land, and to our ances-tree.*

I'd rather not, if you don't mind. You shouldn't follow dreams when they go so badly wrong. Nonetheless, family festivities—there are no family reunions anymore—are something rather special. No one sings any of these songs anymore, of course, but "Nice people to a man we are, and to our family tied" also applies to the younger generation. More or less, anyway.

In those days it was self-evident. Refusal wasn't an option. So far I haven't found any reference to a black sheep in any of the paperwork, nothing that would have given the family council or even the family reunion cause for concern. No fraud, no bankruptcy, no debts, apart from HG's small-scale dodgy deals. No suicide, no divorce, no marriages to Catholics, no promiscuity (at least not known), no illegitimate children, no alcoholism, no brawling, not a whiff of scandal. That's still to come—not all of it, but some. Later. The fall has not yet begun.

They're all still industrious and probably happy to be able to cling to one another beneath the family coat of arms in these grim times. At least I see that coat of arms embossed with ever greater frequency on the fine sheets of writing paper that pass back and forth in the family. Even on letters written by HG, and he's industrious too. He's up to his eyes in Hamburg, but that doesn't prevent him from producing a special issue of the family *Gazette* in 1920: "The Klamroth Family in the World War." Fifteen men served, ten of them as officers. Three are dead, they were the youngest, four were wounded, three are still marked by gas injuries and illness. That's a lot, two-thirds of them. I don't have to broaden this to the millions of human lives that this war cost. Every one of these fates is a reason to mourn.

HG doesn't rebel, not even after his narrow escape. No one in this family rebels. In the preface to his special issue, HG writes: "For almost five years the terrible fire raged, and what our forefathers had been at infinite pains to create, what had been the greatest pride and joy throughout the lives of all true Germans, lay shattered by hatred and rage from without, and from a lack of understanding within. We are back where we started, and despite all the misery and hardship of the time just past and the terrible present, we know that, as before the war, and especially now, the words apply to each of us, and to all our work and our intentions: 'Onward Germany!' The end is for us Klamroths only a new beginning, and if we were Germans before, we are bound now more firmly to our German essence by the blood that has flowed from deep within us for the German fatherland."

HG is twenty-two, and he means every word. Should I stone him for it? Everyone in Germany, and elsewhere, thought like that in those days. In a second special issue of the Klamroth Family Association's *Gazette* a year later, he describes his "Memories of My Cousins," those three boys he played with on Juist in the summer holidays, and who perished so wretchedly in the adults' war. Now HG is twenty-three, and he writes: "They were of my blood, our blood. They shed that blood for our fatherland. We remember them all with love, each individual with loyalty and pride: *Dulce et decorum est pro patria mori.*" About that nonsense I've raged already. I'll stop for now. I can't turn the man into something he isn't.

HG isn't having a good time in Hamburg—we're still in 1920. He is slogging through his apprenticeship with Carl Prior and Co., where the choleric office manager Michaelsen suspects the young dispatch clerk of being "contaminated by socialism" when he points out that a second man is needed for his workload. "Contaminated by socialism" is really a joke to HG, and not one he finds funny. His class consciousness and his honor are in turmoil, and he doesn't feel like sitting in the office until midnight because Michaelsen thinks one cheap worker is still better value than two cheap workers. HG yells at his master—a flash of rebellion, at last!—the master roars back. HG chucks in his job; the master remembers Kurt the Councillor of Commerce and demands that his son stay with the company. Things are smoothed over thanks to Kurt's active intervention, but HG spends his lunchtimes stomping grimly along the banks of the Alster thinking about a new job. What about senator? Now that would be something!

But HG doesn't feel good in his skin. He suffers a severe case of acne. That could be a normal affliction, but in HG's case I rather suspect something stress-related and psychosomatic, although no one would have called it that in those days. So what's getting under his skin? Certainly his troubles with the company are not helping, to such an extent that even Kurt recognizes the connection. He advises HG not to take a narrow-minded company officer so much to heart.

Above all HG is pursued by the death of Gunner Vitt. The court official of Halberstadt district command summons him to "a hearing in the Vitt case" and HG goes weak at the knees. "I couldn't think straight, and my heart was racing madly," he writes to his sister Annie. Kurt goes to the court, he is allowed to see the files, and gives the all clear. HG is needed only as a witness. Franz Vitt's father has applied for "war parents' welfare," and HG is to tell the court whether Gunner Vitt was sufficiently drunk to be unaware of what he was doing according to paragraph 51 of the penal code. Kurt writes to HG: "It has nothing to do with you now. You're dazzling there in the files, your superiors express nothing but pride." But that's not it. HG writes to Annie: "That incident won't let me be. I feel guilty, and no official exoneration will free me from that feeling."

Shortly afterward, HG gets a letter from Erich Hoffmann, the Baltic medical student who worked as an interpreter for HG's squadron in Estonia, and to whom HG "was very attached at the time. He was the one who was with me in Sallotak when the Vitt affair happened, and who all but saved my life by keeping the second marauder off my back." Now Hoffmann needs money. After the postwar confusions in the Baltic he had ended up in Germany, he's sitting his doctor's exam in Königsberg and can't go on doing part-time work in the final term. HG asks Kurt for help. "I'm trying to treat this matter in as purely a businesslike way as possible; if I were to follow my emotions, I wouldn't hesitate to help my old comrade, if I had the funds to do it."

Kurt stands in the way once again: "It's going to involve a considerable sum, which can't even be written off against tax. Consequently one would have to draw on one's private fortune, without knowing whether the sum will ever be paid back. But if we did give the sum, then the gift tax, which is very high where nonrelatives are concerned, would have to be paid by Hoffmann." HG writes to his friend Siegfried Körte, a fellow member of his regiment who also knew Hoffmann in Estonia: "I would so like to give him the support. It would be as if I could extract something good out of the Vitt affair. Vitt's father bothers me, too. I hope he gets the war parents' welfare at least." And a few paragraphs later he writes: "Once again my face is so inflamed and swollen, I wish this business wouldn't keep ambushing me." Whether "this business" refers to Gunner Vitt or the acne, he doesn't say. I reckon that one leads to the other.

HG needs a girlfriend. I take it as given that his body needs one, but he needs one just as urgently for his soul. It's spinning pitifully, and I would really love to grant him the pleasurable view of the world you get when you're in love. But the compulsions of the time are against this, requiring that a person immediately has to think of marriage when all he wants is a pleasant summer. Always the church bells have to ring, when a tinkle would be just as welcome, so HG really tries to fill the deficit in his life with "depth and seriousness."

I have in front of me one of his many attempts to keep a diary. Things like this generally break off after pages and pages of verbal acrobatics, and years ago, when I read this for the first time, I stuck a Post-it note on it: "The boy's dreadful. Precocious, pompous, actually unbearable." He isn't. I just didn't know him yet. Admittedly he writes upsettingly badly, but that disappears, and I'm aware that he's trying to come to terms with himself. On October 26, 1920, the diary gets going in perfect error-free type. HG has turned twenty-two a few days before, and has just finished his apprenticeship with Prior. He writes: "If in what follows I am trying for the third or fourth time to keep a kind of diary, what prompts me to do so is the idea that it's of the greatest importance to observe one's own growth and development in the course of one's experience, and on the one hand years later to follow the details of this past development and explain it to oneself, but on the other hand, and this seems to be the main thing, to learn from it for the times to come."

He actually writes that. In his own diary. I'd like to shake him:

for heaven's sake, man, be yourself! I can't. Instead I read on: "While it may contradict my deep-rooted sense of order and of the completion of anything I set out to do, it may prove—if this remains a fragment—that lots of little fragments finally go to make an edifice which, while it may be outwardly wretched and inadequate, is at least constructed with love, with the love of wishing to know all that it means to be a human being, to live life." On the last side of this fragment I find the key to these flamboyant exercises: "I'm making a carbon copy, so that I can immediately give my parents an image of my life." Nothing surprises me anymore.

First of all HG painstakingly describes the torment of his apprenticeship in Hamburg, and the stress of working for the boor Michaelsen, who sent him on his way with a kindly dishonest reference: "Herr Hans Georg Klamroth entered an apprenticeship with me on May 13, 1919, and within a short time he managed to gain my respect and sympathy." Then HG travels to Halberstadt and, with his father, drinks a bottle of champagne to the "nightmares" that he has just survived. After that he is finally free and has to learn to deal with it. In HG's world it goes like this: "From the conviction that life is a duty, a conviction that my parents must have passed on to me at birth, and encouraged since then with my wise upbringing"—heavens!—"and because of my impressions during my compulsory time in Hamburg, until recently every free minute, every minute that one didn't fill with productive external work, struck me as a luxury, and thus as a waste."

In the course of the next few lazy weeks, however, HG does relax a bit, particularly as there's a lot going on, among other things a trip in the new car to see relatives in Silesia: "It was a wonderful cross-country journey, on which I felt exceptionally well, and even the oft-repeated cries of the wretched pedestrians—'black-marketeer!'—didn't bother me greatly. If one is at least honest with oneself, and honestly feels that one has done and is doing nothing unjust, then other people can get lost." Who is "one"? The car is Kurt's, and HG is just a passenger. The young man is fooling around with ideas above his station.

Visiting also friends in Silesia, HG meets up with an old comrade from his regiment, with whose sister he had a—fairly chaste—affair. Their parents belong to the East Prussian landowners with whom he often went hunting, who supplied him and, more important, Gertrud in Halberstadt with turkeys, cheese, and dry sausage throughout all the years of starvation, and who benignly tolerated HG's flirtation with their daughter Ruth. After an evening canoodling by the pond in the family's park in Labehnen, Ruth probably expected an engagement ring, but HG, having received several severe warnings about this from his father, somehow never got this straightened out.

Now he turns his attention to her brother Heinz, who might be able to help him out of his dilemma—easier than talking directly to the lady. HG writes in his diary: "He was surprised by how seriously I took my relationship with Ruth. In his benevolence he immediately declared himself willing to dissolve my relationship with Ruth. I have no other option, if I don't want to dig the grave for my own spiritual death. And I really don't want that. Heinz refused to hear of any guilt on my part, called it all frivolity and joie de vivre, without knowing exactly what this means to me, a terrible burden of guilt." Joie de vivre equals guilt? Halberstadt is a very Protestant place.

The conversation occurs on the Schleibitz estate, the parental home of HG's close friend Wolf Yorck von Wartenburg, a distant cousin of Count Peter Yorck, who will later have a part to play in the events of July 20. In the photographs, Wolf Yorck is an unusually good-looking, almost girlishly pretty young man. The two of them know each other from their Fahnenjunkers' training in Döberitz in 1917, and HG describes their relationship as one of "a harmony of souls" or "profound, intimate concord." HG considers Wolf Yorck as close to him as his father, he writes on one occasion in a letter to Kurt, and that means something.

HG opens his heart as always: "Of late I have been so constantly engaged with the material side of life that I had completely forgotten what Wolf really meant to me, I had forgotten how deeply I dwelt in his heart. In fact I have never felt that so intensely as I do now." Three other friends of Wolf's are there as well, two girls and a young man, and HG "devotes himself deliberately and yet once more almost submissively to the intellectual bond that surrounded us and which our central figure, Wolf, had tied for us in his heart, so infinitely open to the ideals of life."

HG wants to rave, he wants to admire, and he puts himself down: "I clearly felt the great distance that separated me from these people who lived out their ideals most intensely, these people who are kept always at arm's length from life's harsh reality, which is held in check precisely by the power of ideals. A gap that made me fear all too often, at earlier stages of my life, for my friendship with Wolf—oh me of little faith! Why was I so fearful? During those days I learned to feel that at the summits to which their warmest feelings had elevated me—me, the sober reality man, how amazing!—all human boundaries cease to exist."

It took me a while to understand the meaning that the word "ideals"—always in the plural—had for HG. It represents intellectual reflection or spiritual curiosity. "Ideals" doesn't necessarily mean a model. A person with "ideals" reads books and talks about them, while the kind of "reality man" that HG sees himself as being transports goslings and talks about it, too. The two types don't always sit easily together, and when HG talks about the "ideals" of the other guests, he means precisely that discrepancy. Because when Wolf Yorck was going through his Kant and Fichte phase, HG was still plodding along with Alice Berend and *The Bridegrooms of Babette Bomberling*. He did catch up, though.

Nonetheless, Wolf Yorck's friends are genial with HG—"the others knew that Wolf was very fond of me, and approached me accordingly." But in his insecurity he sometimes—who doesn't?—puts his foot in it. After a piano performance by one of the girls on the first evening by the fireside, the conversation turns to Beethoven, "and for no reason at all I told some extremely stupid anecdotes that might have been more suitable in different surroundings." He wants to use a walk in the park the next morning to tell the other girl "something about myself, but completely failed to do so. I will now have to write to her, and I am keenly awaiting her answer, to be sure that she didn't take my insanely chaotic nonsense amiss."

Poor HG, I sympathize with your red ears. But let me assure you that usually it isn't as bad as you think it is afterward. Because HG is still accepted in this circle, and his longing for a girlfriend doesn't make him look ridiculous. When he understands that the pianist, Dora, is secretly engaged to Jochen, the fourth member of the gang, it does give him "a painful pang." But he suppresses his own freshly germinated emotions: "It was immediately clear to me that Jochen was infinitely more worthy than I to call such a noble human being as Dora his own, and I saw that for me this was only—and when I say 'only' I'm not using it as a qualification—the opportunity I had craved for so long to learn to respect and love 'womanhood' as I imagine doing in my dreams, and then gradually to become worthy, as Jochen is now—on my way to great happiness later on. It is on these terms that I want to remain in contact with Dora as much as possible, I want to become acquainted with her emotions as those of my ideal, without personal desires." Later, without anything about "noble human beings" or yearnings for worthiness, Dora and Jochen Granzow became some of HG's closest friends. They liked one another—it was as simple as that.

Shortly after the trip to the Silesian estates, HG accompanies his mother on a short holiday to the spa in Braunlage. There they meet a "young spinster who takes a great interest in all kinds of intellectual issues." HG engages her in lengthy conversations about Oswald Spengler and his *Decline of the West,* a treatise of cultural philosophy that had excited everyone at the time. They chat about the "need for the education of the great masses" and the "stress on the insignificance of the individual self." However, HG responds just as the rest of us do to difficult best sellers: "I admit that I so far have to base my opinion of *Decline of the West* solely on the introduction to the book and the first chapter."

But the "young spinster" has another subject up her sleeve. She's a hard-line anti-Semite, she tells him. HG: "I told her I was too, with the qualification that I was anti-Semitic in my head, but not in my heart. My opinion on the subject depends upon my mood. Sometimes I can say that with my mind I recognize the Jews as an economic factor, while on the basis of my racial instinct I despise them in my heart. Be that as it may, I see that it's best for me at the moment to keep myself far away from the Jewish question. I am sure that experience, which I will have ample opportunity to collect over the years to come, will bring me soonest to a workable solution."

How am I to deal with this? Aside from the fact that HG has trouble telling his heart from his mind, I shall try to be objective. Anti-Semitism had been socially acceptable since Martin Luther, or at least since Richard Wagner. In 1893 sixteen representatives of the Anti-Semitic Party entered the Reichstag. Hitler simply had to repeat what others had said and written: the chairman of the Pan-German League, Heinrich Class ("Germany for the Germans!"); the Bavarian Cavalry General Konstantin von Gebsattel; the founder of the "Teutonic Order," Theodor Fritsch; the German Gymnastics Association; the Wandervogel; the Reichshammer-bund; the Imperial German Mittelstand Association; both churches—they all agreed on the subject. The list is far from complete. Demands that any commingling of the "Jewish and the Teutonic race" should be liable to punishment, and that a situation should be brought about whereby the Jews had the option of emigrating from Germany, were circling among German opinion makers in 1913. Particular emphasis was placed on the idea that Jews had to transfer their property to the state before leaving the Reich.

After the war, Jews and Social Democrats had to suffer as scapegoats for the right, often in personal union, because the workers' movement had always been considerably influenced by Jewish intellectuals. But anti-Semitism was not yet a national epidemic, the "Jewish question" was just one of many political subjects among bourgeois conservatives, students, and academics. HG is parroting again here, just as he had parroted Oswald Spengler, and it does him credit that he himself admits he doesn't know what he's talking about. Later I've occasionally found things about him that have been too much for me. But anti-Semitism isn't one of them.

In Halberstadt, where HG spends the last of the holidays before his new job in Hamburg gets going, the goats are still romping on the lawn, rabbits and chickens live in the stables, and the huge house can be heated only with a few stoves—there's a coal shortage. There isn't much to eat, either, but lots of people share what little there is—guests are forever arriving. Reading HG's diary I marvel at how Gertrud keeps the household going. She has provided accommodation for three children of landed families from the surrounding area who go to grammar school in Halberstadt—they have to be talked to and comforted when things go wrong, and an eye also needs to be cast over their homework from time to time. Then there's a bedridden old lady to be looked after, a distant relative who couldn't cope on her own in her apartment.

The garden is bedded down for the winter, the roots of the roses are packed with straw, shrubs are cut back, potatoes stored away, the gymnastics equipment from the playground has to go into the tennis pavilion, the big wash is put on to boil, pea soup is cooked for the women who do the ironing, and a mountain of sugar beet is boiled into syrup. In the evenings a stream of young people flows into the house, friends of Annie and Kurt junior, playing music and practicing motets for a concert, and a dance is held in the hall to celebrate the conclusion of Kurt junior's special course in Greek. Gertrud doesn't do it all on her own. She has two maids again, and the gout-ridden gardener Ebeling is still shuffling around in the flower beds. But her head must be spinning, what with organizing and supervising, apart from her extensive correspondence, her work on the committees of several charities, and the many people who need her advice. Could I do that? I wouldn't want to.

Kurt has shifted the core business in the company. There's hardly enough raw material to make fertilizer, so the factory is now taking on paid work for other firms. As a substitute the company has returned to some of its old functions, and it now increasingly distributes seeds, grains, straw, hay, and natural fertilizer. It's going quite well, Kurt's carefully nurtured connections are paying off, and despite constantly rising prices hardly anybody has a sense that disaster is just around the corner in the form of inflation. The Amsterdam-based Curaçao business turns out to be a blessing. It brings in its yields in valuable Dutch guilders, and the personal contacts on the board of directors haven't deteriorated either. In the first session that Kurt attends since the start of the war there is a small, friendly ceremony, at which the member of the English consortium hands him a "peace pipe" stuffed with British tobacco.

A London firm called Kidson also resumes its dealings with I.G. Klamroth, and, moreover, a "rich American uncle" suddenly appears. His name is Ernst Hothorn, and I haven't heard of him before. HG calls him Uncle Ernst. I haven't the faintest idea where he comes from or what he does, but he successfully takes care of I.G. Klamroth's interests in a Belgian company based in the United States, and also sends whatever is in short supply in postwar Germany: thread, tennis balls, condensed milk, Canadian whiskey. Hothorn finds a buyer for HG's bread-slicing machines, and on a visit to Halberstadt he pulls 50,000 marks in cash out of his trouser pocket for Gertrud's Infant School Association—things like that don't happen every day, even in better times.

By now, as the new law requires, the firm has a shop steward elected by all workers and employees as a spokesman for the work-force. Not all the employees, in fact. Kutscher Kückelmann refused to take part in the election: if he wanted something from his lordship, he could make his wishes known to him in person, it had nothing to do with his colleagues. It's the store man for I.G. Klamroth who wins the election, but he's also been with the company for almost thirty years and handles staff matters in perfect harmony with the boss.

Otherwise, after the revolution bureaucratic monstrosities are sprouting up all over the place. In Kurt's branch alone, apart from the War Food Office and the Raw Materials Supplies Authority, there is an impressive range of organizations: the Nitrate Fertilizer Committee, the Assessment Office for Phosphorous Fertilizers, the Assessment Office for Ammonia Fertilizers, the Military Chemicals Joint Stock Company, the Reich Sack Authority—what on earth does it do?—the Reich Association for German Industry, the Sulfuric Acid Committee, the German Industrial Council, the Reich Office for Economic Demobilization, the Consortium of German Industrial and Commercial Employers and Employees, the Registration Office for Phosphorous Fertilizers—I've left out half of them, and you might wonder whether one hand knows what the other's doing here. In almost all these committees Kurt has a seat and vote—in an honorary capacity, obviously. It can't have done any harm to the company.

But there are only twenty-four hours even in Kurt's day, and Berlin isn't just around the corner, so he relinquishes his mandate in the Halberstadt Council Assembly for reasons of overwork. In 1905 he had followed in the footsteps of his father, who had been a member of the town parliament since 1867. Kurt had been the chairman since 1913. In those days it was still a club; there were only three Social Democratic councillors out of a total of forty-two. Since the election of February 1919 the proportions had clearly reversed: twenty-six "reds" against sixteen bourgeois. Kurt: "I do feel melancholy that for the first time in fifty-three years no Klamroth will help to determine the fate of the town." Nonetheless, even the socialist newspaper *Halberstadter Tageblatt* speaks of him with respect: "He was in strong opposition to the extreme left. But opposing views don't mean failing to show respect to one's adversaries, and that was something that Councillor Klamroth never did. So we shall not neglect to stress that in Councillor Klamroth the town is losing an intelligent and conscientious colleague."

In Hamburg, HG's new job with a shipping broker gets going on December 1, 1920. Siegfried Körte picks him up at the station—aside from Yorck, he's HG's other very close friend. They run laughing and joking around the Alster: "As soon as I see Siegfried I'm in a terrific mood." Körte and HG were in the same regiment, and HG often visited the East Prussian estate of Körte's parents, where he particularly admired Siegfried's "estimable mother." Because of Körte, HG gave up his little room at the Bieber family's so that they could move into a flat together when Körte joined him in Hamburg, and the two young men are as thick as thieves. Kurt and Gertrud observe this development with some concern. Discreet reservations arise regularly in Gertrud's letters, because Körte drags HG along to the operetta house on the Reeperbahn—"Let him go on his own, and you go to the concert"—and in Kurt's letters, because he doesn't think Körte is serious where money is concerned—"Try and get him on the right track. He's a loose cannon."

When Wolf Yorck comes to Hamburg on a long visit, Kurt wonders skeptically how the two of them will get on. They're actually very different: the wild and witty Körte certainly hasn't got any "ideals," and has never read a "good book" in his life. But even the earnest young Count is drawn by his charm and his imagination. In one of the few letters from Wolf Yorck that I have found among HG's papers, he describes a boat trip around Hamburg's canals, on which, from the water, Siegfried Körte manages to get them an invitation to a posh garden party being thrown by some shipowners they have never met before. Wolf Yorck writes admiringly: "In response to Siegfried's radiant smile, they almost apologized for not inviting us before."

HG and Siegfried Körte's friendship ends three years later with a crash. Körte had embezzled a considerable amount of foreign currency that an old aunt of Wolf Yorck's had entrusted to him in the middle of the inflation—a disaster! Only months later does Körte pay the money back, after HG had threatened him with serious legal consequences. HG is beside himself that contact between his two closest friends should have wreaked such havoc. And he's in a state of grief because he really loved the hopeless Körte. The tactful Kurt keeps himself from saying "I told you so." He sends HG a card from Berlin: "I sympathize with you. It's hard to lose such a good friend."

Siegfried Körte is the key to Else. They both work for Carl Illies & Co., another Hamburg import-export firm specializing in trade with Japan. Else later: "The amount of military material we shipped to Japan, that ranged from whole submarines to gyrocompasses, everything!" Körte is a dispatch clerk with the company, Else is private secretary to old Illies, a friend of her father's. The two gentlemen must have got along well, because throughout her life Else's spelling was remarkably aberrant. So, Else. Her name is Else Podeus, and she is the daughter of a fine family from Wismar.

SIX

Engaged to be married: HG and Else

HG writes in his diary: "Last night"—that's December 6, 1920—"we had Else Podeus over for a very cosy meal by the advent wreath, which I had decorated. For a long time Siegfried had been wanting me to revise my hitherto rather pejorative assessment of his friend, based on my observation from afar, by getting to know her more closely. And I did so, discovering that this human being really is out of the ordinary. We discussed all manner of things, first of all politics and the Jewish question"—the things people reveal to each other when courtship's at stake!—"and then our general philosophies and finally spiritism. Although many of the things she said struck me as thoroughly well thought out and valuable, in the depths of my heart I cannot rid myself of a certain antipathy toward her." At this point Else is twenty-one.

HG continues: "She's a bit too independent for my notion of the female sex, too much a 'woman of the world,' which is not to say that she overemphasizes this. Perhaps if we meet more often in the future, as we have arranged to do, she will provide the much needed reason to sweep aside an incorrect prejudice that I feel most deeply against a particular kind of person. But for the time being I am not very quick at making this kind of decision, which is quite good too." Five weeks later they're engaged.

With Else, HG hit the bull's-eye. All through my life I have met people whose eyes have lit up over "that" Else: how witty, how quick, how warmhearted, how full of laughter she was. I've only ever experienced that in a partial sense. By the time my memory begins with the big air raid on Halberstadt in April 1945, the house was filled to the brim with people, and Else, who was in charge of the chaos, was hardly available to me as a child. I just joined in with all the other children. Later I was lodged in boarding schools or put up by friends, and whenever Else and I really did live under one roof, she was fighting for our living. She was exhausted and I was going through puberty—not a good mix. After leaving school, as the last of five children, I quickly relieved her of having to support me. Almost three decades followed in which she had lost all enthusiasm for life, and I loved her protectively, chiefly from a distance. I only know the "marvel" that was Else because people have told me about it.

And I am experiencing that marvel now, when I see her peeling away one encrusted layer after another from uptight old HG. By her side, the pompous little boy becomes a proper man, and she falls upon Halberstadt like a bird of paradise, colorful, noisy, and confident. "I was always unimpressed," she says of herself, and it wasn't only HG who loved her for that, Kurt did too. But first things first.

Else the "woman of the world" comes from Wismar, and that's no more the world than Halberstadt is. But Wismar is on the sea, its trade contacts have always been more with Scandinavia, England, or Russia than with Sachsen-Anhalt or Hanover. Else's grandfather Heinrich Podeus, like his father, had been a seafaring man, a cabin boy, a helmsman, then a long-haul captain. He bought his own ships—one of them, incidentally, was called *Hans Georg*—in which he imported large quantities of coal from England. To that end he founded a coal-trading business, adding a shipping company with eleven steamers; a factory making capstans, windlasses, and later ships' engines; an iron foundry, where the parts for railway bridges and stations were manufactured; leading to a rolling-stock factory, the biggest in Germany. As the ships brought not only coal but wood from Scandinavia to Germany, the family set up a sawmill and a planing mill. Else's father, Paul Podeus, later built automobiles—both cars and trucks—and agricultural machinery that was very successful in Japan and South America.

What a blessed century that had been. Entrepreneurs like Heinrich and Paul Podeus in Wismar, and Louis and his son Gustav Klamroth in Halberstadt, could pluck the stars from the sky if they dared to do so. The parallels are striking: big money on one side, great commitment to the workers and the common good on the other. In both cases they're commercial councillors, in both cases they establish foundations for the benefit of their manual and clerical workers, they give their towns paintings, church bells, theater seats, school dinners. There's one striking difference between Kurt Klamroth and Else's father, Paul Podeus: Paul was never a reserve officer. He was, after all, from Mecklenburg, not from Prussia. Nonetheless, he did serve in the war, as a courier. Just as Kurt brought his own horses, Paul came, with a chauffeur, in his own car, built in his own factory.

Else's parental home, Ravelin Horn, was a glory to behold. Another parallel: Kurt built the Halberstadt house in 1911, Paul bought the old villa in 1901 and completely overhauled it. Both had tennis courts; there was a playground with gymnastics equipment in Wismar, too, a huge garden, greenhouses, and servants' quarters. No horses in Wismar, but a sailboat. "Ravelin" is a word from Swedish times, and means something like "fort"; at any rate the house stands on an old defensive mound, and the first owner's name was probably Horn. I've never seen Ravelin Horn; it was sold after Paul's death in the 1920s, and it's now a land registry and changed beyond recognition.

No wonder Else became a "woman of the world." At sixteen, when she leaves school and begins the apprenticeship years of a well-to-do daughter, she is living on the income from a million marks, which are administered by her father but belong to her. She still has these when she meets HG. Soon afterward, with inflation, everything's gone. Until then the money was simply there, lots of money. However, Else is molded by something else. In her parental home, Paul's business associates from all over the world are going in and out; Dagmar, Else's Danish mother, is a cheerful hostess; the house echoes with Danish, English, French, and above all the local dialect, Plattdeutsch—Paul wanted to preserve the Mecklenburg language from extinction, and until their death the brothers and sisters Podeus spoke to one another only in Plattdeutsch.

Else gave readings from Fritz Reuter, the quiet and lovable chronicler of Mecklenburg life in the nineteenth century. Paul himself joined friends and family around the hearth in Ravelin Horn on evenings when Reuter was read. Very late in her life, by which time Else was only a shadow of her former self, I persuaded her to do that again for my friends. Lots of people came, they sat pressed tightly together on the floor of our apartment. Else blossomed. She read "Hanne Nütte," "Ut mine Stromtid," the tales about Fru Pastern, Mining and Lining, and old Bräsig. We all loved her, and the tape recordings of that evening are among my most precious possessions.

Grand Duke Friedrich Franz von Mecklenburg-Schwerin and his wife are, along with their entourage, constant visitors to Ravelin Horn. But the Podeus children spend just as much time charging about in the foundry and the rolling-stock factory; they know all the workers by name and eat potato soup with them in their kitchens. And then there is Denmark. There were huge numbers of relatives there, shipping brokers, shipowners, and traders, who remain my favorite part of the clan. "Stick with the Danes, it'll do you good," is a line spoken by actor Wolfgang Neuss in the old film *Wir Wunderkinder,* and there's a reason why I've remembered that. Else and her brothers and sisters spend their summers in Maribo and in Bandholm on the island of Lolland, with a gaggle of cousins and friends. Later HG becomes part of that community; he feels perfectly at home there.

HG was particularly fond of his mother-in-law Dagmar, who claimed to be the most amusing girl that the island of Lolland had ever produced. The stories about her are legion—she never learned German properly, or perhaps she cultivated her funny double Dutch because she knew that people enjoyed it. "You're the most irritating child to be had by anyone" is a phrase that's entered family lore, along with "*Eeeh,* him I would *not* like to be"—the exclamation of a compassionate soul to fill the awkward silence caused by some unlucky thing. When a sister-in-law told her off for her slovenly way with language, Dagmar coolly shot back, "*Ja,* but me they understand better than you." Once Else's mother sent a long letter to her in revolutionary Berlin, where all hell had broken loose in the streets. Dagmar doesn't mention this, but only scrawls in the margin at the end: "I should really frighten, but always I forget."

She was round as a ball and tiny, just shy of five feet three, and she barely reached the shoulder of her husband, who was six feet four. Else raved about him, even fifty years later: the very incarnation of a gentleman, dazzlingly handsome, stylish in his manners, warmhearted, a humorous family man, "not really educated, but in his field"—he was an engineer—"a distinguished expert." Unfortunately he wasn't a businessman; if he had been he might not have lost the Podeus empire so completely during the time of inflation. Else was grateful that Paul died in 1926, in his late fifties, because "my father without money, that would have been hard to bear."

That danger is still some way off when HG's and Else's paths cross at Christmas 1920. Else has already completed her training, if you can call it that. At the age of sixteen she leaves the Städtisches Lyzeum in Wismar, where by her own account she hasn't learned a thing. After a summer in Denmark, Else lands up at the Erstes Lyceum für Damen, the ladies' college in Dresden, rather than going to study in London, Paris, or even Switzerland, as her older sister had in the days before the war. Here she is taught "global and cultural history, mythology," besides languages, "domestic duties and feminine handiwork"; or rather, that's what she should have been taught. Throughout her life she struggled to sew on buttons. She was probably supposed to become a businesswoman, because she completes some internships in her father's companies, attends business school for girls in Berlin, then spends two terms at business college in the same city, where she listens to Werner Sombart lecturing on national economy, and one Dr. Siebert's disquisitions on "The Moral Life."

This is between April 1918 and Easter 1919, wild times in Berlin. Else throws herself into the fray, attends events held by the Spartacists, demonstrates against the murder of Rosa Luxemburg and Karl Liebknecht, puts a lot of money and time into a social project in East Berlin. She writes election pamphlets for the Social Democrats and argues with a student vicar over the moral status of "free love"—he's for, she's against. Of course it's all a parlor game. When news reaches Wismar that Councillor of Commerce Podeus's daughter has become a red in Berlin, father and daughter indulge themselves in a dozen oysters each and drink a toast to this amusing nonsense.

Because like HG, when the cries of "black-marketeer" from the "wretched pedestrians" didn't trouble him as he sat in his father's car, of course Else doesn't have the slightest notion about the realities of society. That social conditions need to be improved, that there should finally be equal rights for everyone, and that the imperial authoritarian state should be jettisoned—this much is taken for granted. That any of this might affect her, let alone her father, with his major industrial companies, never occurs to her. After all, he's nice to his employees, he pays the highest wages in Mecklenburg, and Else and her brothers and sisters have always brought warm socks and toys to the workers' dwellings at Christmas. And if, after working on the social project in East Berlin, she goes sailing with her wealthy friends on the Wannsee—what possible connection could there be between the two things?

Nonetheless, Paul now reckons that's enough bedlam in Berlin, and Else goes to Copenhagen for a year, to learn to cook. She likes the cheerful Danish way of life, she stays with friends, goes to dances, and "collects admirers the way other people collect stamps," as her father notes, not without pride. She doesn't seek any serious occupation for her fallow intellect. Like HG, she picks up an opinion here and there, and scatters it among people with great charm and even greater self-confidence—"I hadn't read anything, I hadn't really learned anything, presumably I hadn't understood anything," she wrote later for her grandchildren. "But I was always convincing."

Else decides she's done enough messing about, and on July 1, 1920, she starts a job with Carl Illies & Co. in Hamburg. Why she gives it up again on February 28, 1921, I don't know, or what she does afterward.

Else later destroyed almost all of her private documents from the time after her meeting with HG. Her jottings resume only after the end of the Second World War. I can only speculate about why she did that: either she wanted to wipe the slate clean after HG's infidelities, or she wanted to protect him from the Gestapo after his arrest in July 1944. I'm inclined toward the disaster in their marriage. Else was a rigorous person, and what could HG's love letters from the 1920s have had to do with a trial for high treason in the 1940s?

There must have been many such letters. In HG's diaries I find the entry "Wrote to Else" almost every day, even though they saw each other several times a week. HG is head over heels in love. It looks like this: January 2: "Miss Podeus!!!" January 3: "Picked up Else Podeus with Siegfried. Siegfried gawps." January 5: "Else with us in the evening, Siegfried, Jürgen, me, dinner. Hugely enjoyable, ~~played during Test of Vielliebchen~~"—wasn't that a betting game for loving couples involving almonds with double kernels?—"Else and I on first-name terms." January 6: "Lunch with Else, Rosenstrasse. Very elegant! Plans for reading evenings. Walked on her right-hand side." What does *that* mean? It means, in the etiquette of the time: respect, convention, keep a polite distance from the lady, walk on the left side. The husband walks on the right. Right is "testimony of ownership."

Is HG being brazen? In any case, there's no stopping him. January 8: "Else at our house again this evening. I brought her home. Made my position"—and what might that be?—"clear to her. Wonderful walk, the two of us. At home still sitting at Siegfried's bed. First remarks of Siegfried." January 9: "Thought for a long time. What to do?! Position"—yet again!—"Decision. Long letter to father. Said nothing to Siegfried." How do I have to imagine that? First he asks his father, then his intended? January 10: "Lunch with Else and Siegfried. Letter to Else, gave it to Siegfried to read. Wise words. What will come of it?" What comes of it is first of all more and more togetherness every day: with Else in the Kunsthalle, with Else in the Anthropological Museum, with Else at the Vienna Secession exhibition, with Else and Siegfried at a Beethoven concert by the famous pianist Edwin Fischer—the things young love can do! Siegfried and HG had only ever gone to see operettas.

On January 15 Kurt's answer comes. HG: "He advises against. No?! I must trust my desire." Of course his father advises against. His son's suggestion is almost as dangerous as the Iron Cross on the Western Front. HG is just twenty-two, he has an apprentice's certificate, but otherwise he knows nothing, he can do nothing, he owns nothing. But there is something he wants: Else. For three days, HG fights an internal war on three fronts. With Kurt: "I must free myself from father." With himself: "Am I ready to make the big step?" And with Else: "Could I be mistaken? Should I say something?" On January 19 he apparently says nothing at all: "I just stood and stared. Engagement!"

Over the next few days Else, so it seems, is plagued by fears about her own courage. She hides herself away, HG can't get anywhere near her, there are always people there. HG laments in his diary: "What's happened?"—"I'd love to talk to Else!"—"Very bad mood!" It sounds like eternal torment. But after only a week Else kisses her fiancé in the foyer of the Illies office building; that's a demonstration, and things are back where they should be. HG writes delightedly: "Else in red with black fur. Absolutely beautiful!"

Love really is blind. Else had all sorts of qualities, but I really don't think that striking beauty was one of them. She was quite tall for a woman, about the same height as HG, she had a heavyset figure, although with wonderful legs, which she gladly—and rightly—displayed all her life. I particularly remember her beautiful hands, her long, agile, slender fingers, her immaculately pale skin, and her even teeth. She had unruly, spaniel-colored hair, which she stowed away in something knotty at the nape of her neck until short hair came into fashion. Else always wore hats, and because of her flyaway hairdos found this ladies' obligation a blessing. Her face was somehow affected by her extreme nearsighted-ness and the fact that in her youth she didn't "officially" wear glasses. That's why she has that blurred look in photographs—we four daughters, all blind as bats, look exactly the same in photographs from our childhood. What nonsense, but glasses for young ladies were frowned upon.

Else was far from glamorous—more landed gentry than Marlene Dietrich—and apart from the occasional lipstick she never wore makeup. Later on, at least, she did wear bright red varnish on her finely formed fingernails. So it can't have been their first glimpse of her that so captivated HG and others. It probably had more to do with her spontaneity, her surprising cheek combined with impeccable manners, her sense of humor, and her self-confidence. She was anything but modest. She drifted about in castles and cottages as though she were quite at home there, and time and again HG happily records in his diary how people are "astonished" when he introduces her as his fiancée. And he does that—with gay abandon. He's bold as brass now, as all this is going on behind the backs of both sets of parents. They don't know their future son- or daughter-in-law, they haven't been informed, let alone given their consent. Kurt had presumably believed that his argumentative strategy, which had been successful so often in the past, had resolved the matter once and for all, and that his son, ultimately obedient, had complied on this occasion too. When Kurt finds out about HG's high-handed behavior, he wants to pack him off to England—a shame there's no trace of that particular letter.

Kurt treats his son the way his father, Gustav, had once treated him: first it's time for the young fellow to go away for a while. Has Kurt forgotten what life was like for him and Gertrud during the four frugal years of their secret engagement? Besides, he doesn't even know Else, couldn't he at least meet her for tea? No. The shutters go down in Halberstadt. If HG thinks he can present Kurt with a fait accompli, he should see how good he will be at shielding his fiancée from adversity. What Kurt doesn't guess is Else's calmness in this regard and the fact that she and HG, ostentatiously as a couple, are constantly touring their social round. Else writes later: "Where my reputation was concerned, I was the one who made the decisions."

On top of everything Kurt wants to banish his son to England. Forgotten are perfidious Albion, the dumdum bullets, the "bigmouths," the zeppelin bombs to be dropped on the Bank of England. Let's face it: Germany has lost the war, and new contacts with the former enemy wouldn't be bad for business, would they? But HG doesn't want to go to England. HG wants Else. So first of all he travels to Wismar, to beard the lion there in his den. It's Easter 1921, and Siegfried has to go with him. He's been there several times before, and gives HG spiritual reinforcement. HG: "7:20 p.m. via Lübeck to Wismar, first time on this route. Glad Siegfried's with me. Twelve midnight in Wismar, Else and Heinrich at the station"—that's Else's brother. "Anxious. So is she." The next day, Good Friday: "Met the Ravelin Horn bustle. Alchen, Frau von Zitzewitz, Frau Cruse, Heinrich, Paul, etc. No one has any idea about Else and me. Else and I feel somehow strange to one another. In the afternoon to Heiligendamm in two cars, glorious sunny day. On the groyne with Else and Siegfried. Played crazy music in the evening."

The Ravelin Horn bustle is like the one in Halberstadt: lots of people, two big families, Danes and Germans, going in and out all the time, everyone bringing friends. This dovecote, nonetheless, must have been a cosy nest what with all the affection that Paul devoted to his loved ones—Else writes that she and her brothers and sisters couldn't walk past him without getting a big hug. HG sensed this tenderness from the very first day. "Ravelin Horn: a house full of warmth," he writes in his diary.

After twenty-five years, Paul is still dotty about his wife. Else kept some of his letters to Dagmar, all of which begin with a series of Danish endearments—"*min egen,* kæreste, søde lille kone" (my own dearest, sweet little wife) in countless variations. Declarations of love fall like raindrops into his letters. "Yesterday dinner with Commercial Councillor Cramer about export to Chile, *naar jeg dog bare kunde være hos dig nu, min elskede, jeg længes saa forfærdelig efter dig,* he didn't have high hopes for our chances." The Danish interpolation means "If I could only be with you now, my beloved, I yearn for you so terribly." Incidentally, Paul's handwriting is just as extravagant as Else's, while HG writes like Kurt—interesting how important fathers are.

On the next day of HG's introductory visit to Wismar, Easter Saturday, his stomach goes on strike and he can't eat for nervous tension. They go to Schwerin, have a look at the city and curve around Lake Schwerin and to the lakeside town of Möderitz. Else's parents aren't there, but Else's brother Heinrich is—and HG has to tell him, if no one else, about their engagement. "Else pale, me exhausted in the evening, in bed, general sympathy. If only they knew!!" Easter Sunday: "Blazing sun, yet more guests are coming. Mounting nerves, final quick decision on my part, asked P. into his room: request, oof!!! Meanwhile Else's dancing the foxtrot. In the evening everybody at the fireplace, extremely!!! unpleasant position, mother-in-law between Else and me."

I can just imagine. No bells are rung, the conversation burbles along, people laugh, the Danes tell the latest gossip from Copenhagen, in German so that HG isn't excluded. But no one *says* anything, not Paul Podeus, not Dagmar Podeus, certainly not Heinrich. And of course not Else. And there sits HG. On hot coals. "*Eeeeh,* him I wouldn't like to be"—Dagmar could have helped him with that phrase. But she doesn't. Instead, HG and Siegfried drive back to Hamburg on Easter Monday—HG: "Excitement! Excitement! What amazing days!"—and at night he sits down to draft his "written confirmation to P. Podeus."

The next hurdle is to be taken three weeks later: second family reunion in Halberstadt. HG has to attend, Else isn't yet allowed to, until then she fortifies him during nocturnal cab rides when they're coming back from the theater or late dinners. HG is delighted:

"My darling is so sweet!" He travels home apprehensively, communication has been frosty in the meantime, and Gertrud is particularly brittle. HG: "She must be reconciled." Is that because mothers can't let go of their sons as people always say? I have no idea and no son. Jealousy certainly played a part. Relations between Gertrud and Else remained politely strained over the years, and when Else's mother, Dagmar Podeus, that funny and vivacious character, later moved to Halberstadt, Gertrud sometimes saw her as an invader of her tidy surroundings.

HG arrives late enough to find the house already full of overnight visitors, which spares him any arguments with his parents. The family band, Benno Nachtigall, is still rehearsing, HG's quality as a lead singer is required, and at some point it's too late to talk—for today, at least, all problems are circumnavigated.

The next morning the family council first holds its meeting, then the family reunion; the minutes book, punctiliously kept by archivist Kurt, is a record of squandered time. They discuss the state of the kitty—3,266.60 marks— the approval of the chairman and the treasurer, the new arrangements for annual contributions, and so on. Wasn't there something in the "constitution" about "ensuring greater cohesion among family members"? That comes now at the shared lunch. There are sixty-four relatives present, they cackle and chatter, "Haven't seen each other for ages!!" The singing party intones: "When God's blessing falls on us, he sends us off to travel, although with putsches hereabouts, its joys tend to unravel." And it's true: in Saxony and in Schleswig-Holstein, and even in Hamburg, the "Bolshevik hooligans" are out and about, things are particularly violent in Catholic Bavaria, but the Klamroths don't have anything to do with Catholics anyway.

In the afternoon Kurt delivers a lecture about who is related to whom and how and why, family trees are handed around, and HG's turn doesn't come until late at night. "Long discussion with father. Difficult. I'm not going to England. Told him about Wismar." And then, at least: "Father is writing to Paul." A week later the two gentlemen meet in Berlin, they like each other immediately, Paul writes to "min lütt Döchting Elsemaus" (my little daughter Else-mouse) that he has "met a very elegant, kind, and lovable man with whom I spent a very lively evening." The two fathers agree: let's keep things nice and slow. Kurt talks to Paul about HG's stay in England—"at least a year"—as though his son had been talking to the wall when he refused to go. Paul: "I could only agree with everything Herr K. said. You see, concerning your desire to make the engagement public as soon as possible, we two fathers are of quite a different opinion."

HG is furious: "Does this mean war?" The parents could at least travel to Wismar, so that they know what it's all about. Kurt isn't averse, Gertrud is constantly finding new disincentives. She doesn't want the engagement, regardless of who it is with. HG seethes: "Stiff letter to parents. Either with them or without them. I'm not giving Else up." Resistance, bravo! HG is growing up. Kurt sets off to Hamburg to talk to his son. The result: not England, but Curaçao. Not a year, but four months. And before that, Wismar. Immediately.

They travel in May. Ravelin Horn presents itself in all its beauty: Paul's affection, Dagmar's sense of humor, Else's charm, well-brought-up brothers and sisters. Black-tie dinner, Copenhagen porcelain, heavy silver, intelligent people around the table, torches in the garden. No one seems to be trying too hard, everything's casual and perfectly natural. The next day there are tours of the factories, motor-car excursions, picnics by the water, all utterly effortless. The young couple are radiant, Gertrud is experiencing a completely new son, who notes in his diary: "All-around enthusiasm from Mother and Father Kl.—I told them so!" Kurt sticks a photograph of himself and his new daughter, wearing her white dress, into HG's archive pages, with the caption: "We're getting to know 'our' Else." But the official engagement is postponed until autumn 1921, on HG's return from Curaçao.

Until his departure he spends every free day in Wismar. He

loves the atmosphere there, he loves his parents-in-law, loves the house. He often writes: "As always in Ravelin Horn—happiness!" Else lives in a little drawing room with a fireplace in the attic, and clearly no one sees anything amiss in the fact that the couple adjourn there in the evenings. "We're doing things 'the Danish way,'" HG writes ironically in his diary, using quotation marks—admittedly he learns Danish quickly, but we may doubt whether he makes much progress in that direction on Else's sofa. "Have I ever had such a good time?" his diary asks, "very cheerful and happy!," once in Latin, "rideamus" (we're laughing), once in English, "happiness is love." HG has bought engagement rings and organizes a clandestine presentation ceremony with lines that he's worked on for two days—"Else is now wearing the ring."

Besides, HG is evidently very much at home in Ravelin Horn. He is on first-name terms with everyone, and he has been welcomed into the big circle of friends and relations as though he had always been there. I don't know whether he's parked his toothbrush in the guest bathroom, but he will certainly have stowed a suit or two in the wardrobe, for the Podeus family always dresses for dinner. He's also got his stamp albums with him; again and again I read, "sorted stamps in the hall." It must have been a valuable collection in the end, because Else reports that the Gestapo took it away after HG's arrest, and never returned it.

HG brings work with him—"dictated mail to Else," he writes in his diary a number of times. I'm surprised at this: she might have learned shorthand at business school, but her typed letters are all over the place. Love must have blinded HG to this, rectangular as he is. Perhaps he swamped Else with such dictations only so that they could cuddle up together even when they were working. And they write to each other. There are leather-bound, gold-embossed rough-work books, the big sisters and brothers of poetry albums, in which Else and HG share their feelings. Else has cut out most of her pages with a sharp knife, while HG's notes begin on January 20, 1921, only one day after he "just stood and stared" and got engaged.

They begin with Gunner Vitt. HG commits to paper a parable-shaped story about a young man riding around restlessly under the innumerable stars of the Ukrainian night—"alone, quite alone"—in search of the "temple of life." Nothing comes of it, because "Goddess guilt" calls him harshly back. She took care of him "when he fired his pistol half a second too early. Since then she has floated above him wherever he goes, holding before his thoughts and deeds a black cloak: penitence!" It's obvious where the story is going; Else is the new goddess, who will be stronger than the gloomy lady, and when Else exerts her strength, the other woman—HG: "I am praying for it!"—will finally slink away.

I'll have to be careful not to denounce HG. Once again I can read this story only with a groan, but so what? It's his story, and I'm touched that his new happiness with Else and the old trauma about Gunner Vitt are so interwoven. I shall not allow myself the slight suspicion that HG might have used the opportunity to appear as a tragic hero in the eyes of Else.

In these gilt-edged books, HG is often preoccupied with the merging of his soul with Else's—yes, HG the "reality man" has discovered his soul!—with their "twofold perfection," and with his not merely flirtatious self-doubt: "Isn't it a terrible weakness on my part to place all my diffuse, half-thought-out wishes, all my furious yearning for closeness and peace, my own self, so infinitely remote from true manliness, with its incredible incompleteness, next to the heart of the one person I wish to shield so much from all of life's slings and arrows, from all fights and struggles!"

Else endures such phrases, but her view of things is less complicated: "Hans Georg, I love you! At first I expected only to wake up and then to acknowledge the impossibility of being able to marry you. I have woken up, but to the realization that I *can marry only you*. Only you—I want to live with you, become one with you, with you as you are, I don't want to add or subtract a thing, just as you are and all that you will one day become. I will grow thanks to you, I will help you, you will help me, you and I will struggle together, how lovely it is that such a thing exists, that two can be one, it's what we want, my dearest—you."

But Else does want to be careful lest things go wrong with love: "Such thoughts pop into one's head when one takes a closer look at marriages and recognizes what one must bear in mind from the start, so that neither party becomes an intolerable tyrant.—Should it not be possible for the nervous and busy master of the house to control himself at home as well, or *must* the wife suffer as lightning rod, and if she won't, then one of the children? There's nothing uglier than a temperamental man, it's bad enough in a woman, but in a man it's contemptible.

"Is that actually a life for a man, heaped up with public honors, offices, duties, plus his own company to run and an eternal unease, haste, and hurry, when he sees his family briefly at mealtimes, meetings in the evenings, official dinners, or being tired, nervous, and out of control at home. Is that worth the commitment? And what remains of it? A lot of money, an honorable funeral, and the feeling of not having had all that much from 'life,' only one has made oneself a slave and the 'noli me tangere' of the family."

Not much has changed in eighty years, has it? Whom can her invective have been directed at? It can't have been her father, Paul, because he concentrated more on his wife and children than on his companies, which didn't do anybody much good in a time of inflation. But Else isn't deterred: "The final goal of woman is marriage, having children, everything else is unnatural, bluff, substitute, nonsense! But finding the man who suits you is of course not easy. *I've* managed!!!" But Else doesn't find it easy to survive the wait as patiently as her mother-in-law Gertrud had demonstrated before. In the gilt-edged book she complains: "My dear, never travel so far from me again. My dearest dear, I'm not as strong as all that. I have only longing and one sole desire: that you were here again!"

But HG is in Curaçao. Or in Venezuela. Or on a boat. At any rate a long way away. He keeps a travel diary, 153 typed pages, suddenly hardly flowery, and I can tell that he's looking at everything very carefully. He has a go at describing cloud formations—"it must be possible to find words for that, without escaping into images"—and he tries the same with waves and spray, he attempts to catch the colors of night: "Coal-black, slate-black, tar-black, velvet-black, and the strips of light in the roiling water—sea gleam." The journey to Curaçao on a freighter takes almost four weeks, and HG travels with Theo Delbrück, Else's most dependable friend from her youth, who later stood by her for many years from his home in Holland. I remember his teaching me to eat oysters on a street in Amsterdam in the spring. I would have been about seventeen.

Curaçao must have been a bleak patch of earth, in those days at least, a cactus colony in the Dutch Antilles with odd white people, flotsam from all over the world, and a black population that HG calls "niggers," who speak Papiamento, for which there is no written script. HG describes it all curiously and without prejudice, although one homosexual stretches his tolerance to the limit: "He puts on powder like Marie Antoinette, and in this heat the sweat draws weird patterns in his face." The German consul—"They've probably forgotten him here!"—raises his glass to the Dutch queen at the parties he gives, and then to Wilhelm II, who has found shelter in her country.

Here and in Venezuela, HG is passed around from one family to the next. Governor, mayor, U.S. general consul (former enemy!), Spanish traders, Venezuelan oil barons, Hamburg shipping agents—a network operates in the form of letters of recommendation, telegrams to announce his visits from one stop to the next, and wherever he turns up, the people—and this is the amazing thing—have time for him. They make him at home in their houses; they rustle up cars and employees to drive HG around. Let's not forget: this is 1921, Germany has lost the war and has had little to offer ever since, and this young man has nothing at all. Not quite. He has his name, and Kurt came to these parts on a similar tour in 1912. That's nine years ago, when the phosphate company came into being. There can be no talk of such things now, but business-men think in the long term. "The father's blessing establisheth the house of the children," says HG, quoting from the Old Testament.

He has brought a ragbag of reading matter on his journey, such as English children's literature to polish his knowledge of the language: *Little Lord Fauntleroy,* by Frances Hodgson Burnett; Alfred Mason's *Four Feathers,* a huge success at the beginning of the century; *Kidnapped,* by Robert Louis Stevenson; and the wonderful tome *The Scarlet Pimpernel,* by the Hungarian Englishwoman Baroness Orczy. HG rereads Ludendorff's *War Memoirs* immediately before giving it to the governor of Curaçao. He is riled by the *Events Leading Up to the World War* by the arch-conservative German nationalist Karl Helfferisch—"I know all that already." In between come Dostoyevsky's *Brothers Karamazov;* Hermann Count Keyserling's *Travel Diary of a Philosopher,* the metaphysical description of a journey around the world; and Hofmannsthal's youthful work *Thor and Death.* There's also work to be done: the book of trading law, the basic text of national economics, *Letters from a Bank Director to His Son,* by one Argentarius, first in German and then again in English.

HG sometimes feels "peeled out of the real world, which goes on turning and I'm no longer a part of it." He finds that eerie, and clings to the chart room, where "I see that I really am somewhere. Someone has drawn and measured it, and I can lay my finger on it. Paper is becoming more real than the sky and the water around me." To avoid this kind of fantasy, HG teaches himself Danish on the return journey. The freighter comes from Copenhagen, and he irritates everyone from the captain down by addressing them in what he thinks is Danish.

The result is startling. A four-week crossing is enough to make HG reasonably fluent in a language which, while it may be a distant relation of German, is pronounced in a completely different way and bears hardly any similarities in its grammar and vocabulary. Just because you can speak German doesn't mean you can automatically pick up Danish. I'm a good judge of this, because Danish flew into my head when I was a child, and I have letters from HG which he wrote to Danish recipients a few months after his return from Curaçao. They don't contain a single mistake, either in vocabulary or in spelling, and Danish orthography was complicated in those days.

He makes the most of his opportunities. Five days after he and Theo have landed in Bremerhaven, HG is in Denmark, which will later become his second home. Else is waiting at the station in Nykøbing. She writes in the gilt-edged book: "I had so waited for you, and now it was as if you had never been away." HG writes in his diary: "I have so much to say to Else, I love her so!" They don't have the chance to get used to each other In peace and quiet, because there's a diamond wedding anniversary to attend in Bandholm. Else's grandparents have been married for sixty years, and all the world and his wife are on their way to pay tribute to the happy couple.

I know how things like that are celebrated in Bandholm, even today. The tiny, whitewashed little harbor town is decked with bunting, everyone flies the "Dannebrog," the Danish flag, the fences in the few streets are adorned with garlands, and the inhabitants—everyone knows everyone else—stand in their front gardens and applaud as people pass them on their way to church, whether they be newlyweds, a happy couple on their anniversary with their guests, or mourners following a coffin. The party given for the old Cruses, Dagmar's parents, lasts for two days. HG is the only "newcomer" in this practiced circle, and his appearance there is legendary even today. The grandchildren of those guests still tell me the story that has been handed down from parents to children: there was this strange young man, just twenty-three, suntanned, handsome in his tailcoat, a little quiet at first.

After all the speeches had been delivered, before a hundred people, HG jumped to his feet and tapped his glass. First of all he congratulated the anniversary couple with cleverly chosen words, and then came a kind of explosion, a firework sending off showers of wit and cheekiness about the fame and reputation of the assembled company. HG had, he told them, hastened here through storms and wind, to get a foot in the door of this unique family on the illustrious occasion of a diamond wedding. And he would never withdraw that foot, and sooner or later, with Else's help, he would be one of them—they could all rely on that. And all of it in Danish, some of it in verse.

"Who on earth is that?"—"That's Else's fiancé."—"Else's engaged?"—"No, but soon."—"Is he Danish?"—"No, a German."—"A German? But he speaks Danish!" HG was the star of the evening. I know the story by heart, it's always told in the same way. What impresses me about it is HG's chutzpah. He knew hardly any of the hundred or so people in front of him. It was his first time in Denmark, he was speaking a language that he had learned from the crew of a ship—it could all have gone terribly wrong, like someone mistaking the Berlin dialect for German. But that evening he held the whole clan in the palm of his hand. They loved him, even though he later became an occupying officer in their country, and they mourned his death.

When Else and HG return to Wismar, that is in October 1921, the engagement announcements are sent out. There are 250 of them; flowers and presents flow to Ravelin Horn. HG puts on his cutaway and his top hat, Else too puts on her smart clothes, and they pay their official visits to people they've already seen hundreds of times before. What a curious custom! I reluctantly imagine someone's turning up unannounced at noon at my door, to whom I have to devote a quarter of an hour of my precious time, knowing that I will shortly be inviting them to a party anyway. But that was what people did in those days. In etiquette books from this period I find pages and pages filled with the "visiting code": before and after a journey, before and after New Year, hat in hand, never without gloves—later, in Halberstadt, Else kept a visiting book listing everyone who had paid courtesy calls, and whether and with whom they were then invited back.

After the couple had trudged around Wismar and the surrounding area, they had to go through the same procedure in Halberstadt, all over again. This makes sense, because it's Else's first visit to the place that is to be her family home, and no one knows her yet. HG is nervous: "Will Else feel comfortable here?" She is given a warm reception, with a welcome chorale composed by Kurt junior, and a witty performance by the brothers and sisters, but the whole thing is far from simple. "Else is having difficulties finding her way in," notes HG, and it's hardly surprising. The Magdeburger Börde and the surrounding area are a long way away from the airy seaport of Wismar, the people are as heavy as their clods of soil, and no one could have accused them of being "amusing." Else, who signed her name ostentatiously as "Else Klamroth, née Podeus" as long as she lived, later explained to her grandchildren: "I was determined to assert myself."

It has nothing to do with lack of loyalty. Else has always stood by the family. But she doesn't want to give up her own signature. It turns into a stubborn little war, waged under cover of extreme politeness. It gets going right after the engagement. Gertrud censures the couple because they occasionally withdraw to HG's room in the evening—she calls it HG and Else's "independence." HG furiously sets his mother right, Else beams at her: "I love him very much, as you know. That's why I sometimes have to be alone with him, and it's too cold outside." It's November. When Paul Podeus comes to Halberstadt to see "sin lütt Döchting" (his little daughter) in her new surroundings, HG senses some "slight apprehension" beforehand. So all three of them disappear off on autumn hunts in the surrounding family estates, where the men shoot hares and Else shines with a Danish recipe for game.

HG engages in serious arguments with his father, Kurt. While his son was in Curaçao, Kurt has gone over his head to arrange a lengthy trip to the United States for him the following year, and until then he has fixed a place for him as a business assistant in the Union Chemicals Factory in Stettin. HG is speechless. He and Else planned to marry in the spring, HG has a job pending in Hamburg, where the young couple then intended to live, and generally speaking he thinks it's high time that he take control of his own life. The rub is: HG isn't just mentally dependent on Kurt, above all it's a question of finances. The job in Hamburg would hardly feed a single man, certainly not a couple, and Else's money is fast disappearing as prices rise. A year later, after the wedding, Paul transfers 100,000 marks to her—the remains of the original million, now almost totally worthless.

HG finds it difficult to comply. During the crossing to America he broods about "why I'm not strong enough to put up any resistance." The answer is simple: refusal wouldn't have been sensible. In 1921 22 such journeys to the United States were far from easy to organize, and training jobs like the one in Stettin were hardly two a penny. And in the end father and son are pursuing the same goal: HG joining I.G. Klamroth. Stettin and the United States fall under the same heading as training, collecting experiences, extending horizons. HG sees that this isn't wrong. But he doesn't like his father shoving him back and forth like a chess piece. And why does Kurt do that? Because he knows that children will follow on quite quickly after the wedding, and HG's willingness to explore the world will go into steep decline. But the company needs him to do just that, because it has to open itself up to that world if it is going to survive in the new climate.

Kurt apologizes to HG, saying that the decision had to be made quickly and the son in Curaçao had not been accessible. However, after HG's resolutely independent behavior over his engagement, Kurt must have wanted to present him with a fait accompli. HG, however, the obedient son once more, falls back into childish servility that seemed like a thing of the past: "I was strangely passive, the strength that I feel growing within me still won't bear the load."

Over the next few months, HG is pursued by "black birds." Even before, he had sometimes experienced such moods: "very bad humor"—"distempered for no reason"—"sudden gloom." Now the "black birds" fall upon him out of nowhere. Else isn't the reason, quite the contrary. After her initial disappointment at discovering that HG has to travel so far away once again, she tries to bolster him for the American trip. She even convinces him that Stettin is all right: following on from his practical experience with the phosphate mine in Curaçao, it's important for HG to learn what happens to the stuff in the chemicals factory. HG writes in his diary: "Else er den mest henrivende pige paa verden" (Else is the most delightful girl in the world).

The black birds come only when she isn't there. Not because she isn't there. HG and Else have learned to deal with their frequent separations, as long as the mail is delivered promptly and they can make occasional phone calls. But when they come, the black birds, HG falls into a pit of self-doubt, filled with contempt over his own inadequacy: he doesn't know enough, his judgment is without foundation, he isn't in control of himself, he's too easily influenced—"If someone delivers his reasoned judgment to me with great conviction today, I follow him, and then tomorrow someone comes along with the opposite view, to which he also gives sound foundations, then I believe that one." HG's world, which in the army was divided into black and white without room for doubt, his fixed coordinates of right and wrong have vanished into "perhaps" and "on one hand or the other." He learns to his distress that "convictions can change, and that not even experiences are always valid." HG is growing up.

His black birds don't only settle on his "scandalous lack of knowledge," on the fact that he is struggling to learn to ask questions, when before he felt safe with his quick responses. HG doubts the clarity of his character, and in one of the gilt-edged books he bundles it all together for Else in the phrase "I lie!" For pages and pages he wrestles with himself. He doesn't lie to hide shortcomings—he doesn't say "the check's in the mail" when someone asks about a missing payment. And neither does he say "there was a traffic accident" when he turns up late. HG doesn't turn up late. HG invents stories.

"One thing is certain: I didn't lie as a child, and I don't lie now 'with evil intent.' I embellish, I make things up, I fake, I fib—but that's all self-deception. I lie." Since HG has been able to think, he has puffed himself up: "I remember as a little boy that I liked to think up stories and told them to my parents as though I had really experienced them. I had a vivid imagination, and I noticed that my stories were heard with astonishment, amazement, and admiration by the people around me. My imagination was joined by ambition."

HG takes his parents to task: *"Why didn't they beat me so that the first blow would have been enough for me! Why did they just look at me with mild reproach, rather than locking me up in the dark and starving me for days on end, so that the child would have thought with horror and fear of the consequences of his lie? They said, 'What an imagination the boy has!' rather than saying, 'Woe is us, the child lies! How are we to expunge such a thing?'"* HG underlines very rarely. This passage is doubly underlined with strokes of rage. "I remember having a violent sense of envy many years later, when Wolf said to me in Döberitz, in 1917, 'My father would have killed us children if we had ever lied. A Yorck never allows a lie to pass his lips.' Had I been brave enough to talk openly to him then, some things might be different today.

"Lying became an excellent medium for my ambition. I quickly became socially popular among schoolmates and acquaintances and generally.—How? I could chat so entertainingly, make funny stories out of the smallest experiences. Of my stories over the past few years, probably nothing is literally true. I only need to think of the supposed experience with the bride traveling on her own to her wedding, the case with the telephone and the Danes in Hamburg, Father's alleged 'magic trick' with the award, countless supposed wartime adventures—lies, all lies! What a balancing act, what public daring: how often must I anxiously take care to avoid bringing two or more of my acquaintances together, particularly if they are from different periods in my life, because I don't remember precisely what I have told this one and what to the other. Everything becomes a source of danger. But it would all be bearable if only one thing weren't there: my self-loathing!"

The night after Else and he became engaged, HG writes that he stayed awake for a long time, praying: "Let me atone for everything, Lord, but let me stay truthful to her, never let a lie come between Else and me!" But like an addict he then succumbed to temptation, and soon afterward told Else "the 'great' wartime experience. I saw that it made an impression on you, and started boasting, as usual. I lied. Shouldn't I sink into the floor for shame?" And he lists a whole sequence of untruths, all invented to make him seem bigger and more handsome in Else's eyes—"and your trust in me just kept growing." What now? HG worries away at possible causes, from "self-importance" to "mental defectiveness," and asks Else for help. Without her, he says, he can't sort himself out.

With her he can't, either. Else has cut her reply to this confession out of the gilt-edged book, but a few ideas still occur to me. She probably told herself things weren't so bad, and she would bring them under control. Even if Else saw HG's tendency to make things up—experts call it pseudologia phantastica—as a real problem, she could rightly expect that it had been put to an end by having been brought to light. Never again! But it hadn't been brought to an end. When I was still able to question people who knew HG, I heard time and again how witty, how intelligent, how gifted this man was—"but what lies he told!" Even today I can hear the story echoing in my head of how the tennis court behind the house in Halberstadt was turned into an airfield for the complicated landing of a courier plane, during the Second World War.

It all drove Else mad. As a child I was locked in the cupboard, sent to bed without food, beaten with the riding crop, for having "lied"—I was an imaginative child full of stories of the kind invented by HG. Else even came up with the idea of an "arrest" as a punishment for me—at the age of seven I was actually taken to the local jail, where a uniformed man led me away. So sensitized was she, so damaged by HG's form of mental excesses, that she was willing to go to such lengths. It didn't help. I went on puffing myself up with invented stories until they vanished of their own accord.

HG never managed, as far as I know. The fact that Else couldn't even let white lies through—and they save so much time!—leads me to conclude that HG later annoyed her not only with his outrageous stories, but with substantial untruths. The humiliation that a person must bear if their partner's betrayal is accompanied by lies is just as much a betrayal of their intimacy as the actual "misconduct."

Why did HG have to wrap himself in such a cloud of fantasy? In his notes I find the observation "that from childhood I have suffered from an abnormal, tormenting shyness and anxiety, and that my personality and appearance, outwardly so much at odds with this, only arose from the fear of showing that first fear." Elsewhere: "It would be worth examining the effect that shyness and vanity have on one another." HG's craving for recognition also explains, at least to me, why he developed such a tortuous style of writing. But now that, at least, is getting better.

Why does HG choose this particular moment to make his big confession? Else and he had, shortly before, spent the night together for the first time. To celebrate the first year of their engagement, on January 19, 1922, they drive to the snowed-in monastery town of Chorin. They walk for hours through the "wonder-white world. Ice-cold," and they spend the night in the monastery inn. Afterward HG is in a trance. "Yearning, burning, irrational longing for Else," I read in his diary in countless variations. HG phones Wismar almost daily. At that time calls still have to be requested in advance; they're expensive and involve a lot of waiting. But they help, at least temporarily, to combat HG's "torment and great nervousness." Because the black birds are here again: "Can I bind Else to me, the way I am?" The question comes a bit late. The revelation of his lying habits is dated February 3.

HG is ill for a week—he often reacts to mental strain by developing a fever—and his acne blossoms: "Physically I'm a terrible wreck, and mentally it's no better." Then "two very dear, sad letters come from Else. Oh, if I could only be with her." I don't know these letters, but excuse me, what was Else supposed to do? Once she "belonged" to HG, as they said in those days, was she supposed to say to herself and everyone else, "I don't want someone like him"? Was she to tell some possible successor of HG's that the loss of her virginity had been a mistake? Else was very much in control of herself, but not to that degree. In those days it was easier to get a divorce than to break off an engagement where a "defect" was involved. When—unmarried—I lost my virginity, Else wrote to say that I had now ruined my life—and that was, after all, thirty-five years later!

I know I should stay out of it, but I don't like this story at all. If HG really meant what he said about his contempt for the "shortcomings of his character," the revelation should have come first, before the night in Chorin. Then Else would have had the chance to decide whether she should find the whole thing "amusing" or menacing. When she writes her "sad" letters, it suggests that she understood the whole affair for what it really was, an abuse of her trust. But there's no turning back for Else, and presumably she doesn't want to turn back, because she loves HG, and is only too glad to believe his assurances that everything will be different from now on.

So HG travels to America in a state of good cheer. He is leaving a country that is riven by strikes and unrest and whose currency is in free fall. At the end of April 1922 the Reich government announces that since May the previous year 555 million gold marks have been spent in material compensation to the adversaries and 1,294,888,487.62 gold marks in reparations. What is that if you say it out loud? It's actually only one billion, two hundred and ninety-four million, etc., not even close to what is expected, so the French have therefore already occupied Düsseldorf, Duisburg, and Ruhrort as a bargaining chip and are threatening to annex the whole of the Ruhr.

Consequently, in Germany, the terror of extreme right-wing nationalists is growing against so-called republican "appeasers." This "policy of appeasement" had been decided by the Reichstag in May 1921, and meant accepting the Versailles Treaty and the reparation demands without demur. The adversaries, they calculated, would quickly recognize that you can't put your hands in a naked man's pockets, and would reduce their demands accordingly. For nationalists—and there were many of them—this was a thorn in the side of German honor. Three years before, as members of Freikorps associations and student units, they helped put down Social Democratic and Communist uprisings, fought for the maintenance of German predominance in the Baltic and against the Poles in Upper Silesia. Now they were officially dissolved and unemployed. But they hadn't disappeared. Some had nestled down in the new Reichswehr, and though most of them were struggling to lead normal lives, the ones in the Fatherland Associations, the Teutonic Order, the Deutscher Schutz- und Trutzbund, and those in the German National People's Party, were actively seeking to bring down the Weimar Republic with a revolution from the right.

When former finance minister Matthias Erzberger, signatory to the armistice in 1918, was shot in 1921, HG was in Curaçao. The murder of Foreign Minister Walther Rathenau in June 1922 happened when HG was staying in Florida. In both cases the perpetrators belonged to "Organisation Consul," the successors to the Ehrhardt Brigade responsible for the Kapp Putsch. You really have to read Ernst von Salomon's books *Die Geächteten* (The Ostracized Ones) and *Der Fragebogen* (The Questionnaire) to get an idea of the roundwormlike contamination of German elites with nationalist ideas, above all their deep contempt for the republic.

After his release from the prison in which he had been held for six and a half years for involvement in the Rathenau murder and other acts of violence, Salomon will be welcomed with great respect by professors, senior officials, and "society" people as one of their own. He describes the accommodation shown by the State Tribunal for the Defense of the Republic, set up specially after Rathenau's death, toward the "patriotic" murderers. These sons "from respectable families" all appear in Salomon's books, the murderer of Karl Liebknecht and Rosa Luxemburg, Captain Pabst, who was also involved in the Kapp Putsch, commanders such as Captain Lieutenant Hermann Ehrhardt and Manfred von Killinger, whose pamphlets were distributed by the Nazis in editions numbering into the hundreds of thousands. Today antiquarian book buyers will pay a fortune for Killinger's revolting remarks.

In far-off America there's barely a mention of the tumult in Germany after Rathenau's murder. The papers don't even carry much about the Treaty of Rapallo, the first agreement between Russia and Germany after the war, which provoked fury in France and Britain. HG is startled to discover that Americans are hardly interested in Germany, certainly not in North Carolina. Many decades later, as a correspondent in Washington, D.C., I discovered the same thing—the reciprocal interest between the two countries is far from equal, unless Germany happens to be needed for something.

HG doesn't get around to mentioning the war at all. Emotionally, it had only ended yesterday as far as he was concerned, but he hears people saying, "That little war, that was four years ago, nobody thinks about it any more." The fact that Germany is now economically and morally at the bottom of the heap is dismissed with a good-natured laugh: "Well, we did a good job then, didn't we?" The question "Well, how are things now in Germany?" is nothing but a superficial piece of politeness, and HG quickly learns that the speaker doesn't want a proper answer. Instead he draws HG over to the barbecue, where the latest baseball results are being discussed.

The American world throws up all kinds of mysteries for HG. Immediately after his arrival in New Orleans he sees about twenty submarines in a tributary of the Mississippi, all "for sale"—what private individual would want to buy a submarine? Or is this another of HG's "stories"? He'll surely need them from now on if his life is to maintain any color, because he's losing himself in the American pampas. Fertilizer factories aren't exactly built on city boulevards, so he finds himself in places that even today are good only for disciplinary transfers—Atlanta, Georgia; Wilmington, North Carolina; or Bartow, Florida. The last one I haven't even found on a map, but I know the other two and believe me, you wouldn't want to go there.

To begin with, HG is just astonished: "Even in prewar Germany there weren't such things." Everybody has a car—everybody in the family—they all have houses, big houses with several bedrooms and bathrooms, most of them hideously furnished, and the owners are middle managers, grocers, and mechanics. At home this would hardly qualify as HG's social circle, but he doesn't find anything like his circle in the American provinces. The small-town white communities around him are confidently classless, narrow-minded, and affluent. On the beach outside Wilmington HG discovers "aircars," little airplanes in which people arrive to go swimming. "Even young girls fly them!" he notes with amazement. "Is that the future?" Life goes on around him as it always does in the Southern states, slowly, in accordance with the climate. No one is exactly breaking his back in the fertilizer factory—the Morris Fertilizer Company. Everybody walks around in shirtsleeves, the people go to wrestling matches, in the evening they drive slowly down the main drag, and most importantly they go to church.

This isn't to say that Wilmington or Bartow are seats of virtue. On a number of occasions HG is invited conspiratorially to covert cellars where the hosts have hidden their liquor from Prohibition, and often the local dignitaries decide on a visit to the brothel after church. HG bows out of such entertainments like a good fiancé, and he couldn't have afforded them anyway. The prices rob him of his sleep—not the American prices as such, which are moderate enough, but if he pays $1.40 for a haircut, it means he's paying the equivalent of 400 marks. His laundry costs 897 marks, a tram journey 114 marks. The dollar stands at 285 marks and is rising daily, and since HG is given only $50 in expenses by Morris Fertilizer, he has to dig into the 100,000 marks that Kurt has deposited for him in an American bank. HG can foresee how long that's going to last.

None of this contributes to his well-being—without money he is immobile, the people bore him, and the job teaches him nothing new. But he does learn English quickly, spelling included.

Even the girls get on his nerves. "They can drive cars and bake 'pies,' but they don't do anything but chatter inanely. When I recently asked the choirmaster's daughter why she was always giggling, she gave me a disarmingly open look and said, 'Because I've nothing else to do,' and she's right." Letters from home don't help much either: "Father writes that I should 'study the milieu,' and Mother advises 'carpe diem'—but both of those ideas were exhausted long ago." Else's letters make HG sad—"I feel as though I've been banished, and can't find anything in common with her apart from longing."

Why doesn't he leave, why doesn't he have a look at America? I guess that Kurt has lent him to Morris Fertilizer for a specific period of time. HG won't want to disturb business relations between the two companies, and it was kind of the Morris people to take him on in the first place. Another reason is the lack of money—Kurt didn't make that deposit just so that HG could fritter it away. Nevertheless: even in those days HG wouldn't have been the first one to struggle through the United States on his own account. He is wondering himself why he doesn't set out: "Authority—respect—love—fear—discipline?" He also suggests: "Weakness—cowardice. Have I completely lost my powers of decision making?" What powers of decision making?

Salvation comes from outside. Morris's boss sends HG to Chicago and New York, half for work and half for a holiday, so he'll see something of America. In a telegram HG asks Kurt for permission—can you imagine? "Certainly!," Kurt replies, and in no time HG is sitting in the famous Pullman, on those seats that convert into beds at night. I know them only from photographs, because who takes long train journeys in America these days? HG can't get to sleep, there is a "nice-looking woman in the compartment. Great conversations!"—I suspect that his "stories" are flourishing again.

In Chicago, even more so in New York, he can't stop gawking: "This is America!" Morris Fertilizer makes sure that he meets people, and suddenly the "rich uncle" Ernst Hothorn is on the scene again. HG is passed from one person to the next, he goes to Carnegie Hall and the Metropolitan Opera, he sees several Broadway shows, he visits Long Island, plays tennis, goes horse riding. Now he sees properly affluent, tasteful houses, and discovers that white America also has its own class-based society. It doesn't even cost him all that much, because people are always asking him out. Like a parched flower that's finally being watered, HG comes to life and wanders the streets from dawn till dusk. Shouldn't he bring Else over here, shouldn't they stay?

Instead HG receives news from home that Else has found a flat in Bochum—that's the signal. Time to go home. They're going to get married. In Bochum there's a job waiting for him at the Ammonia Sales Association. Not that HG dreamed of being part of an association to distribute Reich German ammonia, but as he writes to his friend Theo Delbrück: "I'd much rather be in Bochum than in Halberstadt, for many reasons, and I hope that even after that Halberstadt won't be our next address quite yet." The "many reasons" are Else's reservations about the strong bulwark of family and stolid Halberstadt society—"There wasn't as much laughter as there was in Wismar," she will later write to her grandchildren.

HG, for his part, doesn't think he's quite ready for the company, or more importantly for his father: "I've got to become strong enough to stand my ground with him."

Most important, the couple finally want to be on their own—speedily, please! The return crossing from New York is booked on a passenger ship called the SS *Manchuria,* and it takes only ten days to get to Hamburg. I don't know how HG paid for this. His crossing on the Norwegian freighter to the United States cost a mere 5 kroner, although even that worked out as 250 marks. The passenger ship crossing must have been much more expensive, because the *Manchuria* was the kind of liner familiar to us from the movies: bridge and deck quoits, black-tie dinner at the captain's table, even a "man overboard," a suicide "from third class."

And a deck romance—that's right, we're in the movies. HG calls her Fatima, there's even a photograph of her, and everything takes its usual course. First a game of bridge together, and "lively conversation." Then a "curious feeling for Fatima" that turns into "in the evening a long time with Fatima on the foredeck." The following day: "Skipped dinner with Fatima. On the foredeck." And next—after all, there isn't much time: "A curious unease draws me to Fatima, even in the morning. Almost silent in the deck chairs, blazing sunshine. Evening with Fatima on the foredeck: moonlight . . . calm . . . long waves . . . sea gleam . . . and so on." The next morning HG has a mental hangover: "I feel terribly stupid, silly, and inconsistent after last night." Why doesn't he just write: it was nice? Shortly afterward the ship docks at the harbor in Hamburg, Else is standing there, Goodbye Fatima, HG's come home.

SEVEN

Else's home, Ravelin Horn

The wedding is arranged for September 15, 1922. That means a lot of stress, but only in Wismar. HG grows increasingly nervous, darting back and forth between a dress-suit tailor in Berlin and a gentlemen's outfitter in Halberstadt, "sorting out his affairs," as though preparing for his demise, and walking for hours with the dogs in the forest "deep in thought." He clings to Horace: "aequam memento rebus in arduis servare mentem" (remember to maintain your equanimity even in difficult times), but it doesn't work. Creeping through the house in Halberstadt in a valedictory mood,

HG does battle with his black birds—"shouldn't I have stayed in New York? The hard thing about the future is that it is so definitive. Gloomy state of mind!!" In short: he's going through what we all go through before getting married.

Ravelin Horn glitters in all its glory. Fifty guests have been invited to a sit-down meal, another hundred or so come to the wedding-eve party, the place is a-bustle with waiters and silver-service waitresses, cooks and sommeliers. Dagmar and her Danish sisters are calm personified and working away over all the bubbling pots simultaneously. After the register office, the wedding ceremony in the red-brick Marienkirche the following day is solemn and festive. Big arrangements of asters and autumn leaves decorate the columns and the altar, four bridesmaids in pink and white, with the bride's male attendants in tails, accompany the couple, and six little children scatter flowers ahead of them. Kurt junior plays a Handel Adagio on his violin, and the vicar preaches on Romans 8:15, as selected by HG: "For ye have not received the spirit of bondage again to fear; but ye have received the spirit of adoption, whereby we cry, Abba, Father!" Then the organ thunders out the tune of "Great God, We Praise Thee!" and with all the chorally experienced Klamroths and the less musical Podeuses, HG joins in with all his heart. Else doesn't sing. She can't.

At home in Ravelin Horn, the two long tables are Dagmar's masterpiece. Everything that the cupboards can provide in terms of porcelain, silver, expensive table linen, is put on display. Candles, flowers, grapes from the house's own greenhouses as decoration, glasses that I still use for my own dinners. When it's time for the speeches, Paul, the head of the house, first of all addresses the foreign guests. This, he says, is a German wedding, and particularly in such dark days it is every German's duty to think first of his fatherland: "I raise my glass to Germany." A few years previously it would have been the Kaiser—how things change . . .

Father-in-law Kurt deals with Else's doubts about joining the Klamroth clan—how does he know? Else can't possibly have mentioned it. He reassures her, saying that family tradition has never meant that new members must feel monopolized: "We give you family security, you give us fresh blood to bless future generations." Before Else can faint in horror, Kurt makes it clear how fully he understands the fact that she comes from elsewhere. "The Podeus clan has always been seafaring people, they are storm-tested, and because of their close connections with people beyond the sea they are agile and quick to make decisions. The blood pulses heavier in the veins of the Harz Klamroths, who"—quoting Field Marshal Moltke—"weigh matters seriously before they take their risks." But that was, in the end, what made the connection so promising for the future, and that was why he was now happy to raise a toast to the Podeus and Cruse families.

Coffee is served in the drawing rooms. Kurt, the archivist, can't help admiring the antiques, the paintings, the carpets, the lush vases of flowers, the crystal carafes with the digestifs, the silent staff. It's the last big festivity in Ravelin Horn, and it radiates the unchallenged serenity of a world that won't admit its decline. Else, later: "We all knew that it was coming to an end. Nonetheless, it was as though that end would never reach us. Ravelin Horn had cast its spell over us once again."

The young couple are the first to leave. When the wedding waltz is danced and the bouquet has been thrown, they leave the wedding feast by car—a shame, actually, but it was what custom demanded. In Wismar the party goes on till five, while Else and HG travel on to the Hotel Stadt Hamburg in Lübeck, "absolutely exhausted, both completely worn out for our wedding night." They recover on their honeymoon. The couple go to the Bavarian Alps, they clamber up and down the mountains from Berchtesgaden in blazing sunshine, and when it rains they spend all day in bed. HG writes in Danish in his diary: "Vi er saa forelskede" (We're so in love!) and in German in Greek letters to fox any potential snoopers: "We love each other very much!" and "Small misfortune." Anyone's guess what that means. I sense only how happy they are.

They're away for three weeks, and it's pure joy. When they come back to Halberstadt, the next party is just around the corner: Kurt and Gertrud's silver wedding anniversary.

That takes place on October 9, and I find six-part choral movements composed by Kurt junior that were sung at the crack of dawn outside the couple's bedroom door—the Klamroths used to do that on feast days. Years later, after the Second World War, when the house was full to the brim with people, on birthdays it must have sounded like the Mormon Tabernacle Choir. I remember songs like "The Sun's First Morning Rays" and "Go out My Heart and Seek Your Joy" at six o'clock in the morning. There was no getting out of it, my soprano was needed. Else, who couldn't sing, stayed gratefully asleep. But now on the morning of the silver wedding, having completed their dawn serenade, the family, dressed to the nines at half past eight, gathers in the hall, where Annie hands over the silver wreath. The chronicle raves about the "deeply moving moment," and reports Gertrud's "quiet tears." Dagmar Podeus saves the day. She hugs Annie and sobs: "You've made even me cry, and I never do!"

The family banner is hoisted in front of the house, and the well-wishers stream in. Anybody of note in the town puts in an appearance: the mayor, the town council, the Chamber of Commerce, a delegation from the former Seydlitz Cuirassiers arrives in full uniform and on horseback, colleagues from the war office in civilian clothes and on foot. The churches send their pastors, and a crowd of deaconesses scurries to the house from St. Cecilia's Convent; the Infant School Association delivers a few verses and I.G. Klamroth's works committee hands over a glass window with the family coat of arms. The gentlemen from the Airedale Club are represented along with their dogs, and even the long-dissolved Halberstadt Air-Fleet Association sends along a little tethered balloon.

There are all kinds of performances, chiefly musical—the family band Benno Nachtigall is kept busy. Everyone dines superbly, this time from Meissen china; forty-six people in evening dress and tails sit around the table, which is decorated with silvered laurel branches and autumn roses. By around two o'clock, when the guests have gone, the family is still gathered around the fireplace, until Kurt junior, as always after evenings spent together, plays the night blessing on the piano: "So legt euch denn, ihr Brüder" (To bed, then, brothers). HG writes in his diary: "A lovely day. Nonetheless, I now see many things differently through Else's eyes."

In early January 1923 the couple move to Bochum. The one-room apartment in the Auguste Viktoria-Allee is the first home of their own—HG hangs up a calligraphic version of Schiller in the hall: "There is room in the smallest cottage for a happy loving couple." They enjoy everything: the coal stove and the cooking box, washing the dishes in a metal bowl and the folding bed next to the tiny wardrobe. Else's untidiness vanishes in a flash; she gets up at five in the morning to make HG's breakfast when he has to travel cross-country for his new employer. HG is "happy!!!" In the Ammonia Sales Association he's a kind of troubleshooter, and is allowed to do all the things he loves: drawing up statistics about fertilizer experiments, viability assessments, and price comparisons. He's concerned with foreign patents and British delivery lists—it sounds dreadful, but HG loves writing down columns of numbers.

The company takes great care of its employees. Because there's often nothing to eat in the strike-plagued Ruhr, the Ammonia Sales Association, by means of a special department, supplies its employees with provisions. In HG's diary he lists at regular intervals: flour given out in the office, canned meat, margarine, eggs, bacon, sugar, chocolate, sausage—at moderate prices which, in view of the soaring costs outside, is a source of salvation to many. Hyperinflation hasn't yet begun, but between early October and early November 1922 the dollar rate has tripled from 2,000 to 6,400 marks, and the carousel is spinning faster and faster.

Things really get going with the occupation of the Ruhr by the French and the Belgians. They invade on January 11, 1923, about

100,000 strong, on the pretext that the German Reich hasn't fulfilled its wood and coal deliveries. The government responds by calling for passive resistance in the Ruhr—that is, a halt to all reparation payments. All of a sudden the Ruhr is paralyzed. The miners stop supplying coal; administration, the postal service, and the railways come to a standstill as soon as the French begin issuing orders. The whole Reich declares its solidarity with the battle in the Ruhr, and as a result the whole Reich is brought financially to its knees—the wages of the strikers must still be paid by the state. It's a bottomless pit, and the Reichsbank keeps pouring in more and more money, freshly printed and worthless.

The occupying powers react with arrests and expulsions; an intensified state of siege is declared with checkpoints on every street corner and nighttime curfews. There are riots; thirteen workers are shot in Essen and four innocent bystanders in Bochum. The newlyweds are right in the middle of it all. They wind their way past checkpoints in search of a grocer's shop selling goods from the back door, because the French often demand the closure of all shops for days on end. Else and HG shiver in their little apartment because of the coal blockade; often there's neither water nor electricity, mail is smuggled via courier through the unoccupied town of Hamm, and they have to sit in the train toilet through the French checkpoint in Scharnhorst, or else the letters will be confiscated. Else is pregnant.

"I feel reverent," HG writes in his diary. And concerned. Else isn't well. She is vomiting all the time, her circulation is falling, and even worse than that, now it is she who is chased by the "black birds." What a time for a baby to be born: the dollar is rising from 10,000 to 20,000 marks, and by early June it stands at 100,000 marks. HG's income has risen sevenfold in a single month; so have prices. The violence in the streets is frightening—it isn't only the French who are fighting in Bochum. Unidentified mobs are lynching supposed collaborators, and far-right Freikorps veterans are launching bomb attacks on military trains and railway bridges. The

Freikorps fighter Albert Leo Schlageter is executed by the French on these charges, leading to violent demonstrations throughout Germany. Not a good environment for a mother-to-be.

It almost breaks his heart—"Tearful farewell!"—but HG takes Else to Wismar. It isn't easy, and only with the help of a friend and a series of complicated train connections does he manage to get her through checkpoints and border harassments to Bremen, where Paul Podeus collects her. HG then fights his way through to Halberstadt, because the future needs to be sorted out. It leads straight to I.G. Klamroth—with a child, everything's different. You don't just go cruising from one experimental station to the next—at least not in those days. Kurt was right to send HG to America before the wedding.

In Halberstadt, they discuss HG's contract as a partner with the firm and possible places to live—a converted apartment is offered in the big company house at the Woort, where the firm's founders used to live. But spending the whole day under the same roof as your senior boss, always available? And then there's an apartment in Grandmother Vogler's house on the Domplatz, and it occurs to Gertrud that they might move into the top floor of the house on Bismarckplatz. Presumably HG hears Else yowling and politely declines.

At Easter, HG makes an adventurous journey to Wismar—the arguments about the railways in the occupied Ruhr have thrown German rail traffic into total confusion. HG rests his head against Else's growing belly, and the baby does him the favor: it kicks. HG is delighted: "What could be more important in life than such a wife and such a miraculous child!" The upper stories in Ravelin Horn are to be rented out, as there are no children left in the house anyway. Else and HG choose the furniture they want to take to Halberstadt, HG with a slightly queasy feeling, "because I don't know how I'm supposed to pay for it." Apparently the valuables will have to be sold, Paul and Dagmar need money.

Throughout the whole of April HG lugs cases and packages to

unoccupied Hamm, clearing the little flat of all but the absolute essentials, eager to get out of the Ruhr. Friends send his things from Hamm to Halberstadt, but getting them there is a test of nerves. At one point there is a "scandalous dispute" with French soldiers who insist that kitchen utensils are an illegal export—HG: "Very dangerous! They're so worked up!" The atmosphere is extremely tense, snipers are taking their toll on the occupying forces, who avenge themselves with the arrest of whole streets. And the dollar is rising and rising—HG spends 4,000 marks on a haircut.

Out of the blue he is sent to Berlin, troubleshooting in the city's branch of the Ammonia Sales Association. That's in late April 1923. He also isn't allow himself any time off. The very day of his arrival in Berlin he goes to his new office and quickly realizes that this is unknown territory, demanding a lot of effort, so he works like a lunatic from early morning till late at night. Months later, when HG is slogging his guts out in I.G. Klamroth, his diary reads: "Fit of rage from Uncle H."—that's the other partner, Heinrich Schultz—"because of my work mania." HG's pace isn't for everyone.

Most people seem to like him. His superiors, including the director of the Ammonia Sales Association, one Dr. Ruperti, call the young man—HG is twenty-four—in for discussions and conferences with business partners. Ruperti, who travels the world on ammonia business, has already used him in Bochum as a personal assistant. Now he appoints HG as his Berlin vice-regent, to stay behind with a notebook full of tasks when Ruperti goes off on another of his jaunts. HG uses the experience for the rest of his life. I come across the names that appear in his diary at this point over and over again as the years pass. HG tends his network, and his extensive correspondence helps to expand it. On the letters he receives, the word "answered" is written in neat script, rarely after more than a week. He even writes to the bores at Morris Fertilizer in Wilmington, North Carolina, and the German consul in Curaçao,

then there is all the people that HG finds important in private—
once he's got somebody in his net, he holds on to him.

One of HG's first visits in Berlin is to Siegfried Körte's
"estimable mother," who has been living there since moving from
East Prussia. He visits her often, and I read about it in his diary:
"Worries about Siegfried"—"talked about the problem child." The
big row with Wolf Yorck's old aunt over the foreign exchange business hasn't yet happened, or if it has HG doesn't know about it, but
there is cause enough for gloomy thoughts. Even during his American trip, HG often received bad news from Else—a loan of 20,000
marks that she had made to their mutual friend hadn't been repaid,
Kurt had resisted an appeal for money from Siegfried, "annoying
letters about Siegfried" had arrived in Bochum, and even now in
Berlin money must have been at the heart of it. HG: "Siegfried is a
dear friend." But he's so fond of him—"He's part of my life"—and
along with Siegfried's mother, HG is "very sad. There's disaster on
the horizon."

There's plenty of that around, anyhow. It's July 1923, and HG
couldn't have chosen a worse moment to start his job as junior
head of the family firm, the fifth in almost 125 years. Inflation is
galloping into the billions, nobody's buying anything, and if anyone
pays a bill, the money's worth only a fragment of its initial value.
There are public food riots, even in Halberstadt. Screeching
housewives take to the streets in protest because there's nothing to
eat. Posters are being plastered up in search of people who have
simply disappeared, the parks echo either with the bawling of the
"Internationale" or with the battle song of the right-wing Ehrhardt
Brigade.

There are endless rumors of putsches, civil war seems to be
breaking out every day, in Saxony and Thuringia the regional governments are deposed by force of arms because legally elected
Communists are involved in them. In Bavaria, however, the Reich
government doesn't dare to move so hard against radical nationalist

uprisings initiated by Hitler and his ilk. The country is in turmoil, and HG's nerves are frazzled. "What on earth's going to happen!" he writes time and again in his diary. "How will we make it through?"—"Awfully nervous! Worries! We haven't enough capital!"—"It's a terribly exciting time!" Kurt, incidentally, seems to be more relaxed about the whole thing. "Father's trying to calm everybody down," HG writes several times. You can't blame the son for being seized by panic, now that he has been given responsibility for the first time—and under circumstances such as these. HG is twenty-five.

At home, Else is left largely to her own devices. Her baby is due shortly, she feels heavy and shapeless, she can't sleep, and she's "a bit homesick," as she admits to her father. The apartment is ready by now, complete with nursery—Else and HG have moved into Grandmother Vogler's house on the Domplatz. She endures the fact that she sees so little of her husband, even though he's not miles away any longer, with "the courage of a war bride," as Paul puts it. "The times are not dissimilar." Else is twenty-four.

They both write to their unborn child. HG pulls out all the stops: "You were created from the burning will of your father and his intense desire to lift himself up, to become immortal in you—and from the fervent desire of your mother to give life, to live for life. Your father's desire and your mother's longing were brought together into the blazing flame that carried us far aloft in our yearning for you—and that's how you came about." Children survive such things. They shrink the drama down to its normal size. Else, the child's mother, is naturally closer to the mark: "My little one, as I write to you, I feel you inside me, telling me with your forceful blows that you want to come out soon and take on life's struggle, that although you are still safe and protected inside me, you are already something of your own, your own little being." She's right.

What I don't read anywhere is whether she's afraid of the ordeal ahead of her. When I had my children, I didn't meet a single mother who had told her daughter the truth about the torture of childbirth. Else didn't warn me. Millions of women have children every day, I was told, and you'll doubtless be able to do the same! Sure. But it doesn't mean you have to enjoy it. Just before the torment ends, HG describes the distraught state of the first-time mother for the still unborn child: "Your mother looked at me with her beloved eyes, so impossibly weary today, and whispered to me, 'I didn't know it would hurt *so* much!'" Poor Else! Home birth, of course, no injections, the whole thing lasted nine hours. But now Barbara's there, it's August 25, 1923, and if HG ever had cause to torture Schubert, here it is: "Now everything, everything must change!"

They're overwhelmed by the miracle child. They're part of creation, God's tools, Mother Earth and Father Spirit, they see the metaphysics of our world in this little mite of a daughter—and they're right. Humble gratitude and jubilant delight at one's participation in the greatness of life are never more intense than in the early weeks of a first child's life. That's not going to last when the baby bawls and has diarrhea and robs you of sleep, when overtired mothers can't see straight and the child's everlasting demands turn daily life upside down more efficiently than anything you had imagined. Then the reflexes swing into action more quickly than devotion—with small children no one has a head for metaphysics. Nonetheless the miracle remains. I look with amazement at my daughters, who are a part of me. And with amazement I realize that without HG I wouldn't be me.

Else finds it hard to recover from the birth. She weeps her eyes out—it's called postnatal depression, and HG is utterly distraught about it: "Why does she cry so intensely? Mother says it has something to do with a change in the body." That's right. But it's also the incredible alertness of the senses that drives these tears, the overwhelming force of responsibility, the loss of sheltered privacy as a couple, the alien, for all your joy, that has made its nest in your life.

All this happens only with the first child. Else has another two in quick succession, and this time she doesn't cry. She knows how to deal with it. And there's something else she knows now: how to have children "like a piece of wet soap" (Else's words). *Shloop* and they're out, none of the next four children took more than an hour after the first contractions. No wonder that Else didn't tell me anything about a trip to hell. She'd presumably forgotten the nine hours she had with Barbara.

HG hardly gets the opportunity to enjoy the child. From dawn till dusk he's at work, shaken by anxiety over the economic situation. The currency is collapsing so rapidly that Else and he twice have to abandon planned outings to the Harz mountains—the money, with drawn yesterday from the bank, won't cover the costs of the trip today. Their daughter is christened at home on November 4, 1923 (Reformation Day), with a "very small party" for twenty people—the men in tails, the family's silver christening cup on the altar in the hall. Stirring account from the father in Barbara's diary: "May this day prove to have been a building block in your life." Into the midst of this explodes Else's furious handwriting: "The roast cost a billion marks, and grandmother"—meaning Gertrud—"was worried about whether it would be enough for everybody." And again, in between HG's neat lines: "Only just!!!"

HG develops a nervous heart condition—"I'm not fit!"—and he feels like Sisyphus: "Did a lot of work with no success whatsoever." He doesn't dare drive for three days to Schleibitz, to attend Wolf Yorck's wedding: "We're living from the morning to the afternoon, I can't leave." He torments himself with stomach pains and sleeplessness: "Signed the first check for a billion, what insane times!!" More and more often the diary says: "I'm irritable with exhaustion"—"profound, bad mood." The black birds are back, and several times HG notes with horror: "I'm torturing Else!"

She must have endured that with loving care. HG gratefully records "how affectionate she is" and that she "shares his political worries." There are good reasons for them. Both Communists and right-wing conservatives are planning a coup. Passive resistance in the Ruhr has to be abandoned because of the total collapse of the economy. In Aachen separatists are declaring a Rhenish republic, the same happens in the Palatinate a short time after. High-ranking military officers in Bavaria plan a march on Berlin against the "Jewish government," which is "messing everything up." Street battles rage, and on November 8, 1923, Adolf Hitler declares the "national revolution" in Munich's Bürgerbräukeller. General Erich Ludendorff—yes, him again!—is involved, and Hitler appoints him commander in chief of the National Army. HG writes with amazement in his diary: "Ludendorff, Hitler—dictators?!!" The putsch ends late on the morning of November 9 under the bullets of the Bavarian regional police at Munich's Feldherrnhalle. Sixteen of Hitler's followers are killed, while he himself gets away, although he's arrested two days later. There is a widespread assumption that this marks the end of Hitler's political career.

The gentlemen in question are given mild punishments, Ludendorff is acquitted of high treason, Hitler and three comrades are condemned to five years' imprisonment and a 200-mark fine. That's the beginning of April 1924, and they're free by Christmas. The court confirms to the putschists that they "had acted in the spirit of the fatherland, and in the most noble and selfless manner"—a moral acquittal that Hitler will exploit. In the fortress of Landsberg he writes *Mein Kampf*.

Else's pregnant again. There are no records telling us how delighted she is about this, less than three months after Barbara's birth. HG celebrates in Danish—"jeg er lykkelig!"—but then he isn't the one who has to go through it all. Nonetheless, the new child is born into politically more peaceful times. The "miracle of the rentenmark," introduced by the unstable Stresemann government on November 15, 1923, eight days before its collapse, consolidates the situation. The dollar stands at 4.2 billion marks, so the Reichsbank fixes the exchange rate at 1 billion paper marks to one rentenmark, or 4.20 rentenmarks to the dollar—simple as that.

The rentenmark is the transitional currency to the reichsmark, and falls like warm rain over the country. "Business is suddenly extraordinarily lively," HG notes in his diary, and Else is buying "eggs and noodles at normal prices" again. The balance sheet for I.G. Klamroth, which had stood at 2.5 billion dubious paper marks the previous year, on January 1, 1924, stands at a solid 703,962.22 gold marks—that's the new state unit that's bringing order in the chaos. It's nothing like prewar figures—of course it isn't, ten years of war and postwar have left their scars. But the company is alive, it's managed its economy satisfactorily throughout that disastrous year, and nobody's emerged with anything worse than a black eye. Not even HG, despite his anxieties. On Christmas Eve, father and son silently drink a glass of champagne together. HG: "He put his hand on my shoulder. We made it!"

After Christmas Else and HG go skiing with friends in the snowy Harz mountains, "carefree, cheerful, wonderful winter weather." All of a sudden the mood in the diary has changed. Games are played once more around the fireplace in Bismarck-platz—"official, tenant, puppy," I vaguely remember that one, some sort of card game. And "numbers," a kind of squabbling patience with figures: "Nümmerchen spielt jedermann, vorausqe-setzt, dass er das kann." (Anyone can play numbers, as long as they know how), the instructions rhyme merrily, and Dagmar Podeus always ends the game victorious by audacious cheating. Else discovers her future passion, doing jigsaws—how many jigsaw puzzles I was given as presents, just so that she could have her fun! And then there was that novelty for Germany, mah-jongg, or Chinese dominoes.

It's not all sunshine yet in the country, not even in Halberstadt. But there are cracks in the clouds: the military emergency is lifted in February 1924, and over the course of the year the Dawes Plan is drawn up. It gets its name from the American banker Charles G. Dawes, whose commission of experts finally brings Germany's reparations into line with her economic capacity. The French are vacating parts of the Ruhr—the French withdrawal isn't definitively finished until autumn 1925.

That calms the political situation, but it doesn't placate the folkish nationals of all shades. Hitler's temporarily forbidden National Socialist Party (NSDAP) is replaced, under a different name and along identical lines, by Alfred Rosenberg and Erich Ludendorff, in the Reichstag elections in May 1924 the German Nationals become the strongest party in the right-wing camp, with ninety-six mandates—only four seats behind the Social Democrats, who are in pitiful decline. Anything "that weakens the reds is fine by HG," and he and Else voted for the German People's Party, Stresemann's (and Kurt's) political home, which has also sustained severe losses. The fact that more than a quarter of German voters choose the antirepublic right sends alarm signals to Kurt at least. HG in his diary: "Father concerned about the weakness of democracy."

The people of Halberstadt don't really have much time to think about the concerns of the Reich. They are happy to notice, as HG writes to his friend Theo Delbrück in Amsterdam, "that things are slowly but constantly improving, if we go on working as hard as before." Business is picking up at I.G. Klamroth, "the spring orders are accumulating, and soon we won't know how to cope with them." The result is a new Steyr car; it must have been a stunner, a convertible, of course, and a little Opel, in which HG likes to flit around the area without a chauffeur. Kurt, on the other hand, still comes to the office on his bicycle. "He was always there at seven in the morning," I was told by an old lady who grew up at the Woort as a daughter of the building superintendents. "The young gentleman turned up two hours later in his sports car!"

New horses are bought as well. Nelly and Lord have vanished from the family records without a word of farewell, and instead there are Minnesieg and Ebony, a crow-black Trakehner gelding that the "rich American uncle" Ernst Hothorn gave to HG. At any rate, HG now goes riding almost every morning at half past six, with his father or the old coachman Hermann Kückelmann—what does that do to the couple's togetherness? Those last minutes of cuddling cut short, not because of an unsettled child, but an unsettled horse? Doubtless Else would have liked to go riding with them. But she can't because of her pregnancy. HG writes, "She grumbles bravely." Who would blame her: two children in a row ruined her figure; for almost two years now Else hasn't fit into her clothes. If she bends down she gets heartburn, and she's dog-tired. The miniature lady Barbara clings to her apron strings as though she understands that this is her last chance to have her mother to herself. But it's all being done for the son, the heir, the scion, the sixth J.G.K.

Ursula is born on July 17, 1924, in three-quarters of an hour. The midwife doesn't get to the house in time, and there's no record of whether and how HG helped Else bring the baby into the world. Did he hold up her knees and support her head, did he pull the child out of her, did he take care that the umbilical cord didn't strangle it? If he had, it would be in his diary. Neither did his diary tell whether one of the two maids assisted Else. Probably not, it would have been too private. Else will have managed on her own while in the adjoining room HG put on his tie, without which he wouldn't have been able to receive Madame Nädler, the midwife. But Else wouldn't have wanted him to help her either. Such a messy, bloody, archaic affair as childbirth was women's business. Men were allowed in again only when mother and child had been washed.

Predictably enough, domestic terror takes over: Barbara is beside herself over the invader; she can't yet walk, but she can certainly pull her little sister's hair. Once Else catches her trying to knock over the pram, and Barbara shrieks and spits when she's prevented from doing so. I could tell you all about it, my daughters are one and a half years apart. There's misery in such a little child's soul, and Else, although not averse to the odd slap on the bum, picks her up and comforts her, cuddles Barbara on the sofa, takes her into bed with them. Ursula, the typical second child, the "cuckoo in the nest," sleeps, crows, demands—and gets—everything she wants, and pays no heed to the hubbub around her.

HG is wild about his daughters, he loves babies, even if he doesn't see that much of them. He disappears off riding at the crack of dawn, breakfasts and showers with cold water, is at the office by nine, comes home for lunch, naps a little, and spends the rest of the day at work. Saturday is a full working day, he goes riding on Sunday too, although in the morning he goes through his mail. In the evenings there are guests in the house, or the young couple are invited out. At night the children whine and cry, Barbara has to be comforted, Ursula gets her bottle from the nursemaid, but—still—both parents are awake.

In the morning Else makes tea for HG before he goes riding, then Barbara bawls, Ursula screams, nursemaids come running, but it's Mama they want. Both children are fed, bathed, put in their diapers, cuddled. Ursula is put in the pram, Barbara wants to be entertained. Meanwhile lunch is discussed—Else doesn't do the cooking herself, but she does do the tasting—shopping lists, laundry appointments, cleaning plans, and please make sure that it doesn't disturb HG's routine. Lunch with her husband and Barbara, and then while he's asleep, quiet, please—finally—descends on the house. Else doesn't nap. In the afternoon she goes shopping with the children in the double pram. After that preparations for the evening, checking on dinner in the kitchen. Else sets the table herself in a particularly stylish way. Children to bed, Barbara wails, Ursula crows; nursemaids are helpful, but Mama's the one they want. Changing, beaming—tired? Who's asking? The evening goes on till midnight, interrupted once or twice by wails from Ursula. And tomorrow? Same thing, all over again.

We've all done that, without staff and usually with a job, on top of everything, haven't we? Well, no, we haven't. They didn't have a vacuum cleaner—Else said the carpets were brushed by hand or beaten outside. Rods of ice were delivered for the cold room, the parquet floors had to be scoured with steel wool because every drop of water left stains. Today we don't preserve vegetables for the winter as they did then, or salt meat when an animal has been slaughtered, and we make jam only for fun. The shopping was done every day at that time, leftovers ended up in pottery jugs in the cellar, there was no washing-up liquid, no hot running water, no tin foil. Certainly no deep freeze, dishwasher, washing machine, or microwave. Bathwater was heated with wood, knife blades cleaned with cork and sand, bed and table linen boiled up in a pot, then starched, bleached on the lawn, darned if necessary, and laid out ready for the wooden mangle.

Else didn't do it all on her own, of course not. Apart from the two domestic maids, laundry maids came to the house, women to do the ironing, servants from the Woort who shoveled coal into the central heating boiler. But Else wasn't sitting with her hands folded, she was her own housekeeper, in charge of planning and budgets; she had to oversee, check, keep the books, draw up lists of linen, silver, and provisions. Did she have to? She was a child of her time and would have permitted no doubts about her domestic management abilities. She couldn't go shuffling around the house in jeans and with her hair a mess during the day, as we might; she constantly had houseguests, and she had to—she really had to—set a good example for the staff and later for the children. And if she wanted to let herself go, there was only one way out. "Else unwell," it says quite often in HG's diary. She went to bed.

Every now and again they escape—to Denmark, to Wismar, to Schleibitz, where Wolf Yorck wants to convert his friend to the German National People's Party. HG resists, even though he considers Wolf to be politically competent. They deliver the children to Bismarckplatz or Ravelin Horn, the two daughters survive the journeys wrapped up warmly in wash baskets on the floor of the open-topped Steyr automobile. The grandparents are happy, so is the nursemaid who travels with them, and HG writes—sheer joy—in his diary: "Alone at last with my sweet wife."

It's usually a short-lived pleasure for him, because he has to get back to the office, but in January 1925, on the fourth anniversary of their engagement, they take a detour to the monastery of Chorin, which is snowed in once again—"memories, memories!"—on their way to ski in Austria. Three weeks altogether, just the two of them. After their restful cross-country skis in the Harz mountains, they're defeated by the steep slopes. HG: "Else gets so furious when she falls. She always falls, and she always gets furious. And she laughs her head off." A skiing instructor comes to their aid. HG to Theo Delbrück: "You can imagine how we're enjoying all the things that Else has been without for two whole years—theater, traveling, guests, sport. We have two lovely children, but now, at last, we have each other as well."

Four weeks later HG writes in his diary: "Jeg ved ikke om at grine eller græde" (I don't know whether to laugh or cry). Else is pregnant again. God alive, how fertile the woman is. How desperate she is, I can't tell. Her diaries have disappeared. She certainly isn't happy, and neither is HG, although he doesn't say so. Because it isn't just Else who's been lacking what we would normally call life, he has too. She can't have been as devoted to him as she had been—being pregnant, a woman tends to be thrown back on her own devices and learns to cope with what is asked of her. I now know that Else had two abortions in 1927. Why not later? She didn't plan for her two youngest children. I suspect that the doctor who had helped her before was no longer in Halberstadt. He was Jewish.

But now she can't even contemplate a termination, anyway. Else knows the demand: a son and heir is required. So fixated is she on this idea that in Ursula's childhood diary in 1925 she writes constantly of her "little brother." I can't begin to imagine how everyone involved would have coped with the disappointment of a third girl—including the third girl. But the Lord above has blessed them: this time they really do get the son they want.

But we're not quite there yet. First they buy a radio, and along with the many guests who are always there, now people come to the house just to listen to the broadcasts—it's a collective event as in the 1950s, when not everybody owned a television. The radio license fee is 24 marks a year. At the beginning of 1924 there are 1,500 paying listeners for the alleged fad in the Reich, by January 1925 there are more than a million.

On the radio they hear of the death of the Reich President Friedrich Ebert on February 28, 1925, shortly before the end of his term of office. This brave and honest man is only fifty-four years old, and dies of appendicitis which he had left untreated. He was waiting for the end of yet another trial concerning an insult to the head of state. Literally harried to his death by more than 150 of these trials, the "November criminal," the "man responsible for the stab in the back of the army," was in truth the representative of the hated Weimar Republic. It wasn't only the folkish and German National right, along with the National Socialists, who were snapping at the heels of the late Ebert. The Communists sent him to his grave with the "curses of the German proletariat"; even among the Social Democrats there had been applications to have him expelled from the party. His own trade union, the saddlers' association, had him thrown out.

His successor is Paul von Hindenburg, the "victor of the battle of Tannenberg" and a convinced monarchist. He's seventy-seven years old, and before running for the highest office in the young republic he requests, in all seriousness, the consent of his former Kaiser in Holland. Thomas Mann had warned: "I would be proud of the political culture of our people if they forbore from electing a warrior of the past as their head of state"—his words go unheeded. The aged general field marshal wins the election, and the result is greeted with jubilation by the radio audience in HG and Else's living room in Domplatz. They applaud the victory of the past, and transfigure earlier times when "everything was better" and they were still unshaken by the miseries of democratic chaos. The fact that Hindenburg stands for war gives him legendary status, and the fact that the war was lost is not a matter for reproach. Everyone knows the reason: the "stab in the back" on the home front. Only Kurt has his doubts. HG: "Father skeptical."

EIGHT

Grandfather Kurt

There's another family reunion in 1925, this time in Berlin-Grunewald, at the home of the banker Walter Klamroth. He's a cousin of Kurt's, a lawyer and the association's treasurer, and I remember that the dueling scars on his face fascinated me just as much as the claim that people used to have such wounds inflicted voluntarily—Uncle Walter was in the Hansea corps. He wore a pince-nez, and as a child I hoped in vain that it would fall off his nose. It's the first time that HG and his wife attend a family reunion together: in 1923 pregnant Else bravely went on her own,

HG was in Bochum; there was no family reunion in 1924, but Else had been pregnant again, as she is this time. HG: "I promised her the prettiest dress for the next family reunion." Forty-six family members come to this one, and the clan sets off in three motorboats "and with a lot of wine," first to the Pfaueninsel in the Havel River, then to the parks of Sakrow and Sanssouci.

Kurt, the archivist, presents them with their "sociological family tree," and delivers a lecture on "the social rise of the Klamroth dynasty through the generations"—from farmer to estate owner, from worker to factory owner, village schoolteacher to vicar, private scholar, once a clerk, now a senior member of the government. He tells them how the "influx of fresh blood" brought in by the wives contributed to the family's impetus, since the men at the top no longer sought their wives in the neighboring villages. He speaks of blood from Hanover and blood from Hessen and Franken, all Protestant blood, incidentally. Else's blood is singled out for approval—not just Mecklenburg, but Denmark, too! Then they sit down in Pschorr's Bierkeller, forty-six Klamroths, ennobled by blood and soil; ten years later they will sing, "From my father's side comes my Klamroth blood, and a good drop of blood it is too (*schrumm schrumm*). So let's raise a toast to our fine pedigree, for noble it is, through and through."

By that time they've lost their innocence. They still find it funny—*schrumm schrumm*—however, by then their blood is part of a trend. But in 1925? The Klamroths weren't folkish, they were strangers to zeal. They weren't anti-Semitic, at least no more than was usual in those days, or befitting to social respectability. Jews weren't their issue. Not yet. They *were* nationalistic, though. Not so much as to rule out a desire for understanding between nations; membership in their social class certainly allowed the Klamroths to cross borders. They were good people, decent, liberal within limits and proud not of their "blood" but of their ancestors' achievement, which imposed a duty upon them. They nurtured their common ground as a family, and that was then called "blood."

Else fits in very well with all this. She is a family animal herself, and the many Danes and Mecklenburgers that she brings with her, who pep up the formality of the Bismarckplatz household with their ready wit and love of mockery, always inspire Kurt and HG's brothers and sisters. Gertrud bravely goes along—"she had no sense of humor!" Else sighs decades later. Else would sometimes unsettle a soiree by expressing "reddish" ideas, saying, for example, that without trade unions workers would be fair game—HG: "Else was a Red Terror again!" But of course she voted liberal-conservative. Gregers Hovmand, a younger cousin of Else's from Bandholm in Denmark, a man whom I loved dearly until his death a few years ago, used to explode with laughter when he spoke of Else's performances: "You wouldn't believe how cheeky she was! She teased everybody. She was so quick-witted, and her poor mother-in-law only ever realized that she'd missed something because everybody was laughing." And HG? "He was as enthusiastic as we were."

In the summer, before the third child is born, they drive to Wismar again. Paul Podeus isn't well, he's suffering from terrible attacks of angina pectoris. Else thinks the loss of his fortune is the reason. I haven't been able to find anything in the documents to explain why the money suddenly disappeared, not even in the Wismar chronicles. Presumably Paul got into difficulties because of the Versailles Treaty, since there were massive export restrictions on certain goods. At any rate, his banks stopped cooperating, and because of a lack of liquidity Paul sold out at a time when the value of money was melting like butter in the sun. That's why Paul and Dagmar have to sell Ravelin Horn as well, but it isn't so easy in these rough times; no one has the money to buy a castle like that. Nonetheless, the mood in the house is unbowed. HG, admiringly, in his diary: "So much warmth, so much laughter, there's no sign of worry."

To the delight of the grandparents, the daughters and a nurse-maid stay in Wismar, while HG and Else spend a two-week holiday in Bandholm. It's his second visit to his chosen homeland, and the affection between the Danes and HG is mutual—Gregers told me that HG announced with a deep sigh at dinner: "Hvis jeg ikke var prøjser, saa ville jeg gerne være dansk" (If I weren't a Prussian, I'd like to be Danish). "Yes, we'd have taken him," said Else's wonderful cousin even half a century later. HG falls in love with Danish cuisine—liver pâté with sweet cucumber salad, crisply fried onions, umpteen sorts of pickled herring, red fruit jelly with cream—"rødgrød med fløde," the tongue twister for all students of Danish. Dagmar Podeus's and Else's handwritten cookbooks are thick tomes with lots of stains, crossings-out, and additions—I'll have to be careful or I'll get stuck reading them. HG flies back to Berlin. His first time in a plane, just four hours from Copenhagen to Berlin's Tempelhof airport. He's impressed.

His son arrives on Saturday, October 17, 1925, at 1:10 in the morning. Once again, Else has had a record labor of just an hour, but this time the midwife is at the house by nine in the evening. "Thank God!" observes HG, and "A boy!!! *Very* happy!" As late as half past two in the morning he reaches for the boy's childhood diary. In it he speaks of this harsh world which his son is just now getting used to, and says that "Mother and Father want to try and make it as lovely as possible for you, and thereby hope for the help of God, who has stood by us all so mercifully in this dark hour. Honor, praise, and thanks to Him!"

I imagine that Else is now relieved. The weight has fallen from her shoulders. She has provided what the dynasty required of her. Like all women in these times she would have believed that it was her failure if she had "only" had girls. How stressful, and what a warped way of thinking in such a confident woman! But that was how it was. It had to be sons—even much later. It didn't occur to anybody, for instance, to think of the highly gifted daughter Barbara as a potential future head of the company.

It isn't the miracle of life that's the subject this time, now it's a triumph: a son, a SON, THE SON! Both grandparents are over the moon, Dagmar is initially disbelieving on the phone in Wismar:

"You fib me!" The next morning, Sunday, all Klamroths, including staff, are gathered for the Thanksgiving service in the Liebfrauenkirche, and HG writes in the childhood diary: "My heart was full to the brim with thanks for the merciful Almighty Father, who has so clearly blessed my life once more with you, my dear boy. Is this His way of saying that my yearning over the past few years has pleased Him? There are moments when man may face his God so closely, and feels His greatness, omnipotence, and goodness in all its strength; now, once again, I have experienced such a moment."

He's gone nuts. And so has Else. She writes in the new diary: "The hour of your birth is one of the loveliest and happiest of my life." What sort of child can do justice to such high-flown expectations? To start with, it is baptized; that is in January 1926. The boy's name is Joachim Gerd Klamroth, known as Jochen, a real I.G.K. for the company—he's scheduled to be sixth in line. But when things reached that point, HG was dead and the company was in ruins. Plans came to nothing. The baptism is celebrated in Bismarckplatz again, once more the family's valuables are piled up on the altar, once again pieces by Handel are played and Bach cantatas sung. Jochen wears an expensive lace christening frock that Dagmar Podeus extracted from the Danish clan. I was christened in it too. The war swallowed it up.

The festivities are impaired by the fact that the child screams his head off. HG addresses the thirty-two dinner guests in verse, culminating in the words: "And by the way—he's *my* son!" In his speech, Kurt points out the baby's unmistakable resemblance to their ancestor Louis Klamroth—poor Jochen, Louis was so ugly! But he was a gifted businessman, and a very tough act to follow. Kurt and HG are experiencing just that, the times aren't made for creativity in business. HG in his diary, on January 1, 1926: "Lack of credit and a shortage of money everywhere, bankruptcy, business investigations, and so on. We're ending our financial year with a loss for the first time; how will it look over the whole year?"

Pretty poor, to start with: the customers aren't paying; on two occasions HG has to borrow major sums from Vogler's bank, just to cover the company salaries. A few days later cousin Vogler cancels the credit, he's clearly not doing too well either, and I.G. Klamroth is 75,000 marks short. Else turns HG's difficulties into a spectacle. She invites fourteen people to a "deflation dinner." The menu: beetroot soup, sauerkraut and salted meat, roasted apples with black-currant sauce—and everything from the cellar, including HG's wine, which "seems to go down pretty nicely."

But the general climate in the country isn't actually that bleak. In October 1925 the Locarno Treaties were signed, paving the way for Germany's return to the circle of the European major powers. The western borders with France and Belgium were settled, in June 1926 the German-Soviet treaty of mutual neutrality was signed, and in September 1926 Germany entered the League of Nations. No talk any longer of winners and losers, now people met at eye level. Though that didn't sweep the reparations from the table, as a reward there were enticing promises of increased foreign credits and an improved international standing. In December 1926 that became tangible: Gustav Stresemann and his French colleague Aristide Briand were awarded the Nobel Peace Prize.

HG mentions none of this. Now, however, he has only five lines a day in his multiyear diary; if he keeps his writing very small, perhaps ten. Berlin and politics are far removed from Halberstadt, when there's a company to be run, when three small children kick up a fuss at home, when you want to keep your friends together and serve "society," and the odd word snatched with your beloved wife on the way out the door isn't enough. HG is twenty-seven—and by now he's grown up.

But he's still young when he rolls in the deep snow with his tiny daughters—what winters they had! They all go pinching carrots from the cellar to present a "snowmen's patrol" to Else, HG takes huge pleasure in "childish games" such as pick-up-sticks, at which he guides Barbara's stubby fingers, or later in a game called Painter

Klecks, which I still know by heart—"Painter Klecks paints snow and ice, his wife grinds coffee, very nice, his son smears paint on walls, alack!, his daughter's hands are inky black," by polishing shoes on the painted card. He goes home at lunchtime, but not just to eat; "cuddled wife and children," it says in his diary, and if he doesn't go riding because of rain, all three offspring creep into his bed in the morning—"lots of laughter."

For 1926 I find the depressing total of three miscarriages in HG's diary—in January, March, and September. And then in 1927 there are the two abortions. That reassures me in terms of their relationship, because Else won't have gotten pregnant every single time. But what on earth are they up to? Even in those days there were ways of avoiding pregnancy, and with a woman as forward as Else they should have made use of them. On each occasion she disappears into the hospital for one or two days, and afterward she's "lackluster" at home. Is that the only way?

At least Else benefits from the new fashion—waistless dresses hide her child-ravaged figure, they're short, which emphasizes her lovely legs, and cloche hats solve the problems with the hairdo. She comes back from Berlin with a pageboy cut, which causes consternation in Halberstadt, particularly in Bismarckplatz—I dimly discern that ideology is at work here: big city versus small town, "modern" versus traditional. A newspaper story from this period reveals that the association Germanness Abroad excludes girls with pageboys as "differently haired." At any rate, there are rows between mother-in-law Gertrud and Else about "frivolity," Else rejects the allegations, and after the failure of his intervention with Gertrud on Else's behalf, HG resolutely takes both wife and pageboy cut under his wing. HG: "At home Else is wailing with rage!"

He's an excellent negotiator, he learned it from his father, but the requirements of the world around him sometimes get out of hand. In the office he is irritated by quarrels between the otherwise so relaxed Kurt and their second partner, brother-in-law Heinrich Schultz—HG: "far too many words!" In Wismar, Else's brother-in-law is bitching because her sister Ursula's inheritance has supposedly been frittered away by Paul, and the man HG's sister Annie is marrying is constantly troubling him with business worries.

Siegfried Körte also makes a reappearance, or rather not Siegfried himself but his "estimable mother." Frau Körte appears in Halberstadt, "a completely broken woman." Körte must have done something nasty again, and HG and Else consult with her about what is to be done—"it's so deplorable, and so difficult to put right." HG writes a number of letters on Siegfried's behalf, probably to get him out of the country. Ten days later the redeeming telegram arrives from Amsterdam: "Siegfried happily departed." Everywhere HG has to smooth things out and come up with solutions, and twice I find him sighing to his diary: "Actually, what does this have to do with me?"

His parents-in-law do have something to do with him, because he loves them, so in July 1926 he travels to Wismar finally to sell Ravelin Horn. He finds a new apartment for them and organizes their move, and when Paul Podeus dies in November, he arranges a dignified funeral and comforts an utterly distraught Else. Until well into the following spring HG spends his evenings sorting out Paul's documents and Dagmar's finances. In the end it seems sensible for Dagmar Podeus to move to Halberstadt, though this doesn't happen until 1932.

No wonder HG is always tired. While reading his diaries, I've been coming across this statement almost daily in variations: "tired," "very tired," "dog-tired"; in English, *utterly tired!*, "completely exhausted." Even so, he still isn't satisfied with what he's doing: "I have an intense desire to be able to work more, achieve more, know more." We're all familiar with that. You break your back, you're completely worn out by the evening, and what have you actually accomplished? Very rarely enough to be able to write in your diary in the evening after a long day's slog: "Very satisfied!"

I've come across only one such entry: HG had thrown all his energy into the election campaign for Halberstadt town council, and the result is: "23 liberal-conservatives, 14 socialists, 2 Communists, 1 center," an almost complete reversal since the last election. And then, underlined in red in the margin: "*Very satisfied!*"

He's also satisfied with his regimental newspaper. It's called the *Prince Albrecht League—Federal Journal of the Associations of Prince Albrecht of Prussia (Lithuanian) Dragoon Regiment No. 1.* The man responsible is Colonel Osterroth (ret.), and HG must write and edit it—must he? He needs the paper for his sense of belonging, just as he needs all those officers' dinners in Berlin, although, or perhaps because, they always end in a terrible drinking bout. This paper appears four times a year, an insignificant pamphlet full of association news and war anecdotes; it's about Wilhelm I and Bismarck, the 1866 battle of Trautenau, in which the regiment played a glorious part, the World War battles in the Baltic and the "heroic retreat from Ukraine."

Everything in the paper yearns for the "proud" past. "A breath of the 1914 spirit blows through the masses" when some standards are being transferred somewhere or other and a 360-strong soldiers' chorus sings "in Old Prussian German." I can't follow HG here, and I don't want to, either. Because I know where it's leading. HG doesn't. Not at this point. I sense his need for marching in step, for flags and rousing music, but that all has to happen *in front of* a company, doesn't it? The "men" are the décor, the living backdrop for his own status, just as the headings in the regimental paper are carefully separated into officers, NCOs, and men. If it weren't so dangerous, it would be ridiculous.

In the regimental paper, whose business base HG has transferred to his company headquarters at the Woort, Franz Vitt puts in an appearance in April 1926. Not Gunner Vitt, of course, but a relation of the same name. The dead man's father has passed away, he writes, the war parents' welfare has long ago come through, and the mother has a small pension as a result. She is well, but her memory of Franz Vitt is still vivid, even though his death is now eight years in the past. HG gets stomach pains and goes home "feeling very ill," "great darkness everywhere." Should he send money? What should he reply? Nothing at all, says Else, and so does Kurt— "Father says it never stops! But don't I have to do something?" Kurt writes back to Franz Vitt, the letter hasn't been preserved. HG is ill for days—"it's all like yesterday." He seeks peace in a long ride through the Harz, falls from his horse, Ebony, and shatters his collarbone.

The gelding is sold, HG can't bear the sight of him anymore. The tireless Ernst Hothorn—I still don't know who he is—finds a replacement and gives HG "the Indian" as a present. Why does he do that, and what does HG do in return? Else is now riding again, and having a hard time with it, as she does with all kinds of sport. She's constantly falling from the horse, and her friend Cläreliese, who writes lovingly about Else in her memoirs, is impressed by her staying power: "Seldom have I seen anyone who skis so miserably, rides so badly, plays tennis so chaotically—but there was no holding her. She's ridden with every hunt, and we've sometimes feared for her life."

Riding with the hunt is the new game in the coming autumn. I've counted eleven hunts in 1927, and that remains unchanged over the next few years; the prerequisite is stubble fields. HG, very good rider, very fast horse, often takes the role of the fox. The pack is lent out for drag hunts, and the landowners around Halberstadt outdo one another in seeking out difficult stretches. Kurt, incidentally, by now almost sixty, bravely keeps up with the considerable pace. It's a festive sight, so many riders in red coats, the ladies in black, hunting horns, hip flasks, a huge amount of fun—riding is an excuse for getting smartly dressed and drinking a lot.

Else doesn't do any real hunting, by which I mean shooting. She goes along with HG when he's visiting the Yorcks in Schleibitz, for example, where the eastern nobility gathers, from the king of Saxony downward. The former king is still called "His Majesty."

Evening dress is worn at dinner, and the same is true at the hunt dinners in Halberstadt. Huge quantities of game are bagged—seven or eight hundred hares, and who's going to eat them all? HG has leased a hunt; in Else's "party book" I find her first hunt breakfast shortly before Christmas 1927: "25 guns, 18 beaters. 280 hares, 1 fox. Bean soup from 10 lbs salted bones, 5 lb salt meat (too much), 15 lb beans (12 would have done), 6 heads of celery and 12 leeks and 25 pairs of sausages. 100 slices of bread (much too much, half is quite enough) with Mettwurst, Leberwurst, meat in aspic, eggs, anchovies, mock hare, quark, tomato, cheese. Punch from 8 bottles of red wine, 6 bottles of tea, 1 bottle of arrack, just enough."

Let anyone try and tell me Else isn't methodical. She records everything—enormous parties with sixty guests and more in Bismarckplatz and small, elegant black-tie dinners. She lists everyone who was there and who wasn't and why ("ill"—"death"—"christening in Kiel"), she records, using terms ranging from "amusing" to "dragged slightly," the course of the evening in question, and how long the whole thing took—"to bed at half past three." People meet at her house for bridge, at several tables, or for musical soirees; she outlines the seating plans in her book and records her errors ("Lieutenant von Arnim and Fräulein von Gilsa—not good"), she weeds out certain people ("not to be invited again"), and lists what there was to eat and drink and how much.

Trained in Danish cuisine, she offers, for large parties at her bridge evenings and at concerts and lectures, "smørrebrød." This doesn't mean the plate-sized creations that used to be seen in Scandinavian restaurants with menus three feet long. What Else makes, or has made for her, is what today we would call finger food. Circles of bread are pressed out with sweet-wine glasses, and on them the most wonderful-looking delicacies are arranged in astonishing combinations. From her I know that disks of potato, with sour cream plus caviar and tiny slices of lemon, are very tasty on black bread. "No onions, Wibke, you'll spoil the caviar, and people will get bad breath!" Her rounds of cheese with black-currant fritters stand enthroned on a base of apple; the hare pâté with Cumberland sauce topped with crispy onions is a poem in itself.

Nowadays any caterer can supply such things. In those days the kitchen maids created these works of art (handmade puff pastry, filled with little pieces of kidney, for example). Else's cookery is famous in Halberstadt, and a source of great pride to HG. "Else's been working her magic again!" And not just in the kitchen. She illuminates the garden with lamps in the bushes and trees, lights loads of candles all over the place, lays the table for a feast, and makes the most opulent flower arrangements out of holly, rowan, and asters (according to the visitors' book). And she is radiant. I've found a photograph of her in which she is just thirty, and in it she's a really beautiful woman.

But it is now, of all times, that her husband betrays her. It creeps up slowly. Perhaps that's normal after six years of an intense marriage, and in the end both of them handle it in a "grown-up" way. With hindsight I wonder if they mightn't have been better off separating. But it's all very well talking about hindsight—they don't know what I know, and how much torment they are in for. They can't guess that this is the beginning of the end. I don't enjoy telling the story. It makes me sad. But this is how it begins: Cläreliese and Helmuth Hinrichs, parents of two small children, the third is on the way, move to Halberstadt in 1928. Helmuth, a dermatologist, takes over the practice of one of the fellow members of his student corps.

After the war Cläreliese writes in her memoirs: "Once on a journey from Magdeburg to Halberstadt Helmuth met a woman who had been the subject of wicked gossip in Halberstadt. This was 'young Frau Klamroth,' the daughter-in-law of Councillor of Commerce Klamroth, whose family was the most respected in the town. She was known for her unusually keen intelligence and the fact that she didn't fit in with ordinary Halberstadt society. Her maiden name is Podeus. Helmuth's first impression of her was that she chain-smoked and had particularly beautiful legs."

The Hinrichses pay HG and Else an official visit; then HG and Else dress themselves up to the nines, top hats and everything, and return the visit. I find the Hinrichses' name in Else's visitors' book for the first time on December 11, 1928, when they come for dinner. Cläreliese in her memoirs: "Having these two people as friends is one of the finest gifts of our life. We have shared everything for many years, joy, troubles and sorrow. Along with our children we almost formed a joint family, and our children are still friends with them." That's all true. I scattered petals at the wedding of the Hinrichses' eldest daughter in 1944, and I danced to Dixieland music with their youngest son, an afterthought like myself, at the Eierschale in Berlin in the late fifties. Else deeply mourned the loss of her friends, who died before she did.

Nonetheless this lovely story is only half true. Cläreliese and HG get involved with each other while Cläreliese is still pregnant. The Hinrichses' daughter, born in the spring of 1929, told me recently that she sometimes worried that HG might be her father. I was able to put her mind at rest. But at some point in late autumn 1929 there is justified concern that Cläreliese might now be pregnant by HG. In his diary, in secret Greek script, he writes about a night in a hotel: "Great fear of pregnancy." Three guesses what happened. Fortunately the problem resolves itself.

Such disasters, and all kinds of other things these people work out as a foursome, because—whether out of defiance or affection—Else and Helmuth have gotten together as well. It's a *ménage à quatre* that amazes me. Till Christmas 1930, for two whole years, they are inseparable. Hardly a day passes, unless one of them is traveling, without a quick morning visit or a shared afternoon nap. If HG and Else have guests, and the Hinrichses happen not to be there, HG goes away for two hours to visit Cläreliese. If Else wants to go skiing in the Harz mountains, she goes with Helmuth.

And they play bridge. Every evening they can spare, and they spare a lot, they play bridge. They don't read anymore, no stamp collecting, HG has stopped playing the piano—they just play bridge. In HG's diary I've stuck small yellow Post-its for every bridge evening, or every bridge *night,* rather, in 1929—I couldn't shut the book anymore. For 1930 I didn't even try. A proper bridge game takes time, and you have to concentrate like mad if you want to get anywhere. There's no room for small talk, let alone serious conversation. So why do the four of them play bridge like people possessed? I think that's exactly why. They aren't able or willing to talk. They're acting as though everything's perfectly normal. They don't want to let go of one another, but neither do they want to quit the field—two on this side, two on that—for their opposite numbers. They want to preserve their marriages plus the fine appearance of their friendship as a foursome.

Of course it doesn't work. In HG's diary I keep finding entries like "problems with Else," "Else on edge," and then expressions of irritation about Cläreliese in Danish—"she's affectionate and dazzlingly beautiful, but I long for my real wife." Nothing comes of it, because Else has thrown HG out of the common bedroom. Something similar has presumably happened at Helmuth and Cläreliese's. HG often visits Cläreliese late at night, and visits her "at her bed." That can hardly have been the Hinrichses' marital bed. How do they manage? Such closeness can't remain hidden from the staff. Cläreliese often picks up HG at his office for an afternoon stroll; "my little vice-wife" waits time and again at the station in Magdeburg or Hanover, where half of Halberstadt gets off the train. I don't even want to imagine how the gossip flourishes in that little town. Where's Kurt?

Twice during this period I find a reference to a dialogue between father and son. Once it was a "serious discussion," once it was "annoying." HG: "I must go my own way." With Cläreliese? I have nothing written by Kurt. Since they are both in Halberstadt and see each other at the office every day, they don't write letters to each other. Else has destroyed her notebooks, Cläreliese's papers went up in flames during a bombing raid on Berlin. I'm dependent on HG's notes, and what I read there reinforces my uneasy feeling:

this gang of four is absurd. Wherever HG and Else go, the Hinrichses are there already. They show up at the houses of Else's friends in Wismar and thereabouts, all of a sudden they're in Denmark, all four of them go on bridge trips for extended weekends with money from their bridge kitty.

Surely they must get on each other's nerves sooner or later! Indeed they do. "Scene with Cläreliese," I read, "major four-way crisis, outwardly we go on playing bridge as though nothing had happened." The mood of the group is "very strained," notes HG elsewhere, "tension with Else." The next day: "Else comes to her senses"—I'd have had him by the throat if he'd written that about me. "I'm very much in love, and still unhappy," he writes. On the day after Helmuth and HG had a man to man conversation about Cläreliese's possible pregnancy, "He's great!" HG writes in his diary, "bridge yesterday evening with the 'four in the know.' How strange it all is—terrible and beautiful!" Else writes: "Bridge with the Hinrichses. Curious evening." The whole thing's sick: between them they have six small children, who go scampering around together on the lawn in Bismarckplatz. The children sleep in one house, then another, the two families swap Danish au pairs, help one another out with ski clothes, cocktail shakers, cello music—we're one great big and oh so happy family, aren't we?

But they can't keep it up. On December 21, 1930, HG and Helmuth go and eat in the Hilarius, a restaurant in Halberstadt that people use for special occasions. The two gentlemen have never done anything like that before, but evidently this is manly business. After that it's all over. Not really over—the Hinrichses appear in the visitors' book in 1931 and later, but not at every party as they did before. HG's diary no longer records nocturnal visits "to Cläreliese's bed." The Hinrichs family kept a silver cigarette box on which HG had engraved the words: "You always return to your first love!" I think that sentence is brazen. But during the 1930s Cläreliese and HG did often seek and find opportunities to revive their former intimacy.

So Cläreliese is probably the first one to try to sort him out when he runs completely out of control: "Serious conversation with C. about my bleakest side. Went home very gloomy." Even if one could perhaps call the affair with the Hinrichses a proper love story such as occurs in the best families, by now one of HG's fuses has blown. Summing up the year of 1934, he establishes that his family is well, and he himself is "incredibly well, but there are often concerns about many other women around me." Whose concerns, please? He keeps meticulous records, even listing overlaps and the resulting conflicts. His records strike me as no different from his hunting successes, which I read about as well: "Overall 520. With 32 hares + one snipe I am king of the hunt." I don't feel like getting involved. He's a grown-up. It's his life. There is just one more story I need to tell that really does take my breath away.

There was, still is, a Danish family, unrelated to us, with whom Else and HG had happy holidays summer after summer. Their three daughters were nannies in Halberstadt, one after the other, and all three of them were among my favorite Danes. The eldest was my substitute mother for years until she died in 1968. The second, Anette, I visited in her nursing home in Copenhagen in 1999 just before her death. She was in Halberstadt in 1934 at the age of seventeen, an absolute beauty. I asked her about HG, and her old lady's face blossomed with radiant happiness. Such charm that man had, how loving he was, and how eternally in love with him she had been: "When he handed me my monthly wages, he asked me to kiss him for every ten marks. Else thought that was annoying, but it was lovely!"

Suddenly: "Jeg gik i seng med ham" (I went to bed with him). Her sister, also an old lady now, was sitting with me by Anette's bed, and we looked at each other in bewildered silence. And then Anette said that HG had asked her to let him know when she came home from her parties—there were always dances with the young lieutenants from the garrison—because in the end he was responsible for her. Else had gone away. One night, after she called "I'm back!" through the bedroom door, he had stretched out his hand and pulled her into bed. She had slept there till morning.

The bliss of that night glowed once more in Anette's face, all of a sudden she was seventeen again and very beautiful. She was also embarrassed, she even turned red, never having told anyone about it before. But now she was going to die soon anyway, and I was to know how wonderful the father had been: "Det var saa skønt og jeg har aldrig glemt det" (It was so beautiful, and I've never forgotten it). Her sister and I agreed that it was an enchanting story. What a man, if people's—particularly women's—eyes still shine at the mention of his name. But of course, and we agreed about this as well, the story was wishful thinking after so many years. Anette dreamed it into being.

She didn't. I find her under February 14, 1934, in HG's diary: "A. spent the night in my bed, very affectionate." Can you believe it? Parents send their underage daughter from the back of beyond in Denmark to Bismarckplatz, entrusting her to HG's and Else's care, and the man, twice her age, tempts the child into his bed! HG doesn't say that he slept with her, he says "in my bed," and I was so surprised that I didn't ask Anette for details. But it may have been just that. And yet—what can he know of a young girl's soul! HG doesn't know his way around his own. And that Anette should glow like that on her deathbed, sixty years later—could HG have known that would happen? Perhaps I'm more of a prude than I think I am. No. I have daughters. Else never found out about that business with Anette, thank God.

NINE

"We sing Hitler songs"

HG and Else have moved in the meantime. The flat on Domplatz was too small with three little children, so they're now stationed on the top floor of the Bismarckplatz house, even though Else has never been able to imagine living under the same roof as her parents-in-law. But it's obviously working fine, there's so much room that they don't even have to meet on the stairs—there are two of them. Flat-sharing is cheaper, because the business is nerve-rackingly wobbly. The international farming crisis has also had a serious effect on I.G. Klamroth; sometimes there's no money at all, sometimes there's too much, the bankruptcies of business partners tear big holes in the Klamroth books. HG, with his tendency to gloominess, notes "deep discouragement," "terrible depression" everywhere, but the crash of the New York Stock Exchange in October 1929 he hasn't even noticed.

Every young I.G. Klamroth needs his own innovation. For Kurt it was the superphosphate mine in Curaçao. HG has discovered the sweet lupine, a new feed plant the development of which requires significant investment and brings in a lot of money. In addition, Curaçao is spewing out decent profits, so there's no reason to feel too sorry for the anxious businessman: he buys a Horch 8, a top-of-the-range model among the cars of the day; soon afterward a black-and-red Mercedes convertible appears, and the company buys three plots of land for new warehouses. The mood in the country, however, is distinctly bleak. The numbers of unemployed are astronomical—in 1932 there are six million of them. The government ran out of money to pay for them long ago and has to enlist the help of a banking consortium. In the wake of the stock market crash in the United States, currency supplies melt away as foreign nations withdraw their loans; on top of everything there's a serious banking crisis, which brings many enterprises to their knees. It's amazing that I.G. Klamroth manages to emerge relatively unscathed.

The National Socialists are enjoying increasing election victories, first on a local, then on a regional level, particularly in the country and among the middle classes. But even so, not many people seem to take them seriously. What counts is class differences: the German Nationals, the major farmers, the Reich Association of German Industry, who advocate restoration, are worlds apart from the mob of the Nazis. You don't sit down at the same table with those people. As late as January 1932 the Ruhr industrialists refuse Hitler the financial aid that he requests.

But it would at least have been worth listening. The National Socialists have always said exactly what they wanted. Joseph

Goebbels on April 30, 1928: "We're entering the Reichstag to arm ourselves from democracy's arsenal. We will become Reichstag members in order to paralyze the Weimar mentality with its own support. If democracy is so stupid as to give us free railway tickets and allowances for this disservice, then that's their business." That's exactly how stupid democracy is. In the Reichstag elections in September 1930, the Nazi vote increases from 800,000 to 6.4 million; in 1928 they had 12 mandates, now they've got 107. Goebbels: "According to the constitution we're obliged only to observe the legality of the road, not the legality of the goal. We want to conquer power legally, but what we will do with that power once we've got it is up to us."

Like so many others, HG and Kurt fail to recognize how dramatic these developments really are. In Halberstadt and in Magdeburg, the Nazis aren't yet much in evidence and they're not their kind of people. Early in 1931 father and son, "out of curiosity," listen to Goebbels in the Berlin Sports Palace, and HG notes: "a ludicrous gathering. Father equally dismissive." From the sitting-room window of the "estimable mother" Körte he watches a street battle between the Brownshirts and the Communists and, repelled, jots a quote from Horace in his diary: "Odi profanum vulgus et arceo" (I hate and shun the common rabble).

Soon after this the rabble enters his house, introduced by Wolf Yorck and his wife, of all people. They show up at HG and Else's with five Brownshirts on their way to Bad Harzburg. How does this happen? In October 1931 the "national opposition" is having its meeting in the little spa town. They're all gathered together—German Nationals, Steel Helmet, Reich Land League (the large farmers), the Pan-German Association, a few industrial emissaries from the Ruhr (to find out how the land lies!), many members of formerly governing families, the ex–Reichsbank president Hjalmar Schacht, the former head of the army General Hans von Seeckt, all bundled together in the "Harzburg Front." They want to restore the Kaiser-Reich, evoking "our elected Reich President Hindenburg, that he might respond to the stormy urging of millions of men and women of the Fatherland, front soldiers," etc., etc. Meaning: we need a truly national government.

Hitler couldn't be excluded from this event, nor did they want him to be. Surely it must be possible to use this guy, with his enormous election victories, to harness the man who is bringing the national idea so skillfully to the simple people, the Pied Piper with his astonishing potential for the common cause? Hitler, just back from an exploratory meeting with Reich President Hindenburg, makes a fool of the assembled conservatives. That the cause is far from common he lets them know the moment his Brownshirts, the first ones to march, have passed the stage in immaculate formation. Hitler isn't interested in the parading Steel Helmet brigade, or whoever else might come along. He disappears ostentatiously, simply leaves without a word of farewell—he has nothing to do with the old conservatives. His is a young movement, forging into the future, that much is clear. He doesn't need the others.

Five of the marchers spent the night before in Halberstadt at the home of HG and Else, a short one, though, because they go on "debating" until the small hours of the morning over copious quantities of Mosel wine. HG: "I'm in a very bad mood." In the guest book they all politely express their gratitude for the "outstanding welcome"; "we'll repay it in the Third Reich," one of them observes correctly. "Billeting! On the occasion of the SA's Harzburg march." They all sign "Heil Hitler," even Wolf and Anne Yorck. The guest book extends from HG and Else's wedding until 1949. It's overflowing with friends, chance visitors, holiday children, family. None of that changes in the Third Reich. But the SA guests and Yorcks are the only ones in all those years to use the Hitler greeting, and HG feels "queasy."

Perhaps it's annoyance over the fact that Wolf Yorck has brought the *profanum vulgus,* the common rabble of Brownshirts, into his house, perhaps he's caught off guard because his friend has always been a political authority for him. But something starts to change from this moment on: no royal hunts with the Yorcks in Schleibitz, no hikes together in the Thuringian Forest. Unlike the Granzows, the "nobles" of Schleibitz, who became reliable friends and who make constant reappearances until the end of the war, the Yorcks creep from the documents, along with Wolf's "ideals." Only once do I find him in the guest book again, that's in 1934—Wolf is by then a Nazi member of the Reichstag. He writes a verse about the proximity of Berlin to Halberstadt, although this time he signs off without "Heil Hitler."

Two years later Wolf Yorck, in his capacity as Reichstag representative of the NSDAP, manages to get HG a ticket for the spectacular special meeting on March 7, 1936, in which Hitler announces the march of German troops into the demilitarized zone on the Rhine. The Reichstag was dissolved once again, so that the German people could give their "solemn agreement" in a new election on March 29. They did so with a 99 percent vote in favor. Whether the two friends ever spoke again after this event is not recorded, but at any rate there is no subsequent mention of Wolf Yorck. He dies in battle in 1944, shortly after HG's death.

After the visit of the uninvited guests, HG writes in his diary: "The Nazis set off for Bad Harzburg very early. Office, cosily drank champers with Schönfeld in the late afternoon and talked a lot, but very tired and rather drunk in the evening." It could be pure chance, but as far as I know, HG has never drunk anything with Dr. Schönfeld before. Schönfeld, the local pediatrician, is a Jew. In 1935 he immigrates to Palestine, and Else writes in the childhood diary: "We're all very sorry, and Jochen in particular is very perturbed about the issue that Jews clearly were human beings too."

HG perceives the atmosphere in the country as "increasingly muggy." The economic situation is disastrous, more and more people are going bankrupt, theaters are closing for lack of money, six of them in Berlin in early 1930, sixteen two years later. One hundred and four cinemas have closed down, and the number is rising. Violent encounters in the streets are getting out of hand: by October

1930 there have been forty-five political murders in Prussia, and that trend is rising too. In a number of federal states bans are introduced on assembly and uniforms. On the eve of the Constitution Day celebrations, some four hundred National Socialists appear in Berlin in standard white shirts and tear down the black-red-and-gold flags in the Schlossplatz, the square in front of Berlin Castle. At the opening of the Reichstag on October 13, 1930, the 107 NSDAP members march into the Plenary Hall in a solid block—wearing the brown shirts of the SA. At the same time troops of thugs are bullying Jewish passersby in the Kurfürstendamm, and demolishing Jewish shops.

These are the years in which the Reich Chancellors Brüning, Papen, and later Schleicher followed one another in quick succession, a bad, a poisonous time. I see HG helpless as he tries to find his bearings. The German People's Party is in its terminal decline following Stresemann's death, and given the general polarization all around, staying out of politics isn't an option. HG attends events held by the Order of Young Germans, a movement seeking, along with dissidents from the German National People's Party, to find a place in the more moderate bourgeois camp. He attends early meetings of the German State Party, which wants to occupy a liberal middle ground. HG visits Heinrich von Gleichen-Russwurm's Gentlemen's Club, an elitist conservative association of economists, politicians, and artists. Even being allowed in is a knightly accolade as far as the club's members are concerned.

I never find HG consorting with Social Democrats or trade unionists. Given his biography perhaps that isn't so strange, but you'd think at least he'd be curious! HG's reading, though, is by no means one-sided. Now that he doesn't have to play so much bridge anymore he gets around to reading again, catching up on Ernst Jünger and wondering about Arnolt Bronnen's novel set in Upper Silesia, *O.S.*—"Is he a fascist or not?!" But HG also wolfs down

Erich Maria Remarque's best-selling novel *All Quiet on the Western Front,* and is furious about Nazi demonstrations against the film: "Mob! And the police just stand and watch!"

One evening in Düsseldorf—HG is constantly traveling because of his sweet lupines—he goes with one of his ladies to a lecture on the poet Heinrich Heine. Anti-Semitic hooligans disrupt the event. HG: "Had to leave by the back door. Disgusting!" In June 1931 he visits an exhibition by Max Liebermann in the Munich Kunstverein: "Nazis hanging about outside the door. Things can't go on like this." The journalist Carl von Ossietzky writes in *Die Weltbühne:* "The National Socialist movement has a noisy present but no future." HG clearly doesn't much feel like helping to give it a future.

In the 1930 election he votes for something called the Deutsches Landvolk, the German Rural People's Party, which fits well enough. In the many elections over the next few years, HG rescues himself each time by opting for the also-rans, only in the town council election in Halberstadt on March 12, 1933, he gives his vote to the Battlefront Black-White-Red, a coalition of German Nationals, Steel Helmet, and nonaligned Conservatives. In this way he probably hopes—in vain—to keep the Nazis at bay in Halberstadt. I sense a strategy of avoidance as far as Hitler's men are concerned. What's he supposed to do, since the way to the Social Democrats or—heaven forfend—the Communists is barred to him? He isn't Catholic, so that excludes the "center," and he has no connections with Bavaria, which rules out the Bavarian People's Party.

In 1931 Else and HG drive without children to Austria and Italy in the black-and-red Mercedes convertible. I don't know how they managed to do this, since strict currency controls have been introduced in the meantime. I also don't know how they managed it without serious trouble brewing, as Else can't have been unaware of Cläreliese's successors. HG even brings some of them back to

Halberstadt, "so that Else can meet them." Odd manners as far as I'm concerned, but I've promised myself to stay out of this, and they both enjoyed the journey.

I'm mentioning this only because apart from references to "a lot of red wine," "magnificent landscape," "fanfare marches of the German marine band in St. Mark's Square, magnificent impression," and a "long night with my very lovely wife," I have encountered the finicky HG once again. He writes down his mileage—"via Quedlinburg-Jena to Hof, 257 km"—he records where they sleep—"Hotel de l'Europe, room 12"—he always does that. This man, unlike everybody else, doesn't take the train "at about ten." He leaves at 9:52 and arrives wherever he's going at 12:17. He picks somebody up from the station at 11:13. I know this persnicketiness from his summer diary for the holidays in Juist, and he was fourteen then. Do these two things fit together—the timetable fanatic and the womanizer? I fear so. There are monstrous examples. There's a lot of room in such a psyche.

The Reichstag election campaign in the summer of 1932 is the worst that Germany has ever experienced. Within six weeks there are 322 terrorist attacks with 72 fatalities and 495 serious injuries in Prussia alone. On Bloody Sunday in Altona on July 17, eighteen people are killed and sixty-eight injured in clashes between National Socialists and Communists. HG in his diary: "Who will create order in the country?!" Most people think the Nazis have what it takes. In the election of July 31 they increase their share of the vote by 19.4 percent, and their number of mandates rises from 107 to 230. They still don't have a parliamentary majority; one man still stubbornly braces himself against Hitler—Hindenburg considers it utterly unreasonable that he should "appoint the Bohemian corporal Reich Chancellor."

Let's cut a long story short. We know what happened. Hindenburg did appoint Hitler Reich Chancellor on January 30, 1933, a Monday, and it's unlikely that anyone in the Klamroth household bothered Schubert on this occasion. But that "everything, everything will change" is beyond doubt. Even in Halberstadt. Even for HG. He's in Berlin when it happens, getting bored at a meeting of the fertilizer committee, "when the sensational news comes in: Hitler is Reich Chancellor!!! In the evening, big torchlight procession in Wilhelmstrasse before Hitler and Hindenburg, which I experience from close range and in a life-threatening crush." And then nothing happens for a while. On Tuesday HG goes to his meetings, and to the cinema in the evening, I won't say with whom; the film's called *FP1 Fails to Reply*. On Wednesday he feels his oats and buys a scandalously expensive horse for 2,750 marks at an East Prussian auction. The animal's name is Lützow, HG didn't have much joy with him, "then home in the Mercedes in 3 hours 55 minutes."

On Thursday it's Else's thirty-fourth birthday—she's pregnant, "we talk a lot about Peter!" Good God! Else is given a photograph of Lützow—a familiar story, like fathers who buy their sons model railways to satisfy their own instinct for play. Guests in the evening, the Hinrichses are there, "to bed at three"—for some time the couple have been sharing a bed again.

On Friday of this week coachman Kückelmann fetches Lützow from Berlin, on Saturday HG rides him in the indoor arena for the first time—"he still needs a bit of work"—on the weekend the man takes to his bed with a bad cold ("read *The Battle for Rome*"—that's by Felix Dahn, a real flu thriller), on Monday he drives to the factory in Nienburg an der Weser, and so on. What did I expect? That HG would be aware of the assault on Julius Leber, editor in chief of the *Lübeck People's Paper* and SPD representative in the Reichstag, who suffers serious injuries when attacked by SS men armed with knives? The same night, seven people are murdered. Should HG prick up his ears because Hitler, upon entering the Reich Chancellery, goes on record as saying, "No power in the world will ever drag me out of here alive"?

HG doesn't hear anything more about Hitler until February 10, when he launches his election campaign—there's yet another election on March 5, supposedly for the last time. On this occasion Hitler delivers a speech in the Berlin Sports Palace—"People of Germany, give us four years and then deliver your judgment upon us." Hitler closes his appeal with the certainty that "the millions who hate us today will stand behind us and will join us in greeting the new dearly acquired German Reich that we have built together, the Reich of greatness and honor, the power and the glory. Amen." Gertrud too sits by the fire listening to the radio. She "is disgusted, there's no calming her." Certainly, nobody's ever used the Lord's Prayer in their election battle before. HG: "Father and I very skeptical."

HG on February 28, 1933: "Alarming news from Berlin, the Reichstag set alight by Communists yesterday, almost burned to the ground! What comes next?" What comes next is the closure of the German Communist Party's office, "protective custody" for all the party's representatives and officials, an emergency decree "for the protection of people and state," the forerunner of Hitler's Empowerment Law. Among those arrested are Carl von Ossietzky, the editor of *Die Weltbühne,* the authors Erich Mühsam and Ludwig Renn, the "frantic reporter" Egon Erwin Kisch, and lawyer Hans Litten. Bertolt Brecht flees to Prague with his family, the publisher Samuel Fischer has already left. In Prussia forty-seven senior administrative officials are suspended from service, the long-standing prime minister Otto Braun goes to Switzerland, Communist Party leader Ernst Thälmann is imprisoned. Goebbels in his diary: "Being alive is a pleasure again."

HG notes on March 4, 1933, a Saturday: "Theo Delbrück comes at 11:02 a.m. Rode Lützow in the afternoon, back to office. Deluge of election speeches on radio. 7 p.m. big torchlight procession through the town, 'Day of the Awakening Nation'—an awful lot of nonsense." Hitler's speech from Königsberg is broadcast on all loudspeakers, and ends with the Dutch hymn of thanks called "We Enter to Pray"—accompanied by the bells of Königsberg Cathedral. The next day is the Reichstag election—the Nazi Party, now amply enriched from the coffers of major industrialists, wins 288 of 647 mandates; 17,280,000 German people have voted for them. Hitler's "concept of legality" has worked. HG quotes Caesar: "Alea iacta est"—the die is cast.

Monday, March 6: "The week of the German counterrevolution has begun, not that we notice it here for the time being. Lots of work in the office, rode Lützow on the track at lunchtime, back to the office in the afternoon, home in the evening. The radio is the first to become entirely National Socialist." Tuesday, March 7: "Things are advancing consistently in politics: Reich commissars of the Nazis first in Hamburg, Bremen, Hessen, Baden, Württemberg. In the evening did the seating plan for our party tomorrow evening. Told Father of the possibility of a new grandchild—he's delighted." What are these Reich commissars about? It's as if the national government wants to depose a regional government and send along its own governor. According to the German constitution they can't do that. Hitler's Reich government could. The regions are being *gleichgeschaltet*—brought into line.

Wednesday, March 8: "At eight o'clock in the morning the local SA and the Steel Helmets fly the black-white-and-red and the swastika flag from the Rathaus—a profoundly significant symbol—but outwardly everything calm. Seventeen guests for dinner, official business, but still quite nice." What do they talk about over their morel soup and saddle of lamb and Italian red wine? Are they still relaxed, or is there already an atmosphere of fear? Do they joke about the brownshirted display of strength, or are they worried that gangs of hooligans might come to their homes, as they are doing all over the country? HG finally got his flag back, is he feeling better now? The two flags together are supposed to symbolize the "glorious past of the German Reich and the mighty rebirth of the German nation," as Hindenburg put it when he signed the Flags Act. Is HG faring well again now?

Friday, March 10: "Lots of work in the office. The whole town is adorned with black-white-and-red flags, in Berlin and some other cities they're burning the black-red-and-gold. But everything's astonishingly peaceful. In the evening, a wild speech by Göring on the radio." Saturday, March 11: "Morning office, after lunch rode Lützow outside for the first time, fell off once. In the evening with Else to a theatrical presentation by the garrison in the Elysium: 'Halberstadt Soldiers from 1650 to the Present Day.' Brilliant performances, marching bands. Afterward with Hinrichses at the SS." There it is again, the enthusiasm for marching bands, whether in St. Mark's Square in Venice or in the Elysium in Halberstadt, for parades in Königsberg or in the Cathedral Square long ago when half the town was on horseback on Sedan Day. But HG is a grown-up now—he's lost me.

Monday, March 13. "Office first, at 11:02 by train to Berlin. There, in the afternoon, discussion with Klemm from Potassium Chemicals, then at the Corn Credit Bank." Hindenburg appoints Joseph Goebbels minister for information and propaganda. Tuesday, March 14: "10:00 to S.E.G."—that's the Saatgut-Erzeugungs-Gesellschaft, or Seed Production Company, of which HG is a board member—"the sweet lupine contract is signed, 11:00 with Hertha"—that's one of his ladies—"round trip in a plane over Berlin, 12:22 back to Halberstadt—the government has ordered three days of flags. Friedenstrasse is called Hohenzollernstrasse again." The new interior minister, Wilhelm Frick, calls upon the regional governments to "avert the immigration of foreigners of Eastern Jewish nationality, and remove immigrants where possible."

HG on March 21: "Big 'national day of celebration'—Reichstag opening celebrated in the Potsdam Garrison Church. According to ruling from Goebbels, all shops must close. Radio transmission of the ceremonial act through loudspeakers in the Holzmarkt. Speeches by Hindenburg and Hitler. We work in the office until lunchtime, the holiday doesn't really accord with the height of the season. In the evening a big torchlight procession through the flag-bedecked streets of the town. Isn't there too much partying going on right now?" The next day: "Reichstag in the Kroll Opera House. The big Empowerment Law has been accepted; the way is now open for the 'Third Reich.'"

HG is slowly growing uneasy. March 29: "The first assembly of the new town councillors takes place today. Magdeburgerstrasse becomes 'Hindenburgstrasse,' Klussstrasse is 'Adolf Hitler Strasse.' At home in the evening, glued in stamps, it's a bit of a distraction from the inflammatory politics." March 30: "Political matters lie like a dark shadow over everything: atrocity propaganda abroad, German defense boycott against the Jews. In the evening spent an hour with old Jacobsohn, for whom I feel infinitely sorry. No solution."

"Atrocity propaganda"—that refers to the keen protests all around the world against the pogroms of the last few weeks. In "revenge" Hitler has ordered his Party formations to begin a general boycott against Jewry at "ten o'clock on the dot" on April 1, against "Jewish shops, Jewish goods, Jewish doctors, Jewish lawyers." The man in charge of the action is Julius Streicher, editor of the anti-Semitic campaigning paper *Der Stürmer,* and chairman of the "Central Committee of the NSDAP to defend against the Jewish atrocity and boycott propaganda." And Jacobsohn? He's HG's colleague in the employers' association. Shortly before Christmas 1932 I still find him mentioned in the diary as the host of a "very enjoyable evening—we always like going there."

When the barbarism breaks out, HG is in Berlin: "From 10:00 official boycott of the Jews with unpleasant acts of terror by the NSDAP. Meetings in the morning, back at 1:48, black-tie birthday with Jüttners, helpless discussion. Should we join the Stahlhelm?" That's the Steel Helmet Organization, the League of Front Soldiers founded in 1918 by Franz Seldte, and not really to be touched with pliers. But no Nazis. Not yet. Franz Seldte is now minister of labor in the new cabinet. The next morning, Sunday, they all travel to Magdeburg to listen to this man Seldte in the Harmonia Hall: "Everybody of any standing was there, but we're still none the wiser." Office in the afternoon, then guests at home—"Mother is profoundly depressed and deeply torn about political developments, Jewish boycott and so on.—Wild times!"

I've been creeping around my computer for days now. I can't go on writing. I'm frightened. I'm frightened about the next entries in HG's diary. Haven't I said over and over again that I can't paint him other than he is? It's his life. He paid for it. I must keep out of it. I'm just telling the story. But I've gone with him for so long, couldn't he just have objected? . . . No. He couldn't. OK, then— April 3: "Evening, employers' association re poss. expulsion of Jew Jacobsohn—sign of the times."

The Jew Jacobsohn. HG isn't an anti-Semite. I can confirm that over the years. And now, the Jew Jacobsohn. HG is on the board of the employers' association—couldn't he have . . . ? No. He couldn't. There's been a ruling bringing everything "into line." The Reich Association of German Industry has just reported its accomplishment: "Semitic members are excluded." What about resigning from the association himself? Who would benefit? I would. April 4: "Afternoon after serious consideration visited Gerlach, new Nazi council chairman, to sound him out. Worked on sales conditions for sweet lupines until ten in the evening."

Wednesday, April 5: "To the office early. Considerable money worries. At lunchtime visited Party member Otto Lehmann, regional representative, to sound him out politically." April 12: "All hell is loose politically. The fire of revolution is blazing, and has now caught me as well!" April 13: "Morn. first office then board meeting of employers' association, in which because of political developments Herr Jacobsohn, as a Jew, must be expelled. Afternoon office till late. Letter to Otto Lehmann about NSDAP." Am I alone in hearing a change in the language? This is HG's private diary, in which he writes "because of political developments . . . Herr Jacobson, as a Jew." Is someone whistling in the dark here, is he paying his dues for initiation?

Thursday, April 20: "Visit by Party members Ogdenhoff and

Lehmann. Evening, Hitler's birthday celebrations in Domplatz and the Municipal Park Hall." The charm of these year-by-year diaries lies in the fact that you can look back and forth to see what happened on the same day in different years. After this, Hitler's birthday isn't mentioned anymore in HG's notes. April 21: "Evening with Otto Heine about Stahlhelm issues." April 23: "Afternoon by car to Wegeleben, discussion of army matters." What's HG up to? And why is he in such a hurry? April 27: "Ogdenhoff at my house in the afternoon; at his request I do sign my application to join the NSDAP, as they're closing membership after May 1. In the evening, chamber music at Otto Heine's. Kurt"—that's Kurt junior, HG's brother—"plays Beethoven very beautifully. Huge party. Goes on till 2:00." The Heines are a similarly lavish family with a lavish house in Halberstadt. It will all have been very festive. HG's celebrating.

And he means it. In Magdeburg he talks to "Party member Fahrenholz about working with the NSDAP," and things really get going on May 1. HG in his diary: "National Labor Day: early ceremonial flag hoisting (swastika!) at the Woort, then a procession through the town, speeches in Domplatz, huge numbers of participants. 12:30 in the afternoon departure of our whole workforce (103 people) in three coaches. Coffee in Trautenstein, dinner in Waldmühle near Blankenburg with music, performances, an address by me and Hitler speech on the radio." Hitler's harnessing the Almighty for the Party again: "Lord, the German nation is strong again in its will, strong in its persistence, strong in its willingness to bear all sacrifices. Lord, we will not abandon Thee! Now bless our fight for our freedom, and with it our German people and fatherland."

Incomprehensible today. I've read Hitler speeches, and more important I've heard them. The effect of the yapping gnome is a mystery to me. But I wasn't there, I was brought up differently, partly thanks to the yapping gnome. Nonetheless, I'd like to know what was driving HG. A few things come to mind. One, that everyone was jostling to be a part of it all. Class difference has ceased to be an issue, the crème de la crème, and not only of Halberstadt society, is falling in line. All the bridge players, the tennis partners, the hunting companions from Else's guest diary have suddenly joined. The ones who might resist at all are workers, Social Democrats and Communists. That's not HG's turf. The churches, or most of them, are jubilating their approval. Not a bad address, either.

If you're going to join, do it early, HG probably thought, like he joined the army just before being drafted, so that he could become a Junker rather than an ordinary soldier. It's too late to be one of the "aristocracy," the ones who have been in the Party since the very start — and SA leader Ernst Röhm and others found out what that was worth when they were murdered in 1934. But we're not quite there yet. So: get in there early, or all the leading positions will have gone. And HG sees himself standing at the head of a company, not in the third or the seventh row among the faceless ranks.

It's not bad for business, either. Not only the local estate owners, but above all the people in the Reichsnährstand, the "Reich Food Estate," a body with which the company will from now on be involved whether it wants to or not, are Party members. But I would be doing HG an injustice if I suggested that he'd joined only out of opportunism. That would have been bad enough. But I don't think he sold his soul for the sake of a practical advantage. He gave them his soul gladly, I fear. He's catching up with something that was interrupted in 1918. There's a straight line linking "Three cheers for Kaiser and fatherland," the war games on Juist, and now the "great national revolution."

There was nothing but humiliation on all sides: the shameful outcome of the war that had ended in dishonor, the return of the regiment to Tilsit at dead of night, the absurd Versailles Treaty, the harassment in the French-occupied Ruhr, the horrors of inflation, and the breakdown of all norms in the years of murder and terror.

The republic ruined HG's faith in parliamentary democracy, if he ever had such a thing, and now a battered nation crowds behind one man who is telling the whole world: We are somebody again, and we're going to show you.

HG has no intellectual defense against this. He's incapable of thinking outside ideas of national greatness and the harm it has suffered. The inhabitants of the "enemy countries" can't do that either. Looking beyond one's own borders is considered "internationalist," and that means Communists. Besides, HG doesn't have the imagination—who did!—to think what this Third Reich might turn into. He had been skeptical for a long time, and he remains so. The "common rabble" hasn't changed in terms of its unscrupulousness and its brutality. But HG thinks—how many people thought the same!—that he might be able to do something. Over the next few weeks and months the diary is full of attempts to contribute. "Party assembly—desolate impression," "badly prepared event—something has to happen." He spends evenings writing papers; once he devotes a whole night to an "open letter to Dr. Goebbels." Whatever may have been in there, I hope he never sent it.

Much later, in the commemorative volume published for the 150th anniversary of I.G. Klamroth in 1940, HG puts into words something that he had struggled to understand: "We sensed the change in the situation against the time just before 1933—regardless of all suppositions and proposed amendments in policy, the National Socialist leadership stuck firmly and unerringly to the principle it had recognized as correct." This refers to crude interventions in agricultural trade, but the pattern's always the same. The Nazis do whatever they want to do. They haven't been waiting for someone like HG. Nothing will come of his supposed leading position within the Party. The man is an ornament for the "movement" because he's prominent in Halberstadt, otherwise he should stay out of it, and above all keep his mouth shut. He's an irritant.

HG: "NSDAP assembly. Sharp public dispute with Party member S about tariff negotiation. Followed by unpleasant conversation." Small wonder. There are no tariff negotiations any longer. Tariffs are decided by the "German Labor Front," period. But keeping his mouth shut is a new one to HG. On May 30: "Dinner at the Association of Central German Employers in Magdeburg with interesting discussion. The national revolution has entered the crisis that everyone expected—but we will help it through." There's something touching about it.

Perhaps that's why HG goes to the SS. It is, after all, the elite of the Party, moreover it's a military group, there's respect for officers there, he's familiar with that. Previously there had been two conversations with senior Party officials "about high-ranking service in the NSDAP," clearly without a result. HG doesn't want to work his way up. He wants to get things moving himself—he doesn't want to be moved. In the SS he is to set up an echelon of riders, and becomes leader of Reserve Storm 4/21. Does he know that he's joining a gang of murderers?

To start with, the SS means hard work for HG. From now on his weekends are completely devoted to it. His boys have to learn to ride properly, and if they get drunk there's trouble. This results in a lot of paperwork, superiors come to inspect HG's riders—why do you need horses to murder people? HG's troop doesn't commit murder, at least not while he's in charge. I'd know. But they do parade. Their uniforms are immaculate, HG had some made for himself. Can that be true? An intelligent, adult man puts on a uniform and that makes him happy? At any rate these uniforms get a mention even though space in the diary is tight: "in SS uniform to Magdeburg," "party in the officers' mess, me in SS uniform," again and again. Nonetheless, there are no photographs of him in this black outfit.

HG gives up the Reserve Storm in July 1934, shortly after the so-called "Röhm putsch," in which the SS were the murderers. I don't know whether his withdrawal has anything to do with this. He doesn't leave the organization, and I can't tell whether he could have done so painlessly. But from this point onward he records almost no SS activity, and barely a single Party event. There are no photographs showing HG wearing the Party badge, and I haven't found a letter from him in which he signs off with the words "Heil Hitler" or "Sieg Heil." Such letters must have existed, both in business and in wartime duty, but privately they didn't.

HG becomes just a name in the files, and blossoms again only in the spring of 1935 with the introduction of universal conscription and the buildup of the Wehrmacht. As a reserve lieutenant he's always off on maneuvers, and is quickly promoted to senior lieutenant, then to captain, no longer with his dragoons, but with the Twelfth Infantry Regiment, which has been based in Halberstadt for generations. He enjoys it, and twice in his diary I find the word "pity!" when exercises are over, in the Senne camp in Münster and elsewhere.

HG declared the burden of business as the reason for his withdrawal from the Party and the SS—and that burden is indeed considerable. The new Reich Food Estate, a conglomeration of all sectors of the food industry, from the farmer to the baker, is choking the companies. With its state "fixed price legislation," all entrepreneurial leeway is blocked, it's hardly possible to make a profit, the agricultural trade is reduced to the sole function of distribution and storage. HG and his colleagues struggle against this on every level, but without success.

In his diary he rages: "fixed price legislation is having a devastating effect!" "We're short of cash. Because we can't economize, there's no money coming in. What am I supposed to pay the workforce with?"—that's a hundred people. "Suggestion from the Agricultural Trade League: fire half the workers." "We can manage a lot, but will we make it through this situation?" "The Agrarian Political Office wants to confiscate our sweet lupines." That'll be the day. HG prevails: "Dreadful negotiations, finally horse-trading over storage capacity. Sweet lupines saved." This time the company nearly went to the dogs.

TEN

On holiday in Denmark

There's a family reunion again, this time in 1933. I can't leave it out, but it's hard for me to write down what's happening now. The clan meets on May 28, 1933, in Kloster Gröningen. That's the property of Kurt's brother Joseph Klamroth and his wife, Minette, known as Nettchen, the one in the song about Auntie Nettchen and Charlemagne. Thirty-five members out of sixty-nine are present, and everything proceeds in an orderly fashion: honoring of the dead, assessment of the budget, foundation funds, weddings, christenings, confirmations, end of the main assembly at 2:10 p.m.

At 7:30 p.m. it is reopened with an emergency application from cousin Willy Busse. But he's already left, and on his behalf HG proposes the adoption of the so-called Aryan paragraph into the constitution of the Klamroth Family Association. HG's explanation according to the minutes: "From the genealogical tables it may be seen beyond dispute that all members of the family association are of purely Aryan descent. We are rightly proud of this racial purity of our clan, which must also be preserved in the future." The purpose of the Aryan paragraph is to ensure that a member who marries a non-Aryan forfeits his membership: "In the present time this is also important for the members since the demonstration of Aryan descent is now often required for particular professions." This is how the urgent nature of the application is explained.

In the following debate, no objections are raised, the motion is carried, the session ends at eight. Note in the minutes: "the formal text of the paragraph should be ascertained from the Reich Interior Ministry, and the chair may make the inquiry." On August 17, 1933, "Aryan Paragraph 9a" is entered in the association registry at Halberstadt local district court: "People shall be deemed 'non-Aryan' if they are descended from non-Aryan, and in particular Jewish parents or grandparents. It is sufficient if one parent or one grandparent is non-Aryan." The Nuremberg Laws will not be passed until two years later.

Thirty-five family members, decent people, aren't they? No objections from anyone. The whole thing is over in half an hour. And what about HG? Couldn't he? Yes, this time he could have said to his cousin Willy Busse, "My dear Willy, you had better do this on your own. And if you ask me, forget this rubbish!" But even in actually delivering Willy Busse's request, HG could have said at the "emergency session": "Cousin Willy wants this, I don't. It is true that the individual Aryan certificate requires work, but our family honor remains undamaged." He doesn't say this. He actually says nothing. In the evening they sing: "May has come, the people have risen, and our family has risen too; so let us all shake hands as before, to the fatherland let us be true." HG and Else's children are allowed to put on a charming little performance. Jochen, who is seven, appears in SA uniform: "Heil Hitler, might you the chronicler be, so devoted to our family tree?"

Jews forbidden—premature obedience. There is no cause, nothing anyone has to react to. Aryan certificate! Kurt could simply produce it from his archive, five and more generations back, if anyone needed it. Emergency? Hitler has been in office for just four months, and even if the Nazis work at a breathtaking pace, couldn't one wait and see before becoming their lackey without any necessity? Good Lord, I thought I'd used up my disgust and rage in all those years, my horror at the indifference, the ingratiation—it took only half an hour! Not a single objection—in HG's diary and Else's childhood diaries the Aryan paragraph isn't even mentioned. And there's nothing about the book burnings, either, which took place less than three weeks ago. Authors they've both just read were among those whose works were destroyed: Remarque, Döblin, Glaeser, Heine, Kästner, Kerr—don't they care?

Instead, the childhood diaries record what an exciting time this is "for you," with almost daily torchlight processions and parades, how festive all the flags look, the marching columns enthusiastically singing the new Hitler songs "which you all know by heart"— the *Storm and Battle Songbook of the NSDAP* is published on March 23, 1933. Six months later, one and a half million copies have been sold. Else suddenly starts writing in old German Sütterlin script, can you believe that? She's always written like her father, asserting her expansive Latin letters against HG's, Kurt's, and Gertrud's Gothic script. And now she's writing Sütterlin. Lucky her hair's so fluffy, or she'd have grown it into plaits!

Are they all out of their minds? What's up with Kurt? First Kurt has in his accurate handwriting eternalized the minutes of the family reunion in the chronicle without personal commentary. But then he composes a nineteen(!)-page letter to a boyhood friend in

America, explaining the German world to him. It was in chaos, he writes, as long as the Jews had a say: "In 1928, in the major banks alone 718 senior posts were occupied by Jews, and among the leaders of the Socialists and the Communists the majority were Jews as well. Jews had the whole of the left-wing press in their hands, the universities were dominated by them, in 1928 40 percent of the professors in the philosophy faculty in Göttingen were Jews, in the law faculty 47 percent. What people would consent to be dominated in the long run by a small minority of foreign origin?"

But now salvation has come, the "national revolution under the leadership of Adolf Hitler" has united the torn and foreign-dominated populace, "as in 1914 the spirit of the German people flares up beneath the black-white-and-red colors, and the unity of the Germans comes powerfully to light." Three cheers for Kaiser and fatherland—oh Kurt! And as to unity, Else too celebrates in the children's diaries: "Big speech of peace by Hitler in the Reichstag on May 17, even the Socialists agree, we are a united people." What she doesn't know is that Interior Minister Frick has brazenly threatened the Social Democrats with the murder of their imprisoned comrades if the faction should dare to abstain on the passage of the peace resolution. What might have made Else suspicious comes a month later: on June 22, 1933, the SPD is banned, and many of its representatives disappear into prison or the concentration camps.

On August 10, 1933, the child that is born isn't Peter, but Sabine, another textbook delivery lasting just an hour. The midwife must have gone to bed fully dressed to be able to help at all. According to the brief descriptions of these births, Else must have felt only a brief dragging pain, then a few contractions, and that was it. Enviable! In HG's diary there's no more word about Peter, just his own "great, great joy and afterward happy walk to the registry office, newspapers etc." Over the next few days he keeps his days in the office short; "went home," he writes, and "marveled at Sabine."

She's christened on October 14 in the chapel of the Liebfrauenkirche, in "a very atmospheric ceremony." Once again it's followed by a dinner for twenty people, not including the bigger children, although the ham in burgundy goes cold because everyone has to listen to Hitler on the radio, explaining Germany's withdrawal from the League of Nations. This in turn has something to do with the Geneva Disarmament Conference, and the growing mistrust of the former enemies about Nazi Germany's fidelity to the treaty. HG calls the speech "impressive," Else finds it "fabulous," and the Germans are asked to go to yet another referendum on November 12 while at the same time electing a new Reichstag. The result is overwhelmingly in favor of the NSDAP—92.1 percent. However, the Nazis are the only party anyone can vote for. The others have all been dissolved.

In his posthumous *Story of a German,* Sebastian Haffner describes how the "entire façade of normal life remained almost unchanged, cinemas, theaters, cafés, all full," and Halberstadt is no different. It's only my horror that in hindsight feels the world should have stopped turning. But the people I'm trailing seem to be in a good mood. They scent the fresh air of a new dawn. Not quite. Twice I find in HG's diary the phrase "defiant optimism," and both instances follow on from meetings with Party members. His account of Sabine's baptism, which turns into a "long and cosy evening until 2:00," even over cold burgundy ham, concludes: "Contrast between inside and outside." Haffner writes: "Of course one couldn't see the secret trait of madness, fear, and tension," and I doubt whether the Klamroths and their friends realized that. Else, however, notes in the children's diary: "We are living in a very intense time, and I am stressed and nervous." She would not have known why.

But the woman really is up to her ears! In the course of 1933, she puts up fifty-one visitors, not including dinner guests—the hardest thing for me would have been having to talk to them all. Despite all this she manages to organize a lot for the children—she can't have invented it all for the diaries, because she's copying it out from her calendar and she hates made-up stories. With the children—lots of children, guests' children, holiday children—she goes skiing, skating, swimming. She complains that horse riding doesn't work with the children, because the horses aren't suitable for children. She plays games with them—grudgingly! I sympathize with her. They play Poch (a card game with counters) and mah-jongg. They do a lot of singing—in harmony, canons, and, most recently, Hitler songs.

Above all Else reads out loud, all year, but of course predominantly in winter. There are rituals, even I experienced them after the war. With the first snowfall, there were baked apples and fairy tales by the fireplace—in my day it was a round iron stove. At Advent each Sunday had its own songs—by heart, please, and all the verses: still a bit rough on the first Sunday of Advent, with "I Saw a Ship A-Sailing," "As Mary Walked through a Thorny Wood," rising to "Every Year Again" and "Raise Up the Door," to "In dulci jubilo," "Quem pastores laudavere," "A Rose Has Blossomed," "A Happy Day Is Born," and "My Heart Leaps with Joy." These last are allowed only just before Christmas.

One candle per Advent Sunday, gingerbread whose dough had been standing for weeks on the shelf already, then gradually a piece of marzipan and candied walnuts—and Christmas tasks. Children aren't allowed to give bought presents, so they get to work cutting and sawing and gluing. I wouldn't want to know how many shriveled, hand-woven needle cases and jigsawed keyboards were distributed every year. Else doesn't do handicraft, Else reads. In 1933 it's *Debit and Credit* by Gustav Freytag—I wonder why all the generations of Klamroth children were tormented with that awful book? In 1934 it's Paul Keller's *Holidays from the Self,* already somewhat tainted by "Strength Through Joy," the state-run worker vacation program.

Christmas Eve is a ritual as well. The tree is decorated on the evening of December 23, but only "grown-up" children beyond their confirmation are allowed to take part. The Christmas room is locked. At half past three on the twenty-fourth there is a family Christmas party in a dark place far from the Christmas room, just the candles burning on the Advent wreath. Songs, recorders, poems. The Christmas story in Luke, Chapter 2, all three parts, each delivered from memory by one of the children, with sung canons in between—"Let Us Go to Bethlehem," "Honor to God in the Highest," and the last song, "Come, Little Children." They don't come, they have to wait, quiet as little mice, until the bell rings in the Christmas room, a heavy, richly decorated brass bell that later summoned my own daughters into the Christmas room each year.

Then off they go through the pitch dark house, up the stairs, down the long, long corridor, slowly please, with the open door at the end of it to reveal the ceiling-high Christmas tree with all its burning candles. HG does duty at the piano: "The Lights Burn on the Christmas Tree," they all sing on the way, five verses before they get there. One more song keeps them in a state of feverish excitement, standing in a half-circle around the tree—they're not allowed to turn around and see what's on the Christmas tables. "The Bells Never Sound Sweeter," HG thunders at the piano, no other Christmas carol can be so easily schmaltzed, and in this highly vocal family the top and bottom voices dance around to make it sweeter.

It still isn't time for presents, because now everyone has to hurry to mass in the cathedral, the incredibly beautiful Halberstadt Cathedral. Again all the carols, the organ roaring away across the big square, enormous bells, lots and lots of people. "Happy Christmas!" On the way home through the crunching snow, the children count the Christmas trees lit up in the windows, and back at the house it's time to distribute the presents, downstairs with grandparents Kurt and Gertrud. They have two Christmas trees, and in between them an impressive crib with filigree wax angels, which float in the branches in their dozens. Above the Sunday stairs hangs the big Moravian Christmas star. Here Gertrud and her harmonium step into action—it's a while before the children can finally pounce on their dolls' houses and rocking horses and the plates of delicious cakes. So that everybody knows which one belongs to whom, there are gingerbread hearts on the present tables, with names written in icing. All through Christmas they are defended against HG, but in vain. He always bites the tips off. All of them.

And there are lots of people, rarely fewer than twenty, each with their own gingerbread hearts. Late in the evening they eat carp in Kurt and Gertrud's big dining room, solemnly, on Meissen porcelain, in dark suits; in 1937 I find them wearing black tie or uniform. Else keeps a Christmas book, painstakingly detailed despite her baroque handwriting—Sütterlin script hasn't made it this far—with names, presents, expenses for every year. I'll take 1934 as an example, but it could be any year. Staff come first, the two maids, Erna and Anneliese, get different presents, but of the same value. Erna: apron—7.65, suitcase—8.90, batiste—6.55, blanket—2.25, dress—4.00, soap—0.95, children's book—3.00: 33.30 reichsmarks altogether. Anneliese is given writing paper and kitchen towels and all sorts of things of that kind, which come to 31.30 reichsmarks. There's a Lucie, an Ella, a Hilde, a Frau Koch. Hermann (that must be coachman Kückelmann) is given a pair of underpants and a shirt, collar, and tie, coming to 3.85 reichmarks; in addition he gets a cake and a hare.

At last I know where all the hares end up, and why HG has put the relevant hunt plus breakfast three days before Christmas. Every Tom, Dick, and Harry is given hares, and it makes sense. Family and friends are in the book—hares, books, games, balls. Nephew Haymo is given "mug, patent shoes" for 50 pfennigs; the Hinrichses' daughter Antje gets a "doll" for 85 pfennigs. The Danish au pair, Anette—exactly! the one with the light in her eyes—gets a "fox-fur" for 15 reichsmarks, "soap, sponge" for 2.30, "collar" for 1.40: 18.70 reichsmarks altogether.

In the book I find a list: married male employees with children, married male employees without children, unmarried male employees without children, married female employees with children, married female employees without children, single female employees without children. The same for the manual workers and for seven business premises, a total of ninety-four people. I haven't counted the children. Everyone gets something, Christmas stollen, books, toys, sweets. Else shares this chore with Gertrud, and everyone gets a handwritten Christmas greeting. They must have started in October.

Else's Christmas book lists the things that the children made for their grandparents and godparents, and there's also a list of forty-three friends who receive either small packages or Christmas greetings. Then there's the lineup of the Christmas pastries: "4 species (roll thinner), Jew-cakes, sugar cookies, shortbread, vanilla crowns, plain nut macaroons, macaroons, coconut macaroons, egg-yolk cakes, sugar cake—½ portion enough, princess almonds, almond mountains, candied almonds, candied walnuts, nougat (too hard), marzipan, stuffed dates—not enough to last till New Year's Eve—gingerbread house." The presents for the children: "Jochen—steam engine for 10 marks, tool box for 7.50, watermill for 3 marks," and so on. Similar expenses for the daughters; HG gets "cuff links for 26 marks, tobacco and pouch for 3.75, patience cards for 3 marks," and so on. NB: Else does this every year. A nightmare!

"We must all help with our feeble powers to make Hitler's heavy burden lighter," Else writes in the children's diary in 1934, and then: "Hitler has just carried out a big, bloody, but doubtless necessary cleansing within the SA and the Party, let's hope that this will be the last act of this kind." HG writes in his diary: "Alarming political news—Chief of Staff Röhm arrested and deposed by Hitler, General Schleicher and his wife arrested and shot, 7 high SA leaders, Heines included, summarily shot for mutiny!!!" Officially eighty-three people, including Röhm, are killed in this bloodbath, among them fifty members of the SA. In fact there were probably more. The background to this is the leadership claim of the SA, with its 4.5 million members, as against the Reich Army, and if you are to believe the newspapers of the day, Hermann Göring spoke from the soul of the people when he addressed the Reichstag: "We always approve of what our Führer does."

Eighty-six-year-old Hindenburg dies on August 2, 1934. HG: "We all feel as though a member of the family is missing." Hitler appoints himself Reich president and Reich Chancellor in one, creating the new position of Führer and Reich Chancellor. On the very same day the soldiers all over the country swear a new oath, and not to the constitution or the fatherland: "I swear by God this sacred oath that I will render unconditional obedience to Adolf Hitler, the Führer of the German Reich and people, supreme commander of the armed forces, and that I shall at all times be ready, as a brave soldier, to give my life for this oath." That's it. It was that oath that made resistance to Hitler so difficult.

But that is not the question now. The Germans are asked again to nod at this one in yet another referendum on August 18, and in fact a considerable number of people refuse to do so. Of the valid votes, 10.1 percent are nays, 4,300,429 altogether. Adding the invalid votes to this—almost 900,000—in 1934 more than five million voted against. But what of the 38 million votes in favor? The majority are celebrating. In the children's diaries Else repeats herself excitedly: "Unity! Who would have thought, five years ago, that the country would come together like this!" But the country is also being drummed together: through loudspeakers, through the radio, with *oom-pah* in the streets. HG and Else's children stand in line at the roadside, waving little flags, they march in step with the Hitler youth, swing clubs with the gymnastics team in the Cathedral Square, and recite vows of loyalty by the nightly campfire.

Every first Sunday in the month they eat stew, and hand over the money they have saved to the Winterhilfswerk—the "winter aid work." If Else can't think of anything to throw into the pot, they all go to the garrison or the SS barracks, where stew is bought from the field kitchen—the children, Else claims, find the cooking equipment exciting. They also hold parties in Bismarckplatz, often and with a certain extravagance. Kurt and Gertrud return from a sea voyage to Curaçao and Trinidad, and are welcomed by seven grandchildren, all transformed with cocoa into little Negroes, with bast skirts around their hips, thick chains around their necks— they look as though professional costume designers have been at work. But seven little Negroes rather than the traditional ten? No problem. Someone rhymes three of them away:

> *Ten little Negroes in South America*
> *They saw Heinz Horn's motorboat*
> *And all then cried "Hurrah!"*

> *Ten little Negroes, and none of the ten*
> *Had ever seen a white gran*
> *Or grandpa until then*

> *Ten little Negroes, all of them start cryin'*
> *One cried too loud and burst*
> *And then there were nine*

> *Nine little Negroes, shark-fishing from a crate*
> *One got eaten up of course*
> *And then there were eight*

> *Eight little Negroes stole the ship's cook's leaven*
> *One got caught and skewered*
> *And then there were seven.*

The seven then relate, in song, of course, what the sea voyage was like, and their song concludes: "Seven little Negroes like white people as much as that / And now they all want to stay in Halberstadt!" It's fun, not only for the children. After the war there were still dressing-up boxes in the attic in Halberstadt—I can see myself in a crinoline as the princess with the swineherd.

Germany celebrates a huge holiday on March 1, 1935—the Saarland has come "home to the Reich" after fifteen years as a League of Nations mandate and a referendum in which 91 percent of Saarlanders—voluntarily, really!—voted in favor. HG in his diary: "Great German victory! Flags out!" Else describes what it looks like: "We've lit up the house, and we all spent the evening at the torchlight procession. You children were there too, it made a very big impression, the big fires in the Cathedral Square, and the torches, which were all lit on command, and the wonderfully illuminated churches and the patriotic songs—none of us will forget it easily!"

To intensify this uplifting feeling, Else and HG, along with the bigger daughters and the Danish au pair, take a whistle-stop tour of "our beautiful fatherland." They really speed through; I suspect that HG wants to try out his new Mercedes—an "11/60," if that means anything to anyone. It's a convertible, as I can see in the film they shot, but I can't tell why they had to drive with the roof down at Easter, wrapped up in caps, blankets, and motoring goggles. What I do see in the film clips: HG has grown a mustache, a real little Hitler 'tache under his nose. It doesn't last, he's just trying it out. He looks revolting.

They don't miss a thing—Marburg, Giessen, Frankfurt, along the Rhine to the "German Corner," up the Mosel to Trier, then to the Saar and the new Franco-German border. Else: "It was really very patriotic feelings that moved us while passing through, and we constantly sang 'German is the Saar' and called out 'Heil Hitler.' " It's the Führer's birthday too, and torchlight processions are marching through the streets everywhere—there you go. I'll have to be careful not to be unfair. Of course they're delighted about the return of the Saar. A wall has fallen after fifteen years. But it still grates! Landau, Speyer, Heidelberg—Else babbles away about who's buried where and who built what, first Reich, second Reich, and then the third one, in Nuremberg.

Apart from the Party rally ground, which is still under construction, they also visit the works of Adam Kraft, Veit Stoss, Peter Vischer the Elder and the Younger, the abundance of wonderful Nuremberg sculptures—what may the war have left of them? HG flies back, Else and the girls eat threefold portions of bratwurst from pewter plates and dawdle home through the Thüringer Wald. They've driven 1,738 kilometers in a week, "without a breakdown"—that's the kind of thing HG records. Else writes: "We have seen a large part of our beautiful, beautiful fatherland and most warmly thank the man who made it all possible, Johannes Georg Klamroth." She actually writes that.

They've been away for Easter; that's unusual, because Easter is another family ritual. On Holy Saturday they read the Easter walk sequence from Goethe's *Faust* by the fireside. According to legend, anyone who happens to be in the house—guests, staff, other people's chauffeurs—is ordered to recite the parts of first, second, third craftsman—I'd like to have been there, just for the fun of it. Who was Faust, and who the poodle? Eggs were painted in the children's collective, with bitter competition for creativity. Else writes in Barbara's diary that her daughter pleaded with Grandfather Kurt to be the one to find her eggs—"he's the only one here who knows anything about art."

Before breakfast they look for the eggs in a restricted area to be sure of finding them—they're raw, the art will vanish when they're boiled, but who wants cold hard eggs? After breakfast the nests, filled with sweets and little presents, are distributed all around the enormous garden. I have a list of the places where Else, HG, Kurt, and Gertrud have recorded their hiding places, thirty-seven nests and little presents: "green nest, 4th black currant bush from the left, about knee height," "picture book for Sabine, in the bucket of sand molds at the bottom." Even so, every year Else finds "lost eggs," a "completely rain-drenched nest" in the garden; in 1934

Jochen and she discover a dozen eggs laid by the family's own bantams, and "eight were still good."

I have my own story about Easter eggs. It happened in 1945, the first time I had blown eggs for the Easter wreath and glued silhouetted figures all over it. The wreath stood on the dining table, and my dangling eggs were the loveliest, of course. When the inferno struck over Halberstadt on April 8, the Sunday after Easter, when that large-scale raid reduced 80 percent of the old town to rubble, the house stood firm, no one died. But the chandelier over the dining table crashed down on the Easter wreath and broke my eggs. The conflagration scorched my memory. Everything that existed before was buried in rubble and horror. Six years were blown away, I know nothing about myself. My life began with my fury at the destruction of my Easter eggs. The chandelier that reduced them to smithereens today hangs in my sitting room.

HG doesn't feel ill at ease with the Nazis, but neither is he a blind follower. On November 1, 1934, he appoints Dr. Hans Litten as a legal adviser to the company—"private secretary" is his official title. Hans Litten is a relative of the liberal-conservative lawyer Hans Litten who defended workers and Communists within the context of Red Aid in the 1920s and put the fear of God into the right-wing judiciary and, most of all, the National Socialists. This Hans Litten was arrested on the night of the Reichstag fire in February 1933, and after five years of brutal torture he took his own life in Dachau Concentration Camp in 1938. Today—it took long enough—streets are named after him, and there are memorial lectures in his name.

The Hans Litten in Halberstadt has, like the lawyer, a Jewish father. He's twenty-four years old when he starts work for I.G. Klamroth. It's no longer possible for him to make his career within the civil service. He becomes HG's closest colleague and confidant, in extreme danger because of his Jewish origins and presumably also because of his kinship and the name he shares with Hans Litten, the "enemy of the state." HG manages to protect "his" Hans

Litten against these threats throughout all those years. Shortly after the outbreak of war he has his colleague categorized as *uk*—"unabkömmlich" (indispensable) to the firm, just before "half-breeds" in the armed forces are exposed to increasing reprisals. I find the Littens mentioned frequently in Else's guest diary; Hans Litten and his non-Jewish wife, Lotte, had married in London in 1938, evading the German proscriptions. Only after HG's arrest in July 1944 is Hans Litten taken away to the forced labor camp of Burg near Magdeburg. He survives, and after the war he will be of inestimable help to Else.

In 1938, HG is denounced by colleagues in Sachsen-Anhalt, who fear his competition when he seeks to open an additional company office in Göttingen. Letters to the NSDAP claim he is still doing business with a Jewish company—and it's true. The Bachmann Company in Göttingen, a business partner of I.G. Klamroth's since 1873, is increasingly getting into severe economic difficulties, which HG's dealings with them help to cushion. The Party in Halberstadt reacts promptly: "This is a serious infringement of the clear orders of the Führer's deputy, to the effect that Party members are to do no business with Jews. I therefore request that Party Member Hans Georg Klamroth be expelled from the Party. Heil Hitler"—signature illegible. The matter comes to nothing.

Not so the case involving B. Lämmerhirt in Mattierzoll, director Dietrich Löwendorf. It's an awful story—HG could do nothing to prevent it. Lämmerhirt is an agricultural trading company with which I.G. Klamroth has had very close business connections over a long period of time. Mattierzoll is halfway between Halberstadt and Wolfenbüttel, after the war just west of the border with East Germany. In HG's diaries I find a visit recorded every spring, extended meals, and invitations back to Halberstadt—a thriving collaboration. The Löwendorfs are Jews, business is clearly getting worse and worse, pressure is growing, and they want to sell, ideally to HG. This way they expect, I read in the files, to have family possessions returned to them from I.G. Klamroth as soon as times are better.

In 1938 I.G. Klamroth tries to buy the company for 65,000 marks, but the regional council of Wolfenbüttel allows only the unit value of 39,900 marks for Löwendorf, with the difference of 25,100 marks to be given to the Reich as a "balancing payment." HG and Löwendorf both protest—Löwendorf must have his money. After three years of arguments, the regional council concedes that the company's market value actually amounts to 65,000 marks, "so that a de-Judaization profit cannot be established." HG pays the whole sum in January 1942, but Löwendorf doesn't get his money.

On the instructions of the Regional Finance president in Hanover, the money is paid into a "limited-availability secure account," from which Löwendorf transfers the tax for the sale of his properties (9,149.95 reichsmarks) and "emigration tax" (11,250 reichsmarks). On November 4, 1942, Dietrich Löwendorf asks the Commerzbank in Braunschweig "to fulfill my home-purchase agreement, drawn up with the Reich Jews' Organization, in accordance with my move to Theresienstadt." That ominous Reich organization is paid 46,500 marks, and Dietrich Löwendorf dies in Theresienstadt on April 13, 1943.

I have been troubled by the question of whether the Mattierzoll branch of I.G. Klamroth was acquired as part of an Aryanization process or whether HG bought it in an orderly fashion. According to the files, he purchased it properly at a price toward the top of the scale—there was a law designed to prevent non-Jews from helping Jewish sellers out of their difficulties by paying extravagant prices. HG had quarreled with the authorities on a number of occasions, because the permit for the sale was delayed for a long time, until Dietrich "Israel" Löwendorf's escape route to Palestine was blocked. There was nothing HG could have done about the fact that the old gentleman from Mattierzoll had no other access to his money but to pay his taxes and buy himself a "home" in Theresienstadt. I'd like to know whether he ever even learned about this tragedy. The Gestapo confiscated HG's diaries from this period. I have the receipt for them right here.

The files contain documents concerning the Löwendorf family's demand for reparations after the war. According to a law promulgated by the British military government in November 1947 concerning the restitution of Jewish property, they had made a claim on the basis of "property values withdrawn without justification." The criterion for "without justification" in this case was that while the seller had indeed received an appropriate sale price, he was "unable to have access to it." The Löwendorf estate had no reason to renounce money they were entitled to get—they had lost quite enough already. That the rain suit hit the wrong company, namely the ailing firm of I.G. Klamroth, which had paid up as it was supposed to and bore no responsibility for the "unavailability" of the money—who would be worried about that? The Jews, after all, had been wronged for twelve years.

But the whole business nearly killed Else. In 1948 she had gone to Mattierzoll in the hope that she might be able to revive I.G. Klamroth in the west along lines laid out by HG. It wouldn't have worked in any case—being so close to the border the small business lacked the hinterland it would have needed to flourish, the general shortage of money after currency reform didn't help, and now there was this lawsuit. Reaching a settlement with the Löwendorf estate, Else paid 42,500 deutschmarks—this was after currency reform—or two-thirds of the purchasing price in reichsmarks. I.G. Klamroth in Mattierzoll went bankrupt. In 1969 a law was introduced concerning damage by reparation payments, and Else was awarded an equalization of burdens totaling 29,150.50 deutschmarks, including interest. But back in the late 1940s she didn't know how she was going to feed her children.

Before the war, Else doesn't have that worry. In 1936 her three older children are thirteen, twelve, and eleven, and very busy in the Hitler Youth. On Saturday—every Saturday is State Youth Day—

there's no school, but compulsory Hitler Youth work instead. In her later career in the Bund Deutscher Mädchen (BDM), the girls' wing of the Hitler Youth movement, Ursula becomes a *Ringführerin,* or ringleader, in which role she is responsible for six hundred girls, and HG explodes with laughter when his chubby daughter, braces on her teeth, has her troops lined up on Bismarckplatz. And then there are camps, training camps, weekend camps—all Hitler Youth camps followed the motto "We are born to die for Germany." As the words of the Hitler Youth anthem had it, "Now let the flags fly in the great dawn, which will light our way to new victories or burn us to death."

Else clearly wasn't upset by this dance of victory and death. I find a note to her daughter Barbara from January 1936, about some problem involving clothes: "You see, what did I tell you about the black BDM jackets? What would become of the solidarity, the *community* and subordination to a single idea of communality, if every little group of girls wanted to follow its own fancy? You leaders must ensure that stress is placed on what is common to the BDM as a whole, not what divides it." Thus speaks Else, the woman with the pronounced tendency to autonomy, who wanted to be "always unimpressed." Incidentally, she's abandoned Sütterlin script, so in her handwriting at least she's herself again.

She has a miscarriage in June 1936, and for the first time she mentions it in the children's diaries. Why does she suddenly engage in so much togetherness with her husband? Just now, HG frequently records "serious row with Else," "depressing argument with E.," "very downcast about a letter from Else to me," "profound disagreement with Else." But in January 1936 he writes, "Afternoon on the lonely island, changes decided"—which suggests that the lost baby may have been a child of reconciliation. But HG's resolutions come to nothing, and a few weeks later another of his playmates pops up again. What do women see in him?

I look at the photographs of him, and nothing really springs to mind. HG is of medium height, a bit thin on top like all the men in the family; he's slim—in those days people weren't as fat as they are today. His teeth aren't great, the acne seems to have cleared up, his hands are quite nice, pianist's hands. So? "He's got a secret glockenspiel," my group of friends used to say when some perfectly ordinary man turned out to be a magnet for women. Where is HG's glockenspiel? Everyone I've been able to ask has raved about HG's charm and his attentiveness, his "concentration on whoever he was talking to." Gregers Hovmand, the much loved Danish cousin, spoke of HG's "intensity," and it must have been bewitching. If a man makes a woman feel like a queen, who wouldn't happily get involved? Perhaps the lack of commitment is another reason. HG's ladies are, as far as I can tell, all married, they've got children, he's the icing on the cake of their everyday life, he's an additional luxury, stolen happiness that doesn't have to be burdened with problems and consequences.

That's not what HG is available for, either. He isn't straying because he's fed up with Else and wants to change his life. He wants everything at home to stay the way it is: his exceptional wife, his delightful children, his position in Halberstadt, his company, his horses, his cars, his friends, his open house. And he wants the rest as well. In my eyes, HG hasn't grown up. I see this straight line that starts with his "abnormal, painful shyness as a child," for which he later compensates with his tortuous prose style and his intellectual exercises. This continues in the endless correspondence which HG uses to stay in touch with his network, to avoid falling into the abyss. He needs his fibs because he lacks confidence in himself, and the many women whom he consumes like drugs must, one after the other, confirm to him that he's better than he thinks he is.

Role playing, borrowed identities—where and when did he lose himself? Yes, as a child he was occasionally slapped, and from early on he had to meet high expectations. Had to, or wanted to? Aren't we all like that, as we grow into an environment that is the way it is? HG wasn't abused, quite the opposite. Kurt was a wonderful father. Is that it? Did the son feel small next to his knowledgeable father, because he had the answers his son was looking for?

HG has spurred the business on, even in the face of Kurt's conservative tendencies. All the heirs to the family company did the same. Nonetheless he seems to worry that he isn't good enough. HG's pathological mania for work goes hand in hand with constant exhaustion. When HG sleeps, he sleeps grimly—a task in itself. Then there are his hysterical anxieties when the firm goes through turbulence. In that respect Kurt was far more relaxed. HG's pedantry—train departure times!—and his passion for the ordered world of the military, his self-doubt about Gunner Vitt, the man's constant need to prove himself—I think the ladies are his form of revolt, HG's outlet.

Why doesn't Else chuck him out? I can only speculate, because she destroyed her diaries from the time with HG. In her postwar diaries I find only occasional references to the way he hurt her. I think Else loves HG—that's one reason. And the children are tenderly, admiringly devoted to their father. Is she supposed to explain to them that their image of him is false? The third point, no less important, is her pride. She won't admit that her husband is just a poor adulterer; her confidence has been damaged to such an extent that she can't show HG up without conceding how humiliated she is. Besides—let's not fool ourselves: then as now, husbands who screw around are dashing fellows, their wives poor wretches. Else couldn't have borne that role.

HG brings at least two of his ladies home, they spend the evening by the fireside, he fiddles with stamps while the concubine and Else glue in photographs. At one point he writes in his diary in earnest: "There are four women for me at home now"—Else, the Danish au pair, one ex, and one current girlfriend. Else keeps up appearances, or does her best to do so—the world and his wife must know what's going on in their house. After all, HG has taken three of Else's supposedly best friends to bed, and he notes it all down as though pedantically recording his train departure times.

In turning myself into Else's advocate, unasked, I've crossed a line, I know. She will have had her reasons when she destroyed her notes. Nonetheless, Mother: your husband is my father, and I have to try my best to understand him—warts and all. The façade of togetherness is manifest in three children: Sabine, the lost baby, and me. Look, people, our marriage exists, we're making babies! In 1943 Else writes in a letter to HG that the two little ones—meaning Sabine and me—wouldn't have been born had she known that the misery would continue uninterrupted. But I think Else also wanted to use the children to hold on to him. HG: "Sabine is my total joy!" She couldn't have foreseen that he wouldn't have the opportunity to delight in my early childhood because he was away in the war.

In May 1935 Else joins the National Socialist Women's Association—perhaps she had to do so, as the wife of a prominent Party member in Halberstadt. Especially since he has completely withdrawn from Party work, he's being hauled in constantly for military exercises. However, she isn't too happy about being appointed as an *Ortsgruppenführerin,* a regional group leader, in 1938. Else in the children's diary: "I don't think I can turn it down, but on the other hand I don't know how I'm going to do it. It involves a huge amount of work, and I'm feeling worse and worse." Else, thirty-nine now, is pregnant again. This time it's me. She never mentioned joining the Party on May 1, 1937. The date is no coincidence; from now on the Party has opened itself once again to new members, after a block on membership was imposed on May 1, 1933. Else has probably been on the waiting list for a long time. I can only guess why she's doing it. It wasn't an urgent necessity for members of the Women's Association, and most of the 2.3 million women in the organization were not in the Party. Else probably feels ennobled.

I can't leave out the 1936 Olympic Games. Off they all go; Barbara, who's now thirteen, has scrimped and saved for a year to buy a season ticket for the track and field athletics competitions. It cost her 30 marks, and she spends the whole period in Berlin. In her letters home the most important question is whether or not she's seen the Führer. HG manages to sell his difficult horse, "Lützow," to somebody from the Olympic team who has been looking after the animal for a few months. To celebrate, he invites his family to dinner at the Kaiserhof, even the children drink champagne, and they write a postcard to Kurt and Gertrud: "It's an elevating feeling, being host to the entire world. Thanks be to the Führer."

Kurt and HG organize the first big ride through the Harz—forty-eight riders spend three days riding across the region. The logistics are difficult, finding accommodation for people and horses, picnics in mown paddocks, jump stretches, speed tests, vets and doctors, line judges, luggage transport—Kurt summons up his experience as a convoy leader in the First World War, and during the weeks of preparation he is completely in his element. Else is lucky, she doesn't have to care for lunch boxes; she's one of the few ladies on the ride, and very proud that her horse "Normandie" jumps three big water-filled ditches without objection. Because it was so nice, this now becomes an annual event, and the last one takes place in the summer before the war.

And it's now that the bar is finally given its official opening—I've been looking forward to this from the outset. The bar is a little hideaway behind the library wall, a two-level cubbyhole, too big to be called a walk-in wardrobe, not big enough to be described as a room. I have no idea why it was originally built, but the thing had a door, glass and mahogany Jugendstil tendrils, decorated with an episcopal purple net curtain. Inside, high stools stood around a very small counter, you could sit on the steps too, there were shelves with bottles and glasses, and right at the back was a sink with running water.

Whatever it might have been before, from May 1937 it's a bar, and in the bar book (even that exists) I read that they drank only strong stuff in there, and they drank it copiously. Until the end of June 1944, they knocked it back, and the book is larded from the first page to the last with scrawled and barely intelligible entries. I know from the war that coffee, alcohol, Pervitin, and Veronal—one a pick-me-up, the other a sleeping tablet—were part of the family's usual diet. In 1937 they're still getting lightheartedly drunk; there's anxiety about war, of course—but the Führer will sort it all out.

That Hitler is actually preparing for war is not felt in these peaceful years of 1936 and 1937. The Germans are doing well. Unemployment has dropped from six million to half a million, the Labor Service and the Hitler Youth are getting the young people off the street. Crime figures have fallen to turn-of-the-century levels, German exports are booming, the label Made in Germany, originally meant as a deterrent, is becoming a big draw all over the world. Cars can be bought at reasonable prices, the 1,450 kilometers of Autobahns already built are a source of wonder, and an additional 1,600 are under construction. Each year the organization Strength Through Joy provides vacations for eight million workers, which they had never been able to afford. Estate after estate of affordable new workers' houses are being built. Brave new world.

Light entertainment is on offer in the country's theaters and cinemas: *Paul and Pauline, Weary Theodor, When the Cock Crows, Angels with Little Blunders.* Paul Linke, Michael Jary, and Ralf Benatzky are composing racy scores, and top-class actors exude serenity: Victor de Kowa, Paul Henckels, Adele Sandrock, Grete Weiser, Hubert von Meyerinck, but also Marianne Hoppe, O. E. Hasse, and Heinrich George.

The motto of May 1 is "Enjoy life!" Albert Speer's Beauty of Labor office is advocating "bright, healthy workplaces, bringing light, air, and sun to the job!" The Reich court officially opposes denunciation: "It would open the door to the kind of bragging that the National Socialist state fights against." Germany is on reasonably good terms with all its neighbors, and state visitors are constantly passing through. Hitler has occupied the demilitarized zone in the Rhineland and reintroduced conscription, both in contravention of the Versailles Treaty, but none of the recent victors protests in any threatening way—the reacquisition of German sovereignty is balm to the German soul, which it feels it owes to its Führer.

But if one takes a closer look, there is serious cause for concern. Jews, citizens of the German state, can't vote or join the army, *Mischlinge*—"half-breeds"—are excluded from being army officers. Jews are stripped of their licenses as interpreters, business inspectors, vets, and chimney sweeps, Jewish cattle traders are forbidden to work. Jews can no longer graduate from university, students are forbidden to learn from Jewish tutors. Jewish doctors can't give people sick notes or issue medical certificates, Jewish welfare organizations lose their tax-free status, the Winter Relief charity no longer looks after Jews, Hebrew is dropped from the curriculum in schools specializing in ancient languages, Germans living in mixed marriages are forbidden to hoist the Reich flag— thus making them visible to everyone. These are some of the new rulings from 1936 and 1937. I could continue the list.

But who's looking? Who, in a population of 70 million, knows a Jewish tutor or a Jewish chimney sweep when there were just half a million Jews in Germany, 125,000 of whom have already left? The Germans are happy about the 1935 Nuremberg Laws, because since their introduction the vandalism of the frequent pogroms has stopped, and relations between Jews and Germans seem somehow to have resolved themselves in an orderly fashion. It hardly occurs to anyone that each of these "pinpricks" is another twist of the garrote, cutting off the air supply to Germany's Jews.

The Halberstadt children travel to Nuremberg for the Party rally in September 1937. They stay with friends and use their sporty ambition to get into events for which they have no tickets. Ursula pretends to be a pretzel seller in the Jungmädel uniform who has left her basket under the grandstand, Barbara becomes the younger sister of a man from the Labor Service who's working as a steward. Their hosts have terrible trouble getting rid of this young workman from Kleve who would dearly love to develop the relationship on a less fraternal basis. For months afterward he writes love letters to Barbara—"Heil Hitler, German maiden!"

The children are deeply impressed by the rally. Ursula, the future *Ringführerin,* at this point she's thirteen, writes home: "So many people, as though they're being pulled on strings, the individual disappears, there's nothing but a disciplined mass. I'll never manage that!" But they do find the speeches boring—twelve-year-old Jochen: "Nobody moves for hours when the Führer speaks, like thousands and thousands of stone statues. And you should have seen the motorbikes: 800 of them, all in formation. Fantastic!!!" We know about this from Leni Riefenstahl's film—extremely dangerous to vulnerable young minds.

In March 1938 German troops enter Austria, and the country comes "home to the Reich." The jubilation in Germany and Austria is indescribable, and the populations of both countries confirm the merger with 99 percent of the votes. Else in the children's diaries: "Of course the march of the troops into Austria was a great risk, but once again it proved that Hitler has chosen the right moment. This triumphal procession through Austria was something the like of which has probably never been seen in history. A Norwegian newspaper wrote that if this was a rape of the Austrians, then 'the Austrians like being raped.'" I don't know what HG thinks about all this. The Gestapo took away his diaries from this period, and until his wartime letters begin in September 1939, there's a gap in the documents.

Else has a hard time with her pregnancy, she finds it almost improper to be having a child at the age of thirty-nine, and she feels accordingly. She isn't as young as forty-year-olds are today, but the idea that it might be a boy this time keeps her going. She's quite certain, and besides, a girl would be quite unbelievable: HG's brothers and sisters have loads of sons, and so do Else's own siblings, so why doesn't she? What do you need sons for? I wanted nothing but daughters, and would have found it hard to cope if I'd had sons. In those days people saw things differently. Back then, the future lay in sons, even for Else, who considered herself a terrific daughter. The disappointment when I was born! Poor Else—she's very brave, HG clearly is too, but that's all now, there aren't going to be any more children. She did enjoy me, though, I was a happy child in a gloomy time. Even now I have to make an effort to put myself in a bad mood, and back then I was a source of carefree cheerfulness for Else.

I too came into the world in record time, on September 8, 1938, and this time it was all over before the midwife turned up. My childhood diary doesn't reveal where HG was. It took weeks to find a girl's name, and Else draws a veil over which boys' names were considered. At one point she thought of "Susanne"—sound bite from Else: "It hadn't occurred to me that it was a thoroughly Old Testament name. But since you have such a fabulous long skull, you really look Aryan, so Susanne didn't work. Father wanted an I.G. combination, but I didn't. Hence Wibke—after visible resistance from Father. But you're such a Nordic child." As I say: the Führer would have been delighted by me, blond, light-skinned, tall, excellent breeding material—oh, Else!

She has an exhausting child-bed period—not something that is practiced today. In those days women who could afford it actually spent six weeks in bed after childbirth. It can't have been healthy, but it does bear out the idea of pregnancy as an illness. This time Else is much too nervous, because in September 1938 Europe is on the brink of war. After Austria, Hitler grabs the Sudetenland as well; these are dramatic times that peak in the Munich Agreement, and in March 1939 the rump Czech republic had been transformed into the "protectorate of Bohemia and Moravia." Czechoslovakia had alliance treaties with the Soviet Union and France, Britain was supposed to support France in the event of a war, but nobody wanted war, not even the Germans. Hitler is said to have studied his only moderately interested compatriots at a military parade in

September 1938 and remarked: "I can't yet wage war with this people."

So the jubilation is all the greater when British prime minister Chamberlain, French premier Daladier, Mussolini, and Hitler save the peace in Munich on September 29. Czechoslovakia pays the bill: she has to abandon the Sudetenland forthwith. At the time nobody thinks that the war has only been postponed, particularly since Hitler and Chamberlain solemnly declare the following day that their two nations will never wage war against each other again. In the children's diary Else writes what most Germans think: "Hitler has won a massive victory without a battle, except a battle of nerves, it was grueling, certainly, but it was also worth it. No one has ever gotten anywhere in the world without taking risks. Faith and admiration in and of our great Führer have strengthened and deepened, even when I had thought that was no longer possible."

But Else is gripped by sheer rage after the pogrom of November 9, known as Kristallnacht: "Synagogues are set alight, the shops and homes of Jews are completely destroyed, we are wreaking worse havoc than the Huns, you are ashamed to be German, and the whole thing is being presented as a spontaneous action, spontaneous in such a rigidly organized country as Germany!! It's a disgrace, and other hostile countries rightly say they don't need to think up any propaganda against us, we ourselves have supplied them with better material than they could ever have come up with on their own. It was utterly depressing, and the memory of it remains so. But there was also general fury in Germany itself. These are cowardly and unworthy fighting methods, unworthy of a highly cultured nation. You young children are just as furious as we are."

Else writes what she thinks, and it would be petty to ask her why her philippic contains not a word of sympathy for the afflicted Jews. She's a warmhearted person, and I don't want to imagine that she's untouched by horror over the fate of others. But it's also clear that she's concerned first and foremost with the honor of the Germans, whose good name is being sullied by other Germans. She goes on to write: "You can imagine how embarrassed I felt with Marylee, it was terrible." Marylee is the English au pair. Hundreds of synagogues and thousands of Jewish shops were destroyed, ninety-one Jews killed, not counting suicides. The pogrom was sparked by the murder of the attaché to the German embassy in Paris, Ernst von Rath, by the Polish Jew Herschel Grynszpan.

About 30,000 Jews disappear into concentration camps. A special tax of 1 billion reichsmarks is imposed on the Jewish community as a whole as "expiation for the base murder," and they themselves have to pay for the damage done to their own property. Jews are to be removed from the universities, Jewish children are not permitted to attend "German" schools; cinemas, theaters, museums, and concerts are forbidden to Jews, and their driving licenses and telephones are taken away from them. They are no longer allowed to run their own businesses or workshops, Jewish company directors and leading executives are to be fired without compensation or support. According to the census in May 1939, 233,973 Jews are living in the "Old Reich."

After Munich, most Germans probably believe that things can go on like this forever: Hitler snaps his fingers and other countries lay their territories at his feet. For that reason the saber-rattling over Danzig, which has been getting louder and louder throughout 1939, is not interpreted as a preparation for war, particularly since Hitler has been presenting himself as the guardian of peace for the past six years. But HG and Else read the London *Times* and the Danish *Berlingske Tidende,* and they are sure that war is on the way.

Else: "For the six months beforehand I was so worried and anxious that it made me very ill. If we hadn't had the foreign newspapers, I could properly have enjoyed those six months like everyone else." The French general consul in Leipzig urgently advises her au pair, Gilberte Rigo from Marseilles, to leave Germany, and she tearfully does so on August 23. HG has already been away on maneuvers along the Polish border since July, and he is called up on August 25. Two days previously, to the bafflement of the world public, Hitler had signed a nonaggression pact with the Soviet Union, until recently the much-hated land of "Jewish Bolshevism."

ELEVEN

HG in Russia, 1942

HG, company commander with the Twelfth Infantry Regiment, writes from the Polish border the day before the outbreak of war, on August 31, 1939: "Dear Else, if I survive these hours I shall certainly think of them every day until I die. With dramatic escalation and inexorable force, fate is striding toward us, and marching over us individual human beings—how small we are! Whether tomorrow evening will still find me alive—what does it really matter? It would be a pity were I to fall, and sad for you and the children—but what are we all compared to the greatness of destiny?" That destiny has a name, which HG doesn't mention—does he know who's kicking off this war?

On September 4, 1939: "My dear ones, everything is in a most excellent state—for days we've been riding right at the front, in enormous marches—the Polack is running away from us brainlessly, without artillery or planes, we have suffered few losses, our planes and tanks are terrific—everything before us is in flames, at night an eerily imposing sight! We have little news from home, because the radio news is poor. What's going on in England and France? Are they attacking us? And what's Italy doing? Send newspapers, the *Berlingske* [the Danish paper] ideally in a sealed envelope. As I write there are ninety of our planes above us: a wonderful feeling! I miss you so terribly, but I mustn't allow myself to think of it. Give my love particularly to Wibke and Sabine!" The troops in Poland don't learn that Britain and France declared war on Germany the previous day, nor about the silence of Italy, which isn't fulfilling its alliance obligations with Germany.

In Halberstadt, by the same token, they hear nothing about HG in Poland, there's a postal blockade, and his letters don't arrive until later. The family feels the effects of the war from the beginning. The blackout has plunged cities, factories, stations, trains into black darkness from the first week. Refugees arrive at Bismarckplatz on September 3, evacuated from the Saarland. Else puts up five, Kurt and Gertrud eight—poor Gertrud, she is experiencing these strains, the hunger, the lack of coal for the second time. Else was a young girl during the First World War. Dagmar Podeus has three people lodging with her, and Else has to supply food for an additional sixteen people every day. That's still manageable, because everyone brings ration cards, but I don't want to imagine how cramped it is, how the washing is done and arguments are avoided. The Saarlanders will stay in Bismarckplatz until after the capitulation of France in June 1940.

The cars are laid up, there's no gasoline left, later they too will be commandeered for military purposes; HG particularly mourns for his new BMW. At I.G. Klamroth, Kurt fights successfully for his trucks: he's also allowed to keep one car, because the company's seven premises, scattered about the surrounding area, are impossible to reach on foot. But the worst thing for Else is waiting for news; the blockade of troop mail is lifted only ten days after the start of the war. Why would they have a postal blockade in the first place? Until then rumors go whizzing around about serious losses to the Halberstadt regiment. At this point Else begins taking sleeping pills.

HG's attitude to the Polish enemy—"the Polack is running from us"—changes after the battle of Kutno, at the bend in the Vistula River, where elite Polish troops from the Danzig Corridor try to prevent the encirclement of Warsaw. HG's battalion, "still 1,000 strong when we moved in, has 200 men this morning. It was the biggest mess I've ever experienced, but the regiment honored its reputation. And the Poles"—not Polacks now!—"fought like heroes and suffered terrible losses." HG leads the battalion as the only surviving captain; "such good friends have fallen, it takes strength to think ahead. But my life has been given to me anew." He sends lists of names of people from the other battalions, asking Else to telephone their families with the news that their husbands are unhurt.

The campaign in Poland has barely begun when SS Einsatzgruppen in the wake of the troops engage in mass shootings of Jews and Polish teachers, lawyers, vicars, and landowners. The Polish elites are liquidated. This is Heinrich Himmler's way of dealing with "the danger that this subhuman people of the East might, through these people of good blood, acquire a ruling class that is dangerous to us because it is equal to us." The Soviets come from the other side and murder thousands of Polish officers—4,143 of them were later found in a mass grave in the forest of Katyn; that too is a deep scar in the Polish soul.

HG is distraught over the suffering of the Polish civilian population. When the besieging forces close in on Warsaw, no food can get through—"they're so hungry, and I've given orders that at least our hosts are allowed to eat with us in the field kitchen, but we can't feed the whole of Warsaw." Also the "shocking destruction of the city, the work of our artillery" causes him trouble. "If they had surrendered sooner, it wouldn't have happened. But the Poles are very proud, you can see that in the dark, closed faces that line the street, they hate us, and I can't blame them. At any rate, we have all responded gratefully to the fact that the war has not come to our country and, I hope, never will." Did HG remember Warsaw when German cities lay in ruins a few years later?

On September 27, 1939, Warsaw capitulates, and from October 13 the fighting troops withdraw, the German military administration in Poland ends on October 27, and General Governor Hans Frank begins his deathly regime. HG notes on a piece of paper all the things he has to think about: "report by tomorrow, how many socks, underpants, shirts for the company to be brought by airplane—nothing for the reservists"—as in the First World War, only conscripts and professional officers are kept supplied—"marches in the form of exercises, also marching at night—no slacking!!—no one on vehicles!—platoon sergeants not in front, but beside the platoons—drivers: whip posture—horses in harness—cyclists: to ride in columns, wheel cycles in drill order, ditto on bad roads—discharge rifle when marching—machine guns under tarpaulin—check mortar carrier." It sounds like an orderly retreat.

Two days later and ninety kilometers farther on: "Today we crossed the Rawka River at a place where apparently serious battles took place in December 1914. On a hill there were big cemeteries on both sides of the road, on the left all German soldiers, on the right the Russian graves with their typical double crosses. And beside the old German cemetery there were a few fresh German graves with bright wooden crosses and steel helmets on top. How many more times must German blood flow over this country?" Why only German blood?

HG's regiment is transferred to Westphalia, where they get

bored to death because they're constantly on exercises—"peaceful army work, but it has to be done if we're to keep our wits about us." Where and what their deployment will be, nobody knows. The war situation is ill defined. What is well defined is the fate of Poland, which Hitler and his vassals immediately set about tackling. The plan is for a huge *Umvölkung* (we would call it an ethnic cleansing): henceforth only Germans are to live on the soil of the German Reich, enlarged by the annexed territories in Poland. Anyone who isn't part of that—Jews, Gypsies, Poles "not of good blood"—is moved into the areas not annexed, known as the General Government, or "exterminated."

Heinrich Himmler sets out how "foreign peoples" are to have their slave status branded on them by having their schooling reduced to four years of primary education: "The sole goal of this primary schooling must be: simple calculation up to 500, writing of own name, a doctrine that it is a divine commandment to be obedient and honest, industrious and well behaved to the Germans. I don't consider that reading is required." Such "subhumans" who cannot be "Germanized" for want of "blood quality" are to be brought to Germany as forced laborers and used in road building, on slag heaps, or in farming.

As regards the treatment of the Eastern Jews, the methods are unclear at first, but the goal is certain: they have no place in the "Great German Reich." By the end of 1939, about 90,000 of them are initially expelled from the now "German" territories into the General Government, to Lodz, Warsaw, and Radom. That's 90,000 individual human beings, with wives, lovers, old parents, a shop on the ground floor. I can see their houses in front of me: porridge still in the pot, the children's schoolbooks on the kitchen table, laundry soaking in the bathroom. Life still breathes in the walls, and an abandoned canary sings into a bright day, as though nothing had happened.

The Nazis are "quick as weasels." SS Hauptsturmführer Adolf Eichmann organizes the transport of a Jewish advance unit from

Moravian Ostrau in Czechoslovakia to the region south of Lublin to build a camp there. The deportations of Jews to Poland begin, from Austria as well as Bohemia and Moravia. In October 1939 the first ghetto is set up. Starvation is one method of murder, poisoning and shooting are others; resettlement plans to Madagascar and the Arctic are discussed. This isn't yet the "final solution of the Jewish question," which won't be implemented till 1942.

Do HG and Else know about this? I don't think so, although they are still reading the Danish newspapers. Did they exist in those days, the kind of reporters who crawl around the dark corners of the planet to reveal the truth? Reports from German concentration camps were published by exiled writers in Amsterdam or Paris. But let's be under no illusions: the German émigrés didn't have much impact on international public opinion, and apart from Nobel laureate Thomas Mann, hardly any of them were given a hearing. Nazi Germany wasn't yet a global outcast, the British hadn't lifted a finger to help Poland, despite their formal agreement to do so, and as to the fate of the Polish Jews, the British had enough on their plates with the refractory Jews in Palestine.

Else and HG won't have known anything about the euthanasia program either. After the Law for the Prevention of Hereditarily Diseased Offspring, meaning compulsory sterilization, of July 14, 1933, Hitler now signs a decree ordering the "Extermination of Unworthy Life." On October 12, 1939, the castle of Grafeneck in Württemberg is seized and equipped with a gas chamber; other killing centers are made operational. The murders are carried out with injections, with dynamite, the patients are shot, and from 1940 onward they are gassed. By the summer of 1941 more than 70,000 mentally ill, handicapped, and disabled people in Germany have been "liquidated." In response to protests from the church, the killing is transferred to the occupied Polish territories.

Could HG and Else have known? It wasn't in the papers, of course. No one in their circle of acquaintances had a disabled child whose being endangered might have alerted them. There was no reason to imagine such things were happening, and surely no one's imagination would have been capable of dreaming up such monstrous acts. For Else and HG, as for most Germans, the state was "clean," honor was the order of the day. As in a religious community, the country operated under the motto One for all, all for one, everyone a part of the proud whole.

Else was a "believer," as I was recently told by one of the Danes who spent a year as a trainee in I.G. Klamroth from 1941 and stayed in Bismarckplatz. Six months after the Polish campaign, HG entered the Abwehr, the German counterintelligence department, and the old Dane, who was twenty-two at the time, describes him as likable and attentive, but "somehow opaque," you could never talk to him about politics. When Else gathered everybody "who had ears" around the radio to listen to Hitler's speeches, HG played the piano, or pored over his company papers, which kept the soldier busy enough on the few occasions when he came home on leave. HG couldn't stop teasing Else when she was awarded the "Mother Cross." She was slightly hurt by this, the Danish gentleman told me, because she was proud of that cross, but at bottom she also found her award for being a "brood mare" quite funny.

"All Quiet on the Western Front," HG writes at the head of his letters from his Westphalian holding pattern—in all likelihood neither he nor the censors know that Remarque's famous book ended up on the bonfire in the book burnings. And HG is right; apart from slight border skirmishes there's nothing going on with Germany's adversaries in the west. These weeks are filled with "nerve-racking waiting," as Else writes. HG is in an extremely bad mood; he is urgently needed by the firm, and at home his youngest daughter is learning to walk without him. On February 5, 1940, he is ordered to the Wehrmacht Senior Command at its Berlin headquarters "on a special assignment."

They send him to Copenhagen—as a civilian, in his capacity as grain salesman. He arrives on March 21. You can only speculate about the purpose and content of this task. The preparations for

Operation Weser Exercise, the occupation of Norway and Denmark by German troops, have been under way since January 1940. On April 9 Denmark is taken without a struggle and Norway is attacked, the German troops ahead of a British invasion by just a few days. There are tussles with British and Norwegian soldiers; on June 13 Operation Weser Exercise is concluded. So what's HG doing negotiating seed trades with the Danes just three weeks before the invasion of German troops? He must have had another mission.

Presumably that's the case. HG knows all and sundry in Denmark, I.G. Klamroth has been doing business with Danish partners for years, HG speaks the language. I've done the rounds of the Danish seed companies that HG writes home about, and I've found someone who used to work for Hertz Frøkompagni—*frø* means seeds. The old gentleman remembers very professional discussions about a deal that HG was to set in motion. This was the foundation of a Dansk Frø-Exportkontor, a Danish seed-export office, which was to "deliver considerable quantities of seeds to the German seed office, 71 Mommsenstrasse in Berlin Charlottenburg, the payment will be made in German nitrogen fertilizer"—as HG writes.

Is that what you write to your wife from Denmark on April 8, when you plan to invade your host country the following day? Yes— when you've got such clandestine instructions that nobody, certainly not your chatty wife, can be informed about it. It's probably the case that German counterintelligence is short of agents in Denmark with local knowledge and a grasp of the language, because they had assumed the strict neutrality of the country in the event of conflict. Now a landing of British soldiers in Norway is imminent, a move that could possibly have brought a British occupation of Denmark in its wake and led to a strategic change throughout the whole of the Baltic region—so there's no time to lose. Someone must have recommended HG. Being summoned to Senior Command for special duty will have come as a surprise to him.

Before his Danish mission, HG has six weeks in Berlin to familiarize himself with his new tasks. That seems a dizzyingly short apprenticeship to me, but the man obviously has talent. Otherwise he wouldn't have been entrusted with counterespionage duties in the Copenhagen Abwehr office, IIIF, clearly an elite unit. He plans a journey to Sweden, no seed business in that country, but the secret services of the region cavort about there, as do the British. In the end HG didn't undertake that trip, because the German occupation kept him busy in Denmark, but he did repeatedly look around in Sweden later on. His disguise in Denmark during those weeks is perfect, down to the notepaper headed "German Seed Office," which he uses for his correspondence to Halberstadt and elsewhere.

There's something else that bothers me: someone's asking you to get involved in the occupation of a country where you've been at home for eighteen years. You are to face your friends, your wife's family, your many acquaintances from Danish high society, in the uniform of the occupying forces, conspicuously recognizable as the aggressor, as a man who is causing deep hurt to the feelings of people he loves. A man who disavows his wife, puts his worshipped mother-in-law in the wrong, and retrospectively betrays decades of hospitality. Can you refuse? Can you say, I'm not doing that?

It was a military order that sent HG to Denmark, and I don't know if he could have put his foot down. People nowadays don't much care to obey orders that go against their own convictions. But I don't even really know whether this order ran counter to HG's beliefs. In the event, it proved to be a stroke of luck that he was there. In 1968, the second in command in the Danish resistance movement, Hans Lunding, wrote in his memoirs that on a number of occasions HG warned the Danes about impending actions by the Germans, putting them in a position to protect their resistance groups. Was that in his mind when he was being given his basic training in Berlin? Did he go to Denmark to prevent worse things from happening?

As part of his disguise HG didn't even have his uniforms with him. However, according to family legend, on April 8, the day before the occupation, he had a formal dinner with unsuspecting friends, and appeared in uniform the following morning at the Phoenix Hotel. In actual fact he flew home a few days later to fetch his uniforms, and from that point onward he was even outwardly recognizable as an occupying officer. I can only guess what HG thinks of the occupation of his adopted country. After the letter of April 8, 1940, his correspondence with Else disappears—I've found a handwritten note from her, in which she says, "Most mail from Denmark destroyed on the instructions of Hans Georg—autumn 1943."

HG stays on in Copenhagen as a counterintelligence officer until February 1942. His reason for having his letters from Denmark destroyed, and why he asks Else to do this only a year and a half later—in that by autumn 1943 HG has already been to and come back from Russia, and is with the Abwehr in Berlin—is one of the difficult pieces in the jigsaw puzzle that I'm trying to assemble. I'm not absolutely sure that I'm putting the pieces together correctly. Does the destruction of the letters have something to do with the fact that the situation in Denmark in the autumn of 1943 is becoming properly "German," meaning properly rough, and HG wants to protect either himself or Danish friends? The activities of IIIF are so secret that the people involved keep their cards extremely close to their chests, and even for the head of the department, Admiral Wilhelm Canaris, this kind of counterintelligence-within-the-counterintelligence department sometimes feels weird. It was an "order of monks," I'm assured by someone who knows more about it than I do. That explains why I've found nothing about HG in Danish archives, and I can assume that HG didn't write anything in his letters home that would later have to be destroyed.

One favorite Dane, Kirsten, for many years our au pair in Halberstadt, writes to Else in April 1940 (she's twenty-five at the time):

"We find it outrageous that we are to be 'protected' without being asked. It's infuriating that the major powers are fighting out their disagreements on the soil of small and uninvolved countries, because they're afraid to battle them out within their own borders. In all the time I spent with you, I never knew how Danish I really was." Else to her daughter Barbara, and I don't think she knows any better: "Please remember always that Father was previously in Denmark as a peaceful businessman for the Seed Office. He still works for it, by the way, except that he has now been caught by Supreme Army Command again. It certainly isn't easy for Father, of course he understands quite well the Danes, and is in an awkward position toward them as their 'protector.' But most of our friends are helping him over this." Kirsten to Else: "It's unbelievable that we didn't defend ourselves!!" Else to Kirsten: "Are you going to defend yourself against an earthquake?"

HG writes to Barbara:

> *A man who fought for victory*
> *To serve his homeland, Germany,*
> *Found himself, unexpectedly,*
> *In the lap of luxury.*
> *Thanks only to the Lord God's whim,*
> *All kinds of goods encircle him,*
> *Fruit, coffee, cigarettes—what glee!*
> *It prompts him to write poetry.*

The western offensive begins on May 10, 1940; Germany descends on neutral Holland, Belgium, and Luxembourg. Holland capitulates on May 14, Belgium on May 28. In order to get the home front in the right mood for the fight against France, on June 5 Hitler orders "that from today throughout the whole of Germany the flags shall be flown for a period of eight days. This is to be a salute for our soldiers. I further order the ringing of bells for a period of three days. Their sound may unite with the prayers with which the German nation will once again accompany her sons from this day forward." There is nothing about this spectacle in Else's children's diaries.

The armistice with France is signed on June 22 in the Forest of Compiègne, in the same railway carriage in which the "shameful" truce between the German Reich and the victorious Allied powers was concluded on November 11, 1918. It comes into force on the night of June 24, 1940, and in the childhood diary Else describes how she woke the whole house so that everyone could hear on the radio how the "all halt" was played—"those were great hours of gratitude."

To hell with the German victories! In both wars they've brought nothing but misery to us and others. But if there has to be war, can we blame Else for listening to the radio all night? Almost every day she learns that the "quite minor German losses" have names and faces. One Halberstadt flying unit is completely lost in the aerial warfare against Britain. A few months previously the young men had danced happily in Bismarckplatz—Else to Barbara: "They were so confident, so convinced of their invincibility!" The fact that in Denmark HG is "far from the firing line, in the truest sense of the word" is a great comfort to Else, particularly since she can see him occasionally on his official flying visits to Berlin, and goes to see him twice on holiday in Denmark, in June 1940 and in September 1941.

They're finally going through a good patch together. In the few letters from Copenhagen that have been preserved, HG writes to Else with longing and affection, in Danish, which presumably the German censors can't read, even in Denmark: "Let me hug you, sweetest woman in the world, and rely on the fact that you are now and will always remain the only one for me, given that we've been through it all: how happy I am that we have talked about it and resolved everything, at least as far as I am concerned. Truly, there are many women here who would be worth sinning for—but no, my darling, you shouldn't think about that." Else doesn't entirely trust the peace—wherever HG mentions a meeting with a particularly attractive woman, Else puts a thick pencil line in the margin. She even marks his raving about the "beautiful Greta Garbo" in the film *Ninotchka*—"I've fallen head over heels in love with her, and hope you won't be cross with me!"—with a grim hand. How hurt she is, and how hard it is to heal!

HG, on the other hand, is untroubled: "I miss you infinitely, all the more in that I'm thoroughly healthy at the moment, and urgently need . . . well, you can probably imagine." On the twentieth anniversary of their engagement, on January 19, 1941, HG sends a poem to Else from Denmark—this she didn't destroy:

Amidst unsettled times
Together let us look back to the past:
That winter day is now so long ago
When once we took each other by the hand
And promised, with the best will in the world,
To build a life together for all time.
And if we now, in peaceful contemplation
Look back over those twenty years of life,
What stands above all else that I can see
Is thanks to you, for having gone with me—
With me, a young and inexperienced man
Who dared to try and reach your noble star
Without quite realizing what it meant
And entered then a strange, new life with you,
And bore within him one sole strong support
Deep in his heart: that I do love you so.

Many years came, all lovely, young and strong,
In which we found our way to one another;
You gave me our children, who bound us
Firmly, and yet more firmly still, together.
Our seed grew tall—and midst the healthy corn

My Father's Country

Weeds flourished too, and sapped the glorious crop.
A storm came then, that almost made us start
From the beginning—shaking to the core
The man in me, in you the woman's soul,
And threatened to o'erturn what we had built.
We stood there, I despairing, you embittered
To view the devastation—hardly daring
To move our hands once more with all their strength
And then, rather than yearning for lost riches,
To sow fresh seed in our beloved field
And clear the rubble all away from it.
But God gave mercy to us, and new strength,
He gave us courage to begin again.
Already we have traveled part the way,
And we may hope: things will be good again!

I wish I could make the sun set over a vast landscape right now, let the orchestra surge and after a while put a succinct "The End" on the screen. I can't. Everything always goes on.

And besides, there's a war on. I'd love to know what HG really was up to in Copenhagen. I don't know much about military matters, and I know nothing at all about the Abwehr, but it's conceivable that there was plenty of subversive activity for a counter-intelligence agent to observe in the region. After all, the Germans in Norway were behaving like vandals, Sweden was interpreting its neutrality any way it chose, and the British were doing everything they could to stir up the Danish resistance.

However, the policy of the German occupation in Denmark—in the early years at least—was different from that in other occupied countries, and quite moderate. The Danish constitution remained in effect, the king in office, parliament and administration continued their work. There was no German military administration as there was in France or Belgium, and no National Socialist Reich commissar as in Norway or Holland. German interests were still represented by the former envoy Cécil von Renthe-Fink. The few Danish Nazis were uninvolved in government and politically irrelevant, and even the little Danish army remained intact and armed. Until late autumn 1943 the seven thousand Jews in the country lived unmolested, and then almost all of them were rescued to Sweden. By that time HG was already at the Eastern Front.

The "soft" occupation of Denmark was an experiment, and the object of constant disagreements among the SS, the Wehrmacht, and the German Foreign Office. The bone of contention was whether the policy of partnership would serve German interests better in the long run than that of oppression, as in Norway, for example. Denmark was strategically important for Germany. Without Danish agricultural exports to Germany the Reich could not exist, as they amounted to between 10 and 15 percent of the total food supply. Apart from the occupying troops, staff costs were small—Werner Best, later the Reich authority in Denmark, got by with 215 clerks and officials. An occupation that left the country with its autonomy would, they assumed, produce less resistance and be less of a drain on the security forces.

Initially it worked quite well, because it was in the Danish government's interest to keep the country intact, with functioning newspapers and universities, free of Nazi agitation centers or any pressure to display flags or take part in parades. Denmark wanted to get through the war as undamaged as possible and without losing face by subservience to Germany. Intelligent men on both sides managed this tightrope act until, starting in 1943, reciprocal acts of violence caused the experiment to founder.

In the years that HG spent in Copenhagen, the local populace and the Germans, comparatively few in number—few, because the occupying troops had soon been cut back—reached a modus vivendi with one another. It was a cool, pragmatic partnership; the Danes didn't exactly love the Germans, but their furious hatred of the occupiers came only later. Government and populace were playing for time, and there were rules to keep: Danish cousin

Gregers Hovmand said he had once shown HG the door after seeing him drive past in an official German car with a uniformed chauffeur. I come across the story once again in Else's letters to Barbara; in her version HG was in a hurry and didn't want to park the car around the corner. Else: "You know how far the next corner in Bandholm harbor is from Gregers's house. If you really want to hide the car, you have to walk a very long way. But you can imagine how awkward that was for Father; after all, he isn't usually tactless."

While on holiday in Denmark in July 1940 Else writes: "I can easily understand how difficult things are for people here. It's like we felt in the French occupation of the Ruhr, except that the French behaved like pigs, while here the German soldiers are displaying blameless conduct. Everyone here confirms that. The Danes had expected vandals and have experienced polite guests, now I hope they'll think twice about other things that they learn about us from hostile propaganda newspapers." Oh, Else!

HG is a "guest" in Denmark—I've found him in the guest books of people of every political hue; his contacts extend from higher-ups in the secret service through to socialists. One of the three favorite Danes—again a former au pair in Halberstadt—was at that time training as a bookseller in a shop directly opposite the British Embassy in Copenhagen. Pelse sees HG going in and out of the building in civilian clothes, "strangely dressed, with a green hat!" It is assumed HG was there to collect the papers of the Hovmand families, honorary consuls for Great Britain with many social and political connections with England. The Hovmands were never questioned by the Germans about their London contacts, even after the British Embassy had been cleared out from top to bottom. Did Pelse talk to HG about it? "He laughed: 'Could you stick to your books rather than checking up on visitors to the English archenemy?' "

From February 1942 HG is at the Eastern Front. But why? There are notes from after the war which suggest—and this is also Else's version—that HG demanded a transfer because he didn't want to share responsibility for the injustice that was being committed in Denmark. But no particular injustice was going on in Denmark during those first years, aside from the occupation itself. Else writes in the children's diary after the start of the Russian campaign: "It's a terrible war. I'm so happy and grateful that Father is in Denmark and doesn't have to take part in this war. Father is sad, of course, and trying everything he can to get away from there, since of course it isn't nice for a man to sit behind the lines leading a comfortable life while his comrades have to endure these trials and difficulties."

I fear that's it: honor! The man is forty-three. At that age his father had grudgingly contented himself with serving as a convoy leader in the First World War, instead of being on the front line with his Cuirassiers. And now it's suggested that HG wants to lead a battalion, i.e., combat troops, untrained as he is. Back in Poland he had understood that it wasn't a job for him. His regiment wanted to make him chief of staff of General Command, and HG wrote to Else "that if the regiment is to continue to be deployed in the west, there are other people who would make equally good or better company leaders at the front than me, while as an old fighter who has by now stood many times in the crossfire, and as a father, I deserve to enjoy a high rank."

Why then does he want to return to the front, and why then to Russia? Perhaps it isn't honor after all. Why did HG have Else destroy his letters from Denmark? Why did she even remove the Sunday letters from Denmark from the children's papers? What happened in the interim? Had HG's collaboration with the Danes come to light, were things getting too hot for him? I don't know, and I will never find out. I couldn't ask Else. Until her death I didn't know what she'd kept and what she hadn't. She never let me open the heavy drawers of her Empire writing desk, where she kept her papers. I had to respect her privacy.

TWELVE

All five at once

By the time HG arrives in Russia, Bernhard is already on the scene. Bernhard Klamroth is HG's second cousin, the son of the banker Walter Klamroth from Berlin-Grunewald, whose pince-nez was such a source of fascination to me after the war—when is it finally going to fall off? In other families, second cousins tend to be rather distant figures, but in the Klamroth family this means closely related. Not so close that Bernhard, born in 1910, couldn't fall head over heels in love with Ursula, HG and Else's second daughter, born in 1924. This sparks in early June 1941. Ursula is then sixteen.

She's plump, with a mouth full of braces, and nothing, nothing at all suggests that she will later be one of the most beautiful women I have ever known. Her eyes, though, huge, dark blue eyes, must already have been so powerful that it was impossible to look away. She was blind as a bat, as we all are; I found an agreement between Ursula and Else, whereby Ursula would earn 30 marks at the end of 1938 if she wore her glasses only at school until then. What nonsense, the child must have gone tapping around the place with her blue eyes—as though you can train nearsighted eyes the way you can train your stomach muscles!

Bernhard is thirty when his path crosses Ursula's—they knew each other before, of course, the way everyone in this extensive family knows everybody else. Bernhard is in Halberstadt for a few days, and what develops is—well, nothing! Nothing develops. It's a bolt from the blue, the original *coup de foudre* that changes everything. Bernhard, the career officer, who joined the Reichswehr as a twenty-year-old in 1930, by now a major on the General Staff of the Fourth Army, dazzlingly handsome in his "red trousers," Polish campaign, French campaign, one military decoration after another, adored by the officers of his Tenth Panzer Division—he and that dizzy, scatterbrained chicklet. I still don't get it.

No one gets it. HG in far-off Denmark writes to Else (she kept it!): "You know how much I love Ursula. But tell me—what does Bernhard want with that one? She's still wet behind the ears, and she has every right to be. I don't want to think about whether there might be an old man's fascination with young flesh involved here." Bernhard is right on the front line in the Russian campaign, yet he still writes to Ursula almost every day, letters of great tenderness, full of dreams for the future. He barely mentions the war, with its mud and daily exertions, and creates a niche in his living quarters in which the two of them alone have a place. On June 22, 1942, it sounds like this: "My darling, a year ago today the campaign in the east began, and this year has changed me. I have met you, and that has given me the strength to endure something that is beyond the power of some of those here. Within myself I am unharmed, and that I owe to you."

In the meantime Bernhard has been busy taking care of things for the two of them. In November 1941 he comes to Berlin for a one-and-a-half-day flying visit; Ursula escapes Gertrud's grandmotherly supervision in Halberstadt—Else is away; and on a park bench opposite his parents' house in Paulsborner Strasse he asks Ursula to marry him. Until now they've seen each other for only four and a half days altogether! Bernhard immediately writes a letter of apology to the furious Gertrud. "So as not to go behind your back, of course I would rather have come to Halberstadt, but I really had only thirty-six hours! Please forgive me!" With the same army post a letter goes out to HG and Else: "I would like to ask your permission for Ursula and me to meet in the future at every possible opportunity (which will usually be unpredictable, sudden, and very short). Even if all further plans seem highly premature in our present situation, I should like to ask you to agree that Ursula and I might consider ourselves engaged with your knowledge."

There's a war on! Every possibility must be exploited, and there aren't many. Bernhard is caught up in the disastrous battles of the Soviet winter offensive—could anything induce parents to stand in the way of their young people's happiness, when there might be a loophole into one day of bliss? Else and HG still try to do justice to their idea of a proper education for their daughter by sending Ursula to the Reich School for Women in Reifenstein-Eichsfeld, where the "maidens" learn how to slaughter chickens, how to put flowers in vases, and all about nourishment for pregnant women. Bernhard teasingly writes to his "*Reichsfrauen* girl," Ursula moans that she could learn everything much better at home, she's surrounded by the high aristocracy, from the daughters of the Hohenzollerns to Habsburg ladies, and the two lovers see the housework for what it is: a tranquilizer for parental nerves.

HG is in total confusion. He suddenly realizes that he basically doesn't know his daughter—she was just turning fifteen when he went to war, and in the years before HG's mind had been so much on other things that she probably was just a part of the domestic hubbub. He writes to both of them, rather helplessly, about the time it would take to turn "Ursula's good foundations into something solid and adult." To Bernhard: "She has never—how could it be otherwise, when she's just seventeen?—had the opportunity for comparison." To Ursula: "If you were three years older, and if you had already proved to me in word and deed that our rather unfinished, unstable little Ursula had become a confident personality with a settled character." To Else: "Does it make sense to wait? Something could happen to Bernhard any day, and then we'll have prevented Ursula's happiness, a brief moment of happiness at least!" HG can't know how right he is—in two and a half years he and Bernhard will die on the gallows in Plötzensee.

Communication is difficult. HG is with Army Group North at the Estonian border, Bernhard is in Army Group Central near Smolensk, Ursula is in Reifenstein, somewhere in the wilds of Thuringia, Else is puttering around in Halberstadt, and letters sometimes take six weeks to arrive. Bernhard can use his General Staff telephone for occasional calls, and sometimes late at night he even calls HG, who has "a curious feeling, talking to this burglar who has broken into my family." They really know each other only "as cousin, friend, and comrade at most," and at a family distance. HG has followed the rapid career progress of his young relative, "always with ill-concealed envy," but he has rarely seen him.

There is to be an engagement after all, the date has been fixed for July 17, 1942, Ursula's eighteenth birthday. Bernhard goes on leave for three weeks in the spring, the first time that he and Ursula have spent any real time together, sheer joy sailing on the Wannsee, enchanted days in the Klamroths' hunting lodge in Britz. Ursula is well behaved with her parents-in-law in Grunewald, and in Halberstadt Else raves about her son-in-law: "Bernhard is a gentleman, both inside and out, he's quite the fellow, and full of life, humor, and youth. The idea of finding a better and a nicer man for

Ursula is quite unthinkable. He's terribly appealing, I hope nothing happens to him, it would be too dreadful!"

Bernhard requests permission from his unit leader, his senior commander, and the army chief of staff to publish his engagement—getting engaged on the quiet is out of the question, at least for an officer. It all goes through without any problems: the high-ranking officers are personally acquainted with either HG or Bernhard, and they pass on their best wishes to his "most gracious little baby-bride." At the wedding, which takes place in January 1943, the story becomes more complicated. Bernhard requires from Ursula: "1. Testimony of Aryan descent (certified by a notary). 2. Certificate of No Impediment (responsible Health Office)—I assume this has something to do with "hereditarily diseased offspring." 3. Police Good Character Report. 4. Three Good Character witnesses with address. 5. Declaration of orderly economic circumstances.

"I have to hand these papers in here, then Lieutenant Colonel von Saldern asks the guarantors if you are a respectable young lady. If the guarantors reply in the affirmative, permission will be applied for from here and with your papers sent to High Command, which will then issue me with the marriage permit that is valid for six months and can, if necessary, be extended to a year. I haven't been able to establish what other papers you need at the registry office. But I don't need anything apart from my pay book and my marriage permit. I suspect that the Certificate of No Impediment [*Eheunbedenklichkeitsbescheinigung*—amazing word!] will take longest, but everything's going to have to be done in a hurry." Bernhard writes this from the wintry steppes of Russia early in October 1942.

"Proof of Aryan status," certified—didn't the Aryan paragraph in the statutes of the Klamroth Family Association make that superfluous? Else also has to bring one of these in for something or other, and curses in a letter written in July 1942: "I'd have to say that my love and respect for my doubtless highly capable forefathers rises and falls with the level of work they create for me. The many long Christian names and the tiny amount of room under the heading, and my handwriting on top of that—I was not amused! And after all that I have to go and have it certified, although Grandfather's work has made it all so much easier for me—what about all those other poor people!!" She doesn't think beyond that. She doesn't think that all her efforts are going into the stigmatization of others. Doesn't she see the people in the street who have had to wear the yellow star since September 1941? Doesn't she reflect that her "proof of Aryan status" is designed to document the fact that she is "of greater value" than they are?

Generally she doesn't think things through. In the children's diary she writes how grateful she is that Sabine and I are enjoying our lives so much despite the war: "The French children, the Russian children, all of them, and the Belgian and Dutch, Greek and Serbian children, have all become acquainted with the horror of war, and you can go on playing unconcernedly because our soldiers are so brave and working so hard for you." Do you believe that? Doesn't it occur to her who brought the horror of war to those children, in a continent overrun by Germany?

The official engagement on July 17, 1942, takes place without a fiancé—Bernhard's brother comes from Berlin to "hand over the steel helmet." I learn that in long-distance marriages during the war a steel helmet symbolizes the absent husband—what a cosy substitution! In Bernhard's documents I find a lot of top brass listed in the congratulatory mail: Colonel Heinz Guderian, the "father" of the German Panzer troops; General Chief of Staff of the Army Franz Halder, the initiator of several planned coups—after July 20, 1944, he is put in a concentration camp; General Field Marshal Friedrich Paulus, the commander of the Sixth Army, whose tragic demise less than six months later at Stalingrad will herald the beginning of the end of Nazi Germany. Incidentally, not one of the well-wishers signs off with "Heil Hitler." The Tenth Panzer Division goes wild, sending perfume and silks from Paris; the officers of

HG's Halberstadt infantry regiment send several cases of Crimean sparkling wine by courier. The Klamroths—honorably—hoist the family flag rather than the swastika.

Bernhard sends fifty red roses via his brother Walter—though in fact they're carnations. Walter has tramped the streets for roses, in vain, and I envisage fifty red carnations in a vase, although I'd rather not. Ursula doesn't care, she sits by the phone, hoping that Bernhard will call, which he does late at night, and now Ursula feels "properly engaged." That's what she sobs on Else's shoulder, and Else writes about it in the next Sunday letter, and HG, on the Estonian border, reads "that I've lost a daughter. Or have I gained a son?" A week later Ursula receives the receipt for a postal transfer of 250 marks—another ritual. This time it's the fulfillment of a contract—the children have given their written undertaking not to smoke until their eighteenth birthday. That's what this money's for, and it's quite a lot for the time; HG has scrimped and saved it in the east. From now on Ursula smokes the way everyone else does: like a chimney.

Nonaggression pact or not, on June 22, 1941, Germany attacks Stalin's Soviet Union with three million men. Napoleon also invaded Russia in June, in 1812. We know what the result was back then, and we know what happens this time. But they're still saying that this war against an opponent who's been taken completely by surprise will be won in a fortnight. Eight months later HG reaches his new posting, and it's not with the fighting troops. He's now an officer with Military Intelligence Third Command in Pleskau, on the border with Estonia, the base of Army Group North, with which HG is directly connected. The job is clearly a tribute to HG, since his predecessor was a lieutenant colonel, and stepping into his shoes as a mere captain is a great honor for which he is congratulated on all sides. HG has ended up in an Armageddon of biblical dimensions, about which Franz Halder, general chief of staff of the army, writes in his diary "this war is beginning to degenerate into a brawl far removed from all previous forms of war." Hitler writes on

March 3, 1941: "This campaign is more than just a battle of arms. It's the battle between two opposed political systems, the clash of two worldviews."

Hitler on March 30: "We must withdraw from any viewpoint of soldierly comradeship. The Communist was no comrade before, and he will be no comrade afterward. It is a battle of annihilation." As in Poland, it is a matter of erasing the elites, and the notorious Commissar's Order of June 6, 1941, culminates in the sentence: "High-ranking political leaders are to be removed." The goal: "the Germanization of the east by the introduction of Germans and the original inhabitants to be treated like Red Indians." There are army leaders who will resist this.

A true hell has been loosed in the east: mass executions, deportations, starvation. Millions, both prisoners of war and the civilian population, have perished. The murder of the Soviet Jews begins on the very first day of the eastern campaign, that's why the Einsatzgruppen of the SS are there, constantly in search of backup teams. In the notes about their "performance-related activity" in the first six months of the Russian war, I read about 600,000 "liquidated" Jews, and the deportations from Western Europe begin in March 1942.

I think of the Jews in Grodno, of Kurt in the First World War, of their battle of wits, along with respect for their opposite number— not one of those Jews will have survived. There is a battle of encirclement at Bialystok, 30,000 Jews in the city, and anyone who survived the carnage will have dug his own grave, to be dispatched, like the rest, with a shot to the back of the neck. Mass shootings in Riga, in Kiev—where did HG end up? Did he know what was going on when he so urgently wanted to get to Russia?

He doesn't write anything about this, of course. Neither does he write that all hell has broken loose among the military leaders at the Eastern Front. The general field marshals in charge of army groups and even whole armies resign, or are replaced by Hitler, who refuses to give an inch during the Soviet winter offensive.

Anyone allowing his troops to retreat is seen as guilty of high treason; Lieutenant General Graf von Sponeck is condemned to death for this, and Colonel General Erich Hoepner is dismissed from the army. Commander in chief General Field Marshal Walther von Brauchitsch hands in his resignation, Hitler takes over.

After the Japanese attack on the American base at Pearl Harbor on December 7, 1941, the United States joins the war. We've been here before: unlimited submarine warfare, the "ruthless exploitation of the occupied territories for the benefit of the Reich," collecting for everyone and everything, gold, money, garbage, the responsibility of the home front. I hear Ludendorff, I hear Hindenburg, I hear the Kaiser. The names are different, the techniques of barbarism have been perfected, but the pattern's the same. In Germany wool and winter clothes are collected for the front, 67 million items altogether, almost four million furs, four and a half million pairs of gloves, and almost eight million pairs of knitted wristlets. Skiers are also roped in, which is hard on the people of Halberstadt, because the town is covered with deep snow, with radiant sunshine and freezing temperatures.

HG also records Arctic temperatures down to thirty-five degrees below zero Fahrenheit and asks the Reich School for Women pupil Ursula whether "smoked sausage and tinned meat are damaged by being frozen." The Sunday letters are back, and the family reads how "they fight the cold in this lousy country. In the morning, cars are regularly deep-frozen, men jack them up, light an open fire under the gas tank, and then they get going again. I'm assured that no cars have blown up so far. Keeping the engines running all day so that they remain warm is impossible because of the gas shortage, so this fire procedure takes place several times a day."

HG's account of what he's up to remains cryptic. He's the leader of this military intelligence unit, which, across the vast expanse of the army with various intelligence troops and numerous secret agents, has its sights on the enemy on both sides of the front. The unorthodox methods of Abwehrkommando III win rapid acceptance within the army and fortify its indispensability. Like Kurt in Grodno, HG brings in chums from Halberstadt, and soon the Bismarckplatz bridge players are sitting together once more. Their business is the battle against partisans—"these people behind the front are extremely dangerous, and they're breeding like cockroaches!" HG's people try to infiltrate them, to raid their command centers to catch them, and they are interrogated at HG's office if caught alive.

His job also involves the interrogation of officers and defectors being held as prisoners of war, and from their statements, along with reports from his own agents, he gets a picture of conditions behind enemy lines. I think it's from them he learned the "information," confirmed several times, "that people are eating people in besieged and starving Leningrad." HG notes this without further comment, but two paragraphs later he writes "that the prisoners of war from the camp, who are working on my building site here, are fighting to come here because we feed them." He and his colleagues work till they drop. They're under pressure, the prisoners have to be interrogated immediately in case the information they have is of acute importance for the German troops. "My radio operators sit day and night by their keys, writing should be forbidden on orders of the Führer," he groans, because even if HG doesn't write all the reports himself, the texts must all pass across his desk.

It doesn't suit him. Else is horrified when HG comes home briefly for Kurt's seventieth birthday on April 22, 1942. He's lost twenty pounds, something to do with his kidneys, and he's "very miserable." Kurt isn't well either. His old amoebic dysentery is acting up again, and his mind is troubled; "it isn't a good time for him," Gertrud writes in her diary. She herself suffered a fractured femur in 1938, shortly after my birth—that's why my second name is Gertrud, to cheer her up. Since then she's been walking with a stick. They're both depressed that HG has been transferred to the

Eastern Front: "it really wasn't necessary for him to transfer." Else tries to explain to them that it's all about Germany, and that everyone must make sacrifices, but her in-laws haven't been able to muster three cheers for some time now. Gertrud writes in her diary: "Hans Georg could have escaped. This war is a different war." It isn't, Grandmother. It's the apocalyptic continuation of your war.

Even so, Kurt's seventieth birthday is a lovely party, almost like the old days. All four children and their partners are there, and any number of grandchildren. Early in the morning "The Sun's Bright Morning Ray" is sung in harmony outside Kurt and Gertrud's bedroom door once more, and soon the well-wishers, many members of the family association, business partners, people from the town, Klamroth employees, are all streaming into the house. Of course there's a performance, praising the many-sided Kurt—the magician, the sculptor, the Cuirassier, the businessman, the archivist, the grandfather. Even I'm allowed to recite my little verse. All the musical instruments are brought out, and a fire blazes in the fireplace: "Warm hearth keeps harm at bay." Gertrud writes happily in her diary: "We've actually forgotten the war."

A few days later HG returns to Russia, rather reluctantly, as he's worried about the firm; Kurt is no longer capable of meeting its demands. "Private secretary" Hans Litten might be worth his weight in gold, and the authorized signatory is a reliable colleague—but HG is indispensable for entrepreneurial creativity in these regulated times. He is the only one in his military surroundings to be shouldering this kind of twofold responsibility: all the others are career officers, "and in the war they are fulfilling their professions, they don't know a reserve officer's worries about his main job or his main business at home, and some of them actually find it contemptible for a reserve officer to speak of the urgent need to look after his civilian life once again."

Early in May HG organizes some business for himself in Reval in Estonia (today it's Tallinn): "400 kilometers of bad roads, a battle-scarred landscape." He finds his way to the castle of Arroküll, where in 1918 he was able to indulge his passion for administrative organization. It's now a housekeeping school along the lines of Ursula's Reich School for Women. HG goes into the room with the sweeping view over the park, where he once lived as an ensign, and "where I thought my life was over." He leaves his enthusiastic driver in the care of the sweet little domestic science students, and travels on to Sallotak, the place where he shot Franz Vitt.

"I walked over the same field where the shots were fired, and stood outside the farmhouse that we carried him into. The Estonian peasants in their Sunday best, watching me with astonishment, might have been the same people who called me for help back then, or their children. I didn't ask them, so they just stared at me in bewilderment, wondering what on earth I wanted in this godforsaken forest village. That was twenty-four years ago, and for me it's as if it was yesterday." HG is "rather silent" as he drives on to Reval, and turns down a dinner invitation from the base leader there. Four weeks later he goes there again. In a handwritten addendum to his Sunday letter to Else he notes: "I have been back to Sallotak, and found the grave. Perhaps I can make my peace with him now."

The family learns some droll things from HG's Sunday letters: his battle with the Army Lodgings Office for three new toilet bowls, his bribing of a Swabian carpenter with holiday vouchers to build him a washhouse, and the garage for fifteen cars, his request for the family to send radish seeds, and the fact that artificial honey has the same effect as castor oil. HG now has colleagues with "powerfully elegant names—Baron Kleist von Budberg and Baron Stackelberg-Livenhof, very Baltic, of course, which means that they know everything better. One of them came yesterday, his name is Baron Mengden von Altenwoga, but he's rather nice even so." HG traveled for five hours by car to present a new officer on the General Staff "to a northern army"; the major there, however, was unable to receive him because of "pressure of work." When HG forced his way into the major's office, he found him sorting his trading cards. Those are the kinds of things somebody writes from this "land of monkeys," when he can't say what's really going on.

HG dreams, too: "What I'd like to do again: at six o'clock one beautiful summer Sunday morning, get on our horses with my wife and my father, go on a terrific ride to Lessing Hill, drink a glass of milk there as the horses rub themselves against the rotten wooden fence—come back home, shave and bathe with my youngest children, breakfast on fried eggs and toast, read the *Deutsche Allgemeine Zeitung* and go to church right on time with my bigger children, after church collect my mail from P.O. Box 42 and pop into the office with it until Else calls 'Will you be home on time for lunch?' and then dash home quickly, happily, hat-wavingly—after Sunday lunch ('Will you carve, or shall I?'), soak in the sun on the lounger on the balcony, be called to tea by Sabine or Wibke, and be surprised by sandcake, then fiddle with stamps while wife and children stick in ex libris tags—after dinner a peaceful little walk with my wife through the garden ('Right here I'd tear everything up and plant *one* big flower bed'), stop in at my parents' veranda, find peacefully sleeping children upstairs and soon afterward go to bed myself, grateful for so much happiness . . . Yes—that's what I'd like to do again."

At home, Else would probably have liked to have a peaceful Sunday like that as well—it would have meant someone's saddling the horses before daybreak, a cook's making the breakfast and putting the roast in the oven at the right time, the children's being put to bed by Marylee or Gilberte or some favorite Dane. Instead, Else is fighting with peas, black currants, and the Foreign Office, which refuses to hand over permits for Sabine and me to spend our summer holidays in Denmark. Nothing comes of it, so Else puts up two children sent to her by the NSV, the National Socialist Welfare Association, so that she can fatten them up—"They're seven and ten, the ten-year-old is smaller than Sabine and fifteen pounds lighter. They told us yesterday that they never got anything hot to eat, both their fathers are at war and their mothers work."

Else, like HG, keeps the scattered family together with numerous carbon copies of the Sunday letters ("How Father manages to conjure up so many legible copies is another of life's unsolved mysteries"). They are all addressed in turn. Barbara, who is by now studying chemistry in Munich: "How was your colloquium? The idea that it's supposed to be so incredibly exciting for a man to make silver out of cadmium is just as baffling to Kirsten"—a favorite Dane—"as it is to Sabine, Wibke, and me. The other way around we might find it more exciting, but we don't even know what cadmium is. Firing at the atomic nuclei does sound exciting. When will you finally smash those things so that one can pull a very long train from here to Berlin with only three pieces of coal?"

To Ursula, the Reich Women's girl in Reifenstein-Eichsfeld: "Did your district leader really talk such nonsense? On occasions like that I'm always sad not to have been there, I would—." She doesn't say what she would do. Later: "Yes, culinary is the word! I shall leave the correction of your mistakes to Father, and then they'll definitely be properly corrected, although Sabine could do it just as well. Where you at the theater—could someone finally tell me how you spell 'where'? *Where* you at the theater or *were* you at the theater? That'll have to be cleared up somehow!!"

To Jochen, at boarding school on the island of Spiekeroog: "How lovely that you're having celebrations like that. Celebrations are an art, and quite definitely an important one. Where would we be if we didn't know how to relieve our heavy, gray, everyday life with a scattering of parties and celebrations? Today it's more important than ever. What do you need a suitcase for, what would I put in it, sand? Empty, it would only be crushed by the time it reached you."

To her future son-in-law Bernhard outside Smolensk: "General Schmidtchen very much regrets that he missed congratulating you on your mother-in-law." To her mother, Dagmar Podeus, who is staying with friends in Wismar: "You don't really think your indiscretions will remain hidden from me! *Jeg var virkeligt fornærmed!*" (I was really annoyed.) To everyone: "So, now I must sort out lunch, however simple it might be. Do you want to know what we're having? Spinach soup and cold mock-rabbit with potatoes cooked in milk and salad on the side. Wibke is just coming skipping up the steps from kindergarten: 'Hallo-ho, hah, I'm so happy again!' And so am I! Goodbye, my beloved, faraway family."

In faraway Pleskau, at seven o'clock each morning after breakfast, HG takes a "stroll through the premises—through the lodgings and across the yard, the motor hall, the pigsty, the kitchen, the men's house, the women's house—those are the prisons—through the radio stations and workshops: All of my men know that they can speak to me on these occasions about their private concerns and worries, and many of them do so, with the result that this early-morning tour sometimes takes up more than an hour." HG does his desk work at night; his day is filled with visitors, a lot of top brass from the army group and the various armies pass through his office, "but, no less interesting, a long stream of human beings passes in front of me, even if the concept of 'human' doesn't seem to have entered the minds of our inhuman enemy in their deployment of them. Old and young men, old women and young girls, even children, are forced onto this path, at the end of which, in accordance with international law, they face death by shooting.

"How often have I recently thought with a shudder how it would be if Barbara, Ursula, and Jochen were also mobilized for such ends—many of these unhappy figures, who face me in the interrogation room with eyes that are either fearful or dull and indifferent, are no older than sixteen, seventeen, or eighteen. A very few of them I see again later, washed and scrubbed and with a cut and trimmed shock of hair, provided by Lance Corporal Birk, with Western European clothing (there's everything in my store, from knickers to bras!) and with a happier, grateful expression in my farmyard, in the laundry, or in the kitchen—but most of them go the way of all flesh.

"At the same time one mustn't go soft. Any inappropriate leniency, any false pity can cost hundreds of German soldiers their lives, and given that alternative it's better if more rather than fewer of these monsters bite the dust. Or perhaps they're human beings too? I don't want to know, for all that matters here is duty."

Bernhard writes to HG from the winter battle for Moscow: "The partisans are a serious threat to supplies. They emerge out of nowhere, often armed with little more than some gas and some matches, apparently quite indifferent to their own lives. They know they will immediately be shot. But their numbers are clearly limitless, just like the enemy soldiers—we take ten thousand of them prisoner, and a few days later there are another ten thousand, again badly armed, but fearless of death. Their sheer mass makes them an inexhaustible reservoir against which we can oppose only our intelligence."

HG in his Sunday letter: "My men and I have been seized by a dogged passion to make our beloved opponents over there show us their trump cards, systematically and one by one. It's like the periodic table, once you've grasped it the next few steps are predictable, and from the birds you catch you can tell who's still missing and search for them successfully. You have to use logic, this isn't a duck shoot.

"It's thrilling to be handed the headphones by a beaming, excited radio operator: 'There he is, Major—No. 763! Three more interceptions and we've got him.' And then when No. 763 stands in front of me a few days later, you can say with satisfaction: once again we've saved the lives of a hundred German soldiers. The regrettable human objects of this enormous game are then generally very surprised by my thorough knowledge of their domestic situation, when I throw it in their faces at the start of their very first interrogation. The fact that these are all people who want to destroy us—and we them—seems irrelevant in the face of our collector's passion, and only becomes briefly visible to me at the end of the game, when I'm handed a neat, numbered parcel of shoes, clothes, and underwear."

I don't know how to respond to this. War isn't a fair-weather business. There were the francs-tireurs, the snipers who were already fighting behind enemy lines during the Franco-Prussian War of 1870–71, the saboteurs, the bomb planters, the murderers. Kurt had come across them in Belgium, when farmers' wives used kitchen knives to slaughter the German officers billeted on them. They appear in every occupied country, they're called terrorists or freedom fighters, depending on whether they win in the end or not. The Jews in Palestine fought against the British in just this way, Tito's partisans in Yugoslavia fought the Germans, the Palestinians fight the Israelis, the list goes on.

Here in Russia, they form a huge fighting corps. The NKWD, the Soviet Secret Police, drive the population of whole villages behind enemy lines into battle. They are parachuted in, they use secret paths to steal behind the front, their fight has no rules, fighting them just once: their death. They are guided and organized, some are cannon fodder, some valuable specialists. Should I be outraged that HG has them shot? No occupying army in the world would let them be, certainly not in war.

HG's promotion to major is celebrated like a children's birthday. Adult men, decked out in stars and aiguillettes, drink themselves stupid right in the middle of the war, and "then things get going, singing in rounds, rocking to and fro together, declamations and magic tricks, ending up in a mad scramble over tables and chairs, followed by playing catch with plates and glasses. Over the rest of the party there hangs a misty veil, but somehow I managed to get home all on my own, and of course I didn't know the password, and should really have been arrested, which I could avert through kind words with the sentries. To celebrate my caterpillars"—those are the things that sit on the epaulets—"my soldiers were given various bottles of vodka, each of my prisoners a packet of the longed-for Machorka tobacco, and so general contentment prevails."

I could continue effortlessly with descriptions of binges in Pleskau, and Gertrud notes anxiously in her diary: "Another of those letters about drunkenness from Hans Georg, that was already a problem in Lithuania, let's hope nothing happens to him!" They all drink, Bernhard and his baby-bride Ursula, when they're together, start the day with Cointreau—of all things! Barbara, not yet twenty, describes orgies of cognac in Munich; in the bar in Bismarckplatz all the soldiers who are home on furlough, or wounded men released from the military hospital, knock back the hard stuff like water. Bernhard tells of the shortage of Pervitin at the front, but Else lives on it, she can't function without sleeping tablets either. Where does she always get it from? They're all sick, but what do you expect, war is sick, the country's sick, why should people be healthy?

Those constant lies! HG in his letters: "profound confidence," "intelligent countermeasures," "quiet certainty," "great trust because the army leadership knows what it's doing," "objectively founded optimism." How on earth can he write that, and why? To calm his family at home, to satisfy the censor? Why doesn't he just say nothing? The Allies, now including the Americans, are landing in Morocco and Algeria, Rommel is reeling from the British attack at El-Alamein, Stalingrad is surrounded, all along the Eastern Front the second Soviet winter offensive is in full swing, hardly a night passes in Germany without heavy British air raids—all in November 1942. But HG is "impressed by the intelligent way in which we are proceeding." Although he really knows better.

In Halberstadt, Jochen has had his medical examination and been pronounced fit for military service—"this child," Else rages, the boy is seventeen. Six months later he gets his "preliminary certificate"—an equivalent to HG's Notabitur in the First World War, which means that he will be sent to the front without finishing school. Else's Sunday letters flutter through her particular cosmos, as always; this one is from November 22, 1942: "The week was completely dominated by Africa and Grandma." If Rommel was forced to retreat for want of supplies, the planners in the Army High Command should take lessons from a housewife: "After all, I wouldn't start cooking if I didn't have any ingredients." Recently, she writes, they had all, children included, pored over the map in search of Marsa Matruk, on the Mediterranean coast of Egypt, to the left of Alexandria—"if one good thing comes out of this war, it's that we're all learning geography!! But we can't find Ordzhonikidze, perhaps there isn't a war going on there?" My atlas has six of them, this one's in the Caucasus, and the war was raging there.

Dagmar Podeus is in the hospital, Else writes, because she's always ill, "but there's nothing wrong with her! I told her she was hysterical, and she threw up in my lap. So there is something wrong with her, because she isn't malicious. But what?" It turns out to be a brain tumor; poor Dagmar suffered terribly. Else's house is full of people again, family children from the Rhineland who have been parked here because of the air raids. Sabine, now nine, has her reading day—"explanation for the menfolk: we have introduced a rule that Sabine is only allowed to read for an hour a day, and a whole day once a month. Since then it's as though the child has been swapped for another one, much more active and affable, when before she had to be dragged away from her books."

She's had a "terrible misfortune" with the dough for her ginger bread: "instead of potash I used Natron, because I'd heard that baking soda and potash were the same thing, but unfortunately it's hartshorn. What's the point of having a daughter take such expensive chemistry courses when she isn't there at such crucial moments? There's nothing I can do about it now—four pounds of flour plus all the other ingredients is too expensive, and if my cakes make you belch, at least you'll know why."

In the evening, as they tinker with their Christmas presents, the family reads Dickens. "I can't see why, even if we're at war with the

British, we should neglect their literature. That would mean telling Barbara she can't go and see Shakespeare in the theater, and what would I do without Oscar Wilde? But it wasn't easy, because *Oliver Twist* always sent Sabine into floods of tears. So I went straight to Dickens's Christmas stories, we'll see how gloomy they are, I can't remember."

Bernhard and Ursula's wedding is supposed to take place on January 5, 1943, and Else later writes in the children's diary: "Ursula is still so young, but there's a war on and every day is precious, so we can't resist any longer." Other people are thinking along similar lines, and for the next six months I find three "children's" weddings among their friends, the brides fresh out of school, eighteen years old, if that. All three husbands will be killed within the year. Else continues: "How am I supposed to feed fifty people for three days, it sometimes takes my breath away, and then everything should also be so pretty and festive, it's barely possible. But I'm so glad of it, because it's such a wonderful distraction."

The increasingly difficult situation at the front also becomes apparent in HG's unit. Sunday letter from November 1, 1942: "298 cases in October against 163 in September and 128 in August. Within three days I've had to go through three detailed hearings lasting twelve, fifteen, and eighteen hours—I can only manage it with a lot of coffee, short nights, and even more cigars than usual. But a few textbook cases have really taken me by surprise—the most interesting one is a little German lieutenant who, after a year as a prisoner with the Russians, and surviving the most appalling treatment over there, was pressed into service against the fatherland, and by pretending to comply he escaped certain death. Clearly separating fact and fiction in such a case, and *proving* the latter, not just through his own subjective statements, but *objectively* with reference to many different parallel facts, was a difficult but rewarding task."

HG continues: "The second textbook case concerned a Russian girl from Leningrad, another student from a special institute with which we are already very familiar, who had come to us by parachute on a very peculiar mission. She speaks almost fluent German, French, English, and Spanish, knows big parts by Goethe, Schiller, Shakespeare, Byron, etc. by heart, is very musical, twenty-two years old, rather attractive to look at—and Communist to the marrow. I'm tempted to see whether we mightn't be able to experiment on such a valuable object, and turn a 'Saula' into a 'Paula.'

"Shooting is a relatively simple and quick solution, but I'm convinced that we can only win this Russian war with the help of the Russians themselves, first and foremost, of course, with Russian intelligence. As its representatives are sown thin on the ground, I think it's wrong simply to hoe up the individual plants of this highly developed species, even if they're still poisonous at the moment, and I would rather cause them to 'mutate' through cross-pollination." Here speaks HG, the seed-breeding expert. "Admittedly these 'breeding experiments' are initially met with considerable mistrust and skeptical tolerance, but I've decided, using successful examples, to make proposals for similar experiments in a wider context.

"This 'Saula' understands, at least for the time being, that she owes her life to me—also for the time being—and has reacted positively to my 'cross-pollination.' Now she sits here every day writing essays in Russian and German on subjects I have set her: 'My first impressions of the fascist aggressors' or 'How must the German Reich influence the Russian people.' These essays are then examined by our propaganda unit and used, among other things, as propaganda flyers. The fact that she has also, not without considerable qualms, provided me with information on a good number of the bombers sent out by her red unit, is another plus for my theory."

I can't say that I like HG in this role, but then he doesn't like the job either. Else writes somewhere in the children's diary: "Father has a rather unpleasant job with the Abwehr in Russia." The third textbook case is a Soviet battalion commander, "very stiff and orderly, thirty-two years old, who has managed to shoot his commissar and then deliver his whole battalion to the German troops. After handing over his men he wanted to join a German unit in its struggle against the partisans. I'd love to tell you what he told me, particularly concerning the motivation of the Russian soldiers, whose extraordinary courage derives from the fact that they can only choose whether to be shot by our people or by their own. After the conclusion of the official hearing I dismissed the interpreter, and the two of us talked about lots of things until the small hours over several bottles of Mosel wine. My Russian is by now almost as good as it was before."

HG also writes letters to "my dear, humble Sabine"—she herself came up with this humility thing—in which he describes how the department's three fat pigs jump in the air when they're allowed into the fresh air, and that the pig called Budyenniy will shortly be slaughtered, because they all have such an appetite for boiled belly pork, and how much he would like to let her have some of it: "Here in this town you see little girls and boys, no bigger than you, running about with wheelbarrows, carrying the German soldiers' heavy luggage for them. They get 5 pfennigs a trip, and we call them the 'Russian taxis.' They wear thick, padded jackets and ragged trousers or skirts and no shoes. They're happy to accept sweets, and by way of thanks they say 'Geil Gitler!' because the Russians can't pronounce the letter *H*." In conclusion: "Goodbye for now, my second-youngest child, and keep some love for your arrogant father."

Another letter is written in "secret" childhood language: 'Deheelifiheelifear Sahalifabiheeline." I get in a state just copying out a single line of this, and he's done a whole typed page of it:

"Thouhoulifasahalifands oholifaf loholifavihilifing greeheel-ifetehilifings, youhoulifour Fahalifathehelifer." She also gets a poem:

> *Sunlight shines and makes*
> *All things lovely here*
> *Brightly you shine too, my daughter*

My Father's Country

In your parents' home
Night flees, and you, the sun, give
Everyone the strength to live
Keep all this in mind and
Let the sun shine bright
All around your youthful sky
My daughter, shun dark cares
Remain steadfast, train your eyes skyward
Only follow the virtuous path
Take no notice of flatterers and
Heed the wise—be good! Goodbye!
YOUR FATHER

HG has lovingly adorned the initial letters of each line, and of course Sabine is delighted to get a poem deriving from her name. A father like that really is the greatest!

At home, Sabine is anxious that they mightn't be able to celebrate Christmas, what with Ursula's wedding lurking just around the corner, but Else the Wonderwoman manages both. She has all five children at home together, the parents-in-law and Dagmar Podeus join in quite successfully, there's a lot of singing, even though HG isn't there. Instead, Ursula plays the piano, Jochen the flute, Else has managed to get hold of some candles from somewhere, and no one complains about the ginger bread made with baking soda. Else's Christmas book lists thirty-three people including children, and she gives them all impressive little gifts, at a time when there's nothing left to buy. They are friends, still astonishing numbers of staff, a whole page of sweets and biscuits, all homemade, eighteen parcels "to the field"—Else is a phenomenon.

As in almost every stressful situation, Else suffers from trigeminal neuralgia, and time and again she is paralyzed for hours. The pains don't disappear until both men, Bernhard and HG, actually walk in through the front door thirty-six hours before the wedding. HG had been held back by a ban on leave, and Bernhard, by now transferred to the Army High Command in Eastern Prussia, had problems with planes, but the hardest part was the short stretch from Berlin to Halberstadt, the railway track had been destroyed the previous day.

It's a glittering party. Just as Else and HG's wedding at Ravelin Horn had been a radiant farewell to past glory, this marriage represents the brilliant end of an era in Bismarckplatz. Once again, the participants are unaware of the fact, or else they sense it and refuse to be defeated. As at Ravelin Horn they are parading their own invulnerability for one last time. Forty-one guests at two sit-down dinners, the prenuptial party plus the wedding, eight staff in the kitchen; Else's party book documents her triumph over the adverse conditions. The army chaplain comes from Tunis, the cook from Naples; both are part of the Tenth Panzer Division, which fought through the murderous previous winter with Bernhard outside Moscow, and their presence is the wedding gift from the division. HG brings along his orderly, Valdemar, an eighteen-year-old Russian, from his Pleskau base, "a very Nordic type," as the incorrigible Else records in the children's diary. HG appointed him as his personal orderly months before, and the two men are very close.

The table is set not only with the family's own Meissen china but also with Dagmar's Royal Copenhagen, and silver belonging to the parents-in-law, Else's own, and Dagmar's. Wafer-thin glasses, linen napkins with the Klamroth monogram, tablecloths woven with the family crest. There are plenty of candles, Else has been collecting apples—Cox's orange pippins—since the autumn, she has grown tulips in the cellar, and distributed fir branches and silver-painted hazelnuts from the garden in crystal bowls. The tables are decorated differently on two successive evenings, at a time of year when there are no flowers. Over the bride's and groom's places hang the oil paintings of Johann Gottlieb, the founder of the company, and his vivacious wife, Johanne, the ancestors of both the betrothed. The ones who got the whole thing started.

Else's party book: "Each of the guests had sent in ration cards for 100 g meat and 30 g margarine, Annie supplied 16 pounds of meat-cards and 6 chickens, 8 loaves, 15 eggs, and 5 liters of milk, Ilse Klamroth 1 pound butter cards, Erika sugar, the same from Mother, and mushrooms, collected for weeks before. Lotte Kl. sent eggs and milk, 2 turkeys and 1 goose came from Nienhagen"—lucky there are so many farmers in the family. It goes on like that for pages: who's sleeping where, where the coal is coming from so that the whole house can be heated—Else provides an object lesson in logistics.

On the evening before the wedding there's ragout of hare with red cabbage; after the official ceremony at lunchtime, "noncompulsory chicken soup with rice for anyone who has time" is served in the hall; in the evening soup à la Wandler—that's a Danish aunt—poultry ragout with mushrooms, roast beef with peas, carrots, sprouts, "salat superb" (white cabbage salad), Altenburg ice cream with pastries, surprise profiteroles. Then at midnight there are canapés with rissoles made of soybeans and minced beef, crabs in aspic, and eggs. Shall I list the wine, too? It's all there, including champagne; Else has called upon her old contacts, about eighty bottles are drunk; Valdemar, in a dark jacket belonging to Jochen and white gloves, pours and keeps people topped up. The one thing missing is real coffee, so the party drinks cereal coffee, but served from Else's silver pot. When the newlyweds leave the house at a quarter to eleven to take the train to Wernigerode, they are pelted not with rice but with peas.

Else manages to dress the flower children (a boy cousin and me), the train bearers (Sabine and a girl cousin), the five bridesmaids and their bridesmen all in equally festive garb. The bride's dress, made with a fabric that Bernhard bought in Paris, is sewn by Suli Woolnough, Else's exotic dressmaker; salt and money are hidden in the hem. The train belongs to the family, all the ladies wear long dresses, the gentlemen black tie or uniform. There are no cars, so Else has got hold of coaches and even horses; two of the landaus previously belonged to Kurt and are now used by the military veterinary hospital. It's a freezing winter's day with a lot of snow, and a long red carpet lies outside the church.

HG dressed in tails—flower children at the front, train carriers, bridesmaids and their escorts behind them—leads his daughter, the baby-bride, through the long Liebfrauenkirche to the groom. He is waiting at the altar, beside Else in his red-trousered gala uniform, the organ thunders out a piece of Bach. Else: "Bernhard isn't the only one who's impressed." While the rings are being exchanged, Kurt junior plays the same movement by Handel on his violin as he did at HG and Else's wedding in Wismar, the Romanesque arches ring once again with a six-part rendition of "Great God We Praise Thee."

The wedding motto, "The Kingdom of God Is Not in Word, But in Power," is appropriate to the needs of the bridal couple, and at this point no one knows how much. Army chaplain Sendler in uniform "speaks well, in a manly, soldierly fashion"—or at least so writes Else in her party book. At Bismarckplatz there are salt and bread at the front door, a fire crackles in the enormous fireplace, Kurt junior and HG's brother-in-law Ulrich thunder out the "Arrival of the Guests" from *Tannhäuser* on two pianos. Speeches, of course, and songs around the table, ninety-four telegrams. I try to imagine what my sister, then still so young, must have felt inside. Years later I asked her. She couldn't remember—"I wasn't there!" The horror of what came later had consigned that time to oblivion.

But now she's all a-twitter. On the honeymoon, the young couple spend two weeks at the Platterhof in Obersalzberg, Hitler's famous hotel in the mountains around Berchtesgaden. Ursula's amused letters about this "posh flophouse" and their new life in Berlin cheer her joy to the world: "It's so wonderful, wonderful, wonderful to be married."

THIRTEEN

Bernhard and Ursula

Since the beginning of 1943, Bernhard has been with the OKH—
Oberkommando des Heeres, or Army High Command—in Mauerwald, East Prussia, near the "Wolf's Lair," the Führer's
headquarters. There he's not quite cut off from the world. Shortly
after arriving he's promoted to lieutenant colonel. He's thirty-two.
His wife gets a job with the OKW—Wehrmacht High Command—
in Berlin, where she listens in to enemy broadcasters in English,
French, and Danish. Else: "What, Ursula, you have to listen to
French as well? I could split my sides!" And the newlywed skips

through her letters: "At eighteen, to be the wife of a lieutenant colonel and an interpreter with the OKW—copy that, anybody, if you can!"

Bernhard comes home every three weeks. Ursula: "It's like a new honeymoon every time. I'm sooo happy!!" He lavishes his young wife with care and attention, and his letters, before the wedding still politely reticent on the subject, are now documents of tender sensuality and wonderful fantasies about their nights together. Ursula gigglingly describes the wives of officers and Reichsleiters around whom she darts like a will-o'-the-wisp: "I CAN'T put the pearls in the safe now, pearls have to be WORN or else they go BLIND!" HG is pleased with that as well, and quotes "Great-grandfather Vogler, who said, 'How much more positive our little womenfolk become in marriage.'"

The capitulation at Stalingrad on January 31, 1943, leaves everyone in Germany shaken. Else is stunned: "Only in the days of the attacks by the Huns and the Mongol invasions can Europe have been as close to the abyss as it is now. It's comparable only to the decline and extinction of the empires of antiquity. That's one thing. The other is the terrible suffering of those who were in the midst of it, and those who knew their loved ones to be in there. I feel in my heart all the torment of parents, wives, and brides, and all the misery and fear and hunger of the soldiers there. So many of our friends are there, so many friends' sons, oh children, it's too horrific."

In Pleskau, HG writes a lot about "setbacks that must be made up for," of "mobilization of forces," and that the "sacrificial death of the comrades in Stalingrad has had a galvanizing effect on all my men, it's making them harder, if that's still possible." After satisfying the censors, HG does at least express a hesitant reservation: "It's pointless to ask whether it mightn't all have come a little earlier." He can only mean the ever more urgent attempts by General Paulus in Stalingrad, since November 1942, to persuade Hitler to grant him permission to retreat, "because otherwise the Sixth Army will march to its destruction." After the disaster Hitler writes to

General Field Marshal von Manstein: "I alone bear responsibility for Stalingrad." So? Two hundred fifty thousand men were encircled, 34,000 injured men were flown out, 91,000 ended up in Soviet captivity, only 5,000 of whom came home. Half of the German soldiers in Stalingrad were dead, having perished in the battles, starved, or frozen. That's not counting the Soviet victims, the hundreds of thousands of soldiers, the civilian population of the city whose evacuation or flight had been forbidden by Stalin.

On the home front the housewives are driven mad by advice in the newspapers: "You will save time and money if you descale your kettle." "When it's time, stop the blackout, save electricity during the day, let in the light." They read admonitions to wash laundry only every five weeks. Motto: Save soap—preserve your linen. Else angrily reports that she has just had her last perm, henceforth they're forbidden—heaven knows why, there are tousled times ahead for wispy-haired Else. Shops are forced to close to gain workers for the armaments industry, and because they're no longer receiving deliveries in any case. After western and northern Germany, it's the turn of Berlin to endure heavy air raids, both the British and the Americans fly over Halberstadt. All occupants of the house receive gas masks, Else has packed little suitcases for the cellar and set up places to sleep down there, she's carried down the Meissen porcelain, the silver, and the linen, in addition she groans about an inventory for the whole house, which will have to be certified by a bailiff to serve as a document for compensation should Bismarckplatz be destroyed by bombs.

It's March 1943, and HG is transferred back to Berlin, to the Foreign Department/Intelligence III in the OKW. He pushed for this move because he wanted to be closer to his family, but also closer to the firm, which is causing him great concern. It isn't easy for HG to leave Pleskau. In a year he has installed an efficient operation there, with highly motivated men. He and his fellow officers in the army groups have not only drunk a lot together, but got on as friends, and news about his successor sounds dubious. HG: "I hope he isn't going to ruin everything I've achieved here."

That's exactly what the new man does. At the end of May HG gets a visit from a former colleague in Berlin, who describes what HG already knows from the many calls for help he has received from Pleskau: "My successor has set up a fantastic business in women, he's laying claim to *droit du seigneur* all over the place, and is tempting his lieutenants to similarly obscene acts. My Saula"— the linguistically gifted spy from Leningrad—"resisted and was shot, they completely demolished my lovely old room with their pistols while dead drunk, and standards are said to be so low that all decent people are requesting to be transferred away. I'm only happy that I got Valdemar out of there!" HG had managed to settle his orderly on a farm in Pomerania because he couldn't obtain any ration cards for him in Berlin. HG visits him there a number of times, and plans "to fetch him to Halberstadt when times are better." With HG's death Valdemar's trail is lost.

HG doesn't feel good in Berlin. Outward circumstances are clearly worse than in Pleskau. HG is no longer "in the field," which means that no one is cleaning his boots or washing his clothes, he has no official car, he has to supply his own lodgings and food, and that's already very difficult in Berlin. The OKW is a ministry like all others, which means that there's plenty of work to be done, and no one cares what goes on outside of office hours. The proximity to Halberstadt proves to be a mixed blessing—he's too far away to intervene when circumstances require it, yet he's near enough to be much more intensely aware of the problems than he was in Pleskau: the difficulties of the firm, worries about the seriously ill Dagmar Podeus and ailing Kurt, Else overworking herself in a house filled to the rafters. Whenever he can, HG goes home for the weekend, but when he does he spends his whole time in the office, and the children and Else feel neglected.

There's also the fact that he's not enjoying his job. HG to his daughter Barbara: "This deskbound work has really nothing to do with my passion as a soldier, and I can't help thinking that if I have to work at a desk then it should at least be my own desk in the firm's office. Here, without any worries about my complete lack of background knowledge, I have been saddled with a considerable amount of responsibility as chief executive of two important departments in the ministry and I sign mountains of documents every day, quite boldly, as 'Head of the Wehrmacht Headquarters, Klamroth.' As I do so that quotation from the old Swedish Chancellor Oxenstierna comes to mind: 'My son, you have no idea how little reason is needed to govern a people.' " Exactly what HG is up to in his office in Jebensstrasse in Charlottenburg remains something of a mystery. Abwehr III is the espionage and counterespionage department, and as far as I can tell, HG's department ("7, Arch Wa A") is monitoring staff and secret protection of the Army Ordnance Office, which is responsible for modern weapon development, from atomic research to missiles—small wonder that HG doesn't much care for it.

But now something else hits HG like a bolt from the blue. Else unpacked his Pleskau suitcases and boxes, which had been delivered to Halberstadt early in April 1943, when HG was already in Berlin. As she did so, she discovered a collection of love letters from a lady called Hanna, and now she goes completely wild. She rages around like a wounded beast, and all the misery from all the years since Cläreliese boils up inside her: "Hans Georg, I can't go on!" I have only the copy of this one very long, despairing letter from Else, dated April 10, 1943. But I can tell from HG's replies that their torment continues until the summer of 1944. It takes a great effort for me to write this down. I want to shake them both and shout at them: "God almighty, you haven't much time left!" But how are they to know that? We all use our time as though it were limitless, we all treat our disputes as though they can still be resolved tomorrow.

I have to speculate, the Gestapo confiscated HG's diaries.

There was a Hanna once before. Tastefully enough, and not for the first time, she and her husband were HG's and Else's close friends. If that's the one, then the matter really is as "ancient," as HG says it is, because that Hanna moved to the remotest corner of Silesia with her husband and many children before the war. It's hard to imagine that the affair could have continued over such a great distance. But why does Hanna write love letters of "such intimacy" to HG in Pleskau, as Else furiously complains? Perhaps she misses him, perhaps she doesn't like it in Silesia and wishes she were back in the good old days in Halberstadt? As there are several letters, it seems certain that HG replied accordingly.

Else recognizes the handwriting, her suspicions are roused, and that's why she reads what she has found. It must be the first time that she learns of this affair—whether it's "ancient" or not—and understands that she has been betrayed—how many times is that now?—by and with a so-called friend. "Hanna's moral standards are her own good fortune," writes Else, and "if Hans"—that's her husband—"if Hans can be difficult, as he doubtless is, at least he's respectable." Bringing the letters home from Pleskau in his luggage isn't just stupid—HG's an Abwehr man, isn't he?—it's unforgivable. What does he expect Else to do? She's been keeping his house going with five children, not an easy feat in wartime. OK, it's her house too, but it was never agreed that she was to look after it single-handed, at least not without reliable support: "Hans Georg, I can't bear the idea that our marriage should be founded on nothing but lies, betrayal, cheating, and broken promises alone! That you should humiliate me and yourself in this fashion! While I long only to find a place somewhere, where I feel safe, where I belong, where I can sometimes relax, sometimes be comforted, and find a little love."

Else thinks about a trial before the officers' court of honor—that would have meant (God almighty!) HG's expulsion from the Wehrmacht. She ponders the scandal in Halberstadt, she considers "traveling to Hanna and wounding her as fatally as you have wounded me." She cancels an appointment with the lawyer at the last minute, she draws up ideas for a housekeeping school to bring her an income in the future, something like Ursula's Reich School for Women in Reifenstein. She writes out her financial needs and those of the children in the event of a divorce, she calculates how much she might make with the sale of the Meissen porcelain, the antiques, the silver, paintings, jewelry—this is 1943, and Europe is ablaze in a murderous war.

But Else is so desperate that she is constantly searching for new ways out, for answers to the unchanging question: "How is it possible that a man who prides himself on standing by his word unconditionally in his business life, has in his private life no moral inhibitions whatsoever, no sense of truth, no sense of obligation toward a promise, no scruples about abusing trust, in short, none of the things that are indispensable to a businessman and an officer?"

Why now? Why, after so many women having passed through HG's and Else's life, is this finally it? Because Else is exhausted, overburdened, finished. Because this humiliation makes one too many. At some point an end must come, and as always it's at the worst possible moment. Because war and Pervitin are taking their toll on Else, because the children are still so small and the outlook for the future so bleak, because there isn't enough money and Else doesn't know how she's supposed to feed that whole crowd at Bismarckplatz day after day, because her mother is dying and in such torment, because Else wants to be loved and appreciated. Because she feels pitifully lonely when HG, after Else's masterstroke at Ursula's wedding, spends the rest of the evening in the maids' room with Valdemar and the other helpers rather than taking his wife in his arms.

HG tries everything to get Else out of this—mockery, affection, rage, resignation: "I can't believe you're torturing yourself and me over such old silliness!" "But you still love me in spite of everything, because otherwise these outbreaks of despair, this constant turn-

ing in circles, would be inexplicable!" "I can't abandon hope that
we will one day be able to talk to each other again like two reasonable human beings." "Good night, my darling, how lovely Venus
looks tonight! May she also shine so beautifully for you—as a star,
and as my love!" "I'm lonely and desperate." HG can't get through
to Else. She doesn't believe a word of it. She doesn't want to see
him in Halberstadt. If he comes, she goes. She travels to a sanato-
rium in Dresden; the doctor says there's nothing wrong with her,
but what is wrong is the lack of comfort for her soul. Else can't
stand the peace there. She escapes back home and continues—
outwardly—as before.

They both act as though nothing is amiss—Sunday letters, children's birthdays, preserving vegetables. Sabine isn't to wear her
shoes out every three weeks, there are no new ones. Barbara, did
you by any chance take my traveling iron? Else has to hand back
her egg cards because of the bantams, but their eggs are so small,
how about getting rid of them instead? Kurt hallucinates and
laments that he "isn't at home," Jochen writes bravely from his
labor service, Wibke has whooping cough, HG gets a tax bill for
27,000 marks—where's he going to get that from? Every night there
are air raid warnings, 30,000 fatalities in attacks on Hamburg, sur-
render of German and Italian troops in North Africa, Allied land-
ings on Sicily, arrest of Mussolini and armistice in Italy, emergency
in Norway, emergency in Denmark. HG to Else: "Our worries and
problems are becoming so overwhelming that we will barely have
time and strength to think of our own little problems."

But they manage. Else manages. HG would rather return to the
past, when Else had "her crises," and then allowed herself to be fit-
ted back into the pattern of their common life, which HG
exploited to tend to their neighbors' gardens. That won't work now,
all of Else's wounds have reopened. HG in his replies to her letters:
"I have neither the strength nor the desire nor the possibility to
jump into one bed, let alone 'a thousand,' as you so tastefully put
it." "It's so sad to find not the loving hug that I so long for from you,

but only ever coldness and rejection. It would be almost surprising if I didn't seek a substitute for that elsewhere." "I can only shake my head sadly over your letter, and although I, like you, almost have the feeling that 'it isn't worth it,' I must fight that resignation, because you are worth it, our 'We' is worth it, you and the children. You are everything that is good and lovable, and that is worth it."

In the world outside the pyres are ablaze. Twenty-three thousand Gypsies are deported to Auschwitz in 1943; 300,000 inhabitants of the Warsaw Ghetto have been hauled off to Treblinka, the uprising of the remaining 60,000 is bloodily put down, no one survives; 42,000 Jews are killed in a mass shooting in the Lublin district of General Government—Aktion Erntefest, it's called, "Operation Harvest Festival," Dutch Jews, Greek Jews, the Baltic Jews are liquidated, in Operation Reinhardt more than 1.6 million Jews are murdered in the camps at Belzec, Sobibor, and Treblinka. I must assume that HG knows much of this, even if the Abwehr is concerned solely with military matters. I would like to believe that Else doesn't know the extent of the slaughter, but they would need only to look outside the front door. The Jews of Halberstadt had already been taken away in 1942. Neither HG nor Else has mentioned that anywhere. Nor the introduction of the wearing of the Jewish star in September 1941. Else, who cheerfully writes all kinds of nonsense in the children's diary, doesn't even write about it after the war, when she describes the downfall of Germany in gloomy tones.

I'm not quite sure how to read this. For a while I consoled myself with the fact that HG and Else couldn't write down anything like dissent at this point, it would have been too dangerous. But they didn't write anything down before, either—since HG's hardships over the expulsion of the "Jew Jacobsohn" from the employers' association in 1933, the treatment of the Jews had not been an issue for him, at least not in his diaries. HG mentions "private secretary" Hans Litten in the firm's chronicle for 1940, and sometimes in letters, but never that Hans Litten's father was a Jew. I know about old Herr Löwendorf from Mattierzoll and his terrible story from the files of the reparations trial, but HG never so much as hints at this affair. Else is furious about the "Jewish boycott" on April 1, 1933, and about the pogroms on November 9, 1938, and she regrets that Dr. Schönfeld, the pediatrician, immigrates to Palestine in 1935—and that's it.

It can't be the case that the progressive brutalization of the living conditions of the Jews, that the forced laborers, the inmates of the concentration camps, all the many death sentences—they're published in the papers as a means of intimidation—that none of this matters to HG, to Else, to their friends. But their friends don't write anything about it, either. In the memoirs of people close to HG and Else, most of them written after the war, they talk about hunger, flight, air raids, chaos above all—nowhere is there any mention of the Jewish star or deportations or concentration camps. There is even one such camp near Halberstadt, where the inmates are destroyed by labor for the Junkers aircraft factory—Langenstein-Zwieberge. If HG and Else, if the others had accepted what was going on around them, which I don't want to believe, they never wrote that down either, although they put everything else on paper. I have no answer.

I must bring Ursula in at this point because of the merriment of the "little Frau Klamroth," as she calls herself. She is working twelve-hour shifts in the OKW, the sirens at night are frightening when she walks home through pitch-dark Berlin after work. Bernhard is usually in East Prussia, and this is what it's like for her: "What does it matter that I don't know how to eke out my bread, what does it matter that I'm always in a hurry, there are days that compensate me a thousandfold for all of that, in which war and my nerve-racking work sink into the background, every day there are even a few minutes when everything else is remote, when the phone rings in the night and I can speak to Bernhard. I'm unimaginably happy, I feel so good, in fact I'm very, very happily married." Or, to her parents: "You too started out in such a tiny flat, but how cosy it is, and how happy I am that Bernhard is so comfortable here as well. He keeps teasing me about doing a bit more dusting, and I'd really like to do that all the time. It's sooo lovely here!" In a post-card to Barbara: "Listen, marriage is great!!"

HG's job in Berlin is putting a strain on him, and burdening his psyche. In July 1943 he writes to Else: "Over the past few days problems have arisen at work again, which have required all my nervous and mental energy. It could be that one becomes dulled to such things over time, and finds them less difficult to bear; but I doubt whether becoming inured like that would be fundamentally a good thing. I have never felt so clearly that we are in a violent bat-tle of ideologies, even within ourselves, in a battle in which the fronts and the right side to be on are not as clearly discernible as the tangible fronts of battle. How many opportunities are opening up now for me to begin new and interesting relationships, to meet leading men and exemplary women, to have access to intellectual movements that will influence our time!"

I can only guess what he means, and I don't think Else under-stands him either. That kind of exchange between them is a thing of the past. If, as I suspect, experiences in his work and conversa-tions with confidants are leading HG to examine his political bear-ings, he won't mention this to Else, because he wants to protect her. In his next letter he asks her to hand over his "black uniforms" to the SS in Halberstadt. "I have special reasons for wanting to donate them. They are hanging in my uniform cupboard, but be careful not to give them the wrong belt." What are these special reasons? Otherwise, HG writes, he's keeping himself out of "the many new trends." He notices that he is living both physically and mentally "on his inner reserves," which he has to be economical with to go on functioning. The all-night air-raid warnings are sap-ping his strength because he can't get enough sleep, "and if only there weren't that constant feeling of hunger!" HG's soul is freezing too: "How lovely it would be if I had you, my love, all to myself again and unreservedly."

In early August 1943 the population of Berlin is requested to leave the city if possible—"All children, likewise women, if not working; men are to remain." HG describes the chaos in the city: "the run on food-card offices, on the railway stations, long lines with lots of luggage at the freight dispatch offices and parcel acceptance desks in the post offices, "and all the grumpy remarks that go with it." Ursula and HG's department remains in Berlin for now, so HG has seen to it, after a conversation with Bernhard, that Ursula is to leave her flat in Brückenallee in the Tiergarten district and move in with him in Schlachtensee, where he is looking after a house for some friends. He reinforces the cellar ceiling with tree trunks from the garden, carts sand from the shores of the lake to the house, takes a fire protection course—"there's a lot you can do!"—and hoards food supplies. "That's what 'love life' is like in Berlin now," he says at the end of his letter, finishing it off with a handwritten greeting to "Enziane Himmelblau" (Gentian Skyblue). Who could that be? I found out in the children's diary. Enziane is one of my imaginary friends, whom I used as a playmate to keep our domestic turmoil at bay.

In November 1943, HG comes back to Berlin late in the evening after a conference at the Zossen office—"thick fog, I was relieved because it means we'll be spared the usual air-raid warning." Instead he gets caught in a major attack, which he and a colleague from the Abwehr sit out in a bunker at Anhalt Station. "Exemplary the great crowd of people there, no panic, deadly silence, while the bombs fell crashing over our heads." Outside he is welcomed by an inferno: "Flames, flames, flames. There was no chance of getting through, the buildings were ablaze on both sides of the street, an enormous rain of sparks was falling and in between time bombs were constantly exploding."

The fire rages from Askanischer Platz to Friedrichstrasse, Unter den Linden, the streets on either side. The Brandenburg Gate is undamaged, but the Tiergarten, "trees, lawns, bushes—everything on fire. The Bendlerviertel is on fire, the beautiful Bellevue castle, the Hansaviertel, the Brückenallee—poor Ursula! Headed on toward Zoo with a curiously silent crowd of people who, like ourselves, had only one goal: to get out of here! Always in the middle of the road, insanely hot because of the fire on both sides. The Gedächtniskirche is on fire, the Ufa Palace, the zoo, the music college, the upper court, last but not least my office in Jebensstrasse. Burning buses and trams in the street, crackling flames, a hurricane of sparks—and no water!"

They find a miraculously undamaged military building in Hardenbergstrasse, "empty apart from an old guard with an excellent air-raid shelter in the cellar with beds, completely unused, no water here either." They sleep there for three hours "despite our hunger, we hadn't eaten anything since the morning, and now, after hours in all that fire, still nothing to drink." At four o'clock in the morning they walk down the brightly burning Kurfürstendamm— "not a soul in the streets, only the flames, without human resistance, getting on with their horrible, thorough work of destruction." At the Avus they flag down a truck which takes them to the west of the city, then there's another hour's march through the less damaged streets of villas, and at half past seven in the morning they enter the house in Schlachtensee. There, "all the windows broken, the roof partly uncovered, there's no gas and no water, but we are safe and so is the house." In five such major raids in two weeks, 2,212 British planes drop 8,656 tons of bombs on Berlin, 2,700 people die, 250,000 are left homeless.

A few days later, HG walks through the city center to find his office. The phones aren't yet working again. "It's admirable the way the sappers have at least cleared the roadways, and are supporting all the buildings in danger of collapse, but the impression of the destroyed streets is simply indescribable! And at the same time I was seething with rage against those pigs of Tommies who have destroyed the work of many generations in a matter of a few hours! Revenge—revenge—revenge!!!" And what about the German air raids on London and other cities, what about Coventry? Perhaps it's asking too much for HG, in the face of these ruins that were once Berlin, to think about which is the chicken and which the egg, to remember the terrible destruction of Warsaw, which so horrified him then. And rage is a therapy for despair.

HG also uses it in his treatment of Else: "Good God, in the devil's name thrice over, drop these old stories and don't bother yourself and me with something that could be long buried and forgotten if it weren't forever being brought artificially back to life." "Incidentally, I should actually confess that if I do ever think of a woman other than you, at the moment I have someone quite different in mind, and that Hanna, along with many others, is far away in the background." "That apart from my work I really have no thoughts left over for Inge or Hanna or any such foolish subjects." "It would be good for us to raise ourselves back up out of this contemptible serving girl's level of jealousy, and turn again into the free and generous human beings that we once were, who have no need of so much talk about trust because it's simply there." "Friday morning. Woke up somewhat crumpled after extremely silly dreams—many delightful women, sailing boats, toboggan run, and then you, as a terribly menacing Gorgon's head, stopping me from grabbing any of them . . . !"

I feel lousy reading all this. They're both at the end of their tethers. Else, shaken like everyone by fear over the course of the war, has the house full of refugees from the bombing raids, family and friends from all over Germany; that means nineteen people sitting down at the table every day. Jochen, who has just turned eighteen, has been consigned to France as a soldier—"a child in uniform," rages Else. Barbara is diagnosed as having a heart murmur, she has to stay in bed, and the appropriate doctors are at the front. In Berlin, Ursula falls from a crowded bus, and Bernhard delivers her to Halberstadt with a serious concussion and having suffered a miscarriage. She's desperately sad, because she has lost her child and her beloved apartment in the Brückenallee. Dagmar Podeus, the irrepressible Dagmar, has developed bedsores and gets pneumonia and still isn't allowed to die. Kurt, knowledgeable Kurt, is driven through the house by attacks of mental derangement, no longer able to find his way. Gertrud, who walks with a cane in any case, falls down the stairs and breaks her ankle. Everything depends on Else.

She can't relax with HG, nor he with her. An unbridgeable gulf has opened up between them; there are open wounds that in spite of the general gloom are not put into perspective, but intensify the unbearability of everything. An additional source of pain—for both of them. Tears come to my eyes when I see that Else can't forgive —she's had to forgive so often! Else—please!—just once more! You'll torment yourself for the rest of your life for leaving HG now, of all times. I do really sympathize with Else after all those outrageous escapades, which were his, not hers. But now they need each other. They are both fighting to the point of emotional exhaustion, they both feel that the loss of the other is more than they can bear. Yet Else is incapable of preventing it. She can't, because she doesn't know that the loss will be definitive and dreadful, and that it will come very soon. She doesn't guess, thinking HG is relatively safe in Berlin. Perhaps she might have acted otherwise if he had been in daily peril at the front. I read in HG's diary: "For Sunday I take my work into the garden, because you don't want to have me at home," and "I reach out my hand, and feel you very close to me." This longing, their mutual longing, will never again be fulfilled.

The building in Jebensstrasse is burned out, and HG's office moves to a temporary lodging in "Tanne." That is the code name for a former NCO school in Eiche, near Potsdam, an uncomfortable, bedbug-ridden place from the 1920s. HG has to take the suburban train to Potsdam and then walk through Sanssouci Park for three-quarters of an hour, which in the long run becomes too much for him, especially now in winter. So he moves completely to Tanne, squeezing himself and his belongings into a tiny barrack room; the unit's shower—"just cold water!"—is around the corner, and HG bravely remembers that the soldiers "in the field" don't fare any better.

One problem is that only duty-related phone calls can be made from here, which makes communication with Halberstadt immensely difficult. If Else has anything urgent to pass on, she has to go through the local commandant in Halberstadt, who then tells HG via the military line. "It was the same when I was in Pleskau," HG says, trying to calm her down, and besides, calls from private phones have in the meantime to be booked at least ten hours in advance. Even in Berlin, HG can't just phone friends or the dentist whenever he feels like it; it's a clear decline in quality of life. The food situation is disastrous; rations for the populace have been cut again, and food in Tanne swallows up ration cards, giving "subterranean quality" in return. In every letter HG writes that he is hungry.

He is promoted to group leader in December 1943, "and with greater authority than any of the other group leaders—me, just about the youngest major among a lot of old warhorses! I realize it means I've put my head in a noose, and I'll have to pull it back out both cautiously and energetically. On the other hand, of course, it's a distinction that everyone envies me for, and I'm being constantly congratulated, although clearly with mixed feelings. Until now I was a furtively blooming violet, being careful to keep a low profile. Now I will be caught in spotlights from every imaginable direction, I'll have to watch out not to be shot down in their glare."

Sure enough, HG has taken over a suicide squad in the shape of Group III W 2, responsible for the preventive nondisclosure protection of military research projects, first and foremost the army's experimental rocket center in Peenemünde, where the so-called V-2 is being built. It's the first midrange rocket, developed over a period of ten years by Wernher von Braun and others. Its real name is Aggregate 4 (A4), but Goebbels quickly rechristened it Vergeltungswaffe 2 (Reprisal Weapon 2). "V-2—the lightning rocket," booms the propaganda, "the terrible effect of V-2"—"the long arm of our offensive," the secret miracle weapon that promises invincibility, last-minute salvation.

There is also a V-1, proper name Fi 103, a jet-propelled "flying bomb," an unmanned plane with a payload of one thousand kilograms of explosives, which was conjured up by the Luftwaffe in just a year and is much less expensive. The V-1 tends to be shot down because it's so slow, while the V-2 liquid-fuel rocket flies at five thousand kilometers an hour—when it flies. Fewer than half of the six thousand completed rockets do what they're supposed to.

In military terms, the two weapon systems prove to be irrelevant, but the public isn't aware of that. Their propaganda value is great and makes the minefield across which HG and the six officers assigned to him are moving all the more explosive. Not only are the long-range German weapons a favorite target for enemy spies and saboteurs. Given the many thousands of technical and civilian staff working in the experimental center itself and with its many suppliers, watertight secrecy, HG's mission, turns out to be a task of Sisyphus.

In addition, as in all the world's armies, the individual branches are not the best of friends: the Luftwaffe, for the V-1, and the army, for the V-2, are bitterly competing for priority in the eyes of Hitler—priority meaning money, raw materials, and labor. Even more dangerous is the power struggle between the Reichsführer SS Heinrich Himmler and the armaments minister Albert Speer. Himmler wants to bring the German arms industry under the control of the SS—including, most importantly, control of the rocket center in Peenemünde.

For this to happen, the influential Wernher von Braun and two of his leading colleagues had to be done away with. All three of them had left no doubt about their preference for the army, not because they were particularly loyal, but because they calculated that they would be given greater freedom of action by the army than by the SS. The fact that von Braun had been a member of the

SS since 1940 had nothing to do with it. The experimental rocket station was an army institution, and it was here that he was able to work. It was impossible to predict whether Himmler's coup would succeed, and von Braun always liked to be on the winning side. This time it doesn't work: early in the morning of March 15, 1944, the three scientists were arrested by the Gestapo and taken to their prison in Stettin, accused of high treason. "Before witnesses," they had expressed defeatist thoughts about the outcome of the war, and openly discussed their urgent desire "to build a spaceship, rather than an instrument of murder."

That could have gone wrong: Wernher von Braun and his colleagues wouldn't have been the first to be "shot while trying to escape." The commander of the experimental rocket center, General Walter Dornberger, is unable to persuade Himmler or General Field Marshal Keitel, head of the OKW, to free his most important staff members. This is where HG is needed. An army officer, he enlists the support of Albert Speer, who has been lying in bed with a knee injury for months, and understands that this is yet another personal attack on him by Himmler. The SS is taking action against the armaments minister.

Speer makes a special request to Hitler, and together the armaments minister and the Abwehr officer bring about the acquittal of the three prisoners after fourteen days. That's what it says in the relevant sources, and that's what it says—cryptically—in HG's diary entry for April 7, 1944: "I've even learned to become personally involved in the inevitable conspiracies that go on in different departments among the authorities, and recently played a downright virtuoso aria on this instrument, which won me the undivided applause of all participants."

The SS had had its foot in the door at Peenemünde for a long time. Since June 1943 there had been a concentration camp there with prisoners from Buchenwald who were initially deployed to build the security fences around the assembly plant for the V-2. On the night of August 17, 1943, the British bombed Peenemünde;

more than seven hundred people died, most of them forced laborers. After this the decision was made to transfer production below ground, to the southern Harz, near Nordhausen. There was a limestone massif there, inside which BASF had dug two tunnels as long ago as the First World War, and with the arrival of the first 107 prisoners from Buchenwald on August 28, 1943, a project began which, under the name Mittelbau Dora, was to become synonymous with hell.

By night and day, the first production sites for the V-2, the so-called Mittelwerk, were built by prisoners and forced laborers in the dark, airless tunnels. It was a perfect factory, "unparalleled even by the Americans," according to Arms Minister Speer. Survivors reported after liberation: "The tunnels were extended by means of heavy compressed air drills, and the removal of even massive chunks of stone had to be accomplished with hands and shovels. Stone dust and gases were constantly being swirled up, and there were no ventilation systems. In the tunnels there was no water for washing or drinking, out of desperation the men urinated in their hands so that they could at least wash the chalk dust from their faces." The sleeping tunnels were cramped, crowded dungeons full of excrement, vermin, and decaying corpses. The transfer to the camp of barracks under construction outside took place gradually until June 1944, meaning that some prisoners spent as long as nine months in that underworld, if they survived at all.

Anyone who was not deployed in the manufacture of the V-2 ended up in the building units. The prisoners were used for enlargement work and new subterranean enterprises, and the construction of the new industrial complex was enormous. Many of the prisoners had no shoes and had to walk barefoot in the debris; they worked in water at subzero temperatures, excavating ditches with hardly any tools except their hands, starving and suffering from exhaustion. Anyone who collapsed was ruthlessly beaten back to work. The mortality rate was higher than in any other concentration camp in Germany. Seriously ill inmates and invalids were deported in liquidation transports to Auschwitz, Majdanek, and Bergen-Belsen. Cautious estimates speak of between 16,000 and 20,000 fatalities between September 1943 and April 1945. Destruction through labor.

Why am I telling this? Because the story can never be told too often. I'm telling it here because HG goes there on several occasions; the V-2 is his job. I'd like to know his attitude toward Mittelbau Dora. The responsible Abwehr officer can't possibly be unaware of who is building this wonder weapon, and under what circumstances. At least once he must have gone underground into the Mittelwerk tunnel building site to learn precisely what he was supposed to protect.

The Dora concentration camp is right next to the Mittelwerk, and impossible to ignore, with its electric fence and its wooden watchtowers. Equally impossible to ignore are the camp slaves in their striped uniforms. HG cannot have overlooked any of the horrifying details of this hell. Of course he doesn't write about it; in his letters I only ever find "Harz" as the destination of his journeys, until he once slips up and names Nordhausen, which I had suspected as being the real meaning of "Harz." Neither will he have spoken to anyone about it, except the officers of his Abwehr group, and they, like HG, must see the many foreign forced laborers—French, Polish, Russian—first of all as a potential secret service risk. None of them, not even HG, can articulate the horror, if they feel any at all.

On his way back from Nordhausen to Tanne, HG drives past Halberstadt, which is just around the corner. By now he has a military BMW "with driver and gas," which frees him from reliance on the chaotic rail connections. How am I to imagine this? Emerging directly from hell for tea with Else, Wibke, and Gentian Skyblue, finally having his hair cut again, popping into the I.G. Klamroth offices, where Hans Litten suggests a constructive solution to avert the next disaster. Back at Bismarckplatz he consoles the desolate Kurt, is pleased that Sabine has come back early enough from a Young Maidens event so that he can play a round of town-country-river with her, and sets off just in time, before all the many house-guests roll in. He wants to get to Tanne before the air-raid siren sounds. And all the time hell is blanked out? The horror doesn't choke him? I have no answer.

Dagmar Podeus dies three days before Christmas 1943, by this stage a blessing for her, a blessing for Else, and yet very sad for everybody. "For first time of my life I am sick and make burden to Else," she had written in the guest book a year previously, and two months later: "as a patient once again, it's an unseemly behavior that I wish to avoid." No avoiding it, though. Dagmar could no longer be left alone in her apartment. She had been sure that she would survive her children. Her parents had become as old as the hills, and all her elder brothers and sisters are at this point still walking about in the best of health—"What will I do when you have all disappeared?" Dagmar lived to the age of seventy-two. For Else, despite all its relief her death is a source of deep sorrow, she already feels homeless after her effective breakup with HG. "I'm an orphan," she writes in the children's diary, "now I have nothing left to give me the illusion of not being alone." She immediately corrects herself: "Of course I'm not alone, because I have you," but sometimes even an adult woman wants to be a child, finding shelter under her mother's apron.

Else and HG don't find a way to reach each other. HG paints red hearts in a letter—"finally I might have a little *coffee* for you—what would you say about that?" He attaches clippings from Danish newspapers about love and marriage: "In a marriage, you can't say, 'he doesn't love me anymore' because he's no longer in the first hot *Sturm-und-Drang* period. It doesn't mean that his love is dead, it has turned into the togetherness that brings warmth for the senses and the soul." "Marriage is a touchstone for one's own character, not for that of the other party. That's just a way of making excuses for oneself." Beneath this HG writes: "I so long to take you in my arms—I'm very lonely and very miserable."

But Else gives neither of them a break. HG on January 27, 1944: "Your letter, the first for a long time, was another splash of cold water poured onto my already less than rosy mood. I will have to recognize by now that the terror and the feeling of anxiety with which I turn each of your letters around in my hands before opening it is clearly not a foolish idiosyncrasy, but rather sadly justified, because your letters actually always contain something that would have been better left unsaid, because it only hurts without healing." Why did Else keep these letters, when she had destroyed just about everything concerning HG since their engagement? I fervently hope she didn't reread them after HG's death. They are testimonies to deep grief and mutual helplessness, and I find them very hard to bear.

FOURTEEN

HG before the People's Court

Halberstadt has been through its first air raid—HG anxiously in spring 1944: "I'm so sorry that I wasn't with you for this emergency, which has now finally reached you too." Such cases are accumulating now. I have in front of me the air-raid maps, stretched out on cardboard with the entry lanes drawn in red. Else writes in the children's diaries that she senses the instability of their nerves: "There are so many people in the house, and I'm sure I shoo them down to the cellar far too often, but I have to have them all together." She herself usually stays upstairs by the radio. The targets are still at the edge of town—the Junkers aircraft factory, the airfield, the freight station, the barracks.

At the same time, life goes on with gratifying banality. The many children parked in the house, all about Sabine's age—she's ten now—have discovered sports, and prefer to walk on their hands. Not me, I'm too small and even then I knew that sports were bad for your health. Down in the air-raid cellar Ursula reads aloud from *Tom Sawyer* and *Huckleberry Finn* and the bomber squadrons can boom away all they like outside, first Tom and Becky have to get safely back out of the cave. To the amazement of all the other children, one of these deposited charges, he's from Nuremberg, has a tapeworm. Else: "Now I know where all our ration cards have gone!" Ursula is expecting a baby, she's radiant, there's lots of singing going on, I suspect they're still Hitler songs.

In the German world, front lines are caving in. Italy has declared war on the Reich; on June 6, 1944, the Allies land in Normandy, 438,000 Jews from Hungary are transported to Auschwitz. The sixty-hour week with a complete ban on leave is the new implementation of the "total war" announced by Goebbels a year ago. In France, the Waffen SS "Das Reich" division liquidates the village of Oradour-sur-Glane: 642 inhabitants are murdered in reprisal for the intensified activities of the French Resistance. Only a few survive.

Early in February 1944, HG travels on Abwehr business to Mauerwald in East Prussia, the base for the OKH when Hitler is residing in the neighboring Wolf's Lair. There he meets the four men along with whom he will end up before the Nazi People's Court half a year later: General Major Hellmuth Stieff is head of the organizational section of the Army General Staff. Bernhard is his group leader II, succeeding Count Claus von Stauffenberg in the post. Then there are Bernhard's colleague Major Joachim Kuhn and Bernhard's close friend Senior Lieutenant Albrecht von Hagen.

These four men are jointly involved in the acquisition of explosives for the attempt on Hitler's life. I can't tell whether they have already discussed it with HG before this evening in Eastern Prussia, or whether this is the first time the subject has been broached. Obviously there are no documents—the essence of conspiracy is secrecy. The verdict delivered by the People's Court against HG and Bernhard states that HG was let in on the plan only on July 10 in Berchtesgaden, but that means nothing. The verdict contains a lot of nonsense. There are many reasons to believe that HG has been informed of the planned assassination attempt, which has been under way for two years, much earlier. There had been other attempts as early as 1938. The list of men executed in connection with July 20 reads like an extract from HG's address book. But being informed isn't the same as being involved. HG hasn't, and I'm quite sure of this, taken part in any of the planning, he was a confidant, not a fellow perpetrator. The same can't be said of the four men he's sitting down with in Mauerwald, they're actively and practically participating.

I don't want to go into the conspiracy of July 20, its military and civilian aspects, the planning of it, and the shortcomings that caused its failure. That has been done competently many times by others. Neither do I want to discuss the political ideas of the opposition for "the postwar period," their rudimentary understanding of democracy, for example, and their reversion to monarchical structures. Rather I remember my impatience in earlier years when I repeatedly wondered: Why so late? It wasn't late. It was unsuccessful. As early as 1939, men like Henning von Tresckow and Fabian von Schlabrendorff had stated "that duty and honor require us to do everything we can to bring down Hitler and National Socialism, and thus to save Germany and Europe from the danger of barbarism." Both later pursued their plans for a coup in Army Group Central, where Bernhard was also based.

Their resistance, and that of many other officers, continued even when Hitler was enjoying his greatest military successes, when he was most widely admired. Things grew increasingly urgent as the SS Einsatzgruppen started following the German troops, sowing hell and destruction around all of Europe, and millions of Jews died in the gas chambers. Resistance was almost impossible in a totalitarian state with its all-powerful Gestapo, its security services, the SS, plus a population that still worshipped Hitler and millions of soldiers who had sworn an oath to him.

If they were to be freed from that oath, Hitler had to be removed. To topple the regime, a military putsch was required with a well-regulated top-to-bottom command structure, assumption of executive power by the Wehrmacht, and the establishment of a state of emergency to prevent civil war. Afterward, a civilian government would lead the country back into the community of civilized nations. Who knows whether it could have worked. Hitler wasn't dead, the putsch collapsed, and the revolution didn't take place.

Admittedly many people had joined the conspiracy—about six hundred were arrested, and that may not have been everyone. But out of millions a vanishingly small number put their consciences above their lives. If they hadn't existed, they or the members of the White Rose, or brave Georg Elser, who all on his own blew up the Munich Bürgerbräukeller on November 8, 1939—I could list some more who refused to cooperate—without them, there would have been nothing for us, their offspring, to cling to in the moral ruins after the war.

I don't know whether it really is Bernhard who lets HG in on the plans for the coup. I tend not to believe it. At any rate, I suspect that whoever put him in the picture was pushing at an open door. He didn't balk at treason in Denmark, on the several occasions when he warned the opposing side of impending German actions. In the summer of 1943 HG writes about the "violent battle of ideologies, even within," about the "intellectual movements that will influence our time"; he gives away his SS uniforms. I think he's finding new bearings at around this time, if not before, and that revolution—high treason, in other words—had crossed his mind.

During interrogation by the Gestapo he mentions Stalingrad as the root cause. It must have been a cumulative development.

It makes sense that HG isn't actively involved in the plans for the coup. He's sitting in his Abwehr office far from any position in which he could have made himself "useful." But what's going on inside him? How does he resolve his conflicts about "murdering a tyrant," about the accusation of the "stab in the back," about his oath? How does he deal with his fear, the fear of all conspirators, that Germany will sink into civil war while at the front line the adversaries step up their pressure? Does he hope the assassination attempt might succeed for the sake of Germany's self-esteem? Is he also convinced that it is necessary, "in the face of history," to cleanse oneself, "coûte que coûte" (whatever the cost), as Henning von Tresckow put it? This was a few days after the Allied invasion of Normandy, and Stauffenberg had asked him whether an assault was still sensible.

HG knows what the regime has turned Germans into. Even if he had seen nothing of the mass murders in Poland because his regiment withdrew so quickly, and Denmark in HG's time was something of a summer holiday, Russia wasn't. His eyes must have been opened there, at least. The fact that he has never written about it doesn't mean a thing. He doesn't write about the Mittelbau Dora concentration camp in Nordhausen either. He doesn't talk to Else about it. She would have remembered, when she wrote in the children's diary, about what it was like when HG came to Halberstadt for the last time on July 21, 1944: "I recall how plausible I found Father's account of the necessity of the assassination attempt, but he said so little, so little. Anything I learned I had to drag out of him. He didn't want me to be burdened with too much knowledge in case of a Gestapo interrogation. He was familiar with their methods."

HG works for military intelligence. Saying nothing has become second nature to him. He writes to Else in April 1944: "For over four years I've been leading a kind of double life, and recently more than ever I'm finding it painful not to be able to talk to you about what's going on in the other half. Precisely because you don't belong to the office, a dialogue with you would clarify much for me, and if things get out of hand, as they are doing at the moment, it makes such demands on me that the other half, the half of my life in which you appear, risks being engulfed, and I no longer know how I can avoid alienation." Whom does HG talk to instead? Nobody, I think. All these men, unless they are sitting in the eye of the hurricane, are condemned to silence. They do their duty, their task is the solution of upcoming problems, not a preoccupation with their own fears. There is a reason almost all of HG's letters from 1944 end with the words "Your lonely husband."

Bernhard, of course, doesn't write to Ursula about the turmoil in OKH either, although she gets mail from him almost every day. His letters are full of poetry and tenderness, pages of detailed plans for the future, when the war is over, anticipation of the child that Ursula is expecting, togetherness: "You know, I think most marriages go flat through thoughtless familiarity. That can't be the case with us, because to me you are a wonder constantly renewed, unknown to me and yet so familiar because it's you. But I'm astonished every time, I discover you in a thousand variations, and time and again I love you anew!"

I find a letter from Bernhard to his father, the awe-inspiring Berlin banker with the pince-nez. Bernhard writes to him on July 13, 1944—a week before the assassination attempt—while on a plane to Budapest: "The idea that I am soon to be a father is just as strange to me as the thought of being married was before my wedding. But if I get used to fatherhood as quickly, and it makes me as happy as life with Ursula, then I will doubtless get used to it *very quickly*, and it will make me *very* happy. Dear Father, when a man's heart is full, his mouth runneth over: again and again I must say that marriage to Ursula is a greater joy to me than anything I have known in the world before, or anything I could have expected. I am sure that Ursula feels exactly the same."

Sometimes Bernhard mentions people from his military surroundings, and on a number of occasions I come across his admiration for Lieutenant Colonel, later Major General, Hellmuth Stieff. In 1942 Stieff had brought Bernhard into the General Staff of the Fourth Army's High Command, and in 1943 to Stauffenberg's former post in the organizational section of the Army General Staff. Stieff is a short, charismatic man, always on the go, whose furious letters about Hitler are startlingly open: "I am filled with utter hatred!" he writes to his wife. Of the starvation of Leningrad: "as though a true devil in human form had invented something that would make even Genghis Khan green with envy." Stieff had surrounded himself with a group of young officers who had been united in their rejection of the regime at least since the fall of Stalingrad. They're the ones sitting with HG on that February evening in Mauerwald.

OKH was always based near the Führer's headquarters, be it the Wolf's Lair or Obersalzberg, in Zossen near Berlin, or wherever Hitler set up camp. Stieff had access to Hitler—had he been prepared to carry out the assassination attempt, as Stauffenberg still seemed to hope in early July, perhaps things might have turned out differently. But Stieff couldn't, wouldn't, have confessed to an "inhibition about killing." Who would blame him? Stauffenberg, seriously hampered by his war wounds—he had lost an eye, one hand, and two fingers on the other—flew from Berlin to the Wolf's Lair, and after the attack it took him a precious three and a half hours to get back to Berlin before he could assume leadership of the coup—another reason for the failure of the conspiracy.

Bernhard doesn't tell Ursula anything about the repeated attempts to get hold of explosives for the attack. She's unaware of his trip to Berlin along with their mutual friend Albrecht von Hagen on May 24, when the two men bring the bomb to Stauffenberg at army headquarters on Bendlerstrasse. Ursula is brave and sends Bernhard what she calls "silly letters," but he senses her anxiety about the birth of the child without him, and the fact that she feels lonely in spite of all the hustle and bustle at home. "You consist entirely of longing, my love," Bernhard writes, setting himself beside her: "So do I, my most enchanting wife. And I'm with you, with you, with you!" On July 1 he and HG come to Halberstadt on a flying visit; Bernhard has to leave the next morning. It's the last time they see him.

I can still cling a little to everyday life on Bismarckplatz. The house is being rearranged once again, because in addition to the numerous relatives, bombed-out strangers are billeted in the house. One of these, an actor called Fischer-Colbrie, fascinates the children by loudly declaiming his parts—what parts, and what for?—and also reciting from a book called *Little Hey, the Art of Speaking,* which was and still is a standard exercise for all would-be Hamlets, full of fiendishly difficult tongue twisters. The children listening outside the door learn as well, and I can imagine the juvenile acrobats parroting these texts as they clamber up and down the stairs on their hands (the latest level of difficulty is two steps at once). Everybody's sad when Herr Fischer-Colbrie finds lodgings elsewhere.

In Goebbels's diaries I find HG mentioned in an entry for June 29, 1944: "Major Klamroth from the Abwehr, whose task it is to ensure the secrecy of our new retaliatory weapons, gives me a detailed presentation on the current state of our retaliatory program. This is more or less as follows"—and here HG tells the propaganda minister about the V-2 and V-1, and that neither of them comes up to the high expectations set for them. He won't have made himself popular with phrases like "the latest experiments have shown that the projectile usually self-detonates at an altitude of 2,000 m" or "two projectiles have inadvertently ended up in Sweden, and another close by the hunting lodge of Reich Regent Horthy"—in Hungary, mind you.

Else has recently got, via HG, a Russian housemaid, one of the parachutists from Pleskau, who has thus escaped the firing squad. Her name is Shenya, everyone calls her Jenny, and at first she weeps her eyes out with homesickness. Else broods in her Sunday letter: "It's a bit like having a serf. If I was awful to the poor child, what would she do? It's actually rather dreadful. But I console myself with the thought that she's certainly never been as well off as she is now." Jenny is soon so much at ease that she actually comes back to the family from a holiday in Russia, and sometimes calls Else Mamutschka. Her trail too is lost after the war.

Gradually Else billets deposited charges with her relatives; she asks friends and long-term family guests to find other places to sleep; she doesn't want any more people on foraging trips in her house—she wants it empty, or at least the part for which she is responsible. There's to be peace and quiet when Ursula has her child. "I was very nervous about all the air-raid warnings, and prayed that we would be spared when the time came," Else writes in the children's diary after the war. "Ursula was very brave, and missed Bernhard terribly, but she consoled me by telling me that she was only one of hundreds of thousands of mothers-to-be, and that they all had to behave like men at the front. Oh, Ursula, how good it was that she didn't know what she would have to put up with."

On July 17 Ursula turns twenty, she gets seven birthday letters from Bernhard, the first ones already written on July 8—he teases her by saying that his "preference for very young girls" takes a "serious crack" when they enter their twenties. He raves about the most beautiful *Frau Oberstleutnant* under the sun, he wishes himself "at least ten decades" with her and dreams of "your head on my shoulder, your breasts, your tender hands, your breath, your lips, all of you, my love." It's Bernhard's last letter, written on July 19, 1944.

HG is often in Halberstadt, so he doesn't write so frequently. In May there's another outburst of fury: "Do try once more to show me what joy it is to be your husband—a joy that I have recently been able to conjure almost exclusively through scant memories of the past and in vague hope of the future!!" But in early June he writes, "Poor thing, it's particularly hard for you because you have succumbed to the impression that I divide myself not only between you and my job, but between you and other women as well; that I consider this view to be both false and unfair does not blind me to the fact that you hold it—and that it's my fault that you came to it. I am so sorry that you therefore feel doubly lonely, and I am searching for every possible way to lift your feeling of loneliness from you. I wish we could take a long holiday together, away from here, all alone, just the two of us; perhaps then you would realize how much I love you!" I find another two pieces of paper from July 1944, obviously sent in packages: "I love you sooooo much!" and "I love thinking about you!"

On July 20 at 12:42 p.m., Stauffenberg's bomb explodes in the Führer's headquarters, the Wolf's Lair. Else learns of this only at night, when Hitler delivers a brief address on the radio. She is woken by Bernhard calling to ask after Ursula and the coming baby. Else in the children's diary: "Bernhard was so curt and so terribly serious on the phone. But he didn't want to wake Ursula." It's Bernhard's last phone call to Halberstadt. Afterward, Else turns on the radio to find out about enemy planes. She hears Hitler saying that officers have attempted to murder him, and knows "in that very instant that Bernhard is involved. How can I describe my worry, my anxiety to you, how can I do that? Words aren't sufficient."

Else doesn't tell anybody about it. Ursula, oblivious, takes a "contractions walk" with her the following evening, July 21, and when they come back, HG is waiting for them in the little temple. Whenever I pass by that little temple in the garden on Bismarckplatz I see HG before me, sitting there on one of the massive sandstone walls on either side of the steps; he's sitting there in uniform, and a mute glance between him and Else focuses their anxiety. Ursula goes into her room, HG tells Else only the most essential part, that Bernhard was "involved" and that he himself knew about it. Shortly after eleven o'clock Ursula goes into labor.

Else writes Bernhard a letter while his child is coming into the world; she started it a few days previously, when it looked as though the baby was due. She writes in installments: "16 July 10:00 p.m. Ursula isn't having pains yet, just vague sensations. She's just gone upstairs to have a bath. She's very calm and cheerful and not at all nervous. I can't say the same about myself. I have a very unpleasant feeling of hollowness in the stomach region, I'm downright terrified. Our telephone wasn't working a little while ago, which was all I needed. I'm thinking lots about you during these hours, Bernhard, I'm very happy that you're Ursula's husband, and the father of our little grandchild, who, we hope, will soon be bawling. In the past year and a half of her marriage Ursula has developed a lot, and the most essential part of that is due to you.

"17 July 8:00 p.m. Unfortunately everything is quiet, it would be so nice, what with its being Ursula's birthday today and the air-raid situation favorable. I suspect that Hans Georg won't come until the baby's here, he's afraid as well! Puha, I wish it was time.

"18 July, 5:00 p.m. We're still waiting. Ursula just collapsed on the balcony with the recliner, perhaps the baby will take that as a request. Father-in-law has been considerably worse for a few days"—that's Kurt, wonderful Kurt!—"one old branch is growing rotten and brittle, and a new young shoot has already begun to grow on the Klamroth tree. It's very curious, that simultaneous experience of becoming and fading away, and in such close proximity. Poor Grandfather's mind is far from clear, and he feels he's being persecuted. Late last night he appeared on the balcony outside the living room, because someone was *guarding* the other door!! And then all of a sudden there was a flash of clarity: 'Else, I'm going mad, it's terrible, but I'm going mad!' I'm seized with boundless pity for this loving old man.

"19 July, evening. Still waiting. It wouldn't be so bad if it weren't for all those damned alarms!

"21 July, shortly after midnight. So now, at last, it's time. The contractions are already coming at quite short intervals, at half past eleven I called the midwife, and she's just turned up, at a quarter past twelve. Radio reports of strike fighters heading for the Brandenburg Marches, and bomber squadrons over western Germany. Will we escape without an air raid? Last night, when you called, Bernhard, I found you so very, very serious on the phone. I didn't want to ask. We're all very agitated about the assassination attempt on the Führer, of course. I listened to the Führer's address last night, and even while you have nothing to do with the whole business, after this speech the whole General Staff is more or less implicated, and that's naturally cause for concern. I haven't said anything to Ursula about it, but during the day she has of course heard about it. There can hardly be a more dramatic moment to come into this world out of joint. Ursula came up to see me at about half past ten, unhappy and in tears. Of course she's frightened, and you're so far away, Bernhard, and the news is so worrying and our anxiety is so great. But then at eleven o'clock Albrecht von Hagen called and passed on greetings from you, and that helped.

"22 July, one o'clock in the morning. The air-raid siren has just started up"—Else has clearly taken the typewriter down to the cellar—"and the contractions are becoming more violent. Enemy planes are over Berlin, on their way back they'll probably pass overhead, according to the wired radio from Dessau. The contractions are coming at brief intervals. My chickenhearted little Ursula, who usually makes such a fuss at the slightest hint of pain, is being so brave, I'm really very proud. Hans Georg, who came this evening, is nowhere to be seen. I'm convinced that the fear of seeing Ursula in pain is greater than his fear of the British. It isn't a pretty sight!! And then there are these heavy, oppressive worries! But Ursula is only occupied with her elemental natural phenomenon, and that's good. It takes the whole person!

"Ursula had to take castor oil this evening, she decided that you should at least share that with her next time, Bernhard! Something to look forward to. The oil has started working, making the contractions more violent. These early contractions are by far the worst and the most unpleasant. Oh, if Ursula could only give birth as easily as

I did. But it does take time with the first child, Barbara was the same. Hans Georg was just running around in desperation, 'But it's not my fault! But it's not my fault!' I tried to comfort him, he wants to try to sleep now, there's nothing he can do anyway. Everything is fine and normal—it's hard and difficult and painful, of course, not easy to watch. I'd rather it was me!! They've just given the all-clear. At least we've managed that.

"½ past 3 a.m. We're still no further on. Ursula has to struggle a lot, she's moaning and whimpering quietly. She dozes a little between the contractions, but only ever for a few minutes. Can poor old Grandfather still grasp that the fourth generation is moving into his house, his great-grandchild? It just occurs to me, I don't think it was customary in the past for a grandmother to witness the birth of her grandchild while wearing long, dark gray trousers and a blue jacket, and with her hands in her trouser pockets. I've just made coffee again.

"10 past 4 a.m. She's up again, and wandering restlessly around. 'Oh *Mutti,* I'm glad Bernhard isn't here! Oh *Mutti, Mutti,* it hurts so much!' That's the refrain. The midwife wants to give her an enema. It's a stupid piece of drudgery, but it helps, it hurries things along. She's had the contractions at brief intervals for five hours now. It's really astonishing that mothers agree to endure these pains three, four, five times and more. But they're forgotten so quickly, that's the good thing, and you know what all this is for.

"It's 5 a.m. Ursula has just been given a deadly nightshade suppository, it should loosen her up and calm her down. Her cervix has so far only dilated to a couple of inches. I always *started* that way, and with Ursula's it's the result of six hours of pain. If only I could help her! We could even have a new air raid before the child is born!

"7 a.m. Ursula had a very hot bath, which gave her some relief. The cervix is now quite widely dilated, the midwife says. But the torture she's going through, the poor child! Her waters still haven't broken! Let's hope there isn't an air raid on the way. I'm so worried!

It's nearly nine o'clock now! She still has to go through this torment. She's lying down again. Now she has to work and press so that the waters finally break.

"8:55. The waters have broken, finally! The worst is over!

"9:48. Bernhard, a boy!! A strong, healthy boy! And Ursula is so radiant and so happy! She's been working so hard over the last three-quarters of an hour—and now he's here, and he started bawling immediately, and everything's forgotten, just vast joy and a great sense of creation. But she's also worked incredibly hard for him this night. He's terrific! I'm so happy and so grateful!

"For completeness sake I should add that three stitches were necessary, one of them very painful, but Ursula was very brave about that as well. The boy weighs eight pounds and is 56 cm long, head circumference 37 cm. Ursula's great joy and radiant happiness when the boy was finally here and gave his first already very forceful cry would have reconciled even you to eleven hours of torment. I'm glad that she held out so bravely, and that she was fully conscious at the moment of that first cry. It's definitely the most intense experience in a woman's life, and it makes an incomparable impression on you, giving you a unique feeling of joy and happiness. Of course you were here with us for the long, hard night. She's waiting for you to come now, so that she can hand your son to you. I hope that will be possible soon."

I don't want to think about whether a woman should put up with eleven hours of torment to "hand his son" to the father, or about the circumstances under which women brought children into the world in those days: at home, with the insane risk to both mother and child. I'm holding in my hand Else's letter to Bernhard, five pages on onion paper, and I see: this is the original. She didn't send it—it was too late. HG phones Berlin in the morning and learns that Bernhard is "away"—it's July 22. In the afternoon HG has to go briefly to Nordhausen, and from there he brings the—incorrect—news that Bernhard was shot with Stauffenberg and the others in Bendlerstrasse on the evening of July 20. Else in the children's diary: "Ursula was gradually growing surprised that she hadn't heard from him, because Bernhard always found ways of contacting her. We told her that Bernhard had suddenly had to travel to Budapest on army business. I didn't want to say anything to her before I knew for certain."

Else again, still in the children's diary: "How hard it was to hide my nagging fear from her! In the midst of it all Grandfather Kurt was wandering around like a ghost, he was quite crazy in those days. Father had never seen him like that, he was so shocked! And then this new little life, how delighted Father was, he's so fond of babies, and what hopes, against all reason, he's placed on this child, for himself and for the company. Early in the morning of July 25 Father travels to Berlin, and we will never see him again. Late the same evening the Gestapo comes and searches the house for four hours. I narrowly manage to keep them from going into Ursula's room, she's already very unsettled, but she doesn't know anything yet." God almighty, the things Else could do! Later she also did the same with the Russians, no one could get past her. She radiated such strength and such determination, I can still see her standing there when the marauding foreign workers had forced their way into the house and threatened her with guns. She laughed in their faces, and they left!

While the Gestapo is in the house, HG phones from Berlin: Bernhard has been arrested in Zossen. Else: "When the people left there was an air raid, Ursula was awake and asked anxiously after Bernhard, and I had to tell her. Ursula's grief tore my heart into pieces, and she was trying so hard to be brave. What a child-bed! What can it be like with a man who adores his wife, and with such a sweet and healthy boy! And what was it like—Ursula, defenselessly abandoned to her thoughts and her fear, it was terrible."

What I would most like to do now is take my leave of this story, simply stop and leave it incomplete. I would like to act as though I were in charge of whether it continued or not. I'm not in charge, and there's no rule that says I have to feel at ease with the story I have to tell. The others, back then, had no choice either.

On August 1, 1944, Bernhard's mother, Marta, is dragged off to a "Labor Education Camp for Women" in Magdeburg. She's sixty-two. The camp is annexed to the Förster sack factory at No. 2 Schillstrasse. The twelve-hour-day hard labor, the orgies of beating, the watery soups, and the terrible hygienic conditions nearly kill Marta Klamroth. The following day Bernhard's father, Walter, who is seventy-two, is sent to jail in Potsdam, where he nearly goes blind. Bernhard's brother Walter junior, he's twenty-seven, is imprisoned in Berlin, and his other brother, Jürgen, a medical student and twenty-five, is put in a punishment battalion. This all happens in early August, two weeks before the trial. Heinrich Himmler, in his notorious speech on August 3, 1944, to Gauleiters in Posen, explains that on the model of the "Teutonic sagas" there was to be *Sippenhaftung,* or "punishment of kin," because "this man has committed treason, his blood is bad, there is traitor's blood in it, it will be eradicated." Ursula is left alone; the rules for "punishment of kin" have never been properly set out, so your fate could be a question of luck or the arbitrary use of power. At the end of October 1944 Bernhard's family is freed, and it is only now that his parents learn what has happened to their son.

Until July 29, Else speaks to HG on the telephone each night, but then she can't reach him anymore. What can they have talked about in those conversations, unaware that they would be their last? What can you say on an official phone when the girl from the switchboard is listening in? So worried were they about Bernhard that they didn't realize the danger HG was in, or at least Else didn't. On his last visit to Halberstadt, HG had told her only that on July 10 he had met Stauffenberg, Stieff, Bernhard, and General Erich Fellgiebel, head of the Signal Corps, in Berchtesgaden— Fellgiebel's task was to block communication from the Führer's headquarters to the heads of the Wehrmacht after the attack. They had talked about the plans for the attempted assassination, after which HG had spent half the night discussing things with Bernhard. Else: "I was naive enough to assume that the self-evident truth that you don't send your own son-in-law to the gallows would also be respected by the other side."

Did HG have any idea that the Gestapo were on his trail? It was impossible they didn't know about that meeting on July 10, at Stieff's table in the officers' mess of the "Frankenstrub," the code name for the OKH near Berchtesgaden. What did the Gestapo know? HG was often in "Mauerwald" or in Zossen, in the Berlin offices of the chiefs of staff, where at every opportunity he met men who were part of the July 20 circle. Was HG aware of that? Were those visits purely related to his work, or were they conspiratorial? How suspicious are occasional meetings with General Quartermaster Eduard Wagner, who shot himself on July 23, or with Artillery General Fritz Lindemann, who is on the run? HG has known both men since the 1920s, and I think he might have met Lindemann in his hometown of Hamburg. If he looked at the list of people already arrested, the avid networker HG must have wondered how many address books belonging to friends and acquaintances involved in the conspiracy contained his name.

His address books were also confiscated by the Gestapo, and HG didn't tell Else anything, certainly because it might have put her in danger, but also because the secretiveness of the Abwehr man had become second nature to him. The original interrogation records of the Gestapo have disappeared, presumably they were burned. The sole source is the Kaltenbrunner reports, and the only thing they contain concerning HG is the July 10 meeting in Berchtesgaden. Ernst Kaltenbrunner was the successor of the murdered Reinhard Heydrich and head of the Security Police, the Security Service, and the Reich Security Main Office, where a July 20 Special Commission involving hundreds of Gestapo officials met immediately after the attempted assassination. In Kaltenbrunner's name this Special Commission dispatched daily files about the progress of the investigations to Hitler's right-hand man, Reichsleiter Martin Bormann. Historically, these reports are extremely dubious, because they are tailored for Hitler's and Bormann's ears, and often contain subjective interpretations on the part of the Gestapo rather than statements from the parties interrogated. But they're all there is.

According to the Kaltenbrunner reports, under interrogation both HG and Bernhard keep strictly to the undeniable facts. HG talks of his initial "doubts, first of all after the loss of Stalingrad, that the war would have a satisfactory outcome for us"; he describes, always without mentioning names, an "overall atmosphere that could almost be called fatalistic" among the staff of the OKH: "Although I cannot quote individual sources, the general mood was more or less *après nous le déluge.* I was and remain unable to judge where this fatalism comes from and what would be the remedy for it."

I notice HG using his years of experience as an Abwehr officer in the hearings. He develops a cooperative relationship with his interrogators, who are given to frequent outbreaks of sarcasm or rage toward the other prisoners. About HG the Kaltenbrunner reports contain phrases such as: "even officers who initially, in a nonnegative sense, had honest concerns about the war and the fate of the people, were gradually drawn into the whirlpool of the conspiracy." Or: "the questions about the overall state of the war raised by Klamroth out of genuine concern," or "Major Klamroth replies most honestly." At the same time his statements are nothing but hot air.

But there must be something concrete. There's the conversation at Stieff's table in the officers' mess in the Frankenstrub, where, in the wake of general depression about the state of the war, Helmuth Stieff struck the table with his hand and said to HG: "You, Herr Klamroth, have been through this grim experience once before. I wasn't there that time. But I wish to assure you of one thing: as on that earlier occasion we won't lose this war, be it with or against this leadership."

Then the reports turn to the conversation between HG and Bernhard in the hotel about the details and extent of the conspiracy. Several times the sentence is quoted: "If there is no other way, we will have to wait for an opportunity when all the 'yes-men' are in one big heap with the Führer, and then all of them will be obliterated at once." By this point HG can't incriminate Stieff and Bernhard any further with his statement—the evidence against them is already overwhelming. Otherwise no names are mentioned. HG talks about himself—in response to the question of why "he didn't immediately try to contradict Stieff," he replies that while Stieff's statement "might have been awkward, his military training prevented him from seeking to correct the general."

It won't just have been that. HG, trained in a cavalry regiment's code of honor, adheres to the rules of the old elites in the Wehrmacht, in the army in particular, where in many respects Prussian tradition and the values passed down from father to son shaped the leadership. Commanders and the members of their General Staff—not all of them—wanted nothing to do with the Party, especially with the rabble of the SS, who were presumptuous enough to claim equal status, and whose infernal bloodlust was sullying the whole of Germany.

In many staffs at the front, and in the home-based Reserve Army, there had been a deliberate recruitment policy: "no 'brown' people"—meaning no hard-line Nazis. They stayed among themselves, and in the Kaltenbrunner reports the interrogators of the July 20 Special Commission repeatedly express their astonishment that despite the openness with which plans for a coup were discussed in the relevant officers' circles, none of it reached the outside world. HG is condemned because he did not report Bernhard. He would never have reported anybody.

HG serves up set phrases to the Gestapo: "Connected to this is the lack of political direction in the officer corps, which I now recognize as corrupt. The majority of officers—and I must count myself among that majority—are helpless to respond to problems that suddenly arise outside of our own field of duty, and inclined to suggest solutions only through the line of command. The order from the next senior officer up will be carried out, and what he doesn't order is no concern of mine."

Nothing but empty words, though the Special Commission uses statements like this to supply subject areas for Bormann and Hitler: "defeatism," "attitude toward the assassination attempt," "foreign contacts of the conspirators," the "apolitical officer." No complete interrogation records are passed on, only extracts from different sessions, which are supposed to establish the coherence of the different aspects of the conspiracy. The prisoners all do the same, they incriminate dead people, where possible, or they charge themselves. Bernhard is quoted speaking about the case, and there's no disputing his involvement in the acquisition of explosives. After the war, his assigned counsel, Arno Weimann, said Bernhard immediately confessed. What else could he have done?

The trials begin in Berlin's People's Court on August 7, 1944. Bernhard, HG, and four other defendants are tried on August 15. No one knows where they were imprisoned for the weeks leading up to the trial. It is documented that after his arrest on July 21 Bernhard was held in a jail in Lehrter Strasse. After that the trail goes cold until his execution in Plötzensee. The papers for these six men have disappeared. The interrogations generally took place in the basement of Reich Security Head Office in Prinz Albrecht Strasse. Could HG and Bernhard have been there, in the Gestapo prison? I don't know where to look for them.

I don't know if they were tortured, Bernhard probably wasn't, because he clearly kept nothing secret. I pray that HG was unharmed too. They made him wait for eleven days after the death sentence. Why, if they didn't hope to force additional information out of him? Fragments of the indictment by Senior State Attorney

Ernst Lautz have been preserved. According to these, they had the greatest problems with HG—presumably rage over HG's silence? What was he supposed to have said?

I have a block in my head and in my soul. I am standing impotently by a black wall that won't let me through to HG in his cell. I don't want to imagine what I've read about the interrogation methods, the shackles that rubbed the prisoners' wrists raw, nor the cries of the torture victims, which could be HG's. I know I must not turn away. But I don't want to know what happened during the "intensified interrogations"—food and sleep deprivation, exhaustion, beating with sticks. Fabian von Schlabrendorff lists all the torture methods in *The Secret War against Hitler*—I can't let myself imagine them being used on HG.

I force myself to look. I don't want to reduce Bernhard and HG to heroes who "go to their deaths with a manly bearing, unbent, punishing their executioners with contempt"—although that was probably the case. But that's not all. I see Bernhard weeping with longing for his wife, who has just given birth to their son—he has been told, I don't know how or when. I see him tortured by doubt over whether he should have married the baby bride, and at the same time try to bring about the collapse of the Hitler regime with every risk of failure. He must be sick with anxiety that something might happen to Ursula; even in the isolation of his cell, or during the hearings, he must know how the Gestapo carry on their work. Did they threaten to take Ursula away, and is that why he immediately confessed?

I see HG in a state of desperate loneliness, far from his wife, whose trust he has squandered. Now, in this cell, she presumably stands by his side, but does he know? He must be wondering how he could actually have believed that Else was infinitely resilient, that their supply of community, which he had wasted in endless escapades, was inexhaustible. In the verdict it says that HG's "betrayal of the Führer" was to be excused neither because of the "difficult family conditions from which he was suffering at the time, nor because his own son-in-law had to be named." What led HG to mention his conflict with Else before the court? To what end? Did he try to explain his "disloyalty" to the Führer with reference to his mental stress because of Else? Or did his strength simply fail him in view of his hopelessness at home and in the court? I can't read that sentence in the verdict without tears, and I thank fate that Else never saw it.

HG's soul has other burdens to bear: he will no longer be able to guide his many children on the path that he thinks is right. He sees his life's work in ruins, his and that of the generations before him. His deranged father can't continue the legacy of the forefathers, and who knows whether his son will survive the war. Does HG reflect that he too helped into being the regime that is about to kill him, that he himself is part of the fate that is now catching up with him? God, I don't want to demand too much of him. I would like to comfort him, if comfort were to be found anywhere. I wish I could make what lies ahead easier for both of them—HG and Bernhard must come to terms with their fear of death, and worse: their fear of a terrible agony.

On August 15, 1944, they are condemned to death by hanging. It's the third show trial of the July 20 plotters; the great hall of Berlin's People's Court is packed with hand-selected spectators in every imaginable uniform. Former Chancellor Helmut Schmidt told me he was ordered there as a young senior lieutenant. Goebbels had decreed that "soldiers of every rank whose National Socialist attitude requires improvement, are to attend the trials at the People's Court so that they know what happens to traitors."

Before the trial, a military "court of honor" called by Hitler, presided over by Field Marshal von Rundstedt, expelled the defendants from the Wehrmacht "in disgrace," so that they would be exposed to the rigors of a civilian court. Hitler: "These criminals should not stand before a court-martial, where their accomplices are sitting, delaying the proceedings!" Not one of the accused had the opportunity to justify himself in person to the honorable gentlemen of this "court of honor," and the court's chairman, Gerd von Rundstedt, should also, as an accessory, have been one of the defended. He had known about the planned coup for months, and had not informed on anyone.

The handcuffs are removed only when the defendants reach the entrance to the courtroom: they're dressed in civilian clothes without ties or suspenders. Two policemen flank them on either side and effectively drag them to their seats by their sleeves. The hall, with its pink quartz rectangles on the wall and the emperor's box above the enormous hearth, is decorated with swastika flags, which have cameras hidden behind them. Hitler's instructions, "They must be brought to trial at lightning speed, they must not be allowed to get a word in edgewise," are implemented to the letter by Roland Freisler, the president of the People's Court. In his bloodred robe, he behaves like a madman, roaring and bellowing and interrupting the defendants as soon as they start to reply. It's a nauseating spectacle, and even Justice Minister Thierack complains to Martin Bormann about Freisler: "He spoke of the defendants as 'sausages.' That did considerable damage to the seriousness of this important assembly."

In HG's and Bernhard's trial, Freisler focuses his hatred on codefendant Adam von Trott zu Solz, legation councillor in the Foreign Office and foreign policy spokesman for the conspirators: "A wretched figure in terms of body, mind, and both physical and intellectual attitude, the type of the pretentious, deracinated, characterless intellectualist from the Roman Café, a Kurfürstendamm phenomenon." Freisler can't always prevent the defendants from expressing themselves unambiguously. During the same trial, Hans-Bernd von Haeften, another member of the Foreign Office and brother of Stauffenberg's adjutant Werner von Haeften, manages to say: "According to my notion of the global historical role of the Führer, namely that he is a great executor of evil—" He gets no further than that, because Freisler roars at him. But Haeften's words have rightly become famous.

According to the court's verdict, all defendants had confirmed their confessions before the court, "although Hans Georg Klamroth repeated his only when he saw that his attempts to dismiss it were collapsing under their internal contradictions." Why was this? Did he play down his nighttime conversation with Bernhard in Berchtesgaden in an attempt to exonerate himself and his son-in-law? In the films of the trial I see them both sitting in the same row; separated by two massive guards, they would have had to really lean forward to see each other. Were they able to glance at each other in solidarity on the way to the courtroom? What did they say? The records of the trial are lost, the films are incomplete, Bernhard doesn't even feature.

HG, very gaunt and very miserable, is asked by Freisler whether he's aware that "to do nothing is treason"? HG reflects, lowers his head, and finally raises it with a defiantly negative gesture. "No!" he says loudly and clearly and shakes his head. Freisler's tirades become incomprehensible. He shouts the word "deviant" a few times, I can just make out "hide and seek" and "national community." That's it. Incidentally, Roland Freisler is killed on February 3, 1945, by a falling beam in the air-raid cellar of Berlin's People's Court building—serves him right.

Bernhard is found guilty of acquiring explosives, HG is guilty because he didn't betray Bernhard and the others. The other defendants on this day, apart from Adam von Trott zu Solz and Hans-Bernd von Haeften, are Count Wolf-Heinrich Helldorf, the prefect of police in Berlin, and Major Egbert Hayessen of the Army Headquarters in the OKH. Freisler's verdict in the name of the German people applies to them all: "Treacherous, dishonorable, and arrogant, rather than following the Führer in a manly fashion, like the whole nation, to fight for victory as no one had ever done throughout the whole of our history, they betrayed the sacrifice of our warriors, people, Führer, and Reich. They set in motion the assassination of our Führer. In cowardly fashion they thought they could deliver our nation to the mercy and disfavor of the enemy, to enslave it to the dark forces of reaction. Traitors to all that we live and fight for, they are all sentenced to death. Their assets pass to the Reich."

In a briefing shortly after July 20, Hitler had also established the manner of death: "They are not to be given the honest bullet. They are to hang like common traitors. And it must be done within two hours of the delivery of the verdict. They must hang immediately, without any mercy." Hitler calls in Freisler and the responsible executioners, and expressly decrees that there should be no clerics present, and that the suffering of the condemned men should not be alleviated in any way: "They are to hang like slaughtered cattle." And so they do. Bernhard's death certificate in Charlottenburg district office gives the time of death as 8:14 p.m. on August 15, 1944. Cause of death: hanging. The witness is the assistant prison guard Paul Dürrhauer, resident at No. 10 Manteuffelstrasse, whom I tried to track down years ago. He died a long while back, and here again he declared that "he was informed about the death on the basis of his own knowledge."

Else writes in the children's diary in February 1947—her first entry in all that time: "We know nothing. The first trial of August 7 and 8 is published in the most repellent form. Stieff is there and Albrecht von Hagen, not Bernhard, we take that as a good sign. On August 7 a soldier collects civilian clothes for Bernhard, in our naïveté we even draw hope from that. Today we know that they had been dishonorably discharged from the Wehrmacht, which was why they had to appear before the court in civilian clothes. Father had civilian clothes in Berlin anyway. The nights are particularly bad, no work to distract us, the heavy night raids on Berlin, and we know that our men are sitting defenselessly in their cells.

"The news from the west is also depressing: serious battles around St. Nazaire, and Jochen is encircled there. Barbara arrives, now at least I have my four daughters around me, but Ursula is in a truly terrible state. And then on the morning of August 17, when

I was still in bed, I was always so exhausted, Aunt Annie [HG's sister] and Uncle Adolf came, and Annie says, 'Else, now you're on your own!' Ah, children, I have forgotten nothing of the torment, nothing! And then Ursula, how was the child to bear it!"

HG's brother Kurt junior learned that the trial had taken place on August 15 via HG's assigned counsel, and that the executions had been carried out immediately afterward. Else receives a message on A5 paper, dated September 29, from the senior Reich attorney with the People's Court: "Former Major Hans Georg Klamroth has been convicted of high treason and condemned to death by the verdict of the People's Court of the Great German Reich. The sentence has been carried out. PP"—illegible. No date of death.

At the end of October HG's assigned counsel finally establishes for certain: HG died on August 26. Else receives two letters that he had written, one on the day of the sentence, the other immediately before his death. She receives the first of these shortly before Christmas, the second in February 1945. Else in the children's diary: "Ten endless days and ten endless nights he had to die, I can never get over that. How Father would have loved to live with us! He had a great deal of trust in God and was deeply religious, please God that gave him strength. He writes to me: 'Teach the children to pray, now I know what it means.' I can't teach you to pray, I can only hope that that mercy is granted to you. It is not given to me. Ursula didn't get a line from Bernhard, and it's probably better that way. Bernhard would have known that this would have been too much for the child."

No one knows what happened to HG during the time between sentence and execution. There is no trace of him during those ten days, no new statement to provide information about a further interrogation. I don't want to think about whether and how the men from the Security Service tried to make him crack, until they finally understood it was pointless. HG is executed along with Adam von Trott zu Solz, Baron Ludwig von Leonrod, and Otto Carl

Kiep. These four men die on August 26, 1944, between midday and one o'clock on a radiant summer's day.

Death by hanging doesn't mean a broken neck, at least not here. Count Helmuth Moltke whispered to his fellow prisoners during the rounds: "Prepare yourselves, it takes twenty minutes." The regulation was to leave the men hanging for twenty minutes, to be sure that they were dead. Further instruction: men to be slowly strangled. I read in Joachim Fest, in Peter Hoffmann, in Ian Kershaw, that the condemned men came to the execution in prisoners' uniforms, that the hangmen put the small noose around their necks, stripped them to the waist, lifted them up, and hanged them on a hook. Then they let the men fall, not especially violently, and, as they struggled with death, they pulled their trousers down. In photographs on Hitler's card table the hanged men were naked. After every execution, which wasn't death yet, a narrow black curtain was drawn in front of the hanged man, and then it was the next man's turn. HG was the second after Adam von Trott zu Solz.

Yes, I do want to look. I want to be there when HG dies. Twenty minutes is longer than hell. I want to tell him he isn't alone, not even after sixty years. Here I am, the one who has gone with him throughout his whole life, and I'm not going to let him go. I would have liked to laugh with you, HG, to enjoy your wit and your warmth that enchanted everyone. I wish I had a vivid memory of you: What did you smell like, and was your beard very scratchy? I would have loved the chance to love you. I was bewildered by your eccentricity as a young man, I find you wonderful because of the good years with Else, I can't understand how you could have fallen prey to the Nazis. It wasn't my time. I'm furious with you for the humiliations you inflicted upon Else, and that's why I find you, the man, ridiculous. Perhaps I should be less presumptuous. I'm distraught about what I have to understand as your indifference to the fate of the Jews, the forced laborers, the mentally ill, the inmates of the concentration camps, Himmler's "Untermenschen" in the occupied areas. Have I misunderstood you, because you never said anything? Now you are dying as an "Untermensch." They deprived you of the cleric you requested. But your Mount of Olives is behind you, and you are a hero in your death. You lived in awful times, and if you wanted things to be better for your children, then you succeeded. You have paid the "blood toll" so that I don't have to. I have learned from you what I must guard against. That's what a father's there for, isn't it? I thank you.

EPILOGUE

I have to go back to Halberstadt once more. Else gets a mound of letters of condolence—many of them anonymous. Not all the friends are still there, some parts of the family are rather restrained. Else is expelled from the Party and the National Socialist League of Women, as is Ursula, the former Ringführerin. On December 2, 1944, the eve of the first day of Advent, they christen Bernhard and Ursula's son, one last time in the house with the family porcelain and Dagmar Podeus's precious christening gown. The boy's name is Jörn Günter, a little I. G. Klamroth, defiant hope in the midst of hopelessness. Jörn's baptismal motto is that of his parents' wedding: The kingdom of God is not in word, but in power.

Back home at last in 1946, Jochen tells the family that he was dishonorably discharged from the Wehrmacht in France in 1944 and put into Punishment Unit 666, a motley collection of criminals and deserters who were assigned to tasks that the brother can't talk about even today. He was nineteen at the time. Twenty-one-year-old Barbara is expelled from the university in Vienna and forced to work for a chemicals factory in Goslar. HG's brother, Kurt junior, born in 1904, previously declared unfit for service and working as a senior privy councillor in the Reich Education Ministry, receives his call-up to a flak unit on the Eastern Front on August 27, 1944, a day after HG's death. On October 27 he is transferred to the notorious Dirlewanger company, a "probation unit" of the Watten-SS, in which at first only serious criminals were used as cannon fodder. From 1944 90 percent of the company were concentration camp inmates, political prisoners who were to be liquidated. HG's parents, Else, Ursula, and the two little children, Sabine and I, are all left unharmed.

Jenny, the Russian forced labor girl, is sent to a munitions factory nearby. She seeks comfort at Bismarckplatz whenever she can. Hans Litten, HG's "private secretary" and the son of a Jewish father, ends up in a forced labor camp in Magdeburg, a disaster also for the company. The house is full to bursting with refugees from the bombs—family, friends, strangers, many carefree children. Almost everybody has head lice and severe chilblains, there's no coal, sirens are wailing day and night. Gertrud writes in her diary: "There are more than fifty of us in the cellar." They read Schiller's *Wallenstein*, distributing the roles, the children learn "The Bell" and "The Sorcerer's Apprentice" by heart—"intellectual property" for when they get carted off to Siberia. Else after the war: "I felt completely petrified amid all the hurly-burly I had to sort out. But we managed. Of course we managed."

The police come to the house another few times. On September 6, 1944, they confiscate the assets—not just the men's, but Else's and Ursula's and the children's. Assets indeed—every teacup and every pair of socks is registered, I find long lists of all the household goods, the books, the paintings, even my toys. Imagine what kind of grim work that involves, and nobody says what it's all for. Will everything be taken out of the house, and where to? When Else wants to donate HG's uniforms, his riding equipment, the outfits for his sports-car journeys to the collection of the "German national sacrifice," she needs a permit. An endless correspondence with the head of the tax office revolves around the payment of bills from the time before the confiscation—telephone, craftsmen, fire insurance, 40.60 reichsmarks for the midwife. Incidentally, neither Else nor Herr Danneberg at the tax office signs off with "Heil Hitler." Presumably the man had known HG as a good taxpayer over the years.

In the meantime the family lives on money from HG's sister Annie and her husband. Kurt and Gertrud are still there too. In the middle of December Else's and Ursula's assets are released, even my toys belong to me once more. This was organized by SS-Obergruppenführer and Waffen-SS General Franz Breithaupt, an absurd phenomenon in an absurd time. Hitler and Himmler themselves had decreed on August 14, 1944—that is one day before HG's and Bernhard's trial, the two men are not yet dead—that the surviving families of the men executed for the July 20 plot should be taken care of by the SS, and Franz Breithaupt already had a track record in this field. In 1934 he "looked after" the families of the men murdered in the so-called Röhm Putsch.

You have to get your head around this one. The men are executed, and then come letters from Herr Breithaupt: "Most honorable gracious lady, The confiscation of your personal assets is an error that calls for immediate correction. Heil Hitler." Breithaupt announces a pension for Else, Ursula, and the underage children, payable from May 1, 1945 (!), plus a "balancing payment" for the months of September to April, 6,300 marks altogether. I don't know whether the money was ever paid. Breithaupt was also the one who sent Else HG's letters: "Most honorable gracious lady, I herewith take the liberty of sending you another letter from your husband. Heil Hitler!" How monstrous can times be?

HG's assets, along with Kurt's money, rest with the company, and to realize them would have meant bankruptcy. Lots of letters from lawyers fly back and forth, claiming that Kurt had not been condemned, and could therefore not be punished. The whole thing gets dragged out, everybody drags it out, neither the police nor the tax office have any desire to get involved in such complicated dealings, just as the end is near. In the major attack on Halberstadt on April 8, 1945, the Woort is destroyed, and with it 155 years of company tradition. The whole mess ends a month later with Germany's capitulation.

One of my first memories of the new era: I got slapped hard in the face. I can't remember who did it, whether it was Else or Barbara, I just remember flying through the kitchen. I had to become an adult before I understood why. Half-pint as I was, I had asked out of the blue, "Where did all the love for the Führer go? Why does nobody say Heil Hitler anymore?" Perhaps I should have asked, "Why did anybody ever say it?"

Acknowledgments

My thanks are due, of course, to my forefathers, who wrote down and kept so much—in times of telephone and e-mail such a wealth of material wouldn't be found anymore, I fear. The members of the family today have rummaged around in cases and boxes and provided me with invaluable documents. I owe my deepest gratitude to the "favorite Dane" Pelse Sonne, who knew HG and guided me through his time in Denmark. I should like to thank my esteemed colleague Heinz Höhne, whose specialist knowledge showed me the way through the thicket of the Abwehr. To everyone at my publishing house, above all Margit Ketterle and Bettina Eltner, let me say that I'm in the best possible hands with all their care and commitment—thank you. For Barbara Wenner, my agent and editor, I would like to invent a new word. Her friendship, her sense of the text, and her outrageous stubbornness have carried the book over the years. To have her at my side is a great gift.

Kurt and Gertrud get married, 1897

Kurt, the family archivist

Baby-faced HG

*HG and Wolf Yorck von
Wartenburg, 1919*

Else Podeus, 1917

Else's parents: Dagmar . . . and Paul Podeus

HG and Else get married, 1922

New blood: Else with Barbara and Ursula, 1925

Family reunion on the Wannsee

HG in the office of I.G. Klamroth

A great couple: Else . . . and HG

The cock of the walk

The family is complete

Kurt's seventieth birthday, 1942

Bernhard and Ursula, 1942

Bernhard, the bridegroom

The young couple

Before the People's Court: Bernhard

. . . and HG with his court-appointed defense lawyer